Public Access ICT across Cultures

Public Access ICT across Cultures

Diversifying Participation in the Network Society

Edited by Francisco J. Proenza

The MIT Press
Cambridge, Massachusetts
London, England

International Development Research Centre
Ottawa • Cairo • Montevideo • Nairobi • New Delhi

Published by the MIT Press. MIT Press books may be purchased at special quantity discounts for business or sales promotional use. For information, please email special_sales@mitpress.mit.edu.

A copublication with
International Development Research Centre
PO Box 8500
Ottawa, ON K1G 3H9
Canada
www.idrc.ca / info@idrc.ca

This book was set in Stone Sans and Stone Serif by Toppan Best-set Premedia Limited. Printed and bound in the United States of America.

Library of Congress Cataloging-in-Publication Data is available.

ISBN: 978-0-262-52737-8
ISBN 978-1-55250-569-4 (IDRC e-book)

10 9 8 7 6 5 4 3 2 1

To Amy Mahan

Contents

To Amy Mahan

Amy Kathleen Mahan's career was marked by a commitment to research and its effective dissemination to improve the communication opportunities of the disadvantaged, as a foundation for human and social development. The focus of much of her work was on telecommunication reform and information and communication technology (ICT) policies, particularly in developing countries.

Although she was a productive researcher, Amy chose to devote most of her activity to helping others through her exceptional skills in research support, editing, and report preparation. She had a rare talent for integrating technical production and substantive content editing to make research results more reader-friendly. She strongly believed the weakest link in the research process was dissemination, and she demonstrated innovation and imagination to improve its effectiveness wherever she worked. She was a team player who preferred to work collaboratively.

Amy Mahan coordinated the Learning Initiatives on Reforms for Network Economies (LIRNE.NET) from Montevideo, Uruguay, and was a member of the Research Working Group of the Global Impact Study of Public Access to Information and Communication Technologies. She was also an active member of the Regional Dialogue on the Information Society (DIRSI) and a founder of Fundación Comunica.

Amy left us at age 47 on March 5, 2009. She left suddenly, giving no warning. She did not want us to be distracted by her illness. She wanted to be known for what she thought, what she wrote, whom she helped.

There are two predominant motivations for investing in and building physical spaces with computers and connections to the Internet: 1) because there is a scarcity *of ICT resources that the endeavor seeks to fill (and perhaps benefit from); and 2) because there is a need to build up* community resources. . . .

The literature assumes the importance of sustainability for community access points. But perhaps what is needed is a more holistic picture which widens the frame to view and accept some public access points as necessarily ephemeral and fleeting. In many instances what is required for adoption is the impetus (and attraction) of introduction to ICT services and applications, rather than a sustained relationship to provide this access. The establishment of a community capacity building access point considers the broader skill base of the community in its evaluations. Likewise, a commercial (or non-profit) enterprise simply seeking to fulfill an access gap should also be posited in context of the community it is serving and in context of shifts in local ICT adoption indicators during its lifespan.

As is often the case for social exclusion (gender being a key example), lack of data is still a key constraint for measuring positive effects and progress generally. If the design for the telecenter or cybercafé does not particularly target women and girls, or poor people, the handicapped, elderly, people who don't speak the official language, or others with special circumstances or needs, it is not likely to collect indicators on the access or use by these subgroups of the premises and ICT services. And, on the other hand, the challenges of simultaneously confronting ICT and a public place may prove insurmountable for some socially marginalized sectors. (From internal memoranda prepared by Amy Mahan, 2008)

Amy Mahan's foremost interest was in ICT as a tool for social inclusion and a means to help women and traditionally marginalized peoples improve their lives and communities. Amy was committed to academic rigor and to learning from field observations and analysis to inform our investments and policy prescriptions, and she understood that rigor required thoroughness and an understanding of context.

At the time of her passing, Amy had made substantial contributions to the research and design of two ICTs for development programs.

It is with deep gratitude for her scholarship, personal courage, and humanity that we honor our friend and colleague by dedicating this book to her memory.

Foreword

Amy Mahan was no stranger to shared Internet use. While living in Quito, Ecuador, in the mid-1990s, she collaborated internationally on various academic and research projects, including editing a book with colleagues in Denmark and Canada via what she called her *sneakernet*—a network configuration that involved putting her shoes on and jogging to the local Internet café to download email, conduct research, and share her findings. She worked from a home office, and shared access was the only option available: Quito's telecom infrastructure was notoriously poor, and commercial Internet access was a monopoly service provided by a bank determined to apply its usurious lending practices to its Internet business model.

At the time, affordable access was often (and naïvely) seen as the only obstacle to the Internet for all initiatives in developing countries. The solutions proposed were equally simplistic: privatize telecoms, invest massively in infrastructure development, and enable telecenters, Internet cafés, and other shared-use solutions for the poor.

Fast forward to 2014, and the world has changed. The mobile phone is everywhere, more than 2.5 billion people are online, and as mobile phones are increasingly Internet-enabled, it seems that the ubiquitous Internet might even be within reach. Why should we worry about shared public access when "everyone" has a smart phone?

The most obvious answer to that question is that in fact not everyone does have a smart phone. The International Telecommunication Union (ITU) estimates that there are 83.7 mobile broadband subscriptions per 100 inhabitants in the developed world but only 19.0 per 100 inhabitants in Africa and 21.1 across the developing world.[1] One of the reasons that shared public access continues to be important is that for many people, it is still the only access available. However, that is far from the only reason. Results from the Global Impact Study of Public Access[2] and from the research documented in this book provide some surprising findings. Even people with home access to computers and the Internet use public access. In some cases this is because the access is faster or the computers better, but other reasons include the technical support provided by staff and other users or simply because Internet cafés offer people a chance to mingle with friends or other people.

The reports in this book take a fresh look at shared public access to computers and the Internet and provide evidence that the benefits of shared public access go far beyond simply providing affordable access to the infrastructure. Public access venues are also places for learning, sharing, working, finding opportunities, empowering, and solidarity. Facebook may be *The Social Network* with more than a billion users globally, but Internet cafés and telecenters are *hundreds of thousands of social networks*, providing tens of millions of users locally with opportunities to improve their livelihoods.

Amy Mahan's foremost interest was in ICT and media as tools for social inclusion and a means to help women, the poor, and traditionally marginalized peoples improve their lives and communities. Her professional involvement in this area included being a key member of the research team for the Global Impact Study of Public Access to ICTs, but she also developed several handbooks and multimedia kits as training tools for the use of ICT in developing countries, co-authored and edited books on subjects as diverse as global media governance and telecommunications regulation reform, and served as production editor of the respected academic journal *Telecommunication Policy*.

Amy was also committed to giving young researchers the opportunity to develop their skills and expertise. The *Amy Mahan Research Fellowship Program* recognizes this commitment to the next generation of researchers, and Amy would have been pleased and honored to have this research dedicated to her. She would, however, have been much happier to have been able to work alongside the young scholars.

Bruce Girard
March 2014

Notes

1. Key ICT indicators for developed and developing countries and the world, International Telecommunications Union. http://www.itu.int/en/ITU-D/Statistics/Documents/statistics/2014/ITU_Key_2005-2014_ICT_data.xls

2. Araba Sey, Chris Coward, François Bar, George Sciadas, Chris Rothschild, and Lucas Koepke. 2013. *Connecting People for Development: Why Public Access ICTs Matter*. Global Impact Study Research Report. http://tascha.uw.edu/publications/connecting-people-for-development/.

Acknowledgments

This book was made possible by the Amy Mahan Research Fellowship Program, a competitive research grant initiative funded by Canada's International Development Research Centre and implemented by Universitat Pompeu Fabra, Barcelona, in collaboration with scholars from the University of San Andrés, Buenos Aires, the University of the Philippines, Manila, and South Africa's LINK Centre at the University of the Witwatersrand, Johannesburg, together with partner institutions from ten participating countries.

Many people helped make the publication of this book possible. The authors gratefully acknowledge the following contributions.

SIRCA colleagues at Nanyang Technological University: Ang Peng Hwa, Arul Chib, Joanna Tan Keng Ling, Naowarat Narula, and Sri Ranjini Mei Hua, as well as IDRC's program officer, Chaitali Sinha, made detailed comments on the draft submission guidelines. All their suggestions were adopted. SIRCA staff shared invaluable resources and experiences, which served as important guidelines in our own program development. Overall, SIRCA staff remained a frequent and reliable source of information and counsel.

The Global Impact Study (GIS) staff—namely, Araba Sey and Christopher Coward (University of Washington) and François Bar (University of Southern California)—helped us, particularly during the early research planning stages. Another GIS team member, George Sciadas, also part of our research team and co-editor of this book, provided a particularly helpful link with Global Impact Study survey research work.

Professor Steven Pace, grounded theory and ICT specialist from Central Queensland University, gave support to the qualitative analysis work of our teams in Chile and Argentina.

Raul Pertierra, anthropologist and ICT specialist from Ateneo de Manila University, assisted our research team working in Thailand.

Ricardo Gomez, Assistant Professor and Chair of the Information & Society Center at the University of Washington's Information School, kindly made available advance copies of his research findings on public access. This material provided an overview of the relative significance of various kinds of public access venues worldwide.

The implementation of the Amy Mahan Research Fellowship Program relied on the assistance of many Universitat Pompeu Fabra (UPF) staff. Special recognition is due to Rector Josep Joan Moreso, Research Vice Rector; Clara Riba, Social Sciences Director; and our colleagues David Sancho, Jacint Jordana, Miquel Oliver, Josep Jofre, Robert Fishman, Willem Saris, and Lorena Camats.

At IDRC, Frank Tulus was instrumental in getting the program underway and accompanied the research by providing guidance and support whenever needed. Laurent Elder championed the initial idea for a complementary capacity-building program to the Global Impact Study and remained supportive of the program throughout its implementation. Raymond Hyma provided assistance with the program's website, especially during the translation process. IDRC's Nola Haddadian and Matthew Smith, and MIT's Marguerite B. Avery and Katherine A. Almeida provided invaluable assistance getting this book published. University of Florida Professor Mario Ariet helped check the proofs. Finally, IDRC's Heloise Emdon, Ben Petrazzini, Michael Clarke, and Florencio Ceballos offered continuous support to the program.

Special thanks are extended to Amy Mahan's family: Bruce Girard, her husband; Danielle Girard, their daughter; and Marilyn Mahan, Amy's mother, for allowing us the honor of naming the program in Amy's memory. Bruce, a renowned specialist in ICT for development, also kindly wrote the foreword to this book.

1 Introduction

Francisco J. Proenza

Abstract

This book presents the findings of ten research teams that worked between 2009 and 2012 across three continents under the auspices of the Amy Mahan Research Fellowship Program to Assess the Impact of Public Access to ICT. It seeks to fill critical gaps in the research literature regarding the impact of public shared access to computers and the Internet. In this introductory chapter, we present the background to the preparation of the book and summarize findings as we overview how the book is organized.

Background to the Preparation of This Book

Worldwide, cybercafés are by far the most prevalent type of public access venue. Cybercafés thrive in urban areas, but their survival is challenged in rural settings by low digital literacy and high maintenance and connectivity costs. Two other common venue types are libraries, most often funded and operated by government, and telecenters, mostly funded by government but at times also by private foundations, nongovernmental organizations (NGOs), or international donors, and run by a broad range of institutions, including public agencies, NGOs, religious organizations, and local groups.

Governments have made large investments in public access, some by equipping libraries as venues, but most by subsidizing telecenters of various types, including commercially oriented centers. These interventions have been driven by the desire to include low-income groups in the digital age by expanding access to the Internet at low cost by sharing resources. There have been urban initiatives, but the more significant efforts have sought to bring the presumed benefits of public access to rural communities. Public interventions are usually based on the presumption that the better-substantiated impacts of Internet use can be obtained through public access, while some of the negative effects of public access are observed and speculated on but largely ignored.

All over the world, cybercafé clients receive services they deem beneficial enough to justify paying for their cost. There is also considerable anecdotal evidence suggesting that public access users—of all types of venues—derive significant benefits. What has been missing is a comprehensive body of scientifically validated knowledge regarding what works and what doesn't and under what circumstances.

This book presents a systematic assessment of the impact of public access across cultures (ten countries in three continents) for a variety of venues operating in different settings for the purpose of informing public policy.

Participating research teams shared three objectives: (1) assess impacts with scientific rigor, (2) acknowledge the reach and limitations of findings, and (3) formulate practical recommendations. Within this broad framework, cybercafés located in urban areas and mid-size towns are examined in the China, India, and Jordan chapters; rural telecenters in the Cameroon and Malaysia chapters; and comparisons across venue types in the Argentina, Chile, Peru, Rwanda, and Thailand chapters. Mixed approaches to data gathering were used in most studies, but qualitative approaches were dominant in Argentina, Chile, Thailand, and Peru, and quantitative approaches were dominant in China, India, Jordan, Malaysia, and Rwanda. Research teams were multidisciplinary: in Thailand the team had expertise in anthropology, sociology, gender studies, and human rights; in China, in economics, systems engineering, marketing and psychology; in Chile, in communications, culture, and gender analysis; in Argentina, in sociology, anthropology, and social communications; and in Malaysia, in education and instructional technology.

The study of different contexts enables the appreciation of differences in policy concerns and under what conditions and to what extent lessons from one setting are applicable elsewhere. Multidisciplinary approaches bring new perspectives and insights. Quantitative methods let us assess the extent of a phenomenon, while qualitative approaches enable a deeper, more nuanced understanding.

In the context of development impact studies, variety in settings and in data and conceptual approaches is an ideal that is seldom achieved in practice because of the high investment and coordination costs involved. The research reported in this book was made possible by the Amy Mahan Research Fellowship Program, a competitive research grant initiative funded by Canada's International Development Research Centre (IDRC) and implemented by Universitat Pompeu Fabra, Barcelona, in collaboration with scholars from Universidad de San Andrés, Buenos Aires; the University of the Philippines, Manila; South Africa's LINK Centre at the University of the Witwatersrand, Johannesburg; and partner institutions from participating countries.

Organization

The book presents the results of field research in three parts. Part I covers public access impacts on users as individuals, part II on society and networks, and part III on women. Part IV contains a single final overview chapter.

Part I: Impact on Personal Achievement and Well-Being

Part I begins with an assessment of cybercafé users in an Arab country: Jordan. It presents the findings of a survey covering 336 users of twenty-four randomly selected cybercafés in Amman. The study finds overwhelming positive perceptions of impact in users' lives in two areas: communications and social networking, and improving education and learning; and less widespread but positive impacts in a third area, income and employment.

The second chapter in this part examines the impacts of ICT training in public access venues on job skills and employment in Rwanda. A purposive survey was taken of 418 white-collar and office workers who occupy positions likely to involve the use of basic computer skills (e.g., secretaries, receptionists, customer service agents, administrative assistants, finance officers, human resource managers, and public access venue employees). Eighty-seven percent in this group report "getting a new or better job" as an objective for wanting to improve their ICT skills. Sixty-seven percent consider that knowledge of the Internet plays a very important or an important role in the job application process, and 41 percent took an ICT skills test during recruitment for their present job. The skills acquired from public access venues differ and affect job prospects differently depending on venue type, location, competence of instructor, duration of the training, and sex of trainees. The training model used by government-sponsored telecenters appears to be most effective, and its expansion should be considered.

Chapters 4 and 5 cover China, the country with the world's largest cybercafé user population. Surveys of 975 café users and 964 nonusers were conducted.

The objective of the first China chapter is to understand user motivations and assess whether personal objectives are fulfilled and the extent to which achievement is affected by Internet café use. A first noteworthy finding of the analysis in this chapter, applicable in China and everywhere else, is that *the goal content of Internet and Internet café use is predominantly intrinsic.* For the most part, people use the Internet and Internet Cafés not because of external pressures or rewards, but as part of their overall search to satisfy basic psychological needs.

Internet café user life goals are not very different from those of nonusers. The goal most highly cherished by both users and nonusers is to "learn more knowledge." Young (under age 35) urban male users and urban male and female student users report statistically significant higher achievement than their nonuser cohorts for this top priority goal. Young (under age 35) urban male users and female urban student users also report higher achievement than nonusers for the goal "have fun, entertain myself." Urban female users report higher achievement for the goals "keep frequent contact with those who don't live nearby" and "relax, relieve tension." As Internet café users gain experience using the technology, the sense of accomplishment appears to wane for the goals "keep frequent contact with those who don't live nearby" by urban females and "have fun, entertain myself" by urban males and urban female students. These are significant findings suggesting that nonusers are missing out in the achievement of goals they cherish and, in the case of learning and communicating, are instrumental and valued by society.

In the second China chapter (chapter 5), we find that Internet addiction is not as widespread as is often reported in the media, and we identify some of the features of users and use practices that seem to increase the risk of overuse.

Part I ends with a review of a quasi-experiment in five rural communities of Cameroon, where *télécentres communautaires polyvalents* (TCPs) are the only places from which students can connect to the Internet. The self-reported academic performance of 1,015 secondary school students interviewed in the five TCPs is used as a yardstick to compare the performance of students who know how to use the Internet and those who do not. Key to academic success are long hours of after-school study and a motivation to learn, but those students who study hard and are motivated to learn get Internet skills in the TCPs in larger proportion than underachievers. The evidence further suggests that, beyond study effort, having access to the Internet gives mid- and upper secondary students a performance edge. There is however some evidence suggesting that spending too much time at the TCP may thwart academic achievement.

Part II: Facilitating Inclusion and Enabling the Buildup of Social Capital

The first chapter of part II examines the ways in which Argentina's low-income urban youth use new technologies in their daily lives. Three venues located in the county of La Matanza are considered: a cybercafé, an access and training center run by a local grassroots organization, and a community technology center run by an organization with government support. The last two centers do not provide access to the public at large, and therefore cannot be considered public access venues. Instead, they focus on providing ICT training services that are valued by our target group of low-income youths. We refer to these two centers as community ICT training centers (CITCs).

The study's main finding is that the cybercafé and the two CITCs contribute to the social inclusion of youth in poor urban environments. They also satisfy training needs that are not met by market-oriented institutes or formal schooling.

Cybercafés are also valuable as social spaces where young people can put into practice what they learn in the community centers and where the main activities revolve around communication and entertainment over the Internet. Women are less frequent visitors to the cybercafés and therefore derive fewer benefits from their use than men. We recommend the establishment of ICT training centers in marginalized communities, where high rates of alienation among young people are observed. We also encourage the strengthening of links between these spaces and the school environment and the promotion of greater participation of women, especially in cybercafés and job training programs.

In Malaysia we consider social connectedness among users of the country's forty-two rural Internet centers (RICs). Social connectedness, defined as the "feeling of belongingness, being linked to and related to a network, community or group that one trusts and interacts with," is a building block of social capital. When a socially connected group establishes trusting relationships, it often finds ways to cooperate in joint activities that are beyond the possibilities of individual members. We examine 300 responses to an online survey on connectedness and find that most RIC users feel a moderate degree of connection, and 27 percent report a relatively high degree of connection with their social network. Nearly 20 percent of respondents feel significantly connected with community leaders.

Part II concludes with an analysis of the impact of public access on the organizational capacity of nine grassroots organizations located in a rural district of Peru's Andean region. Public access venues such as telecenters and *cabinas públicas* (Peru's cybercafés) help make communication processes more effective and facilitate meetings and coordination. These impacts are greatest when the venues have links to the objectives and goals of the organization and when those actors who facilitate information flows with external agents use the Internet to search for funding opportunities. Some organizational skills are more likely to be impacted by information technology (e.g., those related to networking, leadership, infrastructure, and external communications) than others (e.g., supervision, monitoring, and evaluation of plans). The promotion of public access venues as part of universal Internet access initiatives should consider as part of its goal not just the provision of access at the individual level but the inclusion of rural organizations; and initiatives seeking to foster a more productive use of technology by grassroots organizations should focus on developing those capacities that are most impacted.

Part III: Impact on Women

Part III opens with a discussion of why cybercafés are off-limits to most women in two mid-sized towns of Uttar Pradesh. Limitations on access by women surfaced in several chapters where cybercafés were the subject of study. In China, women account for only 27 percent of survey respondents; in Jordan, for only 24 percent. The original focus of our India study was cybercafé user objectives, but when we found only 12 females in our 300-user sample (4 percent), it became evident that the important societal impact was the exclusion of women from this type of venue. Even acknowledging the limited representativeness of our samples, these figures are alarming because cybercafés are by far the most prevalent type of public access venue worldwide. Accordingly, we conducted a supplementary survey of 200 women (100 users and 100 nonusers) to determine why so few women in these towns were using cybercafés.

Most women in Uttar Pradesh are poor and illiterate, and they have minimal participation in the formal economy. The caste system is firmly entrenched and the society is conservative and generally restricts the movement of women outside the family or immediate community. Females in mid-sized towns generally have little decision-making autonomy, power, or financial control within the household. It is mainly working women and female students who come out of their homes. Others rarely come out of their homes, do not talk to strangers, and are always guarded by male family members; when interacting with outsiders, male family members reply on the women's behalf. The environment at the cybercafés is generally considered hostile to women because these venues tend to be crowded with young men. Hence, women and their families do not feel comfortable with the notion of women visiting cybercafés. Generally, illiterate females engaged primarily in household activities felt that cybercafés were not useful to them. Some were not even interested in taking part in the survey. Those who do use cybercafés tend to be better off, educated women from higher castes, and find them useful.

There is an urgent need to increase literacy and enhance awareness of the benefits of the technology among women and their male family members, and to implement programs offering cybercafé operators incentives to make their venues more welcoming and accommodating to women.

The second chapter in this part examines the impact on women of public access through Chile's urban *Quiero mi Barrio* telecenter network. The study is based on interviews with men and women in two centers located in relatively new neighborhoods created as part of government-sponsored housing. Overall, the interviewees feel these centers have had a positive impact on their communities. These facilities are perceived to be particularly valuable for children and young people, as places where they can learn and do their homework conveniently close to home and at no cost. Adult women also appreciate the digital literacy training imparted in these venues. Impact appears to be highest for women because their options to access the Internet from other venues (e.g., cybercafés) are more limited than for men. The analysis suggests that the State should strengthen urban neighborhood telecenters to better serve women's needs, encourage greater participation of women, and help women develop digital skills, realize their aspirations, and meet their everyday needs.

Part III concludes with an assessment of the impact of public access on women migrants from Burma in the border town of Mae Sot, Thailand. The migrant population outnumbers Thais in border towns such as Mae Sot but is excluded from Thailand's ICT development plans. Migrant women in Mae Sot have nevertheless benefited indirectly from two types of venues that facilitate public access: cybercafés and two NGO-operated centers that provide ICT skills training to members of migrant organizations and access to computers and the Internet to their students (i.e. CITCs). These facilities enable dislocated ethnic peoples with families, relatives, friends, and work partners living outside Mae Sot (e.g., Chiang Mai, Bangkok, inside Burma, and in resettled countries) to access the Internet, which for them represents a doorway to a wider space for maintaining and expanding social relationships beyond the geographical boundaries of Mae Sot. Physical distance is partly overcome by the proximity of virtual relationships. Through email and video chat using Skype, Yahoo Messenger, and Gchat, the women in Mae Sot are able to repair kinship ties and extend their familial obligations as daughters, sisters, cousins, and nieces who are physically distant.

Women migrants also use the Internet as a virtual cultural headquarters, providing a space for cultural expression and entertainment. The women express themselves online in their ethnic languages when using email or chat, either in Burmese fonts (which they download online) or in English alphabet. The websites of the community-based organizations advocating for migrants are in Burmese and ethnic languages. The women are also active participants in cultural entertainment—downloading, uploading, and watching and listening to Burmese ethnic music videos and celebrations/festivals.

Use of Internet cafés by migrant women in Mae Sot is in practice limited by direct discrimination of some Thai operators and by the women's own fears of being detected as illegal migrants by Thai police, which could lead to their being detained, harassed, or even deported. Access to computers and the Internet is feasible only for migrant women who have their own computers and home connections, or who connect from their place of work (mainly community-based organizations) or from a few Thai-owned cybercafés that are friendly and accommodating to the needs of Burmese migrants.

Programmatic ICT education needs to be developed and implemented through the cooperation of NGOs, the private sector, and the Thai state. There should also be a concerted effort to influence the Thai government to change policies toward migrants and implement ICT policies for marginalized non-Thais living in Thailand. Without these changes, the welfare of migrants and ICT penetration among migrants cannot progress significantly.

Part IV: A Place to Learn, a Place to Play, a Place to Dream, a Place to Fall from Grace

The book's final chapter highlights findings and draws on prior studies in search for patterns of use and impact across countries to inform critical issues of public access policy.

I Impact on Personal Achievement and Well-Being

2 User Perceptions of Impact of Internet Cafés in Amman, Jordan

Ghaleb Rabab'ah, Ali Farhan AbuSeileek, Francisco J. Proenza, Omar Fraihat, and Saif Addeen Alrababah

Abstract

This study analyzes users' perception of the impact of Internet cafés on three aspects of their lives: social networking, education and learning, and income and employment. The study is based on a sample of 336 Internet café users and twenty-four operators in Amman, Jordan. Internet café users strongly perceive that these venues have improved their lives by expanding their social networks and improving their education and learning. Perceived impact on income or employment was lower than for the other two impact areas but was not insignificant, especially among male users.

The Jordanian government's policy of increasing the number of licenses for private café operators is to be commended. There is, however, an area of major concern. Although women benefit from cybercafés as much as men, comparatively few women use these venues, and those who use them do so infrequently. The disparity is most acute in low-income neighborhoods. Understanding whether the observed gender disparities are culturally determined or the result of the environment prevalent in cybercafés and designing and implementing suitable policies to increase women's use of cybercafés should be high priorities for both researchers and government officials.

Introduction

Jordan's privately owned Internet cafés generally provide basic services for a fee (e.g., Internet access, email, chat, games, and printing) and often also serve hot and cold drinks. Some cafés divide their space into booths or cubicles, allowing privacy and a quiet environment. According to Ministry of Trade statistics (June 6, 2010), there are 546 Internet cafés in Jordan distributed among twelve governorates, about 193 (35 percent) in Amman.

Based on 250 interviews with Internet café users in Jordan and Egypt (200 interviews in Amman and Zarka, Jordan, and 50 in Cairo), Wheeler (2004) found that even people with a high school education or less, not fluent in English, and sometimes unemployed are drawn to Internet cafés, where they surf sometimes as many as forty hours a week. The Internet helped users meet new people and stay in touch with family and friends, and it enabled them to learn new things, including practical skills such as typing and English language use. It was also an important tool for job hunting, checking agricultural prices, or corresponding with potential partners to set up new business opportunities. Wheeler's (2007) study of twenty-five women in five Internet cafés in Cairo gives compelling examples and identifies three kinds of benefits for female users: "1. Increases information access and professional development; 2. Expands or maintains social networks and social capital; and 3. Transforms social and political awareness."

This chapter presents the findings of a survey conducted in twenty-four Internet cafés in Amman in 2010, where 336 users were asked to provide basic personal information and information about their activities while visiting Internet cafés, and to assess the impact Internet cafés were having on their lives. We do not single out or test for the existence of specific negative effects, but instead we focus on the effect of "instrumental" activities. The study does, however, recognize that cybercafé users may experience both positive and negative experiences. We examine user activities, but we also assess user perceptions of impact in three areas commonly regarded as potentially important: education and learning, social networking, and income and employment.

Samples and Data Collection

Of 193 Internet cafés in Amman, a representative sample of twenty-four was selected from three different geographical areas.

When our survey was conducted in mid-2010, half of these establishments had been in business for at least five years, another six had been set up two to five years earlier, and the other six were newer. Fifty-eight percent had between six and fifteen computers, and 37 percent had between sixteen and thirty. About 50 percent charge 0.5 Jordanian dinars (JD) (about US$0.70) per hour, 38 percent 1 JD, and the rest a bit more. Most of these venues offer Internet, printing, typing, CD burning, and scanning services. About 50 percent also offered computer repair services. A few venues offered a variety of other services, including fax, snacks, and public phone, and three offered formal training. Twenty-three of the twenty-four Internet café operators interviewed were men, and one was a woman. Most were between twenty and thirty-four years old and held a BA.

Users visiting these twenty-four cafés were interviewed about their perceptions regarding the impact of these venues on three major areas of their lives: social networking, education and learning, and income and employment. These Internet cafés were visited at two different times of day: morning and evening.

The following procedure was employed. The interviews were conducted in Arabic. The data were collected over eight days (March 10–17, 2010). A team leader arranged for each interviewer to visit three Internet cafés at two time intervals (between 10 A.M. and 2 P.M. and between 3 and 6 P.M.). Permission was obtained from the café operators and visitors. Eight people (seven men and one woman) collected the data.

Participants were told in advance that no names would be revealed, that the study was strictly for research purposes, and that the information collected would be treated confidentially. To encourage participation in the survey, café visitors who agreed to be interviewed were given a prepaid telephone card as compensation for the time spent with the interviewer.

About 30 percent of the women and 10 percent of the men approached in the cafés refused to answer. The reason given was that they were too busy and did not have time to answer the questionnaire. Interviewers were encouraged to stay in the café to try to ensure that a good number of female café users were interviewed. Had there been more female interviewers, some of the women users who refused might have been persuaded to participate.

Except for the observed refusal by some café visitors to be interviewed, there were no major departures from the data-collection plan.

A total of 336 Internet café users (255 men and 81 women) were interviewed. The observed gender imbalance is probably due to Jordanian women's general reticence to visit an Internet café, but it may also be attributed in part to the use of male interviewers and collection of data during the winter season, which witnessed heavy rain. Most women and some men are reluctant to go out in the rain, especially those who do not own a car. Collecting some data in the evening also might have influenced the type of user respondents, with a bias toward a greater number of students ages 16 to 18: most schoolchildren finish their schooling by 1 or 2 P.M., and more young students will be visiting these Internet cafés at these times.

The operators of these twenty-four cafés were also interviewed to understand their perspective regarding the impact on users of these venues. There were three owners operating their Internet cafés and twenty-one operators. In all, complete data were collected from 336 users and twenty-four owner-operators.

Table 2.1
User Survey Respondents by Gender and Age

	Male		Female		All Users	
	#	%	#	%	#	%
Age						
16–19	58	22.7	12	14.8	70	20.8
20–24	106	41.6	40	49.4	146	43.5
25–34	61	23.9	25	30.9	86	25.6
35–49	24	9.4	3	3.7	27	8.0
50–65	6	2.4	1	1.2	7	2.1
Total	255	100.0	81	100.0	336	100.0

Findings

Basic Features of Sample Users

There is considerable gender imbalance in the user sample: 255 respondents were male and only 81 were female. Nearly half the sample (48.8 percent) is made up of young men between the ages of 16 and 24 (table 2.1).

The most frequent age group for both gender cohorts is 20 to 24 years (table 2.1). Proportionately, there are fewer young females ages 16 to 19 (15 percent) than males (23 percent), and more women ages 25 to 49 (35 percent) than men (33 percent).

There were proportionately more women students in the sample than men (58 percent vs. 45 percent; table 2.2). One-third of male respondents and one-fifth of female respondents were employees. Sixteen percent of users were self-employed. Self-employment was more common among men (19 percent) than women (6 percent). About 13 percent of the women interviewed were unemployed, compared with 4 percent of the men.

Nearly all users had completed at least secondary education; only 4 percent of male users had completed only primary (table 2.3). The educational profile of women and men users is similar, with the majority (52 percent for males and 58 percent for females) having undergraduate or even postgraduate degrees (table 2.3).

In a sample composed primarily of young people, most users were single (77 percent), but some were married (20 percent), and a few (about 1 percent) were divorced.

The majority of users (54 percent) are dependent on their families for financial support, more so in the case of women (73 percent) than of men (48 percent). Because family income figures given by a large proportion of survey respondents are based on their perception of what other family members earn, family income figures

Table 2.2
Users by Gender, Age, and Occupation

	Student		Employee		Self-employed		Unemployed		Total	
	#	%	#	%	#	%	#	%	#	%
Male										
16–19	47	42.7	5	6.2	6	12.8	–	–	58	23.5
20–24	58	52.7	32	39.5	10	21.3	2	22.2	102	41.3
25–34	5	4.5	34	42.0	14	29.8	4	44.4	57	23.1
35–49	–	–	8	9.9	15	31.9	1	11.1	24	9.7
50–65	–	–	2	2.5	2	4.3	2	22.2	6	2.4
Subtotal	110	100.0	81	100	47	100	9	100	247	100
%	44.5		32.8		19.0		3.6		100.0	
Female										
16–19	12	26.1	–	–	–	–	–	–	12	15.2
20–24	30	65.2	5	27.8	1	20.0	2	20.0	38	48.1
25–34	4	8.7	10	55.6	4	80.0	7	70.0	25	31.6
35–49	–	–	2	11.1	–	–	1	10.0	3	3.8
50–65	–	–	1	5.6	–	–	–	–	1	1.3
Subtotal	46	100.0	18	100	5	100	10	100	79	100
%	58.2		22.8		6.3		12.7		100	
All	156		99		52		19		326	
%	47.9		30.4		16.0		5.8		100	

thus obtained are subject to a wide margin of error. With that caveat in mind, female respondents appear to come from better-off families: about 42 percent of females but only 26 percent of males reported monthly family income higher than 1,500 JD (table 2.4).

Home Connection, Venue Choice, and Use Patterns

Many cybercafé users have an Internet connection at home (43 percent), but the majority of users (57 percent) do not, and the option to connect from home is least common among adults ages 25 and older (35 percent). Home access also appears more prevalent among men (45 percent) than women (40 percent) (table 2.5).

About 73 percent of users travel less than 2 kilometers (1.25 miles) to the cafés they visit (table 2.6), and about 88 percent visit cafés once a week or more often (table 2.7). The most common reason for choosing to use a particular cybercafé (table 2.8) is that it is close to home (42 percent), but other reasons were also given by respondents:

Table 2.3
Users by Gender, Age, and Educational Achievement

	Primary		Secondary		Post-secondary		Undergrad		Postgrad		All Users	
	#	%	#	%	#	%	#	%	#	%	#	%
Male												
16–19	5	45.5	51	58.0	–	–	–	–	–	–	56	22.2
20–24	2	18.2	21	23.9	14	60.9	68	59.1	1	6.7	106	42.1
25–34	2	18.2	13	14.8	6	26.1	31	27.0	8	53.3	60	23.8
35–49	2	18.2	3	3.4	2	8.7	13	11.3	4	26.7	24	9.5
50–65	–	–	–	–	1	4.3	3	2.6	2	13.3	6	2.4
Subtotal	11	100	88	100	23	100	115	100	15	100	252	100
%	4.4		34.9		9.1		45.6		6.0		100	
Female												
16–19	–	–	12	42.9	–	–	–	–	–	–	12	14.8
20–24	–	–	15	53.6	–	–	24	63.2	1	11.1	40	49.4
25–34	–	–	1	3.6	6	100	13	34.2	5	55.6	25	30.9
35–49	–	–	–	–	–	–	–	–	3	33.3	3	3.7
50–65	–	–	–	–	–	–	1	2.6	–	–	1	1.2
Subtotal	0		28	100	6	100	38	100	9	100	81	100
%	0.0		34.6		7.4		46.9		11.1		100	
All	11		116		29		153		24		333	
%	3.3		34.8		8.7		45.9		7.2		100	

Table 2.4
Users by Gender, Age, and Monthly Family Income

	200–700 JD		700–1,500 JD		>1,500 JD		All Users	
	#	%	#	%	#	%	#	%
Male								
16–19	22	29.7	27	25.7	7	10.9	56	23.0
20–24	26	35.1	41	39.0	33	51.6	100	41.2
25–34	16	21.6	25	23.8	18	28.1	59	24.3
35–49	8	10.8	9	8.6	6	9.4	23	9.5
50–65	2	2.7	3	2.9	–	–	5	2.1
Subtotal	74	100.0	105	100.0	64	100.0	243	100.0
%	30.5		43.2		26.3		100.0	
Female								
16–19	2	11.8	3	10.7	6	18.8	11	14.3
20–24	11	64.7	13	46.4	14	43.8	38	49.4
25–34	4	23.5	10	35.7	10	31.3	24	31.2
35–49	–	–	2	7.1	1	3.1	3	3.9
50–65	–	–	–	–	1	3.1	1	1.3
Subtotal	17	100.0	28	100.0	32	100.0	77	100.0
%	22.1		36.4		41.6		100.0	
All	91		133		96		320	
%	28.4		41.6		30.0		100.0	

JD = Jordanian dinars.

friends also visit (21 percent) or proximity to their place of study (21 percent) or work (16 percent).

Frequent users of cybercafés (i.e., users who visited at least three times a week) account for 78 percent of the men and 44 percent of the women in the sample (table 2.7). Most café visitors spend from one to two hours (44 percent) or two to three hours (32 percent) per visit (table 2.9). Some users were registered members of the cafés they visited (32 percent) or subscribed to monthly plans (3 percent), but the majority (60 percent) paid on a per-visit basis.

User Activities

Survey participants were asked to choose from a list of seventeen activities which may be classified into four broadly defined groups: communication, education and learning, income and employment, and entertainment (tables 2.10a–2.10d). By far the most popular activity among users is communication—primarily by email, an activity in

Table 2.5
Users with Internet Connection at Home, by Gender and Age

	#	# With Data	%
Male			
16–19	34	57	59.6
20–24	47	105	44.8
25–34	22	61	36.1
35–49	9	24	37.5
50–65	1	6	16.7
Subtotal	113	253	44.7
Female			
16–19	6	12	50.0
20–24	16	40	40.0
25–34	10	25	40.0
35–49	–	3	–
50–65	–	1	–
Subtotal	32	81	39.5
All	145	334	43.4
# with data	334		

Table 2.6
Users by Gender, Age, and Distance Traveled to Internet Café

	<1 km		1–2 km		2–5 km		>5 km		Total	
	#	%	#	%	#	%	#	%	#	%
Male										
16–19	28	25.5	18	23.4	11	22.4	1	6.7	58	23.1
20–24	53	48.2	26	33.8	21	42.9	3	20.0	103	41.0
25–34	22	20.0	23	29.9	10	20.4	6	40.0	61	24.3
35–49	6	5.5	8	10.4	6	12.2	4	26.7	24	9.6
50–65	1	0.9	2	2.6	1	2.0	1	6.7	5	2.0
Subtotal	110	100.0	77	100.0	49	100.0	15	100.0	251	100.0
%	43.8		30.7		19.5		6.0		100.0	
Female										
16–19	5	20.0	2	6.5	3	17.6	2	28.6	12	15.0
20–24	12	48.0	16	51.6	9	52.9	2	28.6	39	48.8
25–34	8	32.0	11	35.5	3	17.6	3	42.9	25	31.3
35–49	–	–	2	6.5	1	5.9	–	–	3	3.8
50–65	–	–	–	–	1	5.9	–	–	1	1.3
Subtotal	25	100.0	31	100.0	17	100.0	7	100.0	80	100.0
%	31.3		38.8		21.3		8.8		100.0	
All	135		108		66		22		331	
%	40.8		32.6		19.9		6.6		100.0	

Table 2.7
Users by Gender, Age, and Frequency of Visits to Internet Cafés

	Daily or Almost Daily		Three Times a Week		At Least Once a Week		At Least Once a Month		A Few Times a Year		Total	
	#	%	#	%	#	%	#	%	#	%	#	%
Male												
16–19	36	62.1	13	22.4	4	6.9	5	8.6	–	–	58	100.0
20–24	38	36.2	44	41.9	6	5.7	10	9.5	7	6.7	105	100.0
25–34	29	47.5	18	29.5	10	16.4	2	3.3	2	3.3	61	100.0
35–49	7	29.2	10	41.7	4	16.7	2	8.3	1	4.2	24	100.0
50–65	2	33.3	1	16.7	2	33.3	1	16.7	–	–	6	100.0
Subtotal	112	44.1	86	33.9	26	10.2	20	7.9	10	3.9	254	100.0
Female												
16–19	1	8.3	3	25.0	6	50.0	2	16.7	–	–	12	100.0
20–24	6	15.0	13	32.5	17	42.5	1	2.5	3	7.5	40	100.0
25–34	3	12.0	8	32.0	10	40.0	2	8.0	2	8.0	25	100.0
35–49	–	–	1	33.3	1	33.3	1	33.3	–	–	3	100.0
50–65	1	100.0	–	–	–	–	–	–	–	–	1	100.0
Subtotal	11	13.6	25	30.9	34	42.0	6	7.4	5	6.2	81	100.0
All	123	36.7	111	33.1	60	17.9	26	7.8	15	4.5	335	100.0

which 64 percent of all users engaged, but also chatting (63 percent) and making calls over the Internet (50 percent; table 2.10a). Among activities involving some form of learning (table 2.10b), searching for news was the most popular (33 percent), followed by application for college admission (31 percent) and to a lesser extent typing or printing homework, especially by women (24 percent). Some users engaged in searching (18 percent) and applying for a job (15 percent), but the most popular income and employment activity (table 2.10c) was buying products online (25 percent), especially among female users (42 percent). Entertainment activities were also popular (table 2.10d). Playing computer games was selected by 38 percent of sample users and was particularly popular among young people ages 16 to 19, both men (59 percent) and women (67 percent).

Most websites viewed were in Arabic (64 percent) or English (62 percent). Only rarely were websites in other languages visited.

Using a separate questionnaire, we asked the twenty-four café owners and operators which websites were most frequently used by their customers, and we gave them four options plus a write-in possibility. All twenty-four indicated that networking (email,

Table 2.8
Reason for Using This Venue, by Age and Gender

	Close to Work		Close to Home		Friends Go There		Close to Place of Study		Total	
	#	%	#	%	#	%	#	%	#	%
Male										
16–19	5	6.0	40	48.2	29	34.9	9	10.8	83	100.0
20–24	25	16.6	64	42.4	33	21.9	29	19.2	151	100.0
25–34	16	21.3	34	45.3	15	20.0	10	13.3	75	100.0
35–49	11	39.3	10	35.7	4	14.3	3	10.7	28	100.0
50–65	1	14.3	4	57.1	1	14.3	1	14.3	7	100.0
Subtotal	58	16.9	152	44.2	82	23.8	52	15.1	344	100.0
Female										
16–19	2	11.8	4	23.5	5	29.4	6	35.3	17	100.0
20–24	3	6.1	16	32.7	4	8.2	26	53.1	49	100.0
25–34	6	23.1	10	38.5	3	11.5	7	26.9	26	100.0
35–49	–	–	3	75.0	–	–	1	25.0	4	100.0
50–65	–	–	1	100.0	–	–	–	–	1	100.0
Subtotal	11	11.3	34	35.1	12	12.4	40	41.2	97	100.0
All users	69	15.6	186	42.2	94	21.3	92	20.9	441	100.0

Note: Respondents could select more than one reason. This is why total responses exceed sample size.

Facebook, etc.) was most frequently used. News websites were marked by fifteen operators (62 percent), pornographic sites by five (22 percent), and sport sites by one.

User Perceptions of Impact

Ten indicators were considered, grouped into three categories depending on whether the perceived impact was on social networking, education and learning, or income and employment (tables 2.11a–2.11c). For each indicator, users were given a choice of five options depending on their perception of impact as highly or slightly positive, highly or slightly negative, or no impact.

Social Networking The indicator most frequently ranked highly positive by both men (65 percent) and women (48 percent) was "maintaining communication with family and friends by using social networking" (table 2.11a). The two other social networking indicators—"Meeting new people online" and "Knowing about the culture of other

Table 2.9
Users by Gender, Age, and Hours Spent During Each Visit to Internet Cafés

	1–2 Hours		2–3 Hours		>3 Hours		Total	
	#	%	#	%	#	%	#	%
Male								
16–19	19	35.8	22	41.5	12	22.6	53	100.0
20–24	29	30.2	35	36.5	32	33.3	96	100.0
25–34	29	49.2	15	25.4	15	25.4	59	100.0
35–49	12	52.2	5	21.7	6	26.1	23	100.0
50–65	4	66.7	–	–	2	33.3	6	100.0
Subtotal	93	39.2	77	32.5	67	28.3	237	100.0
Female								
16–19	8	66.7	4	33.3			12	100.0
20–24	28	70.0	7	17.5	5	12.5	40	100.0
25–34	11	45.8	10	41.7	3	12.5	24	100.0
35–49	–	–	3	100.0	–	–	3	100.0
50–65	1	100.0	–	–	–	–	1	100.0
Subtotal	48	60.0	24	30.0	8	10.0	80	100.0
All (with data)	141	44.5	101	31.9	75	23.7	317	100.0

Table 2.10a
Communication Activities Done When Visiting Internet Cafés, by Gender and Age

	Email		VoIP		Chat	
	#	%	#	%	#	%
Male						
16–19	36	62.1	37	63.8	38	65.5
20–24	58	54.7	60	56.6	78	73.6
25–34	41	67.2	31	50.8	36	59.0
35–49	17	70.8	5	20.8	11	45.8
50–65	4	66.7	1	16.7	1	16.7
Subtotal	156	61.2	134	52.5	164	64.3
Female						
16–19	9	75.0	6	50.0	7	58.3
20–24	30	75.0	16	40.0	26	65.0
25–34	17	68.0	10	40.0	15	60.0
35–49	3	100.0	–	–	1	33.3
50–65	–	–	1	100.0	–	–
Subtotal	59	72.8	33	40.7	49	60.5
All users	215	64.0	167	49.7	213	63.4

Note: Percentage figures are in relation to total number of users in the sample.

Table 2.10b
Education and Learning Activities Done When Visiting Internet Cafés, by Gender and Age

	Type or Print Homework		Take an Online Course		Conduct Research		Create Web Page		Search for Local and International News		Apply for College Admission	
	#	%	#	%	#	%	#	%	#	%	#	%
Male												
16–19	6	10.3	5	8.6	0		5	8.6	17	29.3	32	55.2
20–24	37	34.9	5	4.7	1	0.9	14	13.2	37	34.9	45	42.5
25–34	9	14.8	5	8.2	3	4.9	5	8.2	22	36.1	14	23.0
35–49	1	4.2	–	–	5	20.8	–	–	12	50.0	2	8.3
50–65	1	16.7	–	–	–	–	1	16.7	3	50.0	–	–
Subtotal	54	21.2	15	5.9	9	3.5	25	9.8	91	35.7	93	36.5
Female												
16–19	4	33.3	–	–	–	–	–	–	2	16.7	4	33.3
20–24	19	47.5	4	10.0	–	–	–	–	11	27.5	3	7.5
25–34	2	8.0	4	16.0	–	–	4	16.0	5	20.0	6	24.0
35–49	1	33.3	1	33.3	–	–	–	–	1	33.3	–	–
50–65	–	–	–	–	–	–	–	–	–	–	–	–
Subtotal	26	32.1	9	11.1	0		4	4.9	19	23.5	13	16.0
All users	80	23.8	24	7.1	9	2.7	29	8.6	110	32.7	106	31.5

Notes: Percentage figures are in relation to total number of users in the sample.
Creating web pages or searching for local and international news are only indirectly linked to education and learning.

people around the world"—were both ranked highly positive by 38 percent of users and slightly positive by 33 and 38 percent, respectively.

Education and Learning Using the Internet for educational purposes—for example, doing research online, writing homework, or sending emails to teachers—was perceived as slightly or highly positive by 61 percent of respondents (table 2.11b). Ninety-three percent had positive perceptions of improving computer skills and 84 percent of improving English language skills. Attending online classes and workshops was apparently least useful: 63 percent ranked this activity as having no impact.

There are interesting differences in the responses regarding activities performed and perceptions of impact. The number of users who say they use the venue to conduct research (3 percent; table 2.10b) or type or print out their homework (24 percent; table

Table 2.10c
Income and Employment Activities Done When Visiting Internet Cafés, by Gender and Age

	Search for a Job		Apply for a Job		Interview for a Job		Make Money From Online Business		Buy Products Online	
	#	%	#	%	#	%	#	%	#	%
Male										
16–19	4	6.9	2	3.4	–	–	6	10.3	6	10.3
20–24	19	17.9	15	14.2	6	5.7	4	3.8	26	24.5
25–34	20	32.8	20	32.8	3	4.9	1	1.6	14	23.0
35–49	5	20.8	6	25.0	–	–	–	–	3	12.5
50–65	2	33.3	1	16.7	1	16.7	–	–	2	33.3
Subtotal	50	19.6	44	17.3	10	3.9	11	4.3	51	20.0
Female										
16–19	–	–	–	–	–	–	–	–	4	33.3
20–24	1	2.5	2	5.0	–	–	–	–	24	60.0
25–34	10	40.0	6	24.0	1	4.0	1	4.0	5	20.0
35–49	1	33.3	–	–	–	–	–	–	1	33.3
50–65	–	–	–	–	–	–	–	–	–	–
Subtotal	12	14.8	8	9.9	1	1.2	1	1.2	34	42.0
All users	62	18.5	52	15.5	11	3.3	12	3.6	85	25.3

Notes: Percentage figures are in relation to total number of users in the sample. Strictly speaking, buying products online is not an income-generating activity, except in the sense that users may feel it saves them money.

2.10b) is relatively small, but when users are asked instead, "Which of the following has had an impact on you from using the Internet at the Internet cafés?", a larger number of users (38 percent; table 2.11b) report a highly positive impact from "Education (e.g., doing research, writing homework, sending e-mail to teachers)," and an additional 23 percent report a slightly positive impact.

Income and Employment Impact on income or employment was rated much lower than for the other two impact categories (table 2.11c). Nevertheless, 36 percent of men perceived a (highly or slightly) positive impact on finding a job, 24 percent on getting a promotion, and 27 percent on increasing their income. Women's perceptions of impact in this area were lower, perhaps on account of the relatively lower rate of labor force participation of the women surveyed (table 2.2).

Table 2.10d
Entertainment Activities Internet Café Users Engage In, by Gender and Age

	Watch Movies Online		Listen to and Download Music Files		Play Computer Games Online	
	#	%	#	%	#	%
Male						
16–19	1	1.7	23	39.7	34	58.6
20–24	6	5.7	22	20.8	52	49.1
25–34	1	1.6	10	16.4	16	26.2
35–49	1	4.2	3	12.5	4	16.7
50–65	–	–	–	–	–	–
Subtotal	9	3.5	58	22.7	106	41.6
Female						
16–19	1	8.3	6	50.0	8	66.7
20–24	–	–	8	20.0	11	27.5
25–34	–	–	6	24.0	4	16.0
35–49	–	–	–	–	–	–
50–65	–	–	–	–	–	–
Subtotal	1	1.2	20	24.7	23	28.4
All users	10	3.0	78	23.2	129	38.4

Nearly 15 percent of respondents had apparently been negatively impacted with respect to "finding a job." This is the single indicator for which the most negative impact was perceived. Interestingly, however, within the Economic and Employment category, this is also the indicator with the largest proportion of positive impact marks (33 percent; table 2.11c).

Does Having a Home Connection Make a Difference? Because more than 40 percent of café users also had a home connection (table 2.5), it is reasonable to ask to what extent the perceived impact is due to the public access provided—primarily if not exclusively—by the Internet café, as opposed to the impact perceived by café users who had the added convenience of being able to connect to the Internet from their homes.

The one observable marked difference is the negative impact with respect to meeting people online reported by ten female café users, for which there was no counterpart among female users with home connections (table 2.12a). The sample size is small, and we cannot determine whether this difference is statistically significant. Furthermore, because the questions asked refer to online meetings regardless of access place, there is no reason for the place of access to give rise to a difference.

Table 2.11a
User Perceptions of Impact on Social Networking, by Gender

		Positive			Negative				
Perception of Impact on		Highly	Slightly	Highly or Slightly	Slightly	Highly	Slightly or Highly	No Impact*	All Users
Meeting new people online	Male	103	83	186	22	7	29	40	255
	%	40.4	32.5	72.9	8.6	2.7	11.4	15.7	100.0
	Female	24	27	51	4	6	10	20	81
	%	29.6	33.3	63.0	4.9	7.4	12.3	24.7	100.0
	Total	127	110	237	26	13	39	60	336
	%	37.8	32.7	70.5	7.7	3.9	11.6	17.9	100.0
Maintaining communication with family and friends using social networking	Male	166	47	213	13	3	16	26	255
	%	65.1	18.4	83.5	5.1	1.2	6.3	10.2	100.0
	Female	39	27	66	2	3	5	10	81
	%	48.1	33.3	81.5	2.5	3.7	6.2	12.3	100.0
	Total	205	74	279	15		21	36	336
	%	61.0	22.0	83.0	4.5	0.0	6.3	10.7	100.0
Knowing about the culture of other people around the world	Male	105	91	196	13	5	18	41	255
	%	41.2	35.7	76.9	5.1	2.0	7.1	16.1	100.0
	Female	22	36	58	3	3	6	17	81
	%	27.2	44.4	71.6	3.7	3.7	7.4	21.0	100.0
	Total	127	127	254	16	8	24	58	336
	%	37.8	37.8	75.6	4.8	2.4	7.1	17.3	100.0

*Includes respondents who left this question unanswered.

Table 2.11b

User Perceptions of Impact on Education and Learning, by Gender

		Positive			Negative				
Perception of Impact on		Highly	Slightly	Highly or Slightly	Slightly	Highly	Slightly or Highly	No Impact*	All Users
Education (e.g., doing research, writing homework, sending emails to teachers)	Male	91	58	149	8	9	17	89	255
	%	35.7	22.7	58.4	3.1	3.5	6.7	34.9	100.0
	Female	36	19	55	2	8	10	16	81
	%	44.4	23.5	67.9	2.5	9.9	12.3	19.8	100.0
	Total	127	77	204	10	17	27	105	336
	%	37.8	22.9	60.7	3.0	5.1	8.0	31.3	100.0
Improving computer skills	Male	134	104	238	9	2	11	6	255
	%	52.5	40.8	93.3	3.5	0.8	4.3	2.4	100.0
	Female	28	48	76	3	–	3	2	81
	%	34.6	59.3	93.8	3.7	–	3.7	2.5	100.0
	Total	162	152	314	12	2	14	8	336
	%	48.2	45.2	93.5	3.6	0.6	4.2	2.4	100.0
Improving English language skills	Male	105	110	215	11	4	15	25	255
	%	41.2	43.1	84.3	4.3	1.6	5.9	9.8	100.0
	Female	19	47	66	2	1	3	12	81
	%	23.5	58.0	81.5	2.5	1.2	3.7	14.8	100.0
	Total	124	157	281	13	5	18	37	336
	%	36.9	46.7	83.6	3.9	1.5	5.4	11.0	100.0
Attending online classes and workshops	Male	30	37	67	18	9	27	161	255
	%	11.8	14.5	26.3	7.1	3.5	10.6	63.1	100.0
	Female	8	13	21	2	7	9	51	81
	%	9.9	16.0	25.9	2.5	8.6	11.1	63.0	100.0
	Total	38	50	88	20	16	36	212	336
	%	11.3	14.9	26.2	6.0	4.8	10.7	63.1	100.0

*Includes respondents who left this question unanswered.

Table 2.11c

User Perceptions of Impact on Income and Employment, by Gender

Perception of Impact on		Positive			Negative				
		Highly	Slightly	Highly or Slightly	Slightly	Highly	Slightly or Highly	No Impact*	All Users
Getting a promotion at work	Male	24	37	61	13	9	22	172	255
	%	9.4	14.5	23.9	5.1	3.5	8.6	67.5	100.0
	Female	5	7	12	2	1	3	66	81
	%	6.2	8.6	14.8	2.5	1.2	3.7	81.5	100.0
	Total	29	44	73	15	10	25	238	336
	%	8.6	13.1	21.7	4.5	3.0	7.4	70.8	100.0
Increasing your income	Male	26	42	68	27	6	33	154	255
	%	10.2	16.5	26.7	10.6	2.4	12.9	60.4	100.0
	Female	2	6	8	6	2	8	65	81
	%	2.5	7.4	9.9	7.4	2.5	9.9	80.2	100.0
	Total	28	48	76	33	8	41	219	336
	%	8.3	14.3	22.6	9.8	2.4	12.2	65.2	100.0
Finding a job	Male	30	63	93	28	13	41	121	255
	%	11.8	24.7	36.5	11.0	5.1	16.1	47.5	100.0
	Female	4	15	19	3	5	8	54	81
	%	4.9	18.5	23.5	3.7	6.2	9.9	66.7	100.0
	Total	34	78	112	31	18	49	175	336
	%	10.1	23.2	33.3	9.2	5.4	14.6	52.1	100.0

*Includes respondents who left this question unanswered.

Overall, there appears to be no major systematic difference in the perceived impact among Internet café users between those who had Internet at home and those who did not (tables 2.12a–12c). We must conclude that the perceived impacts with respect to the ten indicators result from user access to the Internet, irrespective of the place of access. Internet cafés provide valuable, affordable access to both kinds of users: those who have and those who do not have an Internet connection at home.

Gender Differences

The rate of economic participation among Internet café users—employed plus unemployed as a percentage of the total—is higher among men (55 percent) than among women (42 percent). This lower rate among women users is much higher than for Jordan as a whole, where women's rate of participation in the labor force is about 15 percent (Tabbaa 2010).

Within the limited subsample of non-dependent respondents ages 20 or older, women seem to have a personal income advantage over males, with only 22 percent of men (twenty-seven observations) reporting monthly income of 700 JD or higher compared with 52 percent (eleven observations) of women (table 2.13).

Women users visit Internet cafés less frequently and spend fewer hours there than men. About 56 percent of the women interviewed visited cybercafés once a week or less frequently, compared with 22 percent of men (table 2.7), whereas 61 percent of men spent two or more hours per visit and only 40 percent of women did (table 2.9). The lower frequency and duration of women's visits to cybercafés probably apply to Amman's café user population as a whole and help explain in part our sample's gender imbalance.

There are no major gender-related differences in user perceptions of impact (tables 2.11a–2.11c). The proportion of women (68 percent) positively impacted, either highly or slightly, in terms of education is higher than that of men (58 percent; table 2.11b), but this may be due to the larger proportion of students among women (58 percent, table 2.2) than among men (44 percent).

Table 2.14 disaggregates interviewees by gender in the twenty-four Internet cafés studied. Women visitors are relatively more important in venues situated near the University of Jordan, a female-dominated institution with a student body that is more than 70 percent female. This is the case of the University Center Café and Evolution Café (numbered 10 and 11 in table 2.14). Also, cafés serving high- and upper middle-class areas of Amman, such as Sweifeyeh and Khalda, exhibit a higher proportion of female users. This includes Waves Café, Rehaf Net, Zorona Café, City View Café, and Hanin Net. Altogether, these seven cafés where women users are in the majority account for

Table 2.12a

User Perceptions of Impact on Social Networking, by Gender and Whether User had Internet Connection at Home

		Net at	Positive			Negative			No Impact		All	
Perception of Impact on	M/F	Home	Highly	Slightly	%	Slightly	Highly	%	#	%	#	%
Meeting new people online	M	Yes	50	37	79.8	9	2	10.1	11	10.1	98	100.0
		No	53	46	72.3	12	5	12.4	21	15.3	116	100.0
	F	Yes	13	12	80.6	–	–	–	6	19.4	25	100.0
		No	11	15	54.2	4	6	20.8	12	25.0	36	100.0
Maintaining communication with family and friends using social networking	M	Yes	85	15	90.9	3	1	3.6	6	5.5	104	100.0
		No	81	32	81.3	9	2	7.9	15	10.8	124	100.0
	F	Yes	19	7	83.9	1		3.2	4	12.9	27	100.0
		No	20	20	83.3	1	3	8.3	4	8.3	44	100.0
Knowing about the culture of other people around the world	M	Yes	44	44	80.0	6	2	7.3	14	12.7	96	100.0
		No	61	47	78.8	6	3	6.6	20	14.6	117	100.0
	F	Yes	10	12	71.0	1	1	6.5	7	22.6	24	100.0
		No	12	24	75.0	2	2	8.3	8	16.7	40	100.0

Table 2.12b

User Perceptions of Impact on Education and Learning, by Gender and Whether User Had Internet Connection at Home

Perception of Impact on	M/F	Net at Home	Positive			Negative			No impact		All	
			Highly	Slightly	%	Slightly	Highly	%	#	%	#	%
Education (e.g., doing research, writing homework, sending emails to teachers)	M	Yes	46	31	80.2	5	3	8.3	11	11.5	85	100.0
		No	45	27	71.3	4	4	7.9	21	20.8	80	100.0
	F	Yes	13	8	63.6	4	2	18.2	6	18.2	27	100.0
		No	23	11	68.0	4		8.0	12	24.0	38	100.0
Improving computer skills	M	Yes	66	39	89.7	1	5	5.1	6	5.1	111	100.0
		No	68	64	86.8	1	4	3.3	15	9.9	137	100.0
	F	Yes	12	17	82.9	–	2	5.7	4	11.4	31	100.0
		No	16	31	90.4	–	1	1.9	4	7.7	48	100.0
Improving English language skills	M	Yes	51	50	83.5	1	5	5.0	14	11.6	107	100.0
		No	54	60	80.3	3	5	5.6	20	14.1	122	100.0
	F	Yes	8	14	73.3	–	1	3.3	7	23.3	23	100.0
		No	11	33	81.5	1	1	3.7	8	14.8	46	100.0
Attending online classes and workshops	M	Yes	13	21	55.7	4	9	21.3	14	23.0	47	100.0
		No	17	16	50.0	5	8	19.7	20	30.3	46	100.0
	F	Yes	4	2	42.9	1	–	7.1	7	50.0	7	100.0
		No	4	11	48.4	6	2	25.8	8	25.8	23	100.0

Table 2.12c

User Perceptions of Impact on Income and Employment, by Gender and Whether User Had Internet Connection at Home

		Net at	Positive			Negative			No Impact		All	
Perception of Impact on	M/F	Home	Highly	Slightly	%	Slightly	Highly	%	#	%	#	%
Getting a promotion at work	M	Yes	46	20	48.2	5	2	5.1	64	46.7	73	100.0
		No	45	17	39.0	8	7	9.4	82	51.6	77	100.0
	F	Yes	13	2	35.7	–	–		27	64.3	15	100.0
		No	23	5	43.8	2	1	4.7	33	51.6	31	100.0
Increasing your income	M	Yes	10	18	26.9	7	3	9.6	66	63.5	38	100.0
		No	14	24	27.7	19	3	16.1	77	56.2	60	100.0
	F	Yes	2	–	6.3	1	1	6.3	28	87.5	4	100.0
		No	3	6	18.0	5	1	12.0	35	70.0	15	100.0
Finding a job	M	Yes	12	31	43.4	6	3	9.1	47	47.5	52	100.0
		No	14	32	34.8	22	10	24.2	54	40.9	78	100.0
	F	Yes	1	4	16.1	–	2	6.5	24	77.4	7	100.0
		No	1	11	26.7	3	3	13.3	27	60.0	18	100.0

Table 2.13
Monthly Personal Income of Nondependent Adults Ages 20 or Older, by Gender

	200–700 JD	700–1,500 JD	>, JD	All Non-dependent ≥20 Years
Nondependent users	108	32	6	146
	74%	22%	4%	100%
Nondependent men	98	25	2	125
	78%	20%	2%	100%
Nondependent women	10	7	4	21
	48%	33%	19%	100%

JD = Jordanian dinars.

Table 2.14
Distribution of Interviewees by Gender in the 24 Participating Cafés

#	Café Name	# Computers	Females	Males	Total
1	Another World Café	13	1	12	13
2	Al-Sultan Café	5	2	3	5
3	Chit Chat Café	13	2	11	13
4	Waves Café	12	5	5	10
5	Rehaf Net	15	6	6	12
6	Zorona Café	9	5	4	9
7	Hanin Net	10	6	3	9
8	City View Café	16	7	5	12
9	Square Café	23	5	15	20
10	University Internet Center	37	12	7	17
11	Evolution Café	12	7	5	12
12	Aldawqa Café	12	3	10	13
13	Al-Shmeisani Café	10	2	9	11
14	Al-Tahawor Café	9	1	10	11
15	California Café	20	2	18	20
16	Al-Ekhtessase Café	10	2	9	11
17	Facebook Café	30	3	25	28
18	Ghost Café	24	1	18	19
19	Lojain Café	17	2	15	17
20	Al-Serat Café	18	2	18	20
21	Al-Bader Café	10	1	8	9
22	Pluto Café	10	2	10	12
23	Amman Online	12	1	13	14
24	Kaza Café	20	1	18	19
	Total	367	81	257	336

59 percent of the females in our sample, but they do not cater exclusively to women: about 42 percent of their customers are men. In contrast, the dominance of male users in the remaining cafés surveyed is overwhelming: 87 percent male versus 13 percent female.

Our findings contradict Wheeler's (2004) assertion that in Jordan "most cafés have an equal number of male and female users." Perhaps Wheeler based her observation on a small sample. Gender disparity would not have been detected if only a few cafés were sampled and these happened to be gender balanced.

Conclusions and Recommendations

More than 70 percent of users interviewed report having benefited from using Internet cafés by expanding their social networks, maintaining communications with family and friends, and learning about other cultures. Positive assessments of impact on education and learning indicators were also reported by 60 percent of users. Income or employment impacts were less common but are not insignificant, especially among men. The Jordanian government's policy of increasing the number of licenses for private café operators is commendable and should be maintained.

Our study's findings put the spotlight on a major area of concern. Although women and men benefit equally from cybercafés, comparatively few women use these venues, and those who use them do so infrequently. If the benefits for women so vividly described by Wheeler (2004, 2006, 2007) and confirmed by this study are to be widely achieved and obtained, then the observed imbalance in access must be addressed.

Are these differences culturally determined, perhaps a choice dictated by the norms of a society trying to modernize but not yet comfortable with a more active engagement by women? Or are there features of the cybercafé environment that make women feel at risk of being harassed or disturbed?

The appropriate policy response would differ depending on which of these sets of factors underlies the observed gender imbalance. If it is a matter of culture, campaigns to sensitize families and potential female users to the potential benefits of cybercafés might be in order. However, if the environment of these venues prevents greater use by women, regulatory measures (non-discrimination and a suitable open environment as a requirement for licensing), combined perhaps with incentives to motivate greater use by women (e.g., IT training scholarships to encourage females to use cybercafés), would increase the demand for cybercafé services and at the same time make it in operators' best interest to maintain a female-friendly environment in their cybercafés.

Identifying the obstacles that prevent women, especially low-income women, from using cybercafés and designing suitable policies to overcome them should be a priority subject of research as well as an urgent concern of policymakers. We urge Jordanian researchers and government officials to take up the challenge.

References

Tabbaa, Yasmeen. 2010. *Female Labour Force Participation in Jordan.* Policy paper prepared for the Jordan Economic and Social Council, Amman, Jordan. http://esc.jo/NewsViewer.aspx?NewsId=38#.UvNVzfbRuwo

Wheeler, Deborah L. 2004. The Internet in the Arab World: Digital Divides and Cultural Connections. Lecture presented on June 16, 2004, in Amman, Jordan, at the Royal Institute for Inter-Faith Studies. http://208.112.119.94/guest/lecture_text/internet_n_arabworld_all_txt.htm

Wheeler, Deborah L. 2006. Empowering Publics: Information Technology and Democratization in the Arab World—Lessons from Internet Cafés and Beyond. Oxford Internet Institute, Research Report 11. http://papers.ssrn.com/sol3/papers.cfm?abstract_id=1308527

Wheeler, Deborah L. 2007. Empowerment Zones? Women, Internet Cafés, and Life Transformations in Egypt. *Information Technologies and International Development* 4 (2): 89–104.

3 Impact of Public Access to ICT Skills on Job Prospects in Rwanda

Jean Damascène Mazimpaka, Théodomir Mugiraneza, and Ramata Molo Thioune

Abstract

The Social Economic Development Strategy of Rwanda specifically highlights the creation of an ICT, knowledge-based society as key to the country's development. Public access venues present a way through which ICT skills can be acquired by a large segment of the population. This chapter presents research on users of such venues and assesses the contribution ICT skills make to their job prospects. The research adopted a case study methodology: a questionnaire was administered in both urban and rural areas, and interviews were conducted with key stakeholders. The research finds that ICT skills acquired from such venues help users to get recruited, although the level of impact is modest because of limited job opportunities in the country and users' gap in satisfying other skill requirements of existing jobs. We recommend that government support of telecenters be continued and that the feasibility of supporting training in private urban venues be assessed.

Introduction

Rwanda is a landlocked country in central East Africa with an area of 26,338 km^2 and a population of 10,718,379 inhabitants (2012), 85 percent of whom live in rural areas (National Institute of Statistics of Rwanda 2012). Rwanda has limited resources and identifies its people as its principal asset. Rwanda's development strategy, *Vision 2020* (Republic of Rwanda 2000), acknowledges the shortage of technically qualified people at all levels and lists among its targets to have adequate, highly skilled technicians to satisfy the needs of the national economy.

Access to skills training through schools and universities is common but limited by cost, age, learning timetables, and entry requirements. Formal institutions charge high fees that low-income people cannot afford (Freistadt, Pal, and Alves da Silva 2009). Workers are excluded by inflexible learning timetables. Mature workers in particular seek suitable places where they can learn ICT skills that were not part of the curriculum at the time of their formal education. When low-income people and workers want to acquire ICT skills, their main options are public access venues. In addition, many people who learned basic ICT skills through formal education often further that learning at public access venues.

Rwanda has sought to address this need for low-cost skills training, in part, through a community telecenter project sponsored by the Rwanda Information Technology Authority. By 2012, ninety-four telecenters had been established throughout the country's thirty districts (Republic of Rwanda 2013).

The present study looks at ICT skills acquisition in various types of public venues in Rwanda that provide access to computers and the Internet. A mixed method approach combining qualitative and quantitative methods is used to assess the extent to which the skills acquired in these venues help people get jobs or progress in their career.

Becker et al. (2010) studied the uses of computers and Internet access in U.S. public libraries and found they help users acquire ICT skills that allow them to maintain or obtain employment. Garrido, Rothschild, and Oumar (2009) found that basic ICT skills training combined with assistance in both job search and application process make a significant contribution to job acquisition. Mariscal, Gutierrez, and Botelho (2009) assessed the effect of ICT training provided by NGOs and found that this training offered unique opportunities for integrating marginalized youth into the labor force in Brazil, Colombia, and Mexico.

We find that in Rwanda, ICT skills acquired from public access venues have a positive impact on job prospects, but that the degree of impact depends on the level of education of venue users and on venue type and location, competence of the instructor, duration of the training, and sex of trainees.

Purpose and Methods

Venue Types

Three types of public access venues are common in Rwanda (table 3.1).

Telecenters are government-financed venues that provide public access to computers and the Internet, as well as ICT training and ICT services such as printing. They are generally located in rural areas that are not served by commercial venues. The Rwanda government has also funded mobile telecenters: buses equipped with computers, Internet access, and a power generator. ICT buses take telecenter services to remote areas lacking electricity.

Table 3.1
Basic Features of Rwanda's Public Access Venues

	Telecenters	Cybercafés	Public Secretariats
Total Rwanda	20 (another 10 are being established)	128	130–200
Sponsor	Government	Private firms	Private firms
Rural/urban	Rural	Urban	Urban
Primary service:	Rural access to computers & Internet, including training.	Public access to computers & Internet for a fee.	Office support such as typing, printing, scanning, photocopying. Some also offer Internet access.
Equipment			
Computers	12 small centers have 15 computers; 18 new ones have 40. All have MS Office suite.	Varies widely, from about 4 to 20 computers per center. Usually equipped with MS Office suite.	Varies widely, from 3 in small workroom to 10 in big room shared by individuals, each with one computer, or by several people employed by owner.
Internet	All computers are connected, but quality of connection is low and breakdowns are frequent.	All computers are connected, but quality of connection is low and breakdowns are frequent.	Although some provide public access, only 1 of the 5 visited had Internet connection.
Training services	All telecenters have well-structured ICT training program in basic computer skills. Internet training is mainly on how to use email system.	Café users rely mainly on their friends to teach them and on self-training.	Training is of secondary importance. Staff engage in training only when there is demand and some staff are free to train.
Instructor qualifications	Diploma holders in IT/computer science/electronics, possibly with additional IT training (e.g., Cisco certificate).	Mainly secondary school certificate holders with additional training in basic IT skills.	Mainly secondary school certificate holders with additional training in basic IT skills.

Cybercafés are commercial enterprises that provide public access to computers and the Internet for a fee. In general, cybercafé staff members do not train users: rather, users learn ICT skills on their own by trial and error or with the help of some other person.

Public secretariats are commercial enterprises primarily oriented to ICT services such as typing, printing, scanning, and photocopying. Some also provide access to computers and the Internet to the public at large. ICT training covering word processing, spreadsheet software, and sometimes also Internet use occurs but tends to be a secondary activity.

Cybercafés and public secretariats are found mainly in urban areas, whereas telecenters, in line with government policy, are located mainly in rural areas. In practice, few telecenters (perhaps three) are located in remote small villages; most are located in areas that, although not considered urban, have many characteristics of urban areas: they are reached by the national power line and the national water supply system, and they have secondary schools, health centers, markets, and district and sector offices. These localities are generally unable to sustain commercial venues such as cybercafés, but they can nevertheless accommodate a lot of people and serve a significant user base.

When our survey was conducted in 2010, there were about twenty telecenters, around 130 cybercafés, and a somewhat larger number of public secretariats, possibly 140 or more, in operation in Rwanda.[1]

Research Questions

The impact of public access venues on "job prospects" may be perceived in one of three ways: getting a job as a result of skills acquired from a public access venue (PAV), self-employment in own ICT-based business after acquiring ICT skills from a PAV, or career advancement as a result of acquired ICT skills. The following research questions are addressed:

1. Do acquired ICT skills differ by venue type, venue location, instructor competence, or gender of trainees?
2. How do ICT skills acquired from public access venues affect user job prospects?

Theory of Change

Figure 3.1 shows our view of the process of acquiring ICT skills in public access venues and how these skills impact user job prospects.[2] Inputs include the ICT infrastructure, the instructor, and users' motivation. These inputs enable activities such as learning basic computer skills, Internet-based communication, and online

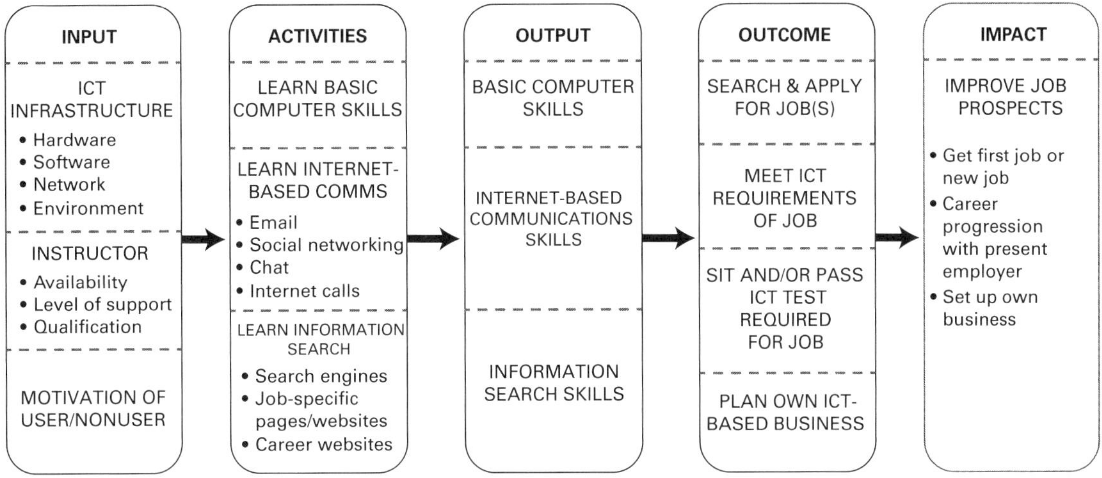

Figure 3.1
Logic Model of ICT skills acquisition in PAVs and impact on job prospects.

information search to take place. The resulting outputs include basic computer skills needed for some jobs, skills for information search over the Internet, and Internet-based communication that can help trainees exchange job-related information. Outputs may lead to outcomes such as searching and applying for a job, meeting ICT competences required for a job, doing ICT tests required in recruitment, and planning one's own business as a result of ICT skills acquired. Finally, the impact is the extent to which the acquisition of ICT skills enhances job prospects, with people either getting their first job or a promotion or setting up their own ICT-based business.

Data

The data used were collected through a formal purposive sample survey (Kumar 2005) complemented by interviews of key stakeholders and observations in public access venues.

Purposive Sample Survey A questionnaire was administered to 418 white-collar and office workers who occupy positions that are likely to involve the use of basic computer skills, including secretaries, receptionists, customer care officers, administrative assistants, finance officers, and human resource managers. Respondents were selected from both public and private institutions where workers occupying these positions are usually found. The sample was drawn from 100 secondary schools,[3] 48 bank branches,

5 provincial government offices, 21 district government offices, 6 ministries, 6 other government institutions, 54 cybercafés, and 48 public secretariats.

Every person surveyed had ICT skills. We classify respondents in three categories:

1. *Primary user-trainees* are those who use PAVs to acquire ICT skills.
2. *Supplementary user-trainees* acquired basic ICT skills elsewhere, but the time they spend at PAVs is more than 50 percent of the time they spend using either the computer or the Internet.
3. *Occasional users* acquired their basic ICT skills from a place other than a PAV, and they use PAVs less than 50 percent of the time they spend using the Internet and the computer.

We refer to the first two categories as *public access user-trainees*.

Table 3.2 shows the distribution of respondents according to rural–urban status, gender, and age and trainee type. Occasional users represent 60 percent of the sample and public access user-trainees (primary and supplementary) account for the remaining 40 percent. About 52 percent of respondents were male and 48 percent female. Respondents between the ages of 20 and 29 make up 49 percent of the sample. Frequent PAV users have more limited formal training than occasional users (table 3.3). Many occasional users are formally educated and either have a university degree or finished secondary school, where ICT training was part of the curriculum. About 60 percent of occasional users have a post-secondary education compared to only about 35 percent of user-trainees.

About 78 percent of user-trainees acquired their ICT skills in urban areas. The 22 percent trained in rural areas include two primary users trained at an ICT bus (table 3.4).

Qualitative Data When we started collecting data, there were twelve fully operational telecenters, each having fifteen PCs. For our qualitative analysis, we visited ten of the twelve existing small telecenters, plus two recently established large telecenters. We also visited five cybercafés and five public secretariats. The smaller sample of commercial venues is due to difficulties experienced when trying to get operation-related information from these centers.

In the sampled venues, we conducted interviews with ICT instructors, made observations, and read the registry of trainees where available. From the registries of trainees, we identified former trainees whom we then met based on their availability. These former trainees answered the questionnaire and had an unstructured interview with us.

Table 3.2
Distribution of Survey Respondents by Age, Gender, and Trainee Type

	Primary		Supplementary		Occasional		All types	
	#	%	#	%	#	%	#	%
Rural—Male								
17–19	–	–	–	–	–	–	–	–
20–29	8	38.1	7	70.0	24	39.3	39	42.4
30–35	6	28.6	2	20.0	17	27.9	25	27.2
≥ 36	7	33.3	1	10.0	20	32.8	28	30.4
Subtotal	21	100.0	10	100.0	61	100.0	92	100.0
Rural—Female								
17–19	–	–	–	–	–	–	–	–
20–29	9	50.0	3	50.0	16	41.0	28	44.4
30–35	4	22.2	2	33.3	11	28.2	17	27.0
≥ 36	5	27.8	1	16.7	12	30.8	18	28.6
Subtotal	18	100.0	6	100.0	30	100.0	63	100.0
Subtotal Rural	39		16		100		153	
%	25.2		10.3		64.5		100.0	
Urban—Male								
17–19	–	–	–	–	–	–	–	–
20–29	18	69.2	22	62.9	24	39.3	64	52.5
30–35	4	15.4	5	14.3	21	34.4	30	24.6
≥ 36	4	15.4	8	22.9	16	26.2	28	23.0
Subtotal	26	100.0	35	100.0	61	100.0	122	100.0
Urban—Female								
17–19	–	4.5	1	3.3	–	–	1	0.7
20–29	9	40.9	22	73.3	40	44.9	71	51.8
30–35	4	22.7	3	10.0	19	21.3	26	19.0
≥ 36	5	31.8	4	13.3	30	33.7	39	28.5
Subtotal	18	100.0	30	100.0	89	100.0	137	100.0
Subtotal Urban	44		65		150		259	
%	17.0		25.1		57.9		100.0	
All respondents	83		81		250		414	
%	20.0		19.6		60.4		100.0	

Note: The number given as "All respondents" includes the number of respondents with complete information on rural/urban status, age, and gender.

Table 3.3

Level of Education of Respondents by User Category

	Primary User-Trainee		Supplementary User-Trainee		Occasional User		Total	
	#	%	#	%	#	%	#	%
Primary school	3	3.4	–	–	–	–	3	0.7
Interrupted secondary	10	11.5	5	6.4	–	–	15	3.6
Finished secondary	44	50.6	45	57.7	101	39.9	190	45.5
Post-secondary	30	34.5	28	35.9	152	60.1	210	50.2
Total	87	100.0	78	100.0	253	100.0	418	100.0

Table 3.4

Distribution of Survey Respondents by User Type, Location (Rural/Urban), Where ICT Skills were Acquired, and Gender

	Gender					
	Male		Female		All	
Rural/urban status	#	%	#	%	#	%
User-trainees						
Rural	22	26.8	12	17.4	34	22.5
%	64.7		35.3		100.0	
Urban	60	73.2	57	82.6	117	77.5
%	52.1		47.9		100.0	
Total user-trainees	82	100.0	69	100.0	151	100.0
%	54.3		45.7		100.0	
Occasional users						
Rural	31	29.0	34	27.9	65	28.3
%	46.3		53.7		100.0	
Urban	76	71.0	88	72.1	164	71.7
%	46.7		53.3		100.0	
Total occasional users	107	100.0	122	100.0	229	100.0
%	46.7		53.3		100.0	

Findings

Inputs

ICT Infrastructure The ICT infrastructure varies from one venue to another. Telecenters are most uniform. Telecenters use their PCs for training and Internet access service, and they usually also have two printers, a scanner, and a server to control the networked computers. In addition, each telecenter has a dish antenna through which it connects to the Internet, but the quality and speed of connection are generally poor. All computers are equipped with Microsoft's (MS) Office suite (Word, Excel, and PowerPoint). In some telecenters (e.g., the Nyabihu telecenter), additional programs such as video editing software are available as a result of the instructor's commitment and users' requests.

Cybercafés and public secretariats differ one from another in terms of ICT infrastructure. All cybercafés have an Internet connection, but apparently few public secretariats do. Given that cybercafés are commercially oriented and their primary interest is in selling Internet-based services, MS Office is not largely used even if it is installed on the computers. Clients normally come in to check their email or search for information on the web. The number of computers in cybercafés ranges from about four to twenty.

While a network of computers including a server is common in cybercafés and telecenters, the standalone workstation is the predominant setup in public secretariats. In one instance, each computer in the secretariat was connected to a printer and a scanner, and several operators could work in the same room. However, most public secretariats have many standalone computers, some of them connected to printers. In these cases, the venue provides training in basic computer skills in addition to typing services. Of the five public secretariats visited, four had no Internet connection and hence do not teach how to use the Internet. Even in the one with an Internet connection, we did not observe people learning how to use the Internet.

Our observations in twenty-two training venues (twelve telecenters, five cybercafés, and five public secretariats) and our interviews with ICT instructors in training venues and with two policymakers in the domain of public access to ICT venues tend to confirm that PAVs have an ICT infrastructure that is adequate for ICT skills training.

Instructor Telecenters have a standardized model. The instructors in three telecenters who agreed to reveal their qualifications are diploma holders with additional relevant certificates such as a Cisco training certificate. This is in line with the following statement from a policymaker interviewed: "Each telecenter has two employees: one with a bachelor's degree in a business administration field who manages the telecenter, and one with a diploma (A1) in an IT field who is an IT technician and instructor."

From direct observation and field visits, we find that the qualification of ICT instructors in cybercafés and public secretariats is lower and not standardized. A cybercafé normally has one or two employees who are in charge of billing and solving computer problems that may occur; they also sometimes teach users depending on how much free time they have and on their personal interest and initiative. The number of employees in public secretariats varies depending on the number of computers they have. Each employee is busy on one computer, handling typing services, but he or she may also be training a person at the same time depending on whether there is a trainee present and how much time the employee has allocated to providing this service.

Primary user-trainees are generally satisfied with the level of support they get from instructors, which they rate as either high (13 percent), moderately high (62 percent), or medium (18 percent) (table 3.5). The level of satisfaction with instructors' support is higher in telecenters than in cybercafés and, to a lesser degree, than in public secretariats. Most people who acquired ICT skills from public secretariats are fairly satisfied with

Table 3.5
Level of Support Received from Instructors by Primary User-trainees, by Venue Used

	Level of Support					
Venue type	High	Moderately High	Medium	Moderately Low	Low	All Primary User-trainees
Cybercafé	1	5	4	3	–	13
%	7.7	38.5	30.8	23.1	–	100.0
Telecenter	7	23	3	1	–	34
%	20.6	67.6	8.8	2.9	–	100.0
Public secretariat	2	15	6	1	–	24
%	8.3	62.5	25.0	4.2	–	100.0
Telecenter and public secretariat	–	2	–	–	–	2
%	–	100.0	–	–	–	100.0
Telecenter, café, and public secretariat	–	1	–	–	–	1
%	–	100.0	–	–	–	100.0
Total	10	46	13	5	–	74
%	13.5	62.2	17.6	6.8	–	100.0

the support they received from instructors. Over time, however, the training role of public secretariats—many of which do not have Internet access—appears to have diminished.

Telecenters were introduced in 2008. A few years previously, when there were only a few cybercafés and no telecenters, public secretariats were the only PAVs people could use to acquire ICT skills. The considerable number of people who reported a high to medium level of satisfaction with the support received from public secretariat instructors are probably those who acquired their training when they had no choice other than public secretariats. Nowadays, the affordability of telecenters, the structured training they provide, and their improving ICT infrastructure due to government support have made them the most-used PAV type for ICT skills acquisition. This is true despite their location in what are predominantly rural (albeit not remote) areas.

Motivation Although the most frequently used media for job advertisement in Rwanda are still newspapers and radio, some job vacancies are posted on institutions' websites. Some employers require that job seekers submit their applications by: (1) email, (2) completing and submitting an electronic form via the employer's website, or (3) filling out an application form downloaded from the website and submitting it in hard copy format. This form of job advertisement and submission is normally used by international NGOs, UN agencies, and some government agencies. These institutions also use the Internet to give feedback to job applicants, although phone calls are more common.

According to survey respondents knowing how to use the Internet is highly important (38 percent) or important (29 percent) in the job application process (table 3.6). This high level of appreciation of the importance of Internet use does not vary by either age or gender.

It is not just Internet use that is attractive to PAV users: they are also interested in other basic computer skills. For instance, many secondary school students interviewed said that attending ICT training in public access venues could help them master computer skills that had recently been introduced to their curriculum but were not well taught. They considered these skills to be among the most sought after in the job market.

PAV users pursue various objectives that lead them to acquire ICT skills. An estimated 82 percent of user-trainees had the objective of improving their skills so they could get a new or better job (table 3.7). The percentage of urban users with this objective is higher than among rural users, and this applies among both user-trainees and occasional users.

Table 3.6
Assessment by All Respondents of the Role of Internet Use in Job Application Process

	Level of Appreciation				
Gender and Age Range	Highly Important	Important	Less Important	Not Important	Total
Male					
17–19	–	–	–	–	–
%	–	–	–	–	–
20–29	49	27	6	18	100
%	49.0	27.0	6.0	18.0	100.0
30–35	15	16	7	17	55
%	27.3	29.1	12.7	30.9	100.0
≥ 36	17	15	6	10	48
%	35.4	31.3	12.5	20.8	100.0
Subtotal	81	58	19	45	203
%	39.9	28.6	9.4	22.2	100.0
Female					
17–19	–	–	–	2	2
%	–	–	–	100.0	100.0
20–29	33	31	11	19	94
%	35.1	33.0	11.7	20.2	100.0
30–35	18	9	8	9	44
%	40.9	20.5	18.2	20.5	100.0
≥ 36	19	16	6	13	54
%	35.2	29.6	11.1	24.1	100.0
Subtotal	70	56	25	43	194
%	36.1	28.9	12.9	22.2	100.0
Total	151	114	44	88	397
%	38.0	28.7	11.1	22.2	100.0

Training Activities

Computer Skills Training A public access venue can teach basic or advanced ICT skills or both. Basic computer skills include an introduction to computers, basic file management operations such as renaming and deleting files, and training in MS Office programs, mainly Word, Excel, and PowerPoint. Advanced skills include software programming, web page creation, troubleshooting hardware, updating antivirus software, and installing basic applications such as Office suites.

Telecenters have a well-structured ICT training program in basic computer skills. Cybercafés, in contrast, have no structured training. Customers are given occasional

Table 3.7
Respondents Who Had "Improving ICT Skills to Get a New or Better Job" as an Objective

	Male		Female		Total	
User Category	#	%	#	%	#	%
User-trainees						
Rural	20	13.4	16	10.7	36	24.2
Urban	44	29.5	42	28.2	86	57.7
Subtotal	64	43.0	58	38.9	122	81.9
Occasional users						
Rural	44	19.8	29	13.1	73	32.9
Urban	50	22.5	78	35.1	128	57.7
Subtotal	94	42.3	107	48.2	201	90.5
Grand total	158	42.6	165	44.5	323	87.1

Note: Percentages are calculated with respect to the number of respondents who answered about the objective of improving ICT skills to get a new or better job (149 user-trainees, 222 occasional users, and 371 total respondents).

help, but cybercafé personnel are primarily engaged in billing and troubleshooting computer problems; they can teach only when they have the time and inclination. In general, if users want to learn basic computer skills at a cybercafé, they bring in a friend who can teach them. Similarly, public secretariats concentrate mainly on ICT services such as typing, photocopying, and printing. They provide basic computer training to a few people occasionally when their staff members have a light workload.

Forty-five percent of the respondents reported that the training they received lasted between one and three months. According to instructors in telecenters, some training can last between three and six months—for example, the IT Essentials certificate (a Cisco-certified training program that includes advanced ICT skills and video editing) offered in four of the twelve visited telecenters. Users who followed this training acquired advanced ICT skills given the content of the material used.

Internet Skills Training All telecenters teach Internet-based communication, mainly how to use email. Other Internet-based communications (such as chatting, web-based social networking, and voice calls over Internet) are not included in the training program. In cybercafés, individuals generally bring friends who can teach them different forms of Internet-based communication, or the cybercafé employees teach them how to use email, but only when the employees are free.

Similar to Internet-based communication, information search is taught at all telecenters. As explained by instructors at two telecenters, training in information search is customized based on each trainee's interest and background, but this is an initiative of the instructor. Cybercafé employees teach information search only when they have the time and inclination, and so individuals tend to bring in friends to teach them. In general, public secretariats do not teach information search because they do not have an Internet connection, and their staff concentrate on other ICT services.

Differences by Type of Venue Telecenters appear to be better equipped than cybercafés and public secretariats to deliver the kind of ICT skills that are useful to trainees wanting to set up their own ICT-based businesses, prepare for recruitment tests, or perform newly acquired jobs.

In cybercafés and public secretariats, priority is given to selling Internet and typing and printing services, respectively, and training is considered an additional revenue-generating service. Telecenters offer solid training in basic and advanced ICT skills and specific types of training that can greatly contribute to job creation; these services are not offered in cybercafés or public secretariats. As well, ICT training certificates issued by telecenters are trusted locally and internationally, which is not the case for those issued by cybercafés and public secretariats. Typical examples are the Cisco-certified IT Essentials certificate and the International Computer Driving License (ICDL).[4] These certificates appear to give trainees who use telecenters an advantage in being recruited and setting up ICT-based businesses compared with trainees who use cybercafés and public secretariats.

Outputs

Basic Skills During our site visits, we observed the training process (including lecture sessions and practical sessions) in four of the twelve telecenters visited. In one telecenter, we saw the results of the test given at the end of ICT training, proving that trainees acquire some ICT skills and are evaluated. No training was taking place in the five cybercafés or the five public secretariats we visited.

The fact that trainees feel confident or feel the need to improve their ICT skills suggests that they have at least basic ICT skills (table 3.8). These basic skills include file management, mastered with confidence by about 90 percent of the respondents, word processing (about 89 percent), and use of spreadsheets (about 77 percent). Basic computer skills taught at PAVs also include identifying different hardware and software components, connecting various computer peripherals, and scanning for viruses, thus allowing trainees to get acquainted with a computer.

Table 3.8
Level of User Confidence in Selected Basic Computer Skills, by User Type

	Not Acquired		Confident		Need to Improve		All	
	#	%	#	%	#	%	#	%
User-trainees								
File management	2	1.2	145	90.1	14	8.7	161	100
Word processing	3	1.9	142	88.8	15	9.4	160	100
Spreadsheet	3	1.9	122	76.7	34	21.4	159	100
Connecting computer peripherals	9	5.5	149	90.3	7	4.2	165	100
Occasional users								
File management	3	1.2	231	92.8	15	6.0	249	100
Word processing	1	0.4	218	87.2	31	12.4	250	100
Spreadsheet	2	0.8	180	72.3	67	26.9	249	100
Connecting computer peripherals	25	10	206	82.1	20	8.0	251	100

Advanced IT Skills Some user-trainees have advanced skills (table 3.9). These people attended the Cisco-certified IT Essentials training program included in the telecenter training curriculum. Others (e.g., those employed in cybercafés) make their own arrangements to learn advanced skills. (Although the IT Essentials program is included in all telecenters' training plans, not all telecenters actually teach it: only five of the twelve visited telecenters delivered IT Essentials training.) User-trainees as well as occasional users have limited advanced skills (table 3.9).

Internet-Based Communications Most user-trainees (88 percent) are able to use email with confidence. Additionally, 70 percent can use the Internet for chatting, and at least 58 percent can communicate using web-based social networking platforms such as Facebook. Nevertheless, fewer than 50 percent can make voice calls using computer programs (table 3.10). In our opinion, the unstable Internet connection and its low speed make it difficult to learn and use Internet-based voice calls.

Information Search In the PAVs we visited trainees practiced information search during their break time. In one telecenter, one trainee was searching prices of agricultural products using the "e-Soko"[5] service available on the Ministry of Agriculture website. Similarly, various users in cybercafés were searching information on the web with the help of others. About 76 percent of user-trainees are confident in their capacity to search for information, whereas 13 percent feel the need to improve this skill

Table 3.9

Level of User Confidence in Select Advanced Computer Skills and Information Search, by User Type

	Not Acquired		Confident		Need to Improve		All	
	#	%	#	%	#	%	#	%
User-trainees - Primary & Supplementary								
Disk formatting	45	27.3	102	61.8	18	10.9	165	100
Disk partitioning	68	42.2	74	46.0	19	11.8	161	100
Configuration of computer peripherals	33	20.0	118	71.5	14	8.5	165	100
Network configuration	73	45.1	59	36.4	30	18.5	162	100
Network troubleshooting	68	42.5	65	40.6	27	16.9	160	100
Website design	126	77.8	13	8	23	14.2	162	100
Program installation	54	32.7	85	51.5	26	15.8	165	100
Information search	18	11.3	122	76.3	20	12.5	160	100
Occasional users								
Disk formatting	112	44.6	112	44.6	27	10.8	251	100
Disk partitioning	142	57.0	84	33.7	23	9.3	249	100
Configuration of computer peripherals	72	28.7	144	57.4	35	13.9	251	100
Network configuration	156	63.2	67	27.1	24	9.7	247	100
Network troubleshooting	146	60.1	65	26.7	32	13.2	243	100
Website design	209	83.9	15	6.0	25	10.1	249	100
Program installation	123	49.6	94	37.9	31	12.5	248	100
Information search	36	14.4	168	66.9	47	18.7	251	100

Table 3.10

Level of Confidence of User-trainees in Internet-based Communication Skills

	Confident		Need to Improve		Estimate with Skills		Total
Skill Type	#	%	#	%	#	%	#
Using email system	141	87.6	12	7.5	153	95.0	161
Chatting	114	70.4	20	12.3	134	82.7	162
Web-based social networking	94	58.4	16	9.9	110	68.3	161
Internet-based voice call	52	32.7	26	16.4	78	49.1	159
Average level of confidence		62.3		11.5		73.8	

Note: The total in each skill type is the total number of respondents who answered about their level in that skill type.

(table 3.9). According to the instructors interviewed, trainees' level of confidence in their information search skills depends on the instructors' commitment because Internet use training generally focuses mainly on using email.

Gender Differences We found no major differences between male and female interviewees in their level of confidence regarding basic computer skills, but there are significant gaps regarding advanced computer skills (table 3.11). Men were more confident than women regarding all advanced skills areas considered, and this is largely due to the significant difference in skills acquisition. The percentage of women that did not acquire skills such as network configuration, file management, network troubleshooting, and program installation, exceeded 50 percent of women users interviewed, but was below 40 percent in the case of men (table 3.11). Apparently, in Rwanda, as happens in many other places, these technical skills are considered the purview of men but not as much of women.

Outcomes

The immediate outcomes that trainees can get from using the PAVs are ICT skills that they can use to search and apply for jobs, meet ICT job requirements, sit and/or pass ICT tests required for particular jobs, and set up their own ICT-based businesses.

Search and Apply for Jobs Many Rwandan institutions have their own websites and these often include job vacancy announcements. Fifty-five percent of survey respondents appreciated the importance of the Internet as a job advertisement and job application channel. In practice, however, out of ten trainees from one of the telecenters visited, only one person had obtained information on job opportunities from the Internet and applied for this job through the Internet.

Meet ICT Requirements of Jobs In most job announcements in Rwanda, the ICT skill most often listed as desirable, if not required, is familiarity with the MS Office suite of programs, particularly Word, Excel, and PowerPoint. This knowledge is mandatory in office or white-collar jobs such as typist/secretary in a private or government institution. In most recruitment tests, the ICT component is part of the evaluation. These ICT skills are obtained from formal schooling and/or PAVs, either exclusively or as a supplement to previously acquired skills. Skills most frequently used are word processing and spreadsheet tasks, and training customers in telecenters and cybercafés in the basics of Internet browsing and using email. For trainees with more advanced skills (e.g., IT Essentials) part- or full-time job opportunities in hardware maintenance, software installation, and network troubleshooting are available.

Table 3.11
Level of User Confidence in Basic and Advanced Skills, by Gender

	Not acquired		Confident		Need to Improve		All	
	#	%	#	%	#	%	#	%
Male								
Basic skills								
File Management	5	2.4	190	90.9	14	6.7	209	100.0
Word Processing	4	1.9	185	88.5	20	9.6	209	100.0
Spreadsheet	4	1.9	165	78.6	41	19.5	210	100.0
Connecting Computer Peripherals	18	8.5	183	85.9	12	5.6	213	100.0
Advanced skills								
Network configuration	81	39.7	87	42.6	36	17.6	204	100.0
Website design	137	70.3	22	11.3	36	18.5	195	100.0
Network Troubleshooting	69	35.6	90	46.4	35	18.0	194	100.0
Program Installation	63	30.1	120	57.4	26	12.4	209	100.0
Information search	16	7.8	156	75.7	34	16.5	206	100.0
Female								
Basic Skills								
File Management	0	0.0	186	92.5	15	7.5	201	100.0
Word Processing	0	0.0	175	87.1	26	12.9	201	100.0
Spreadsheet	1	0.5	137	69.2	60	30.3	198	100.0
Connecting Computer Peripherals	16	7.9	172	84.7	15	7.4	203	100.0
Advanced Skills								
Network configuration	130	69.5	39	20.9	18	9.6	187	100.0
Website design	160	90.9	16	9.1	0	0.0	176	100.0
Network Troubleshooting	126	66.3	40	21.1	24	12.6	190	100.0
Program Installation	104	53.6	59	30.4	31	16.0	194	100.0
Information search	30	15.4	132	67.7	33	16.9	195	100.0

In discussions with ten trainees from public access venues, all expressed their confidence in meeting the ICT requirement of jobs. This is especially true of those trained in telecenters because these venues provide them with widely recognized certificates. Those who had had training in other kinds of PAV also testified that the skills acquired allowed them to get jobs without having to take recruitment tests. They stressed that potential employers who knew they had taken ICT training gave them temporary jobs such as computer maintenance and providing support to clients visiting cybercafés or public secretariats. For instance, a former trainee said he had taken temporary ICT jobs shortly after completing his ICT training at the Kibungo telecenter, and these jobs enabled him to raise the funds he needed to enroll at the Kigali Institute of Science and Technology (KIST). Similarly, a woman trained at the Nyabihu telecenter was subsequently recruited as a computer maintenance technician by a local tea factory. She stressed that the IT Essentials training she received had helped her get this job, which in turn enabled her to finance her studies at the Institute of Higher Education (INES Ruhengeri). Other former trainees attributed their career advancement to their ICT training. For instance, a trainee who was working in a cybercafé got a better job in a company based in South Africa after he completed his Cisco training at the Gicumbi telecenter. As noted by an ICT instructor in one telecenter in the Northern Province, "ICT skills are an added advantage on one's CV and increase [one's] chances of getting a job."

Take ICT Test Required of Job Applicants ICT skills acquired through training in PAVs enable former trainees to take ICT tests required for jobs. These tests typically cover word processing, spreadsheet handling, and Internet use. Former trainees mentioned, for example, tests taken during the recruitment of staff for the recently created microfinance institutions locally known as "Umurenge SACCO."

Plan and Set Up Own ICT-based Business ICT skills acquired from PAVs have also allowed some trainees to plan and set up their own ICT-based business. An example is a former trainee at the Gicumbi telecenter, who set up a cybercafé in Kigali city after successfully completing his training in IT Essentials. Two other trainees trained in IT Essentials and using video editing software at the Nyabihu telecenter (located in a rural area in northwestern Rwanda) were also able to set up their business as a result of their training. One uses the acquired software skill to clean and duplicate photographs in his photo studio. Without the skills, he could not produce many refined photographs in a limited amount of time. Another trainee uses the same software to produce music CDs in his music studio.

Impact

We assess the impact on users' job prospects of ICT skills acquired from public access venues. The indicators measured (table 3.12) are the number of people who: (1) learned about job opportunities via the Internet, (2) submitted their job applications online, (3) took an ICT skills test as part of their recruitment, (4) were recruited mainly because they had ICT skills, or (5) created their own ICT-based business using the skills acquired.

In Rwanda, the use of the Internet to either search for a job or submit an application appears to be minimal. Fewer than 7 percent of the persons surveyed used the Internet

Table 3.12
Job-related Impacts of Using the Internet, by User Type

	Primary User-Trainees		Supp. User-Trainees		Occasional Users		Total	
	#	%	#	%	#	%	#	%
Used Internet to get info about job opportunities	4	4.6	9	11.5	15	5.9	28	6.7
Submitted a job application online	4	4.6	5	6.4	4	1.6	13	3.1
Took ICT skills test during recruitment	27	31.0	32	41.0	114	45.1	173	41.4
Was recruited mainly because had ICT skills	42	48.3	46	59.0	145	57.3	233	55.7
Created an ICT-based business	18	20.7	17	21.8	20	7.9	55	13.2
Sample size	87		78		253		418	

to find job opportunities, and only 3 percent submitted their job application online. However, having ICT skills is an important requirement for getting a job. In many job advertisements, ICT literacy is one of the requirements for being shortlisted, qualifying to take a recruitment test, and getting employed. The proportion of interviewees who took an ICT test during recruitment is significant (41 percent).

Nearly 56 percent of the users interviewed were recruited because they had ICT skills. Primary user-trainees whose ICT skills were acquired at public access venues did not fare as well as supplementary or occasional users. The proportion of user-trainees who took ICT skills test during recruitment was 31 percent, compared with 41 percent among supplementary and 45 percent among occasional users. Similarly, the proportion of primary user-trainees recruited mainly because of their ICT skills was 48 percent, compared with 59 percent among supplementary and 57 percent among occasional users (table 3.12). We do not have enough information to sort out these differences, but perhaps having, on average, a higher formal education degree (table 3.3) gives supplementary and occasional users an edge that allows them to aspire to and get higher level positions than can primary user-trainees.

Nearly 13 percent of all survey respondents were self-employed in their own ICT-based business (table 3.13). Most of these businesses (fifty-three of fifty-five cases) are public secretariats or cybercafés, mainly because a significant number of respondents were drawn purposively from 54 cybercafes and 48 public secretariats. The two non-PAV businesses were established by rural male respondents. Most PAV businesses

Table 3.13
Self-employment in ICT Skills-based Businesses Observed in Sample

	Primary User-trainees	Supp. User-trainees	Occasional Users	Total
Self-employment in ICT-based business				
Rural				
Male	4	2	1	7
Female	2	–	4	6
Subtotal rural	6	2	5	13
Urban				
Male	10	10	4	24
Female	2	5	11	18
Subtotal urban	12	15	15	42
Total	18	17	20	55
Self-employment in ICT non-PAV business				
Rural—Male	2	–	–	2
Self-employment in PAV business				
Rural				
Male	2	–	–	2
Female	2	–	4	6
Subtotal rural	4	–	4	8
Urban				
Male	10	10	4	24
Female	2	5	11	18
Subtotal urban	12	15	15	42
Total	16	15	19	50
PAV as % of total self-employment	88.9	100.0	100.0	96.4
Rural as % of total self-employment	33.3	11.8	25.0	23.6
Female as % of total self-employment	22.2	–	75.0	43.6
Female rural as % of total female self-employment	50.0	100.0	73.3	75.0
Female urban as % of total female self-employment	50.0	–	26.7	25.0
Male rural as % of total male self-employment	28.6	16.7	20.0	22.6
Male urban as % of total male self-employment	71.4	83.3	80.0	77.4
% of males in sample self-employed in ICT	30.4	29.3	4.1	14.8
% of females in sample self-employed in ICT	10.0	14.3	12.0	12.0

(76 percent) were set up by urban respondents. Self-employment using ICT skills acquired was proportionately lowest among occasional users (8 percent) perhaps because of their less frequent contact with PAVs or because these users have higher levels of education (table 3.3) and therefore have access to a broader job market.

The main gender disparity in impact is observed in ICT-based self-employment: nearly 30 percent of male user-trainees set up their own ICT-based businesses (essentially PAVs) compared with only 11 percent of female user-trainees. Oddly, the pattern is reversed among occasional users, with 4 percent of males and 12 percent of females setting up their own business—again, by and large cybercafés and public secretariats. Other than ICT-based self-employment, the data show recruitment of an almost equal number of male and female PAV user-trainees.

Concluding Remarks and Recommendations

The level of ICT skills acquired from PAVs varies from venue to venue, from one venue type to another, and from one trainee to another depending on factors such as instructors' skills, instructors' willingness to take initiative, and the training environment. Venues that include training among their main services deliver a higher level of skills, as do venues that have instructors with good qualifications and a willingness to take initiative, and venues with a good ICT infrastructure, wide training rooms, and well-maintained, up-to-date equipment. In the case of advanced skills, males have more confidence in skills taught than do females.

The ICT skills acquired by users of PAVs appear to have had a positive albeit modest impact on their job prospects (table 3.12). We suspect that impact is dampened by the limited job opportunities in the country, a lack of additional skills such as entrepreneurship that would be useful for self-employment, and, in the case of primary user-trainees, a lack of the level of formal schooling required for some jobs.

The Universal Access Fund implemented by the Rwanda Utilities Regulatory Agency has subsidized the provision of connectivity and equipment to public institutions such as telecenters, schools, and public agencies (Republic of Rwanda 2013). By enabling the deployment of ICT services to rural areas, these subsidies have benefited user-trainees who acquired or strengthened their ICT skills in telecenters and improved their job prospects. On the basis of these findings, we endorse the continuation of policies supporting telecenter development in relatively large rural communities.

Currently, telecenters are the venues best equipped to provide ICT skills training, but this has not always been the case. Prior to the appearance of telecenters, public secretariats served an important training function. One of the strengths of telecenters is that they have developed a solid training program in both basic and advanced ICT skills; they also certify proficiency, awarding trainees with internationally accredited certificates such as the International Computer Driving License (ICDL) and Cisco's IT Essentials. In principle, there is no reason that similar training services could not also be provided by private venues such as public secretariats and cybercafés. If these services are not being provided, it is probably because they are not financially attractive to private entities: urban PAVs may not have enough customers willing to pay for training services.

In the PAVs we visited, especially telecenters, which charge lower (subsidized) fees for services, we observed a strong demand for training. Perhaps there are not many low-income urban users in a position to pay for acquiring marketable ICT skills with their own resources, given their limited knowledge of the returns such an investment would yield. If this is the case, government support may be warranted.

Government subsidies in the form of training scholarships combined with the training of trainers could enable some urban-based public secretariats and cybercafés to develop their own training programs, using the telecenters' experience as a guide. We recommend that the economic feasibility of such a program be examined. This would make it easier to reach a broader audience, likely at a lower cost than through telecenters, which, to avoid unfair competition with private venues, are by design meant to serve rural communities.

Notes

1. According to the Director of Rural Community Access of the Rwanda Development Board (verbal communication), in 2011, there were twelve fully operational telecenters in Rwanda, and some eighteen were being planned or under construction. The estimate of cybercafés is from Ndayisaba (2011). The number of public secretariats changes often but is generally considered to be higher than the number of cybercafés, perhaps more than 130.

2. Figure 3.1 was constructed using materials presented in Innovation Network Inc. (2006).

3. Rwanda is divided into four provinces (Eastern, Western, Northern, and Southern) plus Kigali City, the country's capital and its largest city. The four provinces and Kigali City are subdivided into thirty districts. Our sample was drawn from 100 schools selected out of 1,399 secondary schools, following a proportionate quota sampling with respect to provinces and districts. The forty-eight bank branches were also selected following proportionate quota sampling from groups of bank branches by district. The twenty-one district offices were selected from thirty, again following a proportionate quota sampling with respect to provinces. Six ministries and another six institutions were also sampled randomly. All five provincial offices are represented in the sample.

Considering that the staff of cybercafés and public secretariats have ICT skills, likely learned at PAVs, we also sampled from a pool of fifty-four cybercafés and forty-eight public secretariats following a proportionate quota sampling with respect to cities. At each place, one to three people were surveyed depending on the availability of the desired positions. The institutions were carefully sampled to account for both rural and urban areas.

4. The ICDL is a widely used standard for computer skills. See http://www.icdl.org.za/.

5. http://www.esoko.gov.rw.

References

Becker, Samantha, Michael D. Crandall, Karen E. Fisher, Bo Kinney, Carol Landry, and Anita Rocha. 2010. *Opportunity for All: How the American Public Benefits from Internet Access at U.S. Libraries*. Washington, DC: Institute of Museum and Library Services.

Freistadt, Jay Oliver, Joyojeet Pal, and Regina Helena Alves da Silva. 2009. ICT Centers and the Access Gap to Formal Higher Education for the Poor in Brazil. Paper presented at the Community Informatics Conference 2009: *Empowering Communities: Learning from Community Informatics Practice*. Prato, Italy, October. http://tascha.uw.edu/publications/ict-centers-and-the-access-gap-to-formal-higher-education-for-the-poor-in-brazil/

Garrido, María, Chris Rothschild, and Thierno Oumar. 2009. *Technology for Employability in Washington State: The Role of ICT Training on the Employment, Compensation and Aspirations of Low-skilled, Older, and Unemployed Workers*. Research report. Seattle: Technology & Social Change Group (TASCHA), University of Washington Information School. https://digital.lib.washington.edu/researchworks/bitstream/handle/1773/16298/TASCHA_Washington-State_2009.pdf.

Innovation Network Inc. 2006. Logic Model Workbook. Washington, DC. http://www.innonet.org/client_docs/File/logic_model_workbook.pdf

Kumar, Ranjit. 2005. *Research Methodology: A Step-by-Step Guide for Beginners*. 2nd ed. London: SAGE Publications.

Mariscal, Judith, Luis H. Gutierrez, and José Junqueira Botelho Antonio. 2009. Employment and Youth Inclusion into the Labor Force via Training in Information and Communication Technologies (ICTs): The Cases of Brazil, Colombia, and Mexico. *Information Technologies and International Development* 5 (2): 19–30.

National Institute of Statistics of Rwanda (NISR). 2012. *Statistical Yearbook 2012*. Kigali, Rwanda: NISR. http://www.statistics.gov.rw/system/files/user_uploads/files/books/YEAR%20BOOK_2012.pdf.

Ndayisaba, Jean. 2011. ICT, a Growing Market in Rwanda. *Regulator* 1 (March): 6–8.

Republic of Rwanda. 2000. *Rwanda Vision 2020*. Kigali, Rwanda. http://www.minecofin.gov.rw/fileadmin/General/Vision_2020/Vision-2020.pdf.

Republic of Rwanda. 2013. *Draft (1st Physical Meeting)—WSIS+10: Overall Review of the Implementation of the WSIS Outcomes*. http://www.itu.int/wsis/review/inc/docs/rcreports/WSIS10_Country_Reporting-RWA.pdf.

4 Personal Objectives and the Impact of Internet Cafés in China

Francisco J. Proenza, Wei Shang, Guoxin Li, Jianbin Hao, Oluwasefunmi 'Tale Arogundade, and Martin S. Hagger

Abstract

China has the largest population of Internet cafés in the world. Chinese users of cafés are predominantly young males, but there are also mature users, females, and migrant workers. There are few exclusive Internet café users, as most users connect to the Internet from a variety of places, including cafés, home, school, office, and mobile devices. Users engage in a variety of activities, the most common being chatting, gaming, and Internet surfing.

The Chinese government has an aggressive Internet café policy that aims to protect minors, ensure a safe user environment, and curb Internet addiction and undesirable social behaviors, but it seems to be largely driven by misconceptions about the impact of Internet cafés on users' lives.

The objective of this study is to understand the perceived value of Internet café use to users as individuals and to China as a society. We examine the objectives users pursue when they visit such venues and the extent to which they feel they have achieved their objectives. An understanding of user motives and perceived achievements is key to understanding the phenomenal growth in China's Internet cafés and why China's restrictive policies have been difficult to enforce.

We find that users' objectives for using Internet cafés are reasonable and common among young people. According to self-determination theory, they are the types of goals people pursue to satisfy psychological needs for autonomy, competence, and relatedness.

In the coming years, Internet cafés are bound to remain critical access venues, especially for rural communities and migrant workers. China is rapidly modernizing, but some of its current policies to limit if not prevent use of Internet cafés are controlling and undermining of autonomous motivation and are bound to fail. They also threaten adaptive activities and motives (such as gaining new knowledge), the psychological needs of users, and, by implication, their psychological well-being. Given the difficulties experienced to date with controlling regulatory policies, we recommend that government consider alternative strategies that help advance the country's digital agenda and facilitate self-determination and psychological well-being.

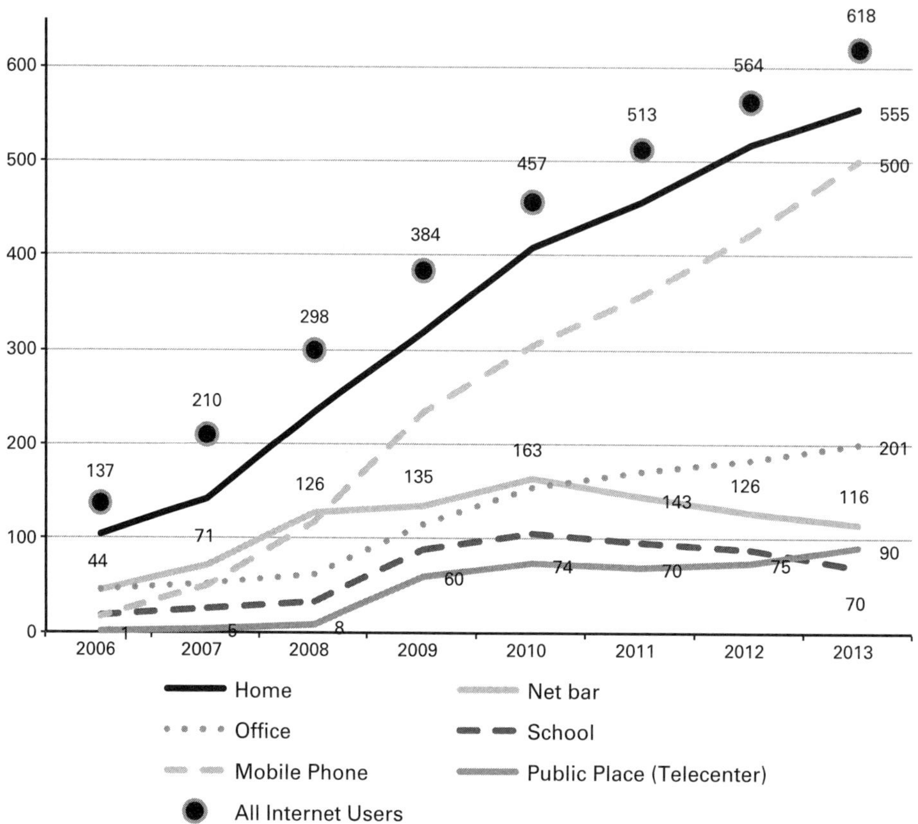

Figure 4.1
China: Millions of Internet users by access mode and in total.

Public Access in China

Internet use in China has experienced phenomenal growth, the equivalent of 24 percent a year between 2006 and 2013 (figure 4.1).[1] Access to the Internet from net bars (as Internet cafés are known locally) reached a peak of 163 million users in December 2010, but has since subsided to 116 million in December 2013 (19 percent of Internet users). However, the number of people connecting from telecenters, negligible in 2006, reached 90 million people or nearly 15 percent of Internet users in 2013. Although hard to ascertain with confidence, the number of users accessing from PAVs (i.e. from either Internet cafés or telecenters combined) may have grown during this period.[2]

With somewhere between 144,000 (Kan 2011) and 136,000 (Jou 2013) Internet cafés and about 116 million users (China Internet Network Information Center 2014), China has the largest population of Internet café users in the world.[3]

Internet cafés are especially important in small cities and rural communities. In 2007, about 28 percent of Internet users in metropolitan areas connected to the Internet from Internet cafés, fewer than in provincial capitals such as Xi'an (51 percent) and Shenyang (36 percent; Liang 2007). Separate data for 2007 show that about 54 percent of rural Internet users connected to the net through Internet cafés, compared with a national figure of only 33 percent of Internet users (China Internet Network Information Center 2007a). Computer ownership is significantly lower in rural (3 percent) than in urban (47 percent) households (China Internet Network Information Center 2007a).

Migrant workers—rural residents who leave their home to work in urban areas—constitute another important group of Internet café users. In 2012, there were about 262.6 million rural migrant workers in China (National Bureau of Statistics of China 2013). About 40 percent of migrants are less than 30 years old (China Labour Bulletin 2013). A large proportion of migrants, especially among the young, regularly surf the Internet as a major leisure activity and to keep in touch with family members. Many migrants live in dormitories provided by their employers and, of necessity, must rely on nearby net bars to access the Internet.

Media accounts of Internet cafés in China usually begin with the story of how in 2002 two boys ages 13 and 14 were refused service in a net bar located in the university district in Beijing (Linchuan Qiu 2009). The disgruntled youths retaliated by setting fire to the Internet café, killing 25 people and injuring many others (*BBC News* 2002; Xinhua 2004). A tightening of regulations and crackdown on unlicensed centers ensued (*BBC News* 2002). Within six months, 90,000 unlicensed net bars were closed, leaving only 110,000 Internet cafés operating (Xinhua 2004). In Beijing, only 30 legal Internet cafés remained open out of more than 2,200 previously in operation (Liang 2002). The crackdown continues to this day, with 7,000 net bars suspended in 2010 (Xinhua 2011).

Government regulations aim to ensure a safe user environment and curb Internet addiction, pornography, and undesirable social behaviors, with the protection of minors a foremost concern (Information Office of the State Council 2010). Regulations are extensive at both national and local levels. In 2003, the Chinese Central Government began to promote Internet café chains, and licenses were issued to only ten chain operators. No increase in the number of licenses issued is foreseen, and existing Internet cafés are expected to join chains or shut down.

Many stakeholders—central and local government officials, Internet café operators, telecom operators, and users—vie for influence over policy regarding licensing and control of Internet café use (Cartier, Castells, and Linchuan Qiu 2005; Linchuan Qiu 2009; Linchuan Qiu and Liuning 2005). Officials in Beijing setting central government policy live in large cities, use the Internet at home and at work, and seldom visit Internet cafés. Their fears about the welfare of minors mirror similar parental concerns in other countries (Livingston and Haddon 2008; Synovate 2009; Turow 1999) and are stoked by sensationalist media accounts.

At the local level where policy is implemented, there tends to be leniency, particularly in small towns. This is partly in recognition of the difficulties of enforcing the policy in the face of a huge demand for Internet café services, but also because of the revenues that licensing generates for local governments. Rent-seeking by public officials also occurs. When asked how he managed to survive, one illegal Internet café operator in Gedong replied, "Well, that's kind of hard to explain." Pressed for an answer, he said the secret was in the "'relationships' between the owner and the police" (Cody 2007).

Restrictive policies appear to have been costly to Internet café patrons but not very effective.[4] As of 2010, only five chains had started operations (Junlong 2010), and these ran at most 40 percent of the country's Internet cafés (Earp 2013; Kan 2011). Many illegal net bars continue to operate (Cody 2007; Hong 2007; Hong and Huang 2005). These are usually standalone, individually run operations, much smaller than chains. All that is needed is a small venue, perhaps 100 m^2, a few computers (as opposed to 300–400 in legal Internet cafés), and broadband connectivity. These centers are set up close to schools and universities, have no clear distinguishing signs, regularly cater to minors, and often run twenty-four hours a day (Hong and Huang 2005). Even if it is illegal, spending the night at a net bar is commonplace.

Negative views of the impact of Internet cafés are not shared by everyone in China (Tian 2010) but are widespread (box 4.1) and are an important force driving policy (Xueqin 2009). They contrast with the vision—articulated for example by Hoffman (2012) and Brynjolfsson and Saunders (2010), and largely shared by the Information Office of the State Council (2010)—of the Internet as a transformational technology that enables people to communicate and learn, firms to innovate and compete effectively, and consumers to benefit from greater access to products and services.

The objective of this study is to understand the perceived value of Internet café use to users as individuals as well as China as a society. We examine the objectives users pursue when they visit Internet cafés, as well as the extent to which users feel

Box 4.1
Sample Negative Perceptions of Internet Café Impact in Chinese Media

"The Internet poses as much danger to young people as illegal narcotics. If this were to continue, the danger would be great here as well as in all of China. . . . As for those who oppose this, I would not pay them any attention. No Internet café owner is going to tell me: 'Internet cafés pose no danger to children!'" (Zhang Guobiao, Fangshan county party secretary; cited in Yu 2006)

"Young people absolutely do not learn new technology or improve the quality of their information at Internet cafés. Improving the quality of information involves the ability to search, add value, judge, apply and distinguish. This is so far removed from the environment and actual experience at Internet cafés! Bill Gates was not nurtured in an Internet café in China." (Chinese scholar; cited in Yu 2006)

"Students who used to indulge in the Internet for hours a day have now returned to school, and are making progress in their studies." (Jiao 2006)

"On July 29, local police ordered all 21 Internet cafés in Guanxian county, Liaocheng of East China's Shandong province, to suspend their business. . . . 'Our purpose is to improve the quality of life for local residents,' Wang Zhenqian, deputy director of the county Party committee's publicity department, was quoted as saying.

"Citizens were concerned about how much time their young children were spending on the Internet. But teenagers also were spending more and more time in Internet cafés and getting weary of studying. This is a serious problem in Guanxian and in the whole country. . . . 'Everyone is clapping their hands in applause for what we have done. Authorities in other places want to do the same thing, but most of them don't dare to,' he said." (Tian 2009)

"Internet cafés have become an important place for juvenile delinquents and in particular for crimes committed by primary and middle school students." (Hongkou District Procurator in Shanghai; cited in Xueqin 2009)

"People's Representative Gao Wanneng called for a 'zero-hour cutoff' for Internet cafés due to long-term Internet addiction in Chinese youth. Gao said such addiction is responsible for high dropout rates and Internet crime and asked the National People's Congress to pass legislation regulating online gaming, reports the Worker's Daily.*"* (Weinland 2010)

"High school seniors gearing up for the massive national college entrance exams in Linchuan in China's central province of Jiangxi have been able to focus only on studying now that all of the town's Internet cafés have closed. . . . 'During this critical period, our goal is to create an educational society for students that is free of distractions,' the official said. 'Besides Internet cafés, there's not much else in town the kids can waste time with.'" (*Sydney Morning Herald*, June 1, 2010)

they have achieved their situational objectives and life goals, and we compare their life goals and achievements with those of nonusers. An understanding of user motives and perceived achievements is key to understanding the phenomenal growth in China's Internet cafés and why China's restrictive policies have been difficult to enforce. Our aim is to contribute to Chinese officials in their deliberations, as they consider alternative policies that are effective and sustainable in dissuading harmful overuse.

Impact Assessment Methodology

Approach to Impact Assessment and Self-Determination Theory

We started with a simple logic model of how a cybercafé could bring about change. The model suggested that user behavior was a key input (i.e., that significant outcomes came about as a result of the uses customers make of the center's services and facilities). Accordingly, it was essential to examine the objectives users pursue when they visit cafés and the achievements they realize. Moreover, finding a way to compare these objectives and achievements with those of nonusers might enable us to detect differences that could be attributed to Internet café use.

The central idea is that nonusers of the Internet will have personal motivations similar to users' but would not define them in terms of online activities. We made the distinction between objectives for using Internet cafés and broader life objectives to which both users and nonusers would aspire but that, in the case of users, might be affected by the experience of Internet café use. A comparison in the perception of users and nonusers regarding achievement of life objectives might help us identify the presence or absence of change.

From the outset, we called the goals used in our surveys *self-determined objectives*. Shortly after data collection started, we stumbled on self-determination theory (SDT) and were drawn to the parallels between our approach and SDT's comprehensive framework, validated in a broad range of spheres (including ICT)[5] and its emphasis on "self-determination" of goals as a motivational force behind everyday activities. We adapted our terminology to make it compatible (e.g., using Vallerand's distinction between *situational goals* and *life goals*) and proceeded to use SDT as our guiding framework.

Personal Goals and Motivation

Goals are central to human behavior. Goals are shaped by personal views of the future and what people expect and feel they can accomplish, taking into account culture, social values, and institutions. When a person visits a cybercafé, he or she is pursuing specific goals (e.g., entertainment, relaxation, communication) that may contribute to or detract from the pursuit of "worthier" objectives (e.g., studying for a test). Long-term goals are a point of reference that drive everyday short-term goals and behavior and in turn help shape people's short- and long-term plans. Goals affect how people view and feel about themselves and their social milieu and help determine their mental health and well-being (Bargh, Gollwitzer, and Oettingen 2010; Deci and Ryan 2000; Freund and Riediger 2006; Greene and DeBacker 2004; Nurmi 1991).

One of the leading approaches to understanding motivation is SDT. According to SDT, people are *intrinsically* motivated when they derive a sense of enjoyment, interest, and personal satisfaction from engaging in an activity. When experiencing activities as intrinsically motivated, no external contingency (e.g., reward, deadline, etc.) is necessary because people will view the cause of their actions as emanating from the self (i.e., they will choose to act of their own free will). In contrast, people are *extrinsically* motivated when they pursue an activity or action to obtain an instrumental reward that is separable from the activity. An extrinsically motivated person acts in recognition of external benefits to which the activity is a stepping stone or in response to parental or peer pressure, government laws and regulations, societal mores, codes of conduct, or school or work requirements such as deadlines. SDT principles have been studied, refined, and validated through numerous experiments in a broad range of human endeavors (Deci and Ryan 2000 2008; Ryan and Deci 2000a 2000b; Vallerand 2007; Vansteenkiste, Lens, and Deci 2006).

Within SDT, intrinsic motivation is proposed as an adaptive motivating force that enhances personal well-being (Ryan and Deci 2000a; Ryan, Kuhl, and Deci 1997). Intrinsic motivation helps people satisfy three innate psychological needs: *autonomy*, *competence*, and *relatedness*. People need to feel autonomous: that they are acting of their own volition to organize personal experiences and that they are doing so on their own initiative. People need to feel they are competent: that their actions have an effect on their environment that yields valued positive outcomes (Deci and Moller 2005; Elliot, McGregor, and Thrash 2002). People also need to feel connected to their significant others: to care for others and feel cared for—what Baumeister and Leary (1995) refer to as "a desire for interpersonal attachment" (see also Moller, Deci, and Elliot 2010; Reis et al. 2000).

Well-being in the form of mental health and vitality—"a positive feeling of aliveness and energy," according to Ryan and Frederick (1997)—is enhanced when people satisfy these three basic needs. In contrast, well-being is undermined when psychological needs are thwarted or unfulfilled (Vallerand 2007). Other psychological needs may influence people's behavior, but research has consistently shown that these three are fundamental (Ryan and Deci 2000b). The need for autonomy has been studied the most, but all three needs make an independent contribution to motivation (Sheldon and Filak 2008), and the satisfaction of all three is necessary for optimal functioning (Deci and Ryan 2000; Sheldon and Niemiec 2006).

Extrinsic motivation is less adaptive because actions are performed and goals pursued for reasons external to the person. People who perform activities for extrinsic motives will continue to be engaged in the activity only so long as the external contingency (i.e., reward or deadline) is present; if not they will desist. Pursuing an extrinsic goal such as fame, wealth, or beauty may undermine well-being, but these goals are still pursued for a variety of reasons, including external parental, social, cultural, or institutional pressures (Sheldon and Kasser 2008), as well as mistaken expectations regarding the benefits they will derive from achieving these goals (Sheldon et al. 2010).

People can, however, *internalize* extrinsic motives (e.g., "I study because doing so will help me pursue the career of my choosing"), and there is a continuum in the degree of autonomy or self-determination of extrinsic forms of motivation. To the extent that individuals view the cause of their behavior as satisfying their psychological needs and emanating from the self, their locus of causality will be perceived to be internal. To the extent that an extrinsic contingency such as a reward is perceived by the individual as contributing to the satisfaction of a basic psychological need, it will be internalized by the individual and become a more effective source of motivation. When external rewards, evaluations, pressures, or punishment are made contingent on a behavior, in situations that the person perceives are beyond his or her control, they tend to undermine intrinsic motivation (Deci, Koestner, and Ryan 1999).

Goals are idiosyncratic, change throughout a person's life cycle, and vary depending on context, culture, and personal experience (Massey, Gebhardt, and Garnefski 2008; Nurmi 1991). Adolescents tend to focus on educational and family-related goals. In middle adulthood, goals are more closely linked to property and children's lives, and as people get older, health, world affairs, and death become important (Nurmi 1992). Goal priorities change even within adolescence, with the importance of leisure peaking early, around the ages of 10 to 14 (Massey, Gebhardt, and Garnefski 2008). Older adults in the United States and Singapore exhibit greater internalization of their social and civic duties than their children (Sheldon et al. 2005). As people mature, personal goals become more intrinsically motivated and autonomous (Sheldon, Houser-Marko, and Kasser 2006).

People in different cultures navigate their environment differently as they choose personal goals to satisfy their psychological needs (Deci and Ryan 2000).[6] Cultural and societal values and institutions may play supportive or undermining roles in satisfying psychological needs.[7] Regardless of the opportunities or constraints that culture and institutions afford, the three basic needs for autonomy, competence, and relatedness are universal. They are operative in every culture,[8] and "in general, some goals are expected to be more closely linked to basic or intrinsic need satisfaction than are others" (Deci and Ryan 2000). Goals validated cross-culturally, including in China, as intrinsically oriented and satisfying basic internal human needs include: community feeling, affiliation (i.e., having satisfying personal relationships), self-acceptance (i.e., feeling autonomous and competent), and physical health, whereas goals validated as extrinsically oriented (contingent on external rewards) include financial success, image, and popularity (Grouzet et al. 2005).

The extent to which goal choice satisfies psychological needs affects mental health and well-being. Kasser and Ryan (1996) found higher levels of well-being among late adolescents who prioritized intrinsic aspirations (community feeling, self-acceptance, and affiliation) over extrinsic goals (financial success). Deci and Vansteenkiste (2004) cite studies showing a positive correlation between people's sense of well-being and their perceived achievement of intrinsic goals but not of extrinsic goals. Furthermore, attainment of intrinsically oriented goals leads to reports of greater psychological well-being, which is not the case for extrinsically oriented goals (Sheldon and Kasser 1998).

Survey Goal Choices

Following Vallerand (2007), situational goals (SGs) are set for specific activities associated with Internet café or Internet use. Life goals (LGs) are construed more broadly as personal aspirations that anyone can pursue.[9] Nonusers will have life goals similar to users', but their situational goals will not be defined in relation to Internet or Internet café activities. The user survey was more extensive than the nonuser survey because users were asked to identify their LGs as well as their SGs for visiting Internet cafés or for using the Internet from home or other venues, whereas nonusers were asked only about their LGs.

We examine situational goals to understand users' motives and perceptions of achievement using Internet cafés. We assess impact by comparing differences between users' and nonusers' life goal choices and achievements.

Situational Goals The starting point for defining users' SGs was the 2009 list of Internet use activities in the Pew Internet Project "Usage Over Time" database (see Pew Internet Project 2012). From this list of activities, we identified likely underlying goals of Internet café users. The complete list of possible SGs constructed this way appears in the left-hand column of table 4.1. The relationship between activities and the objectives thus constructed is indirect. For example, email may be used to keep in touch with family and friends (SG number 13, table 4.1); meet new friends, a mate, or a companion (SG12); get information about physical (SG18) or mental (SG19) health.

Practically all SGs are associated with the use of computers and Internet services accessible through Internet cafés. The one exception is SG14, "Socialize and make

Table 4.1

Situational Goals (SGs) and Life Goals (LGs) Offered as Options in Surveys, Classification of Goals Applying SDT Criteria, and Correspondence Mapping between SGs and LGs

SG no.	List of SGs in order of appearance in user survey	SDT classif.[a]	List of LGs offered as choices in user and nonuser surveys (LG # follows order of appearance in survey)	SDT classif.[b]
1	Improve my performance in school	C	Learn more knowledge (1)	INT
2	Improve my job skills to work better	C		
3	Improve my skills to get better/new job	C		
4	Learn to use computers and the Internet	C		
5	Complete work	C	Get stable, high-paying job, better business opportunities (2)	U
6	Find an additional/new job	U		
7	Better manage my company or farm (e.g., check market info)	C		
8	Make money (e.g., online store, doing web pages, etc.)	EXT		
9	Increase self-confidence	C	Self-realization, enhance self-confidence (3)	INT
10	Search for spiritual comfort	A		
11	Access information (news, weather forecasts, stock info, sports, gossip, etc.)	U	Keep up to date (5)	U
12	Meet new friends or a mate or companion	R	Look for and meet new friends or a mate or companion (12)	INT
13	Keep in touch with family and friends (email, QQ, etc.)	R	Keep in touch with friends and family who don't live nearby (14)	INT
14	Socialize and make friends with people in Internet cafés	R	Get together with friends (face to face) (13)	INT
15	Entertainment(play games, listen to music, watch movies, online video, etc.)	A	Leisure, entertainment (15)	INT
16	Spend time on a hobby or pastime	A	Spend time on a hobby or pastime (16)	INT
17	Relax, relieve tension	A	Relax, relieve tension (17)	INT
18	Get health information to improve physical health	R	Improve the physical health of myself or my family (9)	INT

Table 4.1 (continued)

SG no.	List of SGs in order of appearance in user survey	SDT classif.[a]	List of LGs offered as choices in user and nonuser surveys (LG # follows order of appearance in survey)	SDT classif.[b]
19	Get mental health information to improve mental health	R	Improve the mental health of myself or my family (10)	INT
20	Check public service information (access information, online applications, licenses, etc.)	EXT	Get information on government policies, regulations, and services (6)	EXT
21	Literary and artistic creation (fiction, poetry, music, etc.)	A	Art creation (fiction, poetry, art, music, etc.) (4)	INT
22	Create or update own personal website (home page, blog, microblog)	C		
23	Contribute to other people's web pages or blogs	R		
24	Shop online or get product information online	EXT	Obtain better products and services at lower cost (7)	EXT
25	Online banking or personal financial services (stock trading, online transfers)	EXT		
26	Plan personal or family trips (collect destination info, hotels, maps, directions)	U	Plan a trip (8)	U
27	Promote the community, clubs, interest groups through online activities	R	Participate in community or village activities (11)	INT
28	Support social groups I like (participate in forums, blogs, microblogs)	U		
29	Participate in government website or online policy discussions	U		
30	Other	U	Other (18)	U

[a]SG classification: A: Autonomy; C: Competence; R: Relatedness; EXT: Extrinsically oriented; U: Unclassified

[b]LG classification: INT: Intrinsically oriented; EXT: Extrinsically oriented; U: Unclassified

friends with people in Internet cafés," which is unrelated to access to the venue's equipment or services.

Life Goals The LGs on the right-hand side of table 4.1 were selected because they could be linked with the 29 SGs associated with Internet café use (left-hand side of table 4.1). To illustrate, a person may visit an Internet café to improve school performance (SG1), acquire skills to become a better worker or a better entrepreneur (SG2), get a new or better job (SG3), or learn how to use computers and the Internet (SG4). Once these four Internet-specific SGs were defined, the LG "Learn more knowledge" (LG1, table 4.1) was included in both user and nonuser surveys because it encompasses these four situational goals. The same reasoning was used to define all LGs in user and nonuser surveys. Table 4.1 maps the correspondence between SGs and LGs.

Goal Classification Based on Self-Determination Theory Survey goals were not worded beforehand to fit SDT's taxonomy. However, using SDT as a guiding framework would suggest that these motives are likely to emerge from the data, particularly given recent research showing that people can and do make the distinction between intrinsic and extrinsic motives, even at the implicit, nonconscious level (McLachlan and Hagger 2010, 2011). In the present study, we sought to establish whether the motives identified from common Internet use practices could also be classified following SDT precepts. Once the economist, systems analyst, marketing specialist, and statistician in the team became aware of SDT, they used SDT criteria to classify SGs and LGs and subsequently called on a professional psychologist to join the research effort and confirm the classification.[10]

In table 4.1, SGs are classified as satisfying one of the three psychological needs—autonomy, competence, or relatedness—or as extrinsically oriented. Where SGs might satisfy more than one need, only one dominant need is identified. In the case of SG15, all three needs are probably satisfied,[11] but the goal's wording, "Entertainment (play games, listen to music, watch movies, online video, etc.)," suggests autonomy as the dominant need this goal would fulfill.

LGs are more broadly defined than SGs and are classified as either intrinsically or extrinsically oriented (right-hand side of table 4.1). The LG "Learn more knowledge" used in this study (LG1) is similarly worded (in Chinese and in English) to "Developing yourself and learning new things," a goal that has been validated as intrinsic by Vansteenkiste, Lens, and Deci (2006), and "To grow and learn new things," an intrinsic goal in Kasser's Aspirations Index.[12] LGs 9 and 10, "Improve the physical or mental health of myself or my family," are similar to the aspiration "To be physically healthy" used by Niemiec, Ryan, and Deci (2009). Goals such as "Art creation (fiction, poetry, art, music, etc.)" (LG4) and "Leisure, entertainment" (LG15) imply personal enjoyment and are therefore clearly intrinsically oriented goals.

Goals that imply a contingency, such as the SG "Make money (e.g., online store, doing web pages, etc.)" (SG8) or the LG "Obtain better products and services at lower cost" (LG7), may be readily identified as extrinsically oriented.

Information on the motives behind goal choice was not collected. Both goal content and the underlying motivation determine behavior, and this can make it difficult to classify a goal on the basis of its apparent content. An intrinsic goal may be chosen for controlled reasons, and an extrinsic goal may be chosen for autonomous reasons (Kasser and Ryan 1996; Sheldon et al. 2004). The presence of tangible rewards, threats, deadlines, or coercion may shift the locus of causality, and an ordinarily intrinsic goal may in practice be chosen for extrinsically motivated reasons (Ryan and Deci 2000c). Typically, to "find an additional/new job" (SG6) is a tedious, unattractive, extrinsically oriented goal, especially when it involves offline job seeking, but "looking for a job using the Internet" might be perceived by some to be an engaging and even enjoyable activity. We therefore leave SG6 unclassified. Other goals defy classification because they are too broadly defined or because we know little about the underlying motivation: accessing information (including news, weather forecasts, stock information, sports, gossip, etc.). (SG11), planning trips (SG26 and LG8), helping to improve government (SG29), and participating in social or civic activities (LG11). Given a well-established correlation between content and the motives behind goal choice, goal content is a useful indicator on its own (Sheldon et al. 2004).

The Intrinsic Nature of Internet Café Use Different people will have different life aspirations and articulate them differently. One of the most widely used lists in goal content research is Kasser's Aspirations Index (Massey, Gebhardt, and Garnefski 2008). In 1993, this index included twenty-one goals (Kasser and Ryan 1993). It presently has thirty-five goals, twenty of them intrinsic and fifteen extrinsic.

Of the thirty SGs included in our user surveys, six (including SG30, "Other") cannot be classified, four are classified as extrinsic, and the remaining twenty are intrinsic goals associated with one of the psychological needs: five with autonomy, eight with relatedness, and seven with competence (see left-hand side of table 4.1). Of the eighteen LGs included in user and nonuser surveys, twelve were classified as intrinsic, four were left unclassified, and only two could be clearly identified as extrinsic (right-hand side of table 4.1).

Considering that the survey goals were constructed before SDT criteria were applied, the results of this exercise suggest that the goal content of Internet and Internet café use is predominantly intrinsic.

User and Nonuser Survey Options Users and nonusers of Internet cafés were presented in their surveys with predefined lists of goals (SGs and LGs in the case of users, LGs only in the case of nonusers). They were asked to select their own goals from the lists and indicate the extent of their dedication to achieving these goals (café time spent pursuing each goal in the case of SGs or relative "importance" in the case of LGs) and their perceptions regarding goal achievement in the past twelve months (for both SGs and LGs).

Achieving similar frames of minds of users and nonusers was challenging because for practical reasons the user surveys included cybercafé usage questions before life goal choices were presented. Respondents to nonuser surveys were identified in the vicinity of the Internet cafés and interviewed on Internet café premises because the heat at the time of the survey did not make street interviewing practicable.

Data

Basic Features of Sample Populations The profile of the user sample differs markedly from that of China's general population (table 4.2). More than half the users (56 percent) are males under 25 years old, and most users (81 percent) are urban residents. Men account for 73 percent of users and females for 27 percent. Rural residents comprise 19 percent of sample users. This relatively high number in an essentially urban sample was obtained because we surveyed two cafés located near factories employing migrant workers. (Sampling procedures are described in appendix 4.A.)

The age structures of our samples are compatible with approximate profiles of China's Internet users and nonusers constructed using China Internet Network Information Center (CNNIC) and population data (table 4.3). Urban nonusers under 30 years of age represent 33 percent of our urban subsample (table 4.2) and 29 percent of China's urban nonusers. Fifty-eight percent of China's urban Internet user population is less than 30 years old. Urban café users are even younger; those less than 30 years old account for 90 percent of our urban user subsample (table 4.2).

The nonuser sample is more gender balanced, more in line with China's urban population. Urban females comprise 40 percent of nonuser survey respondents, compared with 45 percent in the case of males. The age structure of the urban nonuser sample is also closer to that of China's population, with urban nonusers 30 years or

Table 4.2
Gender, Rural–Urban Status, and Age Distribution of Respondents of User and Nonuser Surveys

	Users		Nonusers	
	#	%	#	%
Urban male, by age				
< 19	86	8.8	42	4.4
19 to < 25	341	34.9	58	6.0
25 to < 30	78	8.0	32	3.3
30 to < 49	70	7.2	140	14.5
≥ 49	–	–	164	17.0
Subtotal	575	58.9	436	45.2
Urban female, by age				
< 19	33	3.4	57	5.9
19 to < 25	125	12.8	46	4.8
25 to < 30	41	4.2	35	3.6
30 to < 49	12	1.2	140	14.5
≥ 49	–	–	110	11.4
Subtotal	211	21.6	388	40.2
Subtotal urban	786	80.5	824	85.5
Rural male, by age				
< 19	33	3.4	5	0.5
19 to < 25	87	8.9	14	1.5
25 to < 30	11	1.1	8	0.8
30 to < 49	5	0.5	31	3.2
≥ 49	–	–	19	2.0
Subtotal	136	13.9	77	8.0
Rural female, by age				
< 19	17	1.7	4	0.4
19 to < 25	27	2.8	8	0.8
25 to < 30	3	0.3	5	0.5
30 to < 49	7	0.7	30	3.1
≥ 49	–	–	16	1.7
Subtotal	54	5.5	63	6.5
Subtotal rural	190	19.5	140	14.5
All users	976	100.0	964	100.0

Table 4.3

Approximate Profiles of China's Internet Users and Non-users

Summary profile of user population	%	Summary profile of non-user population	%
Urban users < 30 as % of China's population	15.4	Urban non–users < 30 as % of China's population	7.2
Urban users ≥ 30 as % of China's population	11.1	Urban non–users ≥ 30 as % of China's population	17.4
Rural users < 30 as % of China's population	5.7	Rural non–users < 30 as % of China's population	16.0
Rural users ≥ 30 as % of China's population	4.1	Rural non–users ≥ 30 as % of China's population	23.2
Urban users < 30 as % of all urban users	58.1	Urban non–users < 30 as % of all urban non–users	29.3
Urban users ≥ 30 as % of all urban users	41.9	Urban non–users ≥ 30 as % of all urban non–users	70.7
Rural users < 30 as % of all rural users	58.1	Rural non–users < 30 as % of all rural non–users	40.7
Rural users ≥ 30 as % of all rural users	41.9	Rural non–users ≥ 30 as % of all rural non–users	59.3
Urban users < 30 as % of urban population < 30	68.1	Urban non-users < 30 as % of urban population < 30	31.9
Urban users ≥ 30 as % of urban population ≥ 30	38.9	Urban non–users ≥ 30 as % of urban population ≥ 30	61.1
Rural users < 30 as % of rural population < 30	26.2	Rural non–users < 30 as % of rural population < 30	73.8
Rural users ≥ 30 as % of rural population ≥ 30	15.0	Rural non–users ≥ 30 as % of rural population ≥ 30	85.0
All urban users as % of China's population	26.4	All urban non–users as % of China's population	24.6
All rural users as % of China's population	9.8	All rural non–users as % of China's population	39.2
All user penetration rate (= CNNIC rate)	36.2	Rate of non–use in China's population (= CNNIC rate)	63.8

Estimates are based on:

1. World Bank estimate (at time of writing) of China's urban population (51%) http://data.worldbank.org/topic/urban-development
2. Wolfram/Alpha: Age distribution (at time of writing) of China's population: 27.7% < 19; 16.5% 20–29; 55.8% ≥ 30 http://www.wolframalpha.com/input/?i=China+population+distribution
3. CNNIC 28th Statistical Report, July 2011a: Age distribution of Internet users: 27.3% < 19; 30.8% 20–29; 42% ≥ 30; rural users as % of total: 27%; and overall penetration rate: 36.2%.

Table 4.4
Nonusers: Main Reason for Not Using the Internet (# of responses)

	No skills	No time	No need or Interest	No access	Expensive	Other	All
Urban – Male							
<19	6	14	9	5	4	4	42
19 to <30	12	35	23	10	6	4	90
30 to <49	40	35	47	12	4	2	140
≥49	103	14	39	6	1	1	164
Subtotal	161	98	118	33	15	11	436
Urban – Female							
<19	7	24	14	8	3	1	57
19 to <30	4	34	18	12	10	3	81
30 to <49	46	40	36	13	4	1	140
≥49	69	9	21	6	3	2	110
Subtotal	126	107	89	39	20	7	388
Urban – Male & Female							
<19	13	38	23	13	7	5	99
19 to <30	16	69	41	22	16	7	171
30 to <49	86	75	83	25	8	3	280
≥49	172	23	60	12	4	3	274
All Urban	287	205	207	72	35	18	824
Rural – Male & Female							
<19	1	1	3	3	0	1	9
19 to <30	6	15	6	5	3	0	35
30 to <49	20	16	18	4	2	1	61
≥49	16	3	15	1	0	0	35
All Rural	43	35	42	13	5	2	140
All Nonusers	330	240	249	85	40	20	964

older accounting for 57 percent of the subsample. There were no users over 49 years old, but respondents in this age bracket make up nearly a third of the nonuser sample. As in the user survey, only a few (14 percent) rural residents were captured by the nonuser survey. Nearly 90 percent of elderly nonusers (49 years or older) are urban residents. The reasons given by nonusers for not using the Internet are presented in table 4.4.

The 2010 Network World League Cybercafé Survey sampled 8,759 users and found that women represented only about 11 percent of users (TXWM 2011). During fieldwork, a greater willingness by women to participate in the survey was detected, and our estimate of 27 percent may overestimate female representation as users of Internet cafés.

Table 4.5
Places of Access to the Internet of Survey Population

Venue	Use of Venue by Frequency of Use					
	Every Time	Most of the Time	Sometimes	Seldom	Never	All Respondents
Cybercafé	141	341	221	218	55	976
Home	60	201	166	127	422	976
Mobile phone	51	190	229	152	354	976
School	30	141	125	145	535	976
Office	13	49	76	118	720	976
Friend's house	5	14	93	326	538	976
Library	3	22	33	82	836	976
Other	2	6	9	49	910	976

Place of Access, Distance from Home, and Patterns of Internet Café Use Sample users exhibit complex patterns of access to the Internet (tables 4.5–4.7). Out of 976 valid responses, only 90 were from users who used Internet cafés exclusively. Most Internet café users also use other venues; about 50 percent used three or more other types of venues. The other most common place of access (table 4.7) is the home, followed by school.

Predominant Internet café users (i.e., those who report using Internet cafés "all of the time" or "most of the time") represent nearly half (49 percent) of user respondents (table 4.5). Another 31 percent are predominant users of other places of access and do not make as frequent use of Internet cafés (table 4.7). The remaining 20 percent vary in the extent of their commitment to either Internet cafés or other venue types.

There are no Internet cafés in remote rural areas of China, and none of the towns where the surveys were implemented may be considered rural. The surveys' classification of users and nonusers into rural and urban is based on self-reports of interviewees, which would tend to follow China's HuKuo system of registration that identifies a person's place of permanent residence. The user survey was taken in twenty-two Internet cafés and the nonuser survey in the vicinity of those twenty-two Internet cafés (see appendix 4.A). The proportion of users who identified themselves as urban exceeded 50 percent in all but two of these venues.

Most users (90 percent) travel no more than two kilometers to reach an Internet café (table 4.8). About 57 percent visit a café daily or at least once a week (table 4.9), but there are relatively more male daily visitors (19 percent) than female (7 percent). About 70 percent of users visit during the day or at dusk, but some (23 percent) prefer to

Table 4.6
Use of Cybercafés by Survey Population

	Cybercafé Users (All)	Exclusive Cybercafé Users (No Other Venue Used)	Cybercafé Users Who Also Use Other Venue Types			
			1 More	2 More	3 More	Cyber +4 or More
Uses cybercafés all the time	141	60	31	15	16	19
Uses cybercafés most of the time	341	25	74	75	74	93
Sometimes uses cybercafés	221	3	30	42	57	89
Seldom uses cybercafés	218	1	32	47	65	73
Never uses cybercafés	55	1	28	11	4	11
Total	976	90	195	190	216	285

Table 4.7
Predominant Place of Access of Internet Café Users

Predominant Place of Access*	#	%
No predominant place	82	8
Only one predominant place		
Cybercafé	289	30
School	99	10
Home	130	13
Office	25	3
Friend's house	8	1
Library	3	–
Mobile phone	34	3
Predominant mobile users who are also predominant users of:		
Cybercafés	107	11
Home	48	5
School	15	2
Office	2	0.3
Users with two predominant places not including mobiles	87	9
Users with three or more predominant places	46	5
All user respondents	975	100

*A place is considered predominant if the respondent used it to access the Internet. "Every time" or "Most of the time."

Table 4.8
Distance of Usual Internet Café from Home

	All			Urban Males			Urban Females			All Urban Users			Rural Users in Sample		
	#	%	Cum%	#	%	Cum%	#	%	Cum%	#	%	Cum%	#	%	Cum%
< 300 m	291	29.8	29.8	176	30.6	30.6	68	32.2	32.2	244	31.0	31.0	47	24.7	24.7
300–500 m	359	36.8	66.6	215	37.4	68.0	84	39.8	72.0	299	38.0	69.1	60	31.6	56.3
500 m–1 km	161	16.5	83.1	96	16.7	84.7	28	13.3	85.3	124	15.8	84.9	37	19.5	75.8
1–2 km	75	7.7	90.8	40	7.0	91.7	15	7.1	92.4	55	7.0	91.9	20	10.5	86.3
> 2 km	90	9.2	100.0	48	8.3	100.0	16	7.6	100.0	64	8.1	100.0	26	13.7	100.0
Total	976			575			211			786			190		

Table 4.9
Frequency of Visits, Usual Time of Visit, and Amount of Time Spent During Each Visit to Internet Cafés

	All Users		Males		Females		Young Urban Males		Overusers	
	#	%	#	%	#	%	#	%	#	%
Frequency of visits										
Daily or almost daily	151	15.5	133	18.7	18	6.8	15	17.4	36	34.6
At least once a week	408	41.8	296	41.6	112	42.3	36	41.9	43	41.3
At least once a month	222	22.7	152	21.4	70	26.4	26	30.2	13	12.5
A few times a year	195	20.0	130	18.3	65	24.5	9	10.5	12	11.5
Subtotal	976		711		265		86		104	
Usual time of visit										
Morning	89	9.1	66	9.3	23	8.7	9	10.5	9	8.7
Noon	64	6.6	53	7.5	11	4.2	13	15.1	12	11.5
Afternoon	343	35.1	234	32.9	109	41.1	33	38.4	35	33.7
At dusk	194	19.9	134	18.8	60	22.6	10	11.6	17	16.3
Evening	223	22.8	176	24.8	47	17.7	18	20.9	19	18.3
Late night/early morning	15	1.5	9	1.3	6	2.3	1	1.2	3	2.9
Overnight	48	4.9	39	5.5	9	3.4	2	2.3	9	8.7
Subtotal	976		711		265		86		104	
Usual amount of time										
Less than an hour	37	3.8	23	3.2	14	5.3	4	12.1	2	1.9
Around 1hour	145	14.9	87	12.2	58	21.9	9	27.3	10	9.6
Around 2–3 hours	484	49.6	345	48.5	139	52.5	14	42.4	46	44.2
Around 4–5 hours	145	14.9	116	16.3	29	10.9	4	12.1	18	17.3
More than 5 hours	78	8.0	71	10.0	7	2.6	–	–	12	11.5
Not sure	87	8.9	69	9.7	18	6.8	2	6.1	16	15.4
Subtotal	976		711		265		33		104	

1. *Young* here indicates respondents who are less than 19 years old.
2. *Overusers* are sample respondents who answered "sometimes," "every time," or "most of the time" to five or more of the eight questions proposed by Young (1996) to assess Internet addiction. This modified application of Young's criteria will classify a larger number of users as overusers than Young would classify as "addicted."

visit in the evenings, and about 6 percent stay late into the night or even overnight. About two-thirds of all users stay less than three hours when they visit a café. More males (26 percent) than females (14 percent) tend to stay more than three hours.

Young (under age 19) male urban users visit cafés about as frequently as all sample males (i.e., 59 percent daily or almost daily). Contrary to what might be anticipated from the concerns expressed in the media (box 4.1), only 12 percent of these youngsters spend more than three hours per visit to a café, and only 3 percent stay late into the night or overnight (table 4.9).

Overusers[13] visit Internet cafés more frequently (35 percent daily) than users overall (15 percent). Twenty-nine percent of this group spend four hours or longer during each visit, and 12 percent are night owls who stay late into the night or overnight (table 4.9).

Occupation and Income The occupations and incomes of users are quite different from those of nonusers. Students are dominant among users, and income-earning employees are dominant among nonusers (table 4.10). Occupational and income patterns also vary between urban and rural residents. Students represent about 40 percent of urban users and 50 percent of rural users but only 15 and 10 percent of urban and rural nonusers, respectively. There are no retirees among users, but retirees account

Table 4.10
Distribution of User and Nonuser Sample Respondents by Occupation and Urban/Rural Status

	All		Urban		Rural	
	Users	Nonusers	Users	Nonusers	Users	Nonusers
Student	419	142	322	128	97	14
Government employee	20	37	18	33	2	4
Migrant/domestic worker	47	75	30	41	17	34
Business administration	34	22	32	22	2	–
Employee	142	81	123	77	19	4
Technical worker	97	61	81	56	16	5
Factory or service worker	56	72	45	67	11	5
Self-employed	76	160	63	139	13	21
Farmer	3	43	3	11	–	32
Soldier/military	10	3	9	2	1	1
Unemployed	18	79	16	71	2	8
Retired	–	164	–	161	–	3
Other	54	25	44	16	10	9

for 19 percent of urban and 2 percent of rural nonusers. Nonusers earn more than users, and rural users and nonusers have lower incomes than their urban counterparts (table 4.11).

Student users earn less than nonstudent users, as the latter are mostly workers (table 4.12). Student users prefer to access the Internet from cafés and schools. Among nonstudent café users, those who connect mainly from home have higher incomes: about 73 percent of nonstudents connecting predominantly from home earned more than 1,500 yuan per month (approx. US$240), compared with only 57 percent of predominant café users.

Research Questions and Hypotheses

We consider two divergent views of the impact of Internet cafés: one based on media accounts suggesting that impact on users is negative, and a positive view based on Internet impact studies. Self-determination theory guides the analysis.

Situational Goals of Internet Café Users

Are the Motives of Internet Café Users Socially Valuable? (H1a) Media accounts of the impact of Internet cafés (box 4.1) are largely based on the observation that gaming and entertainment are commonplace and a dominant venue activity. We posit that café visitors, even if engaged extensively in entertainment, also engage in many other activities and have multiple objectives when they visit Internet cafés, including some commonly regarded as "instrumental" and socially desirable.

H1a. *The situational goals that Internet café users pursue include common human objectives, some of which have value recognized by society.*

Do Users Learn Computer and Internet Skills in Internet Cafés? (H1b & H1c) In China, it is sometimes claimed, "The Internet cafés are not places where the youth learn Internet skills!" (Yu 2006). This perception runs counter to what is observed in other countries (see e.g., the chapters on Jordan and Cameroon in this book). User experience may also affect the achievement of other situational goals. We therefore propose to test the following hypotheses:

H1b. *The proportion of inexperienced Internet users having computer and Internet training as a situational goal (SG4 in table 4.1) is greater than among experienced users.*

H1c. *Experience in the use of the Internet increases the sense of achievement of Internet-related situational goals reported by users.*

Table 4.11
Distribution of User and Nonuser Sample Respondents by Income and Urban/Rural Status

Monthly Income (in Yuan)	Whole Sample				Urban				Rural			
	Users		Nonusers		Users		Nonusers		Users		Nonusers	
	#	%	#	%	#	%	#	%	#	%	#	%
< 500	240	24.6	194	20.1	170	21.6	159	19.3	70	36.8	35	25.0
501–1,000	220	22.5	133	13.8	173	22.0	98	11.9	47	24.7	35	25.0
1,001–1,500	164	16.8	180	18.7	139	17.7	149	18.1	25	13.2	31	22.1
1,501–2,000	168	17.2	201	20.9	142	18.1	180	21.8	26	13.7	21	15.0
2,001–3,000	127	13.0	163	16.9	113	14.4	152	18.4	14	7.4	11	7.9
3,001–5,000	40	4.1	71	7.4	35	4.5	65	7.9	5	2.6	6	4.3
5,001–8,000	9	0.9	12	1.2	9	1.1	12	1.5	–	–	–	–
> 8,000	8	0.8	10	1.0	5	0.6	9	1.1	3	1.6	1	0.7
Total	976	100.0	964	100.0	786	100.0	824	100	190	100	140	100

Table 4.12

Income by Predominant Place of Access[a] and Student Status

	Students															
Monthly Income (in Yuan)[b]	Cybercafé		School		Home		Office		Friend's House		Library		Mobile Phone		All Students	
	#	%	#	%	#	%	#	%	#	%	#	%	#	%	#	%
< 500	82	51.6	61	46.6	46	47.4	3	60.0	5	83.3	–	–	–	–	219	52.3
501–1,000	59	37.1	63	48.1	41	42.3	2	40.0	–	–	–	–	–	–	167	39.9
1,001–1,500	11	6.9	7	5.3	7	7.2	–	–	–	–	–	–	–	–	21	5.0
1,501–2,000	3	1.9	–	–	–	–	–	–	–	–	–	–	–	–	4	1.0
2,001–3,000	4	2.5	–	–	2	2.1	–	–	–	–	–	–	–	–	6	1.4
3,001–5,000	–	–	–	–	1	1.0	–	–	1	16.7	–	–	–	–	2	0.5
5,001–8,000	–	–	–	–	–	–	–	–	–	–	–	–	–	–	–	–
> 8,000	–	–	–	–	–	–	–	–	–	–	–	–	–	–	–	–
Subtotal	159	100	131	100	97	100	5	100	6	100	–	–	–	–	419	100
	38%		31%		23%		1%		1%		–		–			

	Nonstudents[c]															
	Cybercafé		School		Home		Office		Friend's House		Library		Mobile Phone		All Nonstudents	
	#	%	#	%	#	%	#	%	#	%	#	%	#	%	#	%
> 500	9	2.8	3	7.5	6	3.7	1	1.8	–	–	–	–	2	1.5	21	3.8
501–1,000	32	9.9	5	12.5	13	7.9	3	5.3	1	7.7	1	16.7	6	4.5	53	9.5
1,001–1,500	98	30.3	10	25.0	25	15.2	13	22.8	7	53.8	1	16.7	31	23.1	143	25.7
1,501–2,000	98	30.3	13	32.5	40	24.4	19	33.3	4	30.8	2	33.3	47	35.1	164	29.4
2,001–3,000	62	19.2	6	15.0	55	33.5	13	22.8	–	–	2	33.3	38	28.4	121	21.7
3,001–5,000	15	4.6	3	7.5	15	9.1	6	10.5	1	7.7	–	–	10	7.5	38	6.8
5,001–8,000	2	0.6	–	–	7	4.3	2	3.5	–	–	–	–	–	–	9	1.6
> 8,000	7	2.2	–	–	3	1.8	–	–	–	–	–	–	–	–	8	1.4
Subtotal	323	100	40	100	164	100	57	100	13	100	6	100	134	100	557	100
	44%		5%		22%		8%		2%		1%		18%			

[a] A user may have more than one place of access, and some users will appear in more than one place of access category.

[b] Students were asked to report their cost of living expenses as income.

[c] The classification *nonstudent* refers to occupation. There are probably some part-time students among nonstudents.

Are There Differences in Internet User Goals by Place of Access? (H1d, H1e, & H1f) Using the Internet is not the same as using an Internet café, but Internet use is central to the experience of using an Internet café. Yet Internet café venues in China are singled out for closure or regulation. From a user perspective, do the two activities differ?

We identify common places of access in our sample and examine whether users' SGs vary according to place of access and whether differences in goal achievement are linked to place of access. Our tests take into account that goal choice is affected by demographic differences (Massey, Gebhardt, and Garnefski 2008; Nurmi 1991).

H1d. *There are no major differences in situational goal content between Internet café users and users who access the Internet primarily from other venues.*
H1e. *There are no major differences in situational goal achievement between Internet café users and users who primarily use other venues.*

The data collected should also help assess whether users perceive benefits—over and above the advantages associated with access to computers and the Internet—in socializing with other Internet café patrons.

H1f. *Benefits associated with socializing at cafés are not significant.*

Life Goals of Users and Nonusers

Are User Objectives Different from Those of Nonusers? (H2a & H2b) Given the large differences in the makeup of sample users and nonusers (tables 4.2, 4.10, and 4.11), and that demographic differences are frequently associated with differences in goal content (Massey, Gebhardt, and Garnefski 2008), we expect life goals to vary according to demographics (H2a) but not otherwise (H2b).

H2a. *There are significant differences in the life goals of users and nonusers, and these can be largely attributed to demographic differences, especially age, gender, urban-rural (Hokuo) status, and possibly also occupation (student status).*
H2b. *Holding demographic features constant, there are no major differences in the life goals of users and nonusers.*

Is Life Goal Achievement Affected by Internet Café Use? (H3) To test the two contrasting views of Internet cafés, as places where youth are either corrupted and harmed or changed for the better, we propose H3.

H3. *For demographically similar cohorts, users and nonusers of Internet cafés will report similar life goal achievement.*

Findings

Activities

The 2010 Network World League (TXWM) Cybercafé Survey focuses on user activities. In response to the question, "What is your one main purpose while in a cybercafé?", 55 percent of the users surveyed indicated games, 10 percent downloading resources, 9 percent information search, 8 percent watching movies or listening to music, 7 percent chatting and making friends, 0.7 percent shopping, 0.7 percent email, and 5 percent other activities.

The activities sample users engage in are consistent with the findings of the Network World League Cybercafé Survey, but notice the difference that question wording makes. When users are asked to name their one single purpose for visiting cybercafés, gaming takes top billing, whereas chatting, making friends, and email appear insignificant; but when users are asked to identify all their activities, communication—mainly through chatting but also email—is far more prominent. Gamers tend to be very committed: nearly 49 percent of sample users play games "every time" or "most times." But chatting is even more popular, with 59 percent engaging in this activity just as frequently (table 4.13).

When people visit cybercafés, they engage in not just one activity (of the ten choices offered) but in about 2.8 activities per person either every time or most times, and 4.4 activities if you include activities that users engage in sometimes or more frequently (table 4.14). Understanding variety in cybercafé use is important. It is even more important to understand user motives.

Situational Goal Content and Achievement

User Objectives (H1a) Users pursue multiple objectives with varying degrees of interest when they visit Internet cafés. On average, each user selected 8.4 SGs, and about 57 percent identified with five or more SGs for using Internet cafés. Table 4.B.1 in appendix 4.B lists the thirty SGs ranked by popularity among 935 users with complete data. For each SG, the table gives average self-reported achievement, percentage of cybercafé time dedicated to pursuing each goal, and the goal's classification according to SDT.

There is no reason to expect popular situational goals to be associated with higher achievement, but this correlation is clear from the data. The most popular SGs are also the ones that users spend the most time pursuing while visiting an Internet café, and this probably accounts for the high correlation between goal achievement and goal

Table 4.13

Frequency with Which Users Engage in One of Ten Common Internet Activities When They Visit Internet Cafés

Activity	Every Time (a) %	Most Times (b) %	Sometimes (c) %	Seldom (d) %	Seldom or More Frequently (a + b + c + d) %	Never %
Send and receive email	6.4	7.0	13.9	27.7	55.0	45.1
Chat	26.1	32.8	19.7	10.9	89.4	10.7
Browse the web, surf the Internet	15.3	24.4	23.2	13.7	76.6	23.5
Write blog	2.6	4.6	10.6	20.1	37.8	62.3
Social networking (e.g., Happy Network)	4.4	8.5	12.1	23.2	48.2	51.9
Watch movies or TV	10.2	19.4	29.1	18.5	77.1	23.0
Play online games	23.5	25.1	16.1	13.8	78.6	21.5
Download and listen to music	9.0	16.5	29.0	21.9	76.5	23.6
Watch current events	8.5	11.3	19.1	29.4	68.3	31.8
Shop on the web	1.4	1.8	7.4	20.1	30.8	69.3

Note: One respondent did not engage in any of the ten activities. Accordingly, 975 observations were used to calculate percentages.

Table 4.14
Distribution of Users According to the Number of Activities They Engage in When They Visit Internet Cafés, by Frequency of Engagement

Number of Activities Engaged in	Engagement Frequency: Every Time	Most of the Time	Sometimes	Occasionally	At Least Sometimes	At Least Occasionally	Either Every Time or Most of the Time
1	260	272	225	205	76	37	232
2	111	208	198	210	110	56	243
3	62	126	153	169	161	76	192
4	38	61	84	94	161	78	133
5	19	15	32	41	178	87	57
6	5	8	14	19	120	99	29
7	2	4	5	6	93	159	14
8	5	2	3	6	33	153	8
9	3	–	2	3	18	131	4
10	2	–	2	–	17	99	4
11	–	–	–	–	–	–	–
≥12	–	–	–	–	–	–	–
Number of users	507	696	718	753	967	975	916
As % of respondents	52.0	71.4	73.6	77.2	99.2	100.0	93.9
Av. no. of activities per engagement level	2.1	2.1	2.4	5.9	4.4	10.3	2.8

popularity. On a scale from 3 (full achievement) to 0 (no achievement), the average rating for the top twelve goals ranged from 1.5 to 2.1, compared with a range of 1.0 to 1.5 for the least popular twelve.

The four extrinsic SGs are among the twelve least popular SGs. All of the top twelve SGs are intrinsic, except for one left unclassified (SG11), "Access information (news, weather forecasts, stock info, sports, gossip, etc.)." This is consistent with Kasser's (2002) proposition that, "on average, people are more oriented toward intrinsic values than toward extrinsic values" (p. 31).

As expected by H1a, some of the twelve most popular goals are instrumental goals valued by society (table 4.B.1)—for example, keeping in touch with family and friends (SG13, a goal of 64 percent of users), accessing information (SG11, 51 percent), meeting new friends or finding a mate or companion (SG12, 36 percent), learning to use computers and the Internet (SG4, 36 percent), improving job skills (SG2,30 percent), and improving school performance (SG1, 29 percent).

Next, consider the top twelve situational goals of young urban students less than 19 years old, a cohort of special interest to China's policymakers (table 4.15). The main difference between this group and the entire sample of users is the higher popularity among youngsters of entertaining themselves and having fun, making new friends, socializing in the venue, and improving computer and Internet skills and school performance, and the somewhat lower popularity of enhancing occupational skills. Notice in particular that SG1, "Improve my performance in school," is an objective for using Internet cafés of 29 percent of all users but of 41 to 43 percent of young urban student users.

The top twelve SGs of the 255 women users interviewed (calculations not shown) coincide with those of the whole sample, but women's most popular SG is keeping in touch with family and friends (SG13, 72 percent, compared with 64 percent for the whole user sample), and a greater proportion of women (34 percent, compared with 30 percent for all users) have blogging as an objective (SG23). Among urban student users, blogging is a situational objective of 57 percent of females and 33 percent of males. Rural users' top twelve include eleven of the overall top twelve, but "Increase self-confidence" (SG9) was selected by 31 percent (compared with 23 percent for all users), replacing SG5 on their "top twelve" list.

ICT Training and User Experience (H1b) and Achievement (H1c) When it came to learning how to use computers, Internet cafés and schools were almost equally important (38 and 37 percent, respectively), but Internet cafés were more important when it came to learning how to use the Internet (52 percent for cafés vs. 24 percent

Table 4.15
Proportion of Users Selecting Overall Top-12 Situational Goals (SGs)—All Users and Young Urban Student Male and Female Subsamples

12 Select SGs	% in All Users sample	% in Young (< 19) Urban Student Subsamples	
		Male	Female[b]
Entertainment (SG15, A) [a]	74	81	82
Keep in touch with family and friends (SG13, R)	64	71	75
Access information (news,…gossip, etc.) (SG11, U)	51	49	50
Relax, relieve tension (SG17, A)	43	40	36
Meet new friends or a mate or companion (SG12, R)	36	46	54
Learn to use computers and the Internet (SG4, C)	36	41	50
Socialize and make friends with people in Internet cafés (SG14, R)	33	38	46
Spend time on a hobby or pastime (SG16, A)	33	41	46
Contribute to other people's blogs (SG23, R)	30	33	57
Improve my job skills to work better (SG2, C)	30	25	25
Improve my performance in school (SG1, C)	29	41	43
Complete work (SG5, C)	28	16	29
# of observations in sample/subsample	963	63	28
Average number of significant goals	8.4	8.1	11.4

[a]SDT classification: A: Autonomy, C: Competence, R: Relatedness, U: Unclassified.
[b]The larger number of goals of young female students in part accounts for the higher percentage observed for their SGs.

for schools) (table 4.16). These proportions vary for females: more women in our user sample learned to use computers in schools (43 percent) than in cafés (27 percent), but female users more frequently learned how to use the Internet in cafés (45 percent) than in schools (28 percent). (Calculations are not shown.) It should be noted that because our survey sampled café users, our figures will necessarily overestimate the overall significance of these venues as places for learning computer and Internet use among the ICT user population. But because nearly one-fifth of China's Internet users connect at Internet cafés, these venues are an important place where people are first introduced to ICT. Many users may first learn to use ICT at Internet cafés and afterwards buy their own computer to connect from home.

Table 4.16
Response to "Where Did You Learn How to Use..."

	Computers?		The Internet?	
	#	%	#	%
Internet café	371	38	503	52
School	358	37	238	24
Home	175	18	177	18
Work	39	4	27	3
Friend's house	31	3	27	3
Library	2	0.2	3	0.3
Other venues	–	–	1	0.1
Total	976	100	976	100

Given the rapid growth of Internet café use in China, we expected to survey many novice users. In practice, we sampled well-established user populations, and, after discarding respondents with incomplete data, only eighteen users had less than one year of experience, and another thirty-six had between one and two years. To test H1b, we defined "inexperienced users" as those with less than two years of experience using the Internet. According to this definition, our sample had 52 inexperienced and 911 experienced users.

H1b was tested for the entire user sample and for two subsamples: young users 19 years or less and mature users older than 19 (table 4.17). As anticipated by H1b, the percentage of inexperienced users choosing computer and Internet training as a situational goal is statistically significantly higher than for experienced users. A large number of experienced users have such a goal (35 percent), even if it is not as popular as it is among users with two years of experience or less (52 percent). Within the two subsamples, this goal is more popular among inexperienced than experienced users, but sample sizes are too small to assert statistical significance.

There is little evidence in support of H1c (i.e., the notion that experience [years using the Internet] improves users' SG achievement). Further, none of the main demographic variables (gender, age, urban/rural classification, education, income, student/nonstudent status) are correlated with self-reported achievement of the twelve most popular SGs (table 4.18). Only effort, defined as the proportion of time users reportedly spent pursuing each goal when visiting an Internet café (i.e., less than 25 percent, 25–50 percent, 50–75 percent, or more than 75 percent), is significantly correlated with achievement in the case of ten of the top twelve SGs. The higher the effort, the higher the achievement.

Table 4.17
Test of H1b for Whole Sample and for Subsamples of Young Users and Mature Users

	All Users		Young Users (<19 yrs.)		Mature Users (≥19 yrs.)	
	Inexp.	Exp.	Inexp.	Exp.	Inexp.	Exp.
# of observations	52	911	26	143	26	768
% selecting SG4	51.9	35.0	61.5	53.1	42.3	31.6
Z statistic	−2.4714		−.7903		−1.1468	
Probability that proportions are equal	.0068		.2148		.1271	

1. H1b. The proportion of inexperienced Internet users having computer and Internet training as a situational goal (SG4 in table 4.1) is larger than for experienced users.
2. Calculations based on Mendenhall (1975).

Many institutions conduct formal computer training programs, but in Internet cafés, self-training is the rule. Self-training takes place at the user's own initiative and pace, with occasional help from café operators but mainly from peers, and would thus help satisfy user needs for autonomy and relatedness. To the extent that training is effective, which largely depends on personal effort, it would also satisfy the user's need for competence.

Place of Access and SG Achievement (H1d & H1e) Other venues used predominantly by some café users are the home, the school, and, among those who chose the goal "Shop online . . . " (SG24), mobile phones (table 4.19).

As hypothesized by H1d, there are no major differences in the content of situational goals of predominant café users and predominant users of other venues. The two groups share the same four top SGs, all of which were chosen by at least 44 percent of both groups (table 4.20). The next six most popular SGs of predominant Internet café users were chosen by at least 30 percent in this group, as well as by at least 30 percent of café users who are predominant users of other venues (table 4.20).

As foreseen by H1e, there are no big differences in SG achievement between these two groups (table 4.20). There are, however, four SGs for which statistically significant differences in achievement are observed. For SG15, "Entertainment (play games, listen to music, watch movies, online video, etc.)," predominant users of Internet cafés report higher achievement. In contrast, for SGs 5, 17, and 24, predominant users of other venues report statistically significant higher achievement.

In hindsight, these differences are reasonable. An Internet user primarily interested in entertainment does well to visit Internet cafés where he or she will find fast machines

Table 4.18

Correlation Coefficient for Achievement Level for Twelve Most Popular Situational Goals (SGs) and Demographic Variables and Time Dedicated to SGs

	Male	Age	Urban	Education	Income	Student	Experience	Café Time	#
Entertainment (play games, listen to music, etc.)—SG15	0.105	–0.076	0.019	–0.006	–0.034	0.020	–0.024	0.352**	685
Keep in touch with family and friends (email, QQ, etc.)—SG13	0.024	–0.065	0.018	0.069	–0.117	0.100	–0.108	0.287**	585
Access information (news, sports, gossip, etc.)—SG11	0.028	0.081	0.091	0.182*	0.039	–0.004	0.063	0.187*	466
Relax, relieve tension—SG17	0.023	–0.004	0.090	0.133	–0.031	0.069	–0.004	0.119	393
Meet new friends or a mate or companion—SG12	–0.018	0.021	0.062	0.040	–0.037	0.029	–0.051	0.249**	323
Learn to use computers and the Internet—SG4	–0.015	–0.018	0.086	–0.009	0.057	–0.066	–0.059	0.202**	305
Socialize and make friends with people in Internet cafés—SG14	0.022	0.026	0.104	–0.007	–0.028	–0.016	0.023	0.197**	293
Spend time on a hobby or pastime—SG16	0.122	–0.013	0.064	0.035	–0.080	0.060	–0.041	0.336**	290
Improve my job skills to work better—SG2	0.051	0.032	–0.0005	0.076	0.109	–0.125	0.035	0.189*	266
Contribute to other people's web pages or blogs—SG23	0.087	0.012	0.073	0.128	–0.001	0.010	0.010	0.186*	269
Improve my performance in school—SG1	0.077	0.083	0.009	0.172*	0.044	0.059	0.021	0.159	263
Complete work—SG6	–0.144	0.105	0.130	0.218**	0.135	–0.077	0.105	0.205**	252

Notes: Higher achievement values are indicative of more complete achievement.

Dummy variables are used for "Male," "Urban," and "Student."

Two-tailed statistical significance: *10%, **5%.

Table 4.19
Predominant Users of Other Venues: Distribution of Predominant Venue by Situational Goal Chosen

	Predominant Venue Use			
Situational Goal*	School	Home	Mobile	Library
Improve my performance in school (1)	56	75	84	5
Improve my job skills to work better (2)	34	65	63	2
Improve my skills to get better/new job (3)	35	59	85	–
Learn to use computers and the Internet (4)	67	89	58	1
Complete work (5)	59	66	20	2
Find an additional/new job (6)	39	53	7	–
Better manage my company or farm (e.g., check market info) (7)	21	48	16	1
Make money (e.g., online store, doing web pages, etc.) (8)	25	53	25	2
Increase self-confidence (9)	39	53	20	–
Search for spiritual comfort (10)	47	56	19	4
Access information (news, weather forecasts, stock info, sports, gossip, etc.) (11)	76	114	6	1
Meet new friends or a mate or companion (12)	51	76	–	7
Keep in touch with family and friends (email, QQ, etc.) (13)	90	129	–	5
Socialize and make friends with people in Internet cafés (14)	40	77	–	1
Entertainment (play games, listen to music, watch movies, online video, etc.) (15)	97	147	–	–
Spend time on a hobby or pastime (16)	50	73	–	1
Relax, relieve tension (17)	73	89	–	–
Get health information to improve physical health (18)	35	58	–	2
Get mental health information to improve mental health (19)	29	48	–	–
Check public service information (access information, online applications, licenses, etc.) (20)	31	47	–	–
Literary and artistic creation (fiction, poetry, music, etc.) (21)	25	38	–	12
Create or update personal website (home page, blog, microblog) (22)	36	66	–	4
Contribute to other people's web pages or blogs (23)	42	74	109	6
Shop online or get product information online (24)	41	51	77	6

Table 4.19 (continued)

	Predominant Venue Use			
Situational Goal*	School	Home	Mobile	Library
Online banking or personal financial services (25)	31	54	103	3
Plan personal or family trips (26)	29	49	–	–
Improve the conditions of community (27)	23	43	–	–
Support political or social causes that I find worthwhile (28)	28	53	–	–
Help improve government (29)	17	33	110	–
Other (30)	–	2	–	2

*Number in parentheses shows the order in which SG appears in questionnaire.
Predominant users of other venues are those who did not use Internet cafés "every time" or "most of the time" but instead reportedly used the other venues indicated "every time" or "most of the time."
There were no predominant users of the other two venue categories offered in the questionnaire, namely, "office" and "friend's house."

and high-resolution graphics. A user interested in relaxing, completing work, or getting better products online would best achieve these goals from home or school (if the option is available) or, in the case of getting better products, using a mobile phone.

Do Internet Café Users Benefit from Socializing in the Venue? (H1f) We examine this hypothesis through two questions in the user survey. First, users were asked to state directly their main reason for using Internet cafés. Their responses, tabulated in table 4.21, show that 30 percent of all users frequent cafés to work or be with friends and other people. This is a significant figure, although not as high as the 42 percent of respondents who visit cafés because they have no other option for using computers or the Internet. Better quality equipment was the reason chosen by 19 percent of respondents; only 3 percent of all users indicated getting help from venue staff as their primary reason for visiting cafés.

Different cohorts answered this first question differently. To work or be with friends was popular among urban women, 35 percent of whom chose this response. It was also chosen by 45 percent of café users who predominantly connected to the Internet from home. Thirty percent of this group also chose the availability of better equipment as a reason to use cafés. The group that appears to be most reliant on Internet cafés for access to computers and the Internet (56 percent) is rural residents.

Table 4.20
Predominant Users of Cybercafés or Other Venues: Percentage Choosing Various SGs and Average Achievement of Goals Chosen

	Predominant Cybercafé Users				Predominant Other Venue Users				Achievement Differences & t-test Probability		
	Choice		Goal achievement		Choice		Goal achievement				
	Obs.	477			Obs.	404					
All Users	Rank	%	Mean	Obs.	Rank	%	Mean	Obs.	Diff.	p(t)	
Entertainment (play games, listen to music, watch movies, etc.)	1	77	2.2	365	1	72	2.0	290	0.13	0.030	**
Keep in touch with family and friends (email, QQQ, etc.)	2	63	2.0	300	2	65	2.0	264	–0.08	0.201	
Access information (news, weather forecasts, stock info, sports, gossip, etc.)	3	47	1.7	224	3	56	1.8	227	–0.12	0.116	
Relax, relieve tension	4	43	1.7	204	4	46	1.9	187	–0.19	0.016	**
Meet new friends or a mate or companion	5	38	1.6	182	6	36	1.7	146	–0.07	0.507	
Socialize and make friends with people in Internet cafés	6	34	1.7	164	10	34	1.5	138	0.13	0.232	
Improve my job skills to work better	7	32	1.5	152	12	31	1.5	126	–0.01	0.960	
Spend time on a hobby or pastime	8	31	1.8	149	7	36	1.8	144	–0.03	0.795	
Learn to use computers and the Internet	9	31	1.7	146	5	43	1.8	172	–0.08	0.383	
Contribute to other people's web pages or blogs	10	30	1.7	144	11	32	1.8	129	–0.08	0.467	
Search for spiritual comfort	11	29	1.6	137	14	27	1.4	110	0.15	0.186	
Improve my skills to get better/new job	12	28	1.2	132	15	27	1.2	108	0.04	0.746	
Improve my performance in school	13	27	1.5	127	9	35	1.5	142	0.02	0.867	
Create or update own personal website (home page, blog, microblog)	14	26	1.6	123	13	28	1.6	115	0.01	0.946	
Increase self-confidence	15	25	1.6	118	16	25	1.5	102	0.02	0.864	
Find an additional/new job	16	24	1.1	114	19	24	1.1	95	0.06	0.647	
Support social groups I like (participate in forums, blogs, microblogs)	16	24	1.7	114	21	22	1.6	89	0.10	0.484	

Table 4.20 (continued)

	Predominant Cybercafé Users				Predominant Other Venue Users				Achievement Differences & t-test Probability		
	Choice		Goal achievement		Choice		Goal achievement				
	Obs.	477			Obs.	404					
All Users	Rank	%	Mean	Obs.	Rank	%	Mean	Obs.	Diff.	p(t)	
Complete work	18	24	1.6	113	8	35	1.8	143	–0.26	0.030	**
Make money (e.g., online store, doing web pages, etc.)	19	21	1.1	100	22	21	1.0	86	0.12	0.454	
Check public service information (access information, online applications, licenses, etc.)	20	18	1.3	88	25	20	1.3	81	0.03	0.827	
Get health information to improve physical health	21	18	1.4	87	18	25	1.5	99	–0.10	0.465	
Online banking or personal financial services (stock trading, online transfers)	21	18	1.4	87	20	23	1.4	94	0.02	0.889	
Promote the community, clubs, interest groups through online activities	21	18	1.4	87	28	17	1.2	68	0.15	0.395	
Get better products or services for myself or my family	24	18	1.3	86	17	25	1.5	102	–0.25	0.082	*
Get mental health information to improve mental health	25	18	1.4	84	23	21	1.4	83	0.04	0.779	
Plan personal or family trips	26	17	1.2	83	24	20	1.2	82	0.06	0.727	
Better manage my company or farm (e.g., check market info)	27	17	1.2	79	26	18	1.1	73	0.09	0.585	
Participate in government website or online policy discussions	28	16	1.1	76	29	13	0.9	52	0.12	0.521	
Literary and artistic creation (fiction, poetry, music, etc.)	29	15	1.2	71	27	17	1.3	69	–0.11	0.555	
Other	30	1	0.6	7	30	–	2.5	2	–	–	

Table 4.21
Main Reason for Visiting Internet Cafés

									Predominant Users of:					
	All		Urban Male		Urban Female		Rural		Internet Cafés		Home		Mobile	
Reason Given	#	%	#	%	#	%	#	%	#	%	#	%	#	%
1: No other option for computer access	251	25.7	132	23.0	41	19.4	78	41.1	143	36.1	12	6.7	10	29.4
2: No other option for Internet access	157	16.1	90	15.7	39	18.5	28	14.7	71	17.9	16	9.0	7	20.6
3: To work or be with friends, other people	295	30.2	169	29.4	75	35.5	51	26.8	80	20.2	81	45.5	8	23.5
4: To get help from venue staff	28	2.9	17	3.0	4	1.9	7	3.7	7	1.8	6	3.4	1	2.9
5: Better equipment than home or work	188	19.3	131	22.8	39	18.5	18	9.5	69	17.4	54	30.3	8	23.5
6: Other, please specify	57	5.8	36	6.3	13	6.2	8	4.2	26	6.6	9	5.1	–	–
Total	976		575		211		190		396		178		34	

Note: A user is defined as a "predominant Internet café user" or "predominant home user" if he or she reports using one of these venues "most of the time" or "some of the time" and uses other venues less frequently (except for mobiles, which may be used as frequently). A "predominant mobile user" is one who connects by mobile "every time" or "most of the time" and more frequently than from elsewhere.

Second, we also included as a possible SG choice SG14, "Socialize and make friends with people in Internet cafés." This is the seventh most popular SG, chosen by 33 percent of all users (appendix 4.B, table 4.B.1). It is also the ninth most popular goal among young male students (38 percent) and the eighth most popular among female students (46 percent) (appendix 4.B, table 4.B.2). It was selected as a goal for using cafés by 34 percent of predominant users of Internet cafés and in the same proportion by café users who predominantly use other venues (table 4.20).

Life Goal Content and Achievement

Content (H2a & H2b) Notwithstanding major demographic differences and contrary to expectations (H2a), there is remarkable agreement in the LGs endorsed by users and nonusers (table 4.22).

Five LGs stand out as most popular (i.e., were chosen as either "most important" or "very important" by at least 30 percent of both users and nonusers).

	% of Users	% of Nonusers
Learn more knowledge (LG1, I)	53	44
Leisure, entertainment (LG15, I)	46	32
Keep in touch with friends and family who don't live nearby (LG14, I)	40	45
Keep up to date (LG5, U)	31	37
Get stable, high-paying job, better business opportunities (LG2, U)	31	32

There is also agreement on three LGs not prioritized by at least 25 percent of respondents.

	% of Users	% of Nonusers
Plan a trip (LG8, U)	15	23
Art creation (fiction, poetry, art, music, etc.) (LG4, I)	8	7
Participate in community or village activities (LG11, I)	4	15

Three differences in LG priorities stand out. Improving the physical health of self or family was a high priority for 57 percent of nonusers but only 25 percent of

Table 4.22

Life Goals (LGs): Rank of LGs Chosen as Either "Most Important" or "Very Important," Average Achievement, and Achievement Differences between Users and Nonusers

LGs Chosen as Either "Most Important" or "Very Important"[a]	Users # Obs. 846 / # LGs 4.4		Users Average Achieve.[b]		Nonusers # Obs. 927 / # LGs 4.9		Nonusers Average Achieve.		Difference in Achievement, t-test, and Stat. Significance		
	Rank	%	Av.	#	Rank	%	Av.	#	Diff.	P(t)	Sig.
Learn more knowledge (1, I)	1	53	1.7	450	3	44	1.5	405	0.2	0.0001	**
Leisure, entertainment (15, I)	2	46	2.2	388	6	32	2.1	294	0.1	0.0514	*
Keep in touch with friends and family who don't live nearby (14, I)	3	40	2.1	341	2	45	2.1	417	–	0.4033	
Relax, relieve tension (17, I)	4	35	1.9	295	14	19	1.7	179	0.2	0.0029	**
Get stable, high-paying job, better business opportunities (2, U)	5	31	1.1	266	7	32	1.3	293	–0.1	0.1258	
Keep up to date (5, U)	6	31	1.9	261	4	37	2.1	341	–0.2	0.0017	**
Spend time on a hobby or pastime (16, I)	7	30	2.0	250	9	26	1.9	244	–	0.4670	
Self-realization, enhance self-confidence (3, I)	8	28	1.7	239	11	25	1.5	228	0.2	0.0208	**
Get together with friends (face to face) (13, I)	9	26	1.9	219	12	23	2.0	214	–0.1	0.3612	
Improve the physical health of myself or my family (9, I)	10	25	1.8	212	1	57	2.0	531	–0.2	0.0001	**
Look for and meet new friends or a mate or companion (12, I)	11	24	1.8	202	15	17	1.7	162	0.1	0.2365	
Get information on government policies, regulations, and services (6, E)	12	17	1.8	147	10	26	1.7	238	0.1	0.5061	
Improve the mental health of myself or my family (10, I)	13	17	1.8	143	5	36	1.9	333	–0.2	0.0294	**
Plan a trip (8, U)	14	15	1.4	126	13	23	1.8	210	–0.4	0.0005	**
Obtain better products and services at lower cost (7, E)	15	14	1.8	118	8	27	1.9	251	–0.1	0.3876	
Art creation (fiction, poetry, music, etc.) (4, I)	16	8	1.4	67	17	7	1.5	68	–0.1	0.7084	
Participate in community or village activities (11, I)	17	4	1.7	36	16	15	2.0	139	–0.3	0.0655	*
Other (18, U)	18	1	2.1	9	18	1	1.5	6	0.6	0.3111	

[a]The first number in parenthesis indicates LG identifying number; the second number stands for goal classification according to SDT: I = intrinsic goal, E = extrinsic goal, U = unclassified.

[b]Full achievement = 3, No achievement = 0.

Shading: Unshaded LGs are those that are popular with 30% or more of the user or nonuser samples. Dark shaded LGs are those popular with fewer than 25% of user or nonuser samples. Light shaded LGs are those popular with 30 to 25% of user or nonuser samples.

users. Mental health (LG10) was a high priority for 36 percent of nonusers but only 17 percent of users. Being relaxed and relieving tension was a priority for 35 percent of users but only 19 percent of nonusers.

As anticipated by H2b, when the comparison is between similar cohorts, salient differences in goal priorities dissipate—for example, in our priority policy group, urban male students less than 19 years old, a subsample comprised of 39 users and 30 nonusers. The two LGs rated "most important" by this group were "Learn more knowledge" (LG1), chosen by 64 percent of users and 60 percent of nonusers, and "Leisure, entertainment" (LG15), selected by 33 percent of users and 40 percent of nonusers (table 4.23).[14]

Achievement (H3) To test H3, we focus on the top five LGs of users and the top five of nonusers (table 4.24). Because two goals are among the top five of both groups, a total of eight LGs are considered.[15]

Scholars have argued that the Internet has radically improved our ability to learn on our own (Hiemstra 2006), find information to improve our health (Boase et al. 2006), communicate with family and friends (Wang and Wellman 2010), entertain ourselves (Duffy, Liying, and Ong 2010), and relax (Russoniello, O'Brien, and Parks 2009). Choi et al. (2004) found "stay informed about what is going on" and "get up-to-date information" to be important components of a general motivation to use the Internet for "Surveillance Information Seeking," a motivation that in practice might confer an advantage to Internet users over nonusers.

Do the purported positive impacts of the Internet carry over to Internet café use? Do these positive impacts make a difference in user perceptions of life goal achievement? If they do, the performance of café users in their achievement of LGs 1, 5, 9, 10, 14, 15, and 17 would be enhanced, in contradiction of the negative view of cafés common in Chinese media (box 4.1). We have no expectations regarding LG 2, but because it is also a top LG, we also subject it to scrutiny.

H3 was refined and tested as follows:

H3. *For similar demographic cohorts, users will report the same levels of achievement of LGs 1, 5, 9, 10, 14, 15, and 17 as nonusers.*

Table 4.22 reports on tests—over the whole sample—of differences in mean reported achievement of users versus nonusers. Those tests suggest that Internet café use is associated with higher achievement of LG1, "Learn more knowledge," LG15, "Leisure, entertainment," and LG17, "Relax, relieve tension." In contrast, lower user achievement appears associated with LG5, "Keep up to date," and LG9 and LG10, "Improve the physical and mental health of myself or my family." There are, however,

Table 4.23
Young (< 19) Urban Male Student Users and Nonusers: Percentage Choosing Various Life Goals (LGs) as Most Important

	Users		Nonusers	
	# Obs.	39	# Obs.	30
	Av # LGs	2.9	Av # LGs	2.5
LG Chosen as Most Important	Rank	%	Rank	%
Learn more knowledge (1)	1	64.1	1	60.0
Spend time on a hobby or pastime (16)	2	33.3	2	40.0
Leisure, entertainment (15)	3	30.8	10	13.3
Relax, relieve tension (17)	4	28.2	12	10.0
Keep in touch with friends and family who don't live nearby (14)	5	23.1	9	13.3
Self-realization, enhance self-confidence (3)	6	20.5	3	23.3
Look for and meet new friends or a mate or companion (12)	7	17.9	11	10.0
Keep up to date (5)	8	15.4	7	13.3
Improve the physical health of myself or my family (9)	8	15.4	5	16.7
Get together with friends (face to face) (13)	8	15.4	13	6.7
Obtain better products and services at lower cost (7)	11	10.3	8	13.3
Improve the mental health of myself or my family (10)	11	10.3	6	16.7
Get information on government policies, regulations, and services (6)	13	5.1	–	–
Get stable, high-paying job, better business opportunities (2)	14	2.6	–	–
Art creation (fiction, poetry, music, etc.) (4)	14	2.6	–	–
Plan a (leisure) trip (8)	–	–	4	16.7
Participate in community or village activities (11)	–	–	–	–
Other (18)	–	–	–	–

Table 4.24
Five Most Popular Life Goals (LGs) of Users and Nonusers

	Users		Nonusers	
Popular LGs	Rank	#	Rank	#
Learn more knowledge (1, I)	1	450	3	405
Leisure, entertainment (15, I)	2	388	6	294
Keep in touch with friends and family who don't live nearby (14, I)	3	341	2	417
Relax, relieve tension (17, I)	4	295	14	179
Get stable, high paying job, better business opport. (2, U)	5	266	7	293
Keep up to date (5, U)	6	261	4	341
Improve the physical health of myself or my family (9, I)	10	212	1	531
Improve the mental health of myself or my family (10, I)	13	143	5	333

In parentheses: number showing position of LG in the questionnaire and its SDT classification (see table 4.1). See also table 4.22.

confounding factors influencing these tests. For example, the higher popularity and achievement of LG9 and LG10 among nonusers might be linked to greater concern for health because nonusers are on average older than users.

To distinguish the effect of Internet café use from that of other factors, we ran regressions on perceived achievement for each of the eight top goals, using as independent variables user/nonuser status, HuKuo residency status (urban/rural), student/nonstudent status, income, education level, age (in logarithmic form), gender, years of experience using the Internet, relative importance of the LG, and Internet overuse. We also included two control variables: the total number of life goals chosen and the relative importance of each goal. Notice that the user, over-user, and experience variables need to be considered jointly because a nonuser cannot have experience with or overuse the Internet.

Regressions were run for the whole sample and for key subsamples (listed in appendix 4.C, table 4.C.1). Results are reported in appendix 4.C, tables 4.C.2 through 4.C.9, and summarily depicted in table 4.25.

Regression analysis confirms the positive relationships between achievement and Internet café use for LG1, LG15, and LG17, previously identified through tests of differences in mean achievement (table 4.22), but makes evident the need to take demographic differences into consideration.[16] Regression analysis lends support to H3 in the case of four of the seven life goals for which we anticipated a positive effect: LG1, LG14, LG15, and LG17. Nevertheless, the effect of café use on achievement varies depending on LG, gender, age, student occupational status, and HuKuo status.[17]

- Urban male Internet café users less than 35 years old and urban male and female students report statistically significant higher achievement than nonusers for LG1, "Learning more knowledge."
- Urban male users less than 35 years old and female urban student users also report higher achievement than nonusers for LG15, "Leisure, entertainment."
- Urban female users report higher achievement for LG14, "Keep in touch with friends and family who don't live nearby," and LG17, "Relax, relieve tension."
- As users gain experience using the technology, part of the "enthusiasm" in their sense of accomplishment appears to wane. Achievement reports become lower with Internet use experience, with statistical significance in the case of LG14 ("Keep in touch with friends and family who don't live nearby") by urban females and of LG15 ("Leisure, entertainment") by urban males and urban female students.
- Among urban male nonstudents, a group made up largely of workers, there is a negative relationship between Internet café use and perceived achievement of LG2, "Get stable, high-paying job, better business opportunities." This troubling result deserves greater scrutiny in future studies. Male urban nonstudent users may be reporting lower achievement than the nonuser cohort because they are wasting time using the Internet, or it could be that those workers who visit Internet cafés are dissatisfied with their work and want to relax or change their situation.
- Rural residents who are overusers of the Internet report higher achievement of LG2, "Get stable, high-paying job, better business opportunities," than rural users and nonusers.
- Among rural residents, Internet café use is associated not with higher but with lower achievement of LG10, "Improve the mental health of myself or my family." Rural Internet overusers' achievement perceptions of LG10 are higher than those of users but still lower than those of nonusers.
- Urban male Internet overusers less than 35 years old and urban male overusers who are not students report lower achievement of LG5, "Keep up to date," than users and nonusers.

An extensive discussion of the effect of demographic variables on goal achievement is beyond the scope of this study. These variables were included in the regressions to avoid biasing tests of hypotheses. The LGs in the surveys are limited to those that could be linked with Internet café use, whereas in practice, people may have other aspirations and express them differently. For completeness, we briefly highlight the most salient links between demographic variables and goal achievement.

- Rural residents report lower achievement than urban residents regarding LG1, "Learn more knowledge," and LG5, "Keep up to date" (tables 4.C.2 and 4.C.4).[18]

- Notable gender differences are a higher sense of achievement by males regarding LG5, "Keep up to date," and LG15, "Leisure, entertainment" (tables 4.C.4 and 4.C.8).
- Students in general (users and nonusers) perceive higher achievement than nonstudents for LG1, "Learn more knowledge," and LG2, "Get stable, high-paying job, better business opportunities" (tables 4.C.2 and 4.C.3) but lower achievement for LG15, "Leisure, entertainment" and LG5, "Keep up to date" (tables 4.C.8 and 4.C.4).
- As urban women age, their sense of achievement is higher for LG2, "Get stable, high-paying job, better business opportunities" (table 4.C.3), but lower for LG14, "Keep in touch with friends and family who don't live nearby" (table 4.C.7), and LG15, "Leisure, entertainment." Reported achievement of urban males decreases with age for LG17, "Relax, relieve tension" (table 4.C.9). Among urban males less than 35 years old, reported achievement increases with age for LG1, "Learn more knowledge" (table 4.C.2). Among rural residents, perceived achievement decreases with age for LG10, "Improve the mental health of myself or my family" (table 4.C.6).
- Respondents with higher levels of education report lower achievement for LG9, "Improve the physical health of myself and my family" (table 4.C.5), and, in the case of urban males less than 35 years old, for LG1, "Learn more knowledge" (table 4.C.2).
- A respondent's income affects reported achievement: positively for LG1 and LG2 (tables 4.C.2 and 4.C.5), but negatively in the case of male urban students for LG15 (table 4.C.8).

There is no reason to expect a priori that users will outperform nonusers with respect to LG achievement. People pursuing intrinsic goals are generally more effective at achieving their objectives (Bargh, Gollwitzer, and Oettingen 2010), but our achievement comparisons are across goals shared by users and nonusers. Using the Internet or an Internet café is not indispensable for satisfying basic psychological needs. The goal of acquiring more knowledge could perhaps be satisfied by reading books or attending lectures or cultural activities. The Internet is an attractive entertainment medium as well as a way to relax, but a young man might be able to satisfy his psychological needs in other ways (e.g., board games, dancing, or sports).

If nonusers can in principle accomplish these LGs through other activities, why do they report lower achievement than café users do?

We cannot rule out that the environment where interviews took place (i.e., an Internet café) affected perceptions of achievement. We cannot claim, for example, that young males and student female users outperform nonusers in school. To do so would require a comparison of actual school performance not self-reports of achievement.

Table 4.25
Statistically Significant Relationships Observed between Internet Café Use on Reported Life Goal (LG) Achievement, by Life Goal and Subsample

	LG1	LG2	LG5	LG9	LG10	LG14	LG15	LG17
All	o^+		o^-			$+e^-$	$+e^-$	+
Urban	+		o^-				$+e^-$	+
Urban males								
Urban males < 35 yrs. old	+		o^-				$+e^-$	
Urban male nonstudents		–	e^-o^-					
Urban male students	$+o^+$							
Urban females						$+e^-$		+
Urban female students	+						$+e^-$	
Rural		o^+			$-o^+$	$+e^-$		

+	Positive relationship between Internet café use and achievement
–	Negative relationship between Internet café use and achievement
e^+	Positive relationship between Internet use experience and achievement
e^-	Negative relationship between Internet use experience and achievement
o^+	Positive relationship between Internet overuse and achievement
o^-	Negative relationship between Internet overuse and achievement
LG1	Learn more knowledge (Intrinsic)
LG2	Get a stable, high-paying job, better business opportunities (Unclassified)
LG5	Keep up to date (Unclassified)
LG9	Improve the physical health of myself or my family (Intrinsic)
LG10	Improve the mental health of myself or my family (Intrinsic)
LG14	Keep in touch with friends and family who don't live nearby (Intrinsic)
LG15	Leisure, entertainment (Intrinsic)
LG17	Relax, relieve tension (Intrinsic)

We suspect that goal contagion (Aarts and Hassin 2005; Loersch et al. 2008) is playing a part, the goal in this case being to visit Internet cafés. Users perceive cafés as places that help them achieve some of their intrinsic SGs and LGs. Regular café users may be playing an informational role among peers, priming synchronistic behavior by first-time users, and this priming is likely to be particularly effective given the intrinsic nature of most Internet use SGs (Friedman et al. 2010). Once novice users become familiar with the technology, the enhanced perception of achievement of self-endorsed intrinsic LGs is bound to become a powerful autonomous motivational force. The more a person satisfies his or her psychological needs and feels self-determined by going to an Internet café, the more inclined he or she will be to return.

Goal contagion may explain the popularity of Internet cafés, but the question remains: why the difference in achievement? If Internet cafés help users achieve their LGs, why is it that nonusers do not join in? In fact, most of them do. Only about 32 percent of China's young (under age 30) urban population does not use the Internet (table 4.3). In China, the Internet is very much part of the youth culture, and evidence suggests that young people view Internet cafés as places where they can have fun and accomplish goals they cherish.

Not everyone has to use the Internet to achieve self-determination and thrive. Some young (under age 30) urban nonusers gave autonomous reasons for not using the Internet—for example, 23 percent had no need for the Internet, and 39 percent had no time (table 4.4). However, it is important to bear in mind that these responses come from a group that represents only about one-third of China's urban youth.

Discussion and Policy Considerations

Users engage in many activities and pursue multiple objectives when they visit China's Internet cafés. They entertain themselves (SG15, chosen by 73 percent of users), keep in touch with friends and family (SG13, 63 percent), become better informed (SG11, 51 percent), relax and relieve tension (SG17, 42 percent), and meet new friends or a mate or companion (SG12, 35 percent). Considering that urban youths (especially males) are the dominant user group, this list of goals is hardly surprising.

Internet cafés are often people's first place of contact with ICT. More café users learned how to use computers and the Internet in cafés than in any other type of venue. We expected the desire to learn computer skills (SG4) to emerge as important among new users, and this is the case for about half of inexperienced users, but one-third of more experienced users also pursue this objective. Contrary to expectations, we found no evidence linking SG achievement with user experience. SG achievement is linked to the amount of time users spend pursing these goals when they visit cafés, but we found no evidence of a link between years of use and achievement.

Users' goals for visiting cybercafés vary according to their gender, place of residence, working/student status, and stage in life. About 41 percent of adolescent students who visit cafés do so in part to improve their school performance (SG1), compared with only 28 percent for the user population as a whole.

We found no major differences in the goals pursued by predominant users of Internet cafés and café users who are predominant users of other venues, but we detected sensible differences in goal achievement between these two groups. Predominant users of cafés do better than predominant users of other venues with regard to SG15, "Leisure, entertainment," whereas predominant users of other venues (mainly home and school and, in the case of SG24, mobiles) outperform café users when it comes to SG5, "Keep up to date," SG17, "Relax, relieve tension," and SG24, "Shop online or get product information online."

Most user motives for visiting cafés are reasonable, socially valuable, and common among young people (Choi et al. 2004; Gabrielsen, Ulleberg, and Watten 2012). The classification of user SGs according to SDT criteria suggests that these goals are pursued because they help users fulfill important psychological needs for autonomy, competence, and relatedness.

There is considerable overlap in the LG choices of users and nonusers, particularly for cohorts with similar demographics. For the whole sample, LG1, "Learn more knowledge," is the most popular goal among both users (53 percent) and nonusers (44 percent). Among young urban male students, LG1 is also the most popular LG of both groups, with a high proportion of both users (64 percent) and nonusers (60 percent) selecting this LG.

Internet café users report higher achievement than nonusers in their pursuit of some LGs. Young (under age 35) male users and male and female student users reportedly "learn more knowledge" (LG1) than nonusers; young male users and female student users report higher achievement than nonusers for LG15, "Leisure, entertainment"; and urban female users report higher achievement than nonusers for LG14, "Keep in touch with friends and family who don't live nearby," and LG17, "Relax, relieve tension." Some of these achievement advantages wane with age and Internet use experience, but findings that some users outperform nonusers in achievement perceptions of four intrinsic LGs (LG1, LG14, LG15, and LG17) suggest that nonusers who do not visit Internet cafés are missing out by not engaging in activities that facilitate the satisfaction of human needs.

We also detected some negative effects associated with Internet café use. Among the urban working (nonstudent) subsample, nonusers reported higher achievement than users for LG5, "Get stable, high-paying job, better business opportunities." We cannot tell, however, if users are reporting lower achievement than nonusers because they are wasting time using the Internet or because the workers who visit Internet cafés are those who are dissatisfied with their present work situation. Among rural users, lower perceptions of achievement were reported for LG10, "Improve the mental health of myself or my family." Our rural sample was too small to venture an interpretation, but this finding deserves further scrutiny, perhaps through a study exclusively focused on rural residents using urban cafés. In the few instances of overuse observed in our sample, overuse also adversely affected achievement of LG5, "Keep up to date," mainly among young urban males under age 35, particularly nonstudents.

User perceptions of the impact of Internet café use and media accounts stigmatizing these facilities are difficult to reconcile. The two views are separated not just by different perceptions but by age, limited experience with Internet use on the part of mature adults, and differing concerns, each appropriate to people at different life stages. To help bridge these divides, government may want to consider fostering greater diversity in the customer base of Internet cafés, which would encourage the pursuit of a broader range of LGs. We also hypothesize that diversity would be conducive to informed understanding on the part of parents, authorities, and the media of the value of Internet cafés; improved rapport among authorities, users, and Internet café operators; and café environments perceived by parents as more wholesome and by users as more supportive of their self-determination.

Many ways to promote diversity in café use can be envisaged. We outline one possible approach:

- Diversity in café use could be promoted as part of government's Internet development strategy. China's Internet development frontier is largely rural, but even in urban areas, there is room for expansion, particularly among older (over age 30) urban nonusers, who represent 27 percent of China's nonusers overall and 71 percent of its urban nonusers (table 4.3). A few respondents in this group indicated they had no need (26 percent) or no time (18 percent) to use the Internet, but the most common reason given (47 percent) was lack of skills (table 4.4).
- Fear of technology is common among mature adult (over age 30) nonusers,[19] and overcoming that fear often requires the implementation of digital literacy programs. That a significant proportion of the urban nonuser population does not use the technology because of a lack of skills represents an opening that government and café operators could seize to expand Internet use in a supportive environment—for example, through an adult literacy education program imparted in urban cybercafés and implemented in partnership with operators. Such a program could begin with a small pilot focused on the mature adult urban population, especially women, and local authorities. It would also help foster diversity in Internet café use.

Notwithstanding the importance that government assigns to Internet café policy, there does not seem to be much open scientific discussion of the underlying issues. China is rapidly becoming a modern society but appears to be relying primarily on control techniques that go counter to what we scientifically know about human nature and well-being. The majority of respondents' top-ranked goals are autonomous-oriented, suggesting that ICT and cybercafé use is an autonomous-oriented activity for most users (and potentially also nonusers) in China. However, the policies to stymie and limit use of cybercafés in China are controlling and undermining of autonomous motivation and, therefore, threaten the psychological needs of users (and, by implication, their psychological well-being). Given the difficulties experienced with controlling regulatory policies, the time may be ripe to consider alternative strategies that support user self-control, help advance the country's digital agenda, and facilitate self-determination and psychological well-being.

Notes

1. Figure 4.1 was constructed using CNNIC data on the total number of Internet users and the proportion of those users who access the Internet from home, Net bars, office, school, public places, or through their mobile phones. These data are available in China Internet Network Information Center (2007a, 2008, 2009, 2010, 2011a, 2012, 2013, 2014) reports published in January and based on surveys conducted in December of the previous year.

2. We cannot estimate the total number of PAV users by simply adding the number of users of Internet Cafés to the number of telecenter users because there is no way of determining how many Internet users use access the Internet using both modes.

3. The estimate of 136,000 Internet cafés in 2012 reported by Jou (2013) was produced by *Tencent* and covers only licensed cafés. Unlicensed cafés are not mentioned.

4. Xueqin (2009) gives an insider view of the difficulties experienced by the Chinese government in its attempts to regulate Internet cafés.

5. Self-determination theory has informed understanding of the motivation of users of social networks (Miller and Prior 2010), communities of practice (Palmisano 2009), virtual worlds (Verhagen et al. 2009), online learning (Hartnett, St. George, and Dron 2011), and video games (Ryan, Rigby, and Przybylski 2006; Wang et al. 2008; Rigby and Przybylski 2009; Przybylski et al. 2009; Przybylski, Ryan, and Rigby 2009, 2010); and of the effects of the Internet on adolescent video game overuse (Wan and Chiou 2007), personal relationships (Séguin-Lévesque et al. 2003), the pursuit of e-learning in schools (Sørebø et al. 2009) and the workplace (Roca and Gagné 2008) and, in combination with the theory of planned behavior, of the effectiveness of ICT skills training in rural public access centers in Thailand (Techatassanasoontorn and Tanvisuth 2008).

6. In low-wealth rural societies, where children represent an important resource for family survival, early economic independence is discouraged, whereas in high-income urban settings, independence and economic self-reliance are encouraged. Adolescents in both societies can satisfy their need for autonomy and relatedness: in an urban culture by internalizing the value of independence and living on their own early in life, and in an agrarian setting by deciding,

of their own volition, to remain close to help and work alongside their family (Kagitcibasi 2005).

7. Kasser and Ryan (1993, 1996), Kasser et al. (2007), and Kasser (2011) show how capitalism undervalues basic needs satisfaction, especially as practiced in the United States and the UK, where financial rewards and prestige are often contingent on performance. For example, remuneration for long hours of work undermines a worker's ability to spend time with family or on vacation with friends (adversely affecting relatedness). The limited participation of employees in decisions regarding work schedules and processes undermines worker autonomy. Similarly, militaristic dictatorships or very rigid religious traditions are prone to undermine citizen's abilities to satisfy their need for autonomy.

Institutional pressures may also affect behavior and well-being in more confined spheres. The inordinate pressures that legal schools in the United States generate and the detrimental effects on students are well documented. Self-determination theory has shown how these pressures undermine basic needs satisfaction, intrinsic motivation, and well-being and shift the value orientation of students from goals such as helping the community toward extrinsic goals such as image and fame. Moreover, the specific approach that a school follows also affects behavior. Students at a school that is supportive of autonomy, gives students choices, and is focused on satisfying student concerns will perform better than students in an environment that is insensitive to their preferences (Sheldon and Krieger 2004, 2007).

8. According to Zhou, Ma, and Deci (2009):

People's need for relatedness leads them to want, to some degree, to be dependent on trusted others rather than fully independent of them, but their need for autonomy also leads them to want to experience a sense of volition and choice about their dependence and their behavior. In eastern countries such as China which stress conformity, SDT maintains that it is the degree of subjective endorsement and ownership of the norms that determines whether the conformity constitutes authenticity and self-determination versus alienation and coercion. As a consequence, in the process of acting in accord with societal norms and expectations, one does not necessarily feel controlled in one's actions (and hence might not experience low levels of self-determination).

9. Vallerand (2007) also speaks of an intermediate level of *contextual goals* that are defined over broad domains such as education, personal relations, and sport. Contextual goals were not considered in this study.

10. Goal classification is grounded on the work of Kasser and Ryan (1996), Sheldon et al. (2004), Grouzet et al. (2005), Vansteenkiste, Lens, and Deci (2006), Sebire, Standage, and Vansteenkiste (2008), and McLachlan and Hagger (2011).

The intrinsic nature of the health goal was confirmed through personal correspondence with Tim Kasser. The psychologist on our team introduced the link between psychological needs and SGs. Because LGs are more broadly defined and in some instances may be linked to more than one SG (see table 4.1), each associated with a different need, for LGs we kept the more broad classification between intrinsic and extrinsic that is widely used by SDT researchers—for example, by Kasser and Ryan (1996), Sheldon et al. (2004), and Grouzet et al. (2005).

11. According to Przybylski, Ryan, and Rigby (2010), "the industry started with games tailored to meet competence needs through games focused on challenges and goals to be mastered. Over time, video game developers have broadened game designs and environments to better meet the autonomy need by providing flexibility in goals, choice over strategies, and opportunities for action in novel environments. Along with expanding autonomy, games have also increasingly been apt at satisfying relatedness needs by providing opportunities for engaging in online interactions and communities."

12. This goal appears in the revised version of the Aspirations Index first developed by Kasser and Ryan (1996). The scale and its description are available on the following website: http://faculty.knox.edu/tkasser/aspirations.html.

13. Young (1996) proposed to classify an Internet user as addicted if he or she answered yes to five or more of the following eight questions:

1. Do you feel preoccupied with the Internet (think about previous online activity or anticipate next online session)?
2. Do you feel the need to use the Internet with increasing amounts of time in order to achieve satisfaction?
3. Have you repeatedly made unsuccessful efforts to control, cut back, or stop Internet use?
4. Do you feel restless, moody, depressed, or irritable when attempting to cut down or stop Internet use?
5. Do you stay online longer than originally intended?
6. Have you jeopardized or risked the loss of a significant relationship, job, educational, or career opportunity because of the Internet?
7. Have you lied to family members, therapist, or others to conceal the extent of involvement with the Internet?
8. Do you use the Internet as a way of escaping from problems or relieving a dysphoric mood (e.g., feelings of helplessness, guilt, anxiety, depression)?

Our user survey includes the eight-item questionnaire proposed by Young (1996) (validated in Chinese by Cao et al. 2007) but allowed a graduated response to each question: 1. Usually; 2. Most times; 3. Sometimes; 4. Seldom; 5. Never. Our "overuser" variable assigns a value of 1 to respondents who answered 1, 2, or 3 ("Usually," "Most times," or "Sometimes") to five or more of Young's eight questions. This is a lax criterion that will tend to classify more respondents as "overusers" than Young would classify as "addicted." A total of 104 overusers so defined were found in our sample.

Internet addiction in China is the subject of the next chapter in this book.

14. User and nonuser surveys gave interviewees the option to assign one of five levels of importance to the various LGs presented: "Most important," "Very important," "Important," "Less important," and "Not so important." Percentages in table 4.22 and the regressions in appendix 4.C consider LGs that respondents identified as either "Most important" or "Very important." Observations that identified LGs but gave no information on achievement were discarded. The average number of LGs chosen by the two groups and the number of observations for each choice group are given below.

Average # of LGs Chosen as:

	Most Important	Most or Very Important	Total LGs Chosen
Users	1.2	3.9	7.4
Nonusers	1.6	4.7	6.8

Number of Observations with At Least One LG Chosen as:

	Most Important	Most or Very Important
Users:	494	846
Nonusers:	1.6	4.7

Many interviewees did not mark any LG as "most important," whereas others chose more than one goal as "most important," which suggests that the distinction between choosing a goal as "most important" or "very important" is highly subjective. Furthermore, in the regressions reported in appendix 4.C, we include a control independent variable identifying the choice as most important when this is the case.

When making comparisons among a small subsample, such as the young urban male student subsample in table 4.23, for the sake of precision, we focus on the choice of "most important" LG.

15. The focus on popular goals allows us to cover important goals but is also necessary given the large differences in user and nonuser demographics known to affect goal priorities. For example, there are no users older than 49 and very few nonusers younger than 19 years old, and the LGs and achievements of these two groups are bound to differ, making it difficult to disentangle the effects attributable to demographic differences from those that could be associated with Internet café use. By focusing on goals popular for both groups, we increase the number of overlapping user/nonuser observations and enhance our ability to make meaningful comparisons.

16. Apparently other factors lie behind the seemingly positive relationship (suggested by the results presented in table 4.22) between Internet use and achievement for LG5, "Keep up to date," and LG9, "Improve the physical health of myself or my family," while masking the positive relationship among urban females for LG14, "Keep in contact with friends and family who are not nearby," and the negative relationship among urban working males for LG2, "Get stable, high-paying job, better business opportunities."

17. We only point out differences found to be statistically significant, with at least a 10 percent probability that a regression coefficient is not equal to zero.

18. The top five LG priorities of rural users and the top five of rural nonusers are all in the list of eight top goals under consideration. Nevertheless, with few observations (table 4.2) on a heterogeneous group (tables 4.10 and 4.11), the rural subsample contains limited information to assess LG achievement differences within the group.

Notwithstanding these limitations, some differences in the effect of achievement variables stand out. High-income rural residents have a higher sense of achievement of LG1. Rural residents with higher incomes have a greater sense of achievement of LG2 as do Internet overusers. Being a user has a detrimental effect on the sense of achievement of mental health objectives (LG10), yet overusers apparently fare better than users. Internet users report higher achievement than nonusers with respect to LG14, "Keep in contact with friends and family who don't live nearby." This effect wears off with time: rural experienced Internet users report lower LG14 achievement than novice users. Better-educated rural users apparently have a higher sense of achievement of LG17, "Be relaxed, relieve tension."

19. "Respondents told us that they were embarrassed about their lack of computer skills, and some were intimidated or worried that they would need to already know certain skills, like typing, before they could learn to use the Internet. A novice user we interviewed told the story of going to get his hair cut and being told by the woman behind the counter at the hair salon to sign in on a computer terminal in the waiting area. He was deeply embarrassed when he could barely figure out how to use the keyboard to punch in his name, and resolved then to come to the Community Technology Center in his apartment complex to learn to type, use computers and the Internet." (Lenhart et al. 2003, p. 12)

References

Aarts, Henk, and Ran R. Hassin. 2005. Automatic Goal Inference and Contagion: On Pursuing Goals One Perceives in Other People's Behavior. In *Social Motivation: Conscious and Unconscious Processes*, ed. Joseph P. Forgas, Kipling D. Williams, and Simon M. Laham, 153–167. Cambridge, UK: Cambridge University Press.

Babbie, Earl R. 2008. *The Basics of Social Research*. 4th ed. Belmont, CA: Thomson Wadsworth.

Bargh, John A., Peter M. Gollwitzer, and Gabriele Oettingen. 2010. Motivation. In *Handbook of Social Psychology*, 5th ed., ed. Susan T. Fiske, Daniel T. Gilbert, and Gardner Lindzay, 268–316. New York: Wiley.

Baumeister, Roy F., and Mark R. Leary. 1995. The Need to Belong: Desire for Interpersonal Attachments as a Fundamental Human Motivation. *Psychological Bulletin* 117 (3): 497–529.

BBC News. 2002. China Gets Tough on Internet Cafés. December 27. http://news.bbc.co.uk/2/hi/asia-pacific/2608305.stm.

Boase, Jeffrey, John B. Horrigan, Barry Wellman, and Lee Rainie. 2006. *The Strength of Internet Ties*. Washington, DC: Pew Internet and American Life Project.

Brynjolfsson, Erik, and Adam Saunders. 2010. *Wired for Innovation: How Information Technology Is Reshaping the Economy*. Cambridge, MA: MIT Press.

Cao, Fenglin, Linyan Su, Liu TieQiao, and Gao Xueping. 2007. The Relationship Between Impulsivity and Internet Addiction in a Sample of Chinese Adolescents. *European Psychiatry* 22: 466–471.

Cartier, Carolyn, Manuel Castells, and Jack Linchuan Qiu. 2005. The Information Have-Less: Inequality, Mobility, and Translocal Networks in Chinese Cities. *Studies in Comparative International Development* 40 (2): 9–34.

China Internet Network Information Center. 2007a. *Statistical Survey Report on the Internet Development in China*. January. 19th Survey Report. Beijing: Author. http://www.apira.org/data/upload/pdf/Asia-Pacific/CNNIC/19threport-en.pdf.

China Internet Network Information Center. 2007b. *Survey Report on Internet Development in Rural China*. August. Beijing: Author. http://www.apira.org/data/upload/pdf/Asia-Pacific/CNNIC/2007_Survey_Report_on_Internet_Development_in_Rural_China2007.pdf.

China Internet Network Information Center. 2008. *Statistical Survey Report on the Internet Development in China*. January. 21st Survey Report. Beijing: Author. http://www.apira.org/data/upload/pdf/Asia-Pacific/CNNIC/21streport-en.pdf.

China Internet Network Information Center. 2009. *Statistical Survey Report on the Internet Development in China. January. 23rd Survey Report.* Beijing: Author.

China Internet Network Information Center. 2010. *Statistical Survey Report on Internet Development in China. January. 25th Survey Report.* Beijing: Author.

China Internet Network Information Center. 2011a. *Statistical Report on Internet Development in China*. January. 27th Survey Report. Beijing: Author. http://www1.cnnic.cn/IDR/ReportDownloads/201209/P020120904420388544497.pdf.

China Internet Network Information Center. 2011b. *Statistical Report on Internet Development in China*. July. 28th Survey Report. Beijing: Author. http://www1.cnnic.cn/IDR/ReportDownloads/201209/P020120904421102801754.pdf.

China Internet Network Information Center. 2012. *Statistical Report on Internet Development in China*. January. 29th Survey Report. Beijing: Author. http://www1.cnnic.cn/IDR/ReportDownloads/201209/P020120904421720687608.pdf.

China Internet Network Information Center. 2013. *Statistical Report on Internet Development in China*. January. 31st Survey Report. Beijing: Author. http://www1.cnnic.cn/IDR/ReportDownloads/201302/P020130221391269963814.pdf.

China Internet Network Information Center. 2014. *Statistical Report on Internet Development in China*. January. 33rd Survey Report. Beijing: Author. http://www1.cnnic.cn/IDR/ReportDownloads/201404/U020140417607531610855.pdf.

China Labour Bulletin. 2013. Migrant Workers and Their Children. http://www.clb.org.hk/en/content/migrant-workers-and-their-children/.

Choi, Junho, James Watt, Ad Dekkers, and Sung-Hee Park. 2004. Motives of Internet Uses: Cross-cultural Perspectives—the US, the Netherlands, and South Korea. Paper presented at the annual meeting of the International Communication Association, New Orleans, Louisiana, May 27. http://citation.allacademic.com/meta/p_mla_apa_research_citation/1/1/2/8/3/pages112833/p112833-1.php/.

Cody, Edward. 2007. Despite a Ban, Chinese Youth Navigate to Internet Cafés. *The Washington Post*, February 9. http://www.washingtonpost.com/wp-dyn/content/article/2007/02/08/AR2007020802389.html.

Deci, Edward L., Richard Koestner, and Richard M. Ryan. 1999. A Meta-Analytic Review of Experiments Examining the Effects of Extrinsic Rewards on Intrinsic Motivation. *Psychological Bulletin* 125 (6): 627–668.

Deci, Edward L., and Arlen C. Moller. 2005. The Concept of Competence: A Starting Place for Understanding Intrinsic Motivation and Self-Determined Extrinsic Motivation. In *Handbook of Competence and Motivation*, ed. Andrew J. Elliot and Carol S. Dweck, 579–597. New York: The Guilford Press.

Deci, Edward L., and Richard M. Ryan. 2000. The 'What' and 'Why' of Goal Pursuits: Human Needs and the Self-Determination of Behavior. *Psychological Inquiry* 11 (4): 227–268.

Deci, Edward L., and Richard M. Ryan. 2008. Facilitating Optimal Motivation and Psychological Well-Being Across Life's Domains. *Canadian Psychology* 49 (1): 14–23.

Deci, Edward L., and Maarten Vansteenkiste. 2004. Self-Determination Theory and Basic Need Satisfaction: Understanding Human Development in Positive Psychology. *Ricerche di Psicologia* 27 (1): 23–40.

Duffy, Andrew, Tan Liying, and Larissa Ong. 2010. Singapore Teens' Perceived Ownership of Online Sources and Credibility. *First Monday* 15 (4).

Earp, Madeline. 2013. *Throttling Dissent: China's New Leaders Refine Internet Control*. Washington, DC: Freedom House.

Elliot, Andrew J., Holly A. McGregor, and Todd M. Thrash. 2002. The Need for Competence. In *Handbook of Self-determination Research*, ed. Edward L. Deci and Richard M. Ryan, 361–387. Rochester, NY: University of Rochester Press.

Freund, Alexandra M., and Michaela Riediger. 2006. Goals as Building Blocks of Personality and Development in Adulthood. In *Handbook of Personality Development*, ed. Daniel K. Mroczek and Todd D. Little, 353–372. Mahwah, NJ: Lawrence Erlbaum.

Friedman, Ron, Edward L. Deci, Andrew Elliot, Arlen C. Moller, and Henk Aarts. 2010. Motivational Synchronicity: Priming Motivational Orientations with Observations of Others' Behaviors. *Motivation and Emotion* 34:34–38.

Gabrielsen, Leiv E., Pål Ulleberg, and Reidulf G. Watten. 2012. The Adolescent Life Goal Profile Scale: Development of a New Scale for Measurements of Life Goals Among Young People. *Journal of Happiness Studies* 13 (6): 1053–1072.

Greene, Barbara A., and Teresa K. DeBacker. 2004. Gender and Orientations Toward the Future: Links to Motivation. *Educational Psychology Review* 16 (2): 91–120.

Grouzet, Frederick M. E., Tim Kasser, Aaron Ahuvia, Miguel Fernández Dols José, Youngmee Kim, Sing Lau, Richard M. Ryan, Shaun Saunders, Peter Schmuck, and Kennon M. Sheldon. 2005. The

Structure of Goal Contents Across 15 Cultures. *Journal of Personality and Social Psychology* 89 (5): 800–816.

Hartnett, Maggie, Alison St. George, and Jon Dron. 2011. Being Together: Factors that Unintentionally Undermine Motivation in Co-located Online Learning Environments. *Journal of Open, Flexible, and Distance Learning* 15 (1): 1–16.

Hiemstra, Roger. 2006. Is the Internet Changing Self-directed Learning? Rural Users Provide Some Answers. *International Journal of Self-directed Learning* 3 (2): 45–60.

Hoffman, Donna L. 2012. Internet Indispensability, Online Social Capital, and Consumer Well-Being. In *Transformative Consumer Research for Personal and Collective Well Being: Reviews and Frontiers*, ed. David Glen Mick, Simone Pettigrew, Cornelia Pechmann, and Julie Ozanne, 193–223. New York: Routledge.

Hong, Cheng. 2007. Police Raid Sees Closure of 20 Illegal Net Cafés. *China Daily*. April 6. http://www.chinadaily.com.cn/china/2007-04/06/content_844599.htm.

Hong, Junhao, and Li Huang. 2005. A Split and Swaying Approach to Building Information Society: The Case of Internet Cafés in China. *Telematics and Informatics* 22: 377–393.

Information Office of the State Council. 2010. *The Internet in China*. White paper prepared June 8. http://english.gov.cn/2010-06/08/content_1622956.htm.

Jiao, Wu. 2006. Internet Café Ban Sparks Wide Debate. *China Daily*, October 9. http://www.chinadaily.com.cn/china/2006-10/09/content_703501.htm.

Jou, Eric. 2013. China's Internet Cafés Are Disappearing: What's Going On?! *Kotaku*. http://kotaku.com/chinas-internet-cafes-are-disappearing-whats-going-o-1479419777/.

Junlong Culture Communication Co. Ltd. 2010. *China Internet Café Holdings*. Investor presentation presented at China Rising Investment Conference, December. http://a.eqcdn.com/junlongculturecommunicationcoltd/media/18c09d90db0ee3883808e8db089dc0d1.pdf.

Kagitcibasi, Cigdem. 2005. Autonomy and Relatedness in Cultural Context: Implications for Self and Family. *Journal of Cross-Cultural Psychology* 36 (4): 403–422.

Kan, Michael. 2011. China Closes 130,000 Internet Cafés as It Seeks More Control. *PCWorld*, March 18. http://www.pcworld.com/article/222531/china_shuts_net_cafes.html.

Kasser, Tim. 2002. *Handbook of Self-determination Research*. Ed. Edward L. Deci and Richard M. Ryan, 123–140. Rochester, NY: University of Rochester Press; chap. 6.

Kasser, Tim. 2011. Capitalism and Autonomy. In *Human Autonomy in Cross-Cultural Context: Perspectives on the Psychology of Agency, Freedom and Well-Being*, ed. Valery I. Chirkov, Richard M. Ryan, and Kennon M. Sheldon, 191–206. Dordrecht: Springer.

Kasser, Tim, Steve Cohn, Allen D. Kanner, and Richard M. Ryan. 2007. Some Costs of American Corporate Capitalism: A Psychological Exploration of Value and Goal Conflicts. *Psychological Inquiry* 18 (1): 1–22.

Kasser, Tim, and Richard M. Ryan. 1993. A Dark Side of the American Dream: Correlates of Financial Success as a Central Life Aspiration. *Journal of Personality and Social Psychology* 65 (2): 410–422.

Kasser, Tim, and Richard M. Ryan. 1996. Further Examining the American Dream: Differential Correlates of Intrinsic and Extrinsic Goals. *Personality and Social Psychology Bulletin* 22 (3): 280–287.

Lenhart, Amanda, John Horrigan, Lee Rainie, Katherine Allen, Angie Boyce, Mary Madden, and Erin O'Grady. 2003. *The Ever Shifting Internet Population: A New Look at Internet Access and the Digital Divide*. Washington, DC: Pew Internet and American Life Project.

Liang, Guo. 2002. The Internet: China's Window to the World. *YaleGlobal Online*, November 18. http://yaleglobal.yale.edu/content/internet-chinas-window-world/.

Liang, Guo. 2007. Surveying Internet Usage and Its Impact in Seven Chinese Cities. Center for Social Development, Chinese Academy of Social Sciences, November. Funded by Markle Foundation. http://www.markle.org/publications/1291-surveying-internet-usage-and-its-impact-seven-chinese-cities/.

Linchuan Qiu, Jack. 2009. *Working Class Network Society: Communication Technology and the Information Have-less in Urban China*. Cambridge, MA: MIT Press.

Linchuan Qiu, Jack, and Zhou Liuning. 2005. Through the Prism of the Internet Café: Managing an Ecology of Games. *China Information* 19 (2): 261–297.

Livingston, Sonia, and Leslie Haddon. 2008. Risky Experiences for European Children Online: Charting Research Strengths and Research Gaps. *Children & Society* 22 (4): 314–323.

Loersch, Chris, Henk Aarts, B. Keith Payne, and Valerie E. Jefferis. 2008. The Influence of Social Groups on Goal Contagion. *Journal of Experimental Social Psychology* 44:1555–1558.

Massey, Emma, Winifred A. Gebhardt, and Nadia Garnefski. 2008. Adolescent Goal Content and Pursuit: A Review of the Literature from the Past 16 Years. *Developmental Review* 28:421–460.

McLachlan, Sarah, and Martin S. Hagger. 2010. Associations Between Motivational Orientations and Chronically-Accessible Outcomes in Leisure-Time Physical Activity: Are Appearance-Related Outcomes Controlling in Nature? *Research Quarterly for Exercise and Sport* 81 (1): 102–107.

McLachlan, Sarah, and Martin S. Hagger. 2011. Do People Differentiate Between Intrinsic and Extrinsic Goals for Physical Activity? *Journal of Sport & Exercise Psychology* 33: 273–288.

Mendenhall, William. 1975. *Introduction to Probability and Statistics*. 4th ed. North Scituate, NC: Duxbury Press.

Miller, Lucy M., and Daniel D. Prior. 2010. Online Social Networks and Friending Behaviour: A Self-Determination Theory Perspective. In *Proceedings of the Australian and New Zealand Marketing Academy Conference (ANZMAC 2010), Doing More with Less*. Christchurch, New Zealand, November 29–December 1. http://anzmac2010.org/proceedings/pdf/anzmac10Final00230.pdf.

Moller, Arlen C., Edward L. Deci, and Andrew J. Elliot. 2010. Person-Level Relatedness and the Incremental Value of Relating. *Personality and Social Psychology Bulletin* 36 (6): 754–767.

National Bureau of Statistics of China. 2013. Statistical Communiqué of the People's Republic of China on the 2012 National Economic and Social Development. http://www.stats.gov.cn/english./NewsEvents/201302/t20130222_26962.html#/.

Niemiec, Christopher P., Richard M. Ryan, and Edward L. Deci. 2009. The Path Taken: Consequences of Attaining Intrinsic and Extrinsic Aspirations in Post-College Life. *Journal of Research in Personality* 43: 291–306.

Nurmi, Jari-Erik. 1991. How Do Adolescents See Their Future? A Review of the Development of Future Orientation and Planning. *Developmental Review* 11 (1): 1–59.

Nurmi, Jari-Erik. 1992. Age Differences in Adult Life Goals, Concerns and Their Temporal Extension: A Life Course Approach to Future-oriented Motivation. *International Journal of Behavioral Development* 15 (4): 487–508.

Palmisano, Jay. 2009. Motivating Knowledge Contribution in Virtual Communities of Practice: A Self-Determination Theory Perspective. In *Proceedings of the Fifteenth Americas Conference on Information Systems*. San Francisco, California, August 6–9. AMCIS 2009 Doctoral Consortium.

Pew Internet Project. 2012 (and ongoing). Internet Usage Over Time. Excel spreadsheet available for download. http://www.pewinternet.org/data-trend/internet-use/internet-use-over-time/.

Przybylski, Andrew K., Richard M. Ryan, and C. Scott Rigby. 2009. The Motivating Role of Violence in Video Games. *Personality and Social Psychology Bulletin* 35 (2): 243–259.

Przybylski, Andrew K., Richard M. Ryan, and C. Scott Rigby. 2010. A Motivational Model of Video Game Engagement. *Review of General Psychology* 14 (2): 154–166.

Przybylski, Andrew K., Netta Weinstein, Richard M. Ryan, and C. Scott Rigby. 2009. Having To versus Wanting To Play: Background and Consequences of Harmonious versus Obsessive Engagement in Video Games. *Cyberpsychology & Behavior* 12 (5): 485–492.

Reis, Harry T., Kennon M. Sheldon, Shelly L. Gable, Joseph Roscoe, and Richard M. Ryan. 2000. Daily Well-Being: The Role of Autonomy, Competence, and Relatedness. *Personality and Social Psychology Bulletin* 26 (4): 419–435.

Rigby, C. Scott, and Andrew Przybylski. 2009. Virtual Worlds and the Learner Hero: How Today's Video Games Can Inform Tomorrow's Digital Learning Environments. *Theory and Research in Education* 7 (2): 214–223.

Roca, Juan Carlos, and Marylène Gagné. 2008. Understanding e-Learning Continuance Intention in the Workplace: A Self-Determination Theory Perspective. *Computers in Human Behavior* 24:1585–1604.

Russoniello, Carmen V., Kevin O'Brien, and Jennifer M. Parks. 2009. The Effectiveness of Casual Video Games in Improving Mood and Decreasing Stress. *Journal of Cyber Therapy and Rehabilitation* 2 (1): 53–66.

Ryan, Richard M., and Edward L. Deci. 2000a. Intrinsic and Extrinsic Motivations: Classic Definitions and New Directions. *Contemporary Educational Psychology* 25:54–67.

Ryan, Richard M., and Edward L. Deci. 2000b. The Darker and Brighter Sides of Human Existence: Basic Psychological Needs as a Unifying Concept. *Psychological Inquiry* 11 (4): 319–338.

Ryan, Richard M., and Edward L. Deci. 2000c. Self-Determination Theory and the Facilitation of Intrinsic Motivation, Social Development and Well-Being. *American Psychologist* 55 (1): 68–78.

Ryan, Richard M., and Cristina Frederick. 1997. On Energy, Personality, and Health: Subjective Vitality as a Dynamic Reflection of Well-Being. *Journal of Personality* 65 (3): 529–565.

Ryan, Richard M., Julius Kuhl, and Edward L. Deci. 1997. Nature and Autonomy: An Organizational View of Social and Neurobiological Aspects of Self-Regulation in Behavior and Development. *Development and Psychopathology* 9:701–728.

Ryan, Richard M., C. Scott Rigby, and Andrew Przybylski. 2006. The Motivational Pull of Video Games: A Self-Determination Theory Approach. *Motivation and Emotion* 30:347–363.

Sebire, Simon J., Martyn Standage, and Maarten Vansteenkiste. 2008. Development and Validation of the Goal Content for Exercise Questionnaire. *Journal of Sport & Exercise Psychology* 30:353–377.

Séguin-Levesque, Chantal, Marie Lyne N. Laliberté, Luc G. Pelletier, Céline Blanchard, and Robert J. Vallerand. 2003. Harmonious and Obsessive Passion for the Internet: Their Associations with the Couple's Relationship. *Journal of Applied Social Psychology* 33 (1): 197–221.

Sheldon, Kennon M., and Vincent Filak. 2008. Manipulating Autonomy, Competence, and Relatedness Support in a Game-Learning Context: New Evidence That All Three Needs Matter. *British Journal of Social Psychology* 47: 267–283.

Sheldon, Kennon M., Alexander Gunz, Charles P. Nichols, and Yuna Ferguson. 2010. Extrinsic Value Orientation and Affective Forecasting: Overestimating the Rewards, Underestimating the Costs. *Journal of Personality* 78 (1): 149–178.

Sheldon, Kennon M., Linda Houser-Marko, and Tim Kasser. 2006. Does Autonomy Increase with Age? Comparing the Goal Motivations of College Students and Their Parents. *Journal of Research in Personality* 40: 168–178.

Sheldon, Kennon M., and Tim Kasser. 1998. Pursuing Personal Goals: Skills Enable Progress, but Not All Progress Is Beneficial. *Personality and Social Psychology Bulletin* 24 (12): 1319–1331.

Sheldon, Kennon M., and Tim Kasser. 2008. Psychological Threat and Extrinsic Goal Striving. *Motivation and Emotion* 32:37–45.

Sheldon, Kennon M., Tim Kasser, Linda Houser-Marko, Taisha Jones, and Daniel Turban. 2005. Doing One's Duty: Chronological Age, Felt Autonomy and Subjective Well-Being. *European Journal of Personality* 19:97–115.

Sheldon, Kennon M., and Lawrence S. Krieger. 2004. Does Legal Education Have Undermining Effects on Law Students? Evaluating Changes in Motivation, Values, and Well-Being. *Behavioral Sciences & the Law* 22:261–286.

Sheldon, Kennon M., and Lawrence S. Krieger. 2007. Understanding the Negative Effects of Legal Education on Law Students: A Longitudinal Test of Self-Determination Theory. *Personality and Social Psychology Bulletin* 33 (6): 883–897.

Sheldon, Kennon M., and Christopher P. Niemiec. 2006. It's Not Just the Amount That Counts: Balanced Need Satisfaction Also Affects Well-Being. *Journal of Personality and Social Psychology* 91 (2): 331–341.

Sheldon, Kennon M., Richard M. Ryan, Edward L. Deci, and Tim Kasser. 2004. The Independent Effects of Goal Contents and Motives on Well Being: It's Both What You Pursue and Why You Pursue It. *Personality and Social Psychology Bulletin* 30 (4): 475–486.

Sørebø, Øystein, Hallgeir Halvari, Vebjørn Flaata Gulli, and Roar Kristiansen. 2009. The Role of Self-Determination Theory in Explaining Teachers' Motivation to Continue to Use e-Learning Technology. *Computers & Education* 53:1177–1187.

Sydney Morning Herald. 2010. Internet Cafés Close Ahead of Exams in China. June 1. http://news.smh.com.au/breaking-news-technology/internet-cafes-close-ahead-of-exams-in-china-20100601-wvjw.html.

Synovate Ltd. 2009. *Staying Safe Survey 2009: Young People and Parents' Attitudes around Internet Safety*. Department for Children, Schools and Families, United Kingdom. Research Report DCSF-RR183.

Techatassanasoontorn, Angsana A., and Arunee Tanvisuth. 2008. The Integrated Self-Determination and Self-Efficacy Theories of ICT Training and Use: The Case of the Socio-Economically Disadvantaged. *Special Interest Group on Global Development Workshop*, Paris, France. December 13. http://www.globdev.org/files/23-Paper-Techat-Integrated%20Self%20Determ.pdf.

Tian, Lan. 2009. Shandong County Closes Cyber Cafés. *China Daily*, October 15. http://www.china.org.cn/china/2009-10/15/content_18706149.htm.

Tian, Lan. 2010. Young Internet Addicts on the Rise. *China Daily*, February 3.http://www.chinadaily.com.cn/china/2010-02/03/content_9417660.htm.

Turow, Joseph. 1999. *The Internet and the Family: The View from Parents, the View from the Press.* Report No. 27. Annenberg Public Policy Center of the University of Pennsylvania. http://www.asc.upenn.edu/usr/jturow/Report99.pdf.

TXWM (Chinese Cybercafé Industry Portal). 2011. Cybercafé Users' Consumer Behaviour and Online Behaviour Survey (in Chinese). March. http://www.txwm.com.

Vallerand, Robert J. 2007. Intrinsic and Extrinsic Motivation in Sport and Physical Activity: A Review and a Look at the Future. In *Handbook of Sport Psychology*, 3rd ed., ed. Gershon Tenenbaum and Robert C. Eklund, 59–83. Hoboken, NJ: Wiley.

Vansteenkiste, Maarten, Willy Lens, and Edward L. Deci. 2006. Intrinsic versus Extrinsic Goal Contents in Self-Determination Theory: Another Look at the Quality of Academic Motivation. *Educational Psychologist* 41 (1): 19–31.

Verhagen, Tibert, Frans Feldberg, Bart van den Hooff, and Selmar Meents. 2009. Understanding Virtual World Usage: A Multipurpose Model and Empirical Testing. Research paper presented at the Seventeenth European Conference on Information Systems (ECIS).

Wan, Chin-Sheng, and Wen-Bin Chiou. 2007. The Motivations of Adolescents Who Are Addicted to Online Games: A Cognitive Perspective. *Adolescence* 42 (165): 179–197.

Wang, Chee Keng John, Angeline Khoo, Woon Chia Liu, and Shanti Divaharan. 2008. Passion and Intrinsic Motivation in Digital Gaming. *Cyberpsychology & Behavior* 11 (1): 39–45.

Wang, Hua, and Barry Wellman. 2010. Social Connectivity in America: Changes in Adult Friendship Network Size from 2002 to 2007. *American Behavioral Scientist* 53 (8): 1148–1169.

Weinland, Don. 2010. China: New Regulation Proposed for Internet Cafés. *Global Voices Online*, March 8. http://globalvoicesonline.org/2010/03/08/china-new-regulation-proposed-for-internet-cafes/.

Xinhua. 2004. Experts Warn of 'Internet Syndrome' Among Teenagers. *China Daily*, February 2. http://www.chinadaily.com.cn/english/doc/2004-02/12/content_305555.htm.

Xinhua. 2011. China Shuts Down 130,000 Unlicensed Internet Cafés. *China Daily*, March 18. http://www.chinadaily.com.cn/bizchina/2011-03/18/content_12193024.htm.

Xueqin, Wang. 2009. Internet Cafés: What Else Can Be Done in Addition to Rectification? In *Good Governance in China—A Way Towards Social Harmony: Case Studies by China's Rising Leaders*, ed. Wang Menkui, 86–97. London: Routledge.

Young, Kimberly S. 1996. Internet Addiction: The Emergence of a New Clinical Disorder. *Cyberpsychology & Behavior* 1 (3): 237–244.

Yu, Zhou. 2006. The Internet Cafés of Fangshan: Fangshan County Party Secretary Shuts Down Internet Cafés. *EastSouthWestNorth*, October 15. http://www.zonaeuropa.com/20061016_1.htm.

Zhou, Mingming, Wei Ji Ma, and Edward L. Deci. 2009. The Importance of Autonomy for Rural Chinese Children's Motivation for Learning. *Learning and Individual Differences* 19: 492–498.

Appendix 4.A Sampling Procedures and Overview of Cybercafés Sampled

A multistaged cluster sampling method was used in the study (Babbie 2008). The target research population consisted of users of Internet cafés in China. The sampling frame of Internet cafés was provided by Hintsoft & Pubwin Media Corporation, currently the biggest Internet café administration system provider, with around 60 percent of Internet café market share in China.

In the first sampling stage, we randomly stratified select large urban communities and less densely populated areas as clusters according to the GDP levels of different cities and counties. In the second stage, we conducted simple random sampling from the list of all operating Internet cafés using the Hintsoft & Pubwin system for every selected area. Because there are no Internet cafés in China's truly rural areas, we considered that rural residents could be reached in the county nearest to where they live. The distinction between rural and urban residents was determined by the subjects' self-reports. Finally, twenty Internet cafés were randomly selected from ten cities and nearby counties. Users going to these Internet cafés on a specific survey day (or two days) were asked to answer the questionnaire. In each Internet café, about fifty users' answers were collected.

The survey was administered by volunteers from a university: most were undergraduate students majoring in marketing science, while others were undergraduate students in other management-related majors. Two meetings were arranged before the survey was implemented. At the first meeting, held in July and attended by all the volunteer investigators, the project and the survey were explained, and the questionnaire and data input software were introduced and discussed. The second meeting was an online meeting held just before survey implementation. The final version of the questionnaire was distributed, and information and experiences from the pilot survey were discussed. After the investigators went into the field, they kept in touch with one of the research team members, who provided help and suggestions as and when they met difficulty in the field.

The questionnaire was piloted at a small Internet café near Zhongguancun Area, Beijing. Ten users answered the questionnaire; two of them self-reported as rural residents. Some questions and options were rephrased to make them easier to understand, and the wording of some options was revised. The final version of the questionnaire

Table 4.A.1
City Population, Sample Size, and Number of Rural Residents in Internet Cafés Surveyed

Café Code	City Population	Sample Size	Rural Res. #	Rural Res. %	Café Code	City Population	Sample Size	Rural Res. #	Rural Res. %
No. 1	4,316,600	50	5	10.0	No. 12	3,262,548	50	17	34.0
No. 2	1,368,500	43	–	–	No. 13	231,853	50	4	8.0
No. 3	1,368,500	6	1	16.7	No. 14	2,187,009	50	8	16.0
No. 4	7,677,089	46	9	19.6	No. 15	3,318,057	50	8	16.0
No. 5	10,635,971	50	1	2.0	No. 16	2,552,097	50	–	–
No. 6	834,437	50	21	42.0	No. 17	2,117,000	52	13	25.0
No. 7	4,414,681	40	9	22.5	No. 18	4,613,873	50	29	58.0
No. 8	10,357,938	46	–	–	No. 19	4,613,873	50	12	24.0
No. 9	10,357,938	46	–	–	No. 20	14,047,625	51	12	23.5
No. 10	8,004,680	50	11	22.0	No. 21	4,472,001	45	24	53.3
No. 11	723,958	50	6	12.0	No. 22	–	1	–	–

was administered during the summer vacation. Answers to questionnaires were input into SPSS data management software and cleaned. Questionnaire results with incomplete answers were deleted, leaving 976 valid questionnaires. Among the collected questionnaires, 20 percent of the subjects were rural users.

There were huge differences in our randomly selected venues, ranging from small, shabby Internet cafés to luxurious Internet cafés in downtown areas. This is consistent with the diversity of cafés in China. Among the twenty Internet cafés sampled, the number of seats per center ranged from 56 to 561, but most cafés had approximately 100 seats. Half of the Internet cafés surveyed had private rooms (or cubicles)—on average, thirteen per venue. Overall occupancy of Internet cafés was reportedly 53 percent. The list provided by Hintsoft & Pubwin and used to draw our sample listed four of the twenty Internet cafés sampled as located in rural areas; however, the division between rural and urban is sometimes vague. We used the café users' self-reported answers to determine whether they were rural or urban residents.

Table 4.A.1 shows the population of the city where each cybercafé is located, the sample size, and the number of rural residents in the cafés from which the sample was drawn.

Appendix 4.B Situational Goal Popularity

Table 4.B.1
Situational Goals (SGs): Popularity Ranking, Achievement, Percentage of Café Time Spent Pursuing Goal, and SDT Classification

	Choice		Average SG Achievement[b] & % Café Time Spent Pursuing SG			
	Obs.	963				SDT
SGs[a]	Rank	%	Obs.	Achieve	% time	Classification[c]
Entertainment (play games, listen to music, watch movies, online video, etc.) (15)	1	74	713	2.1	47	A
Keep in touch with family and friends (email, QQ, etc.) (13)	2	64	617	2.0	38	R
Access information (news, weather forecasts, stock info, sports, gossip, etc.) (11)	3	51	491	1.8	30	U
Relax, relieve tension (17)	4	43	418	1.8	37	A
Meet new friends or a mate or companion (12)	5	36	349	1.6	33	R
Learn to use computers and the Internet (4)	6	36	346	1.8	36	C
Socialize and make friends with people in Internet cafés (14)	7	33	321	1.6	33	R
Spend time on a hobby or pastime (16)	8	33	315	1.8	36	A
Contribute to other people's web pages or blogs (23)	9	30	291	1.7	33	R
Improve my job skills to work better (2)	10	30	290	1.5	32	C
Improve my performance in school (1)	11	29	283	1.5	33	C
Complete work (5)	12	28	274	1.7	33	C
Search for spiritual comfort (10)	13	27	260	1.5	35	A
Create or update own personal website (home page, blog, microblog) (22)	14	26	255	1.6	33	C
Improve my skills to get better/new job (3)	15	26	252	1.2	30	C
Increase self-confidence (9)	16	24	232	1.5	34	C

Find an additional/new job (6)	17	23	221	1.1	27	U
Support social groups I like (participate in forums, blogs, microblogs) (28)	18	22	216	1.6	32	U
Shop online or get product information online (24)	19	21	205	1.4	32	EXT
Get health information to improve physical health (18)	20	20	195	1.5	36	R
Make money (e.g., online store, doing web pages, etc.) (8)	21	20	194	1.1	34	EXT
Online banking or personal financial services (stock trading, online transfers) (25)	22	20	193	1.4	31	EXT
Check public service information (access information, online applications, licenses, etc.) (20)	23	19	185	1.3	29	EXT
Get mental health information to improve mental health (19)	24	19	180	1.4	33	R
Plan personal or family trips (collect destination info, hotels, maps, directions) (26)	25	18	175	1.2	31	U
Better manage my company or farm (e.g., check market info) (7)	26	17	164	1.2	29	C
Promote the community, clubs, interest groups through online activities (27)	27	17	163	1.3	35	R
Literary and artistic creation (fiction, poetry, music, etc.) (21)	28	15	148	1.2	31	A
Participate in government website or online policy discussions (29)	29	14	137	1.1	26	U
Other (30)	30	1	10	1.0	27	U

[a]Number in parentheses shows the order in which SG appears in questionnaire.

[b]Goal fully achieved: 3, No achievement: 0.

[c]SDT classification: A: Autonomy, C: Competence, R: Relatedness, U: Unclassified, EXT: Extrinsic.

Table 4.B.2

Top 12 Situational Goals (SGs) of Young (<19) Urban Student Users of Internet Cafés, by Gender

SGs[a]	Rank	%	# Obs	SDT Classification[b]
Male (63 observations)				
Entertainment (play games, listen to music, watch movies, online video, etc.) (15)	1	81	51	A
Keep in touch with family and friends (email, QQ, etc.) (13)	2	71	45	R
Learn to use computers and the Internet (4)	3	56	35	C
Access information (news, weather forecasts, stock info, sports, gossip, etc.) (11)	4	49	31	U
Meet new friends or a mate or companion (12)	5	46	29	R
Improve my performance in school (1)	6	41	26	C
Spend time on a hobby or pastime (16)	6	41	26	A
Relax, relieve tension (17)	8	40	25	A
Socialize and make friends with people in Internet cafés (14)	9	38	24	R
Search for spiritual comfort (10)	10	33	21	A
Create or update own personal website (home page, blog, microblog) (22)	10	33	21	C
Contribute to other people's web pages or blogs (23)	10	33	21	R

Table 4.B.2 (continued)

SGs[a]	Rank	%	# Obs	SDT Classification[b]
Female (28 observations)				
Entertainment (play games, listen to music, watch movies, online video, etc.) (15)	1	82	23	A
Keep in touch with family and friends (email, QQ, etc.) (13)	2	75	21	R
Contribute to other people's web pages or blogs (23)	3	57	16	R
Meet new friends or a mate or companion (12)	4	54	15	R
Learn to use computers and the Internet (4)	5	50	14	C
Access information (news, weather forecasts, stock info, sports, gossip, etc.). (11)	5	50	14	U
Create or update own personal website (home page, blog, microblog) (22)	5	50	14	C
Socialize and make friends with people in Internet cafés (14)	8	46	13	R
Spend time on a hobby or pastime (16)	8	46	13	A
Improve my performance in school (1)	10	43	12	C
Support social groups I like (participate in forums, blogs, microblogs) (28)	11	39	11	
Increase self-confidence (9)	12	36	10	C
Search for spiritual comfort (10)	12	36	10	A
Relax, relieve tension (17)	12	36	10	A
Shop online or get product information online (24)	12	36	10	EXT

[a]Number in parentheses shows the order in which SG appears in questionnaire.
[b]SDT classification: A: Autonomy, C: Competence, R: Relatedness, U: Unclassified, EXT: Extrinsic.

Appendix 4.C Regression Analysis to Test Hypothesis of No Effect of Cybercafé Use on LG Achievement

Notes to the Tables

1. Figures given are regression estimates of the coefficient for each independent variable, the corresponding t-statistic, and the probabilities that the coefficients depart from zero (i.e., that the independent variables have an effect, positive or negative, on reported achievement).

Significant probabilities are marked as follows:
< 10%: •
< 5%: *
< 1%: **
< 0.1%: ***

2. The dependent variable is the perceived achievement of each LG, with achievement measured as 3 = All to 0 = None. Only those respondents choosing a goal as either "most important" or "very important" are considered.

3. The following independent variables are considered:

User = 1 for users, 0 for nonusers.
Exp ("experience") is the number of years using the Internet.
Import1,..., Import17 are dummy variables to acknowledge that goal choices for "most important" goal (= 1) may be more valued by the respondent (and imply greater effort by the respondent) than "very important" LGs.
NumLGs is the number of goals that a respondent selected as one of his or her life goals. Respondents were able to choose up to 18 LGs and assign them varying levels of importance.

Urban and *Male* are dummy variables (Urban = 1; Rural = 0; Male = 1; Female = 0). *UMS* stands for "urban male students," *UFS* for "urban female students."
LNAGE is the logarithm of the respondent's age.
Student = 1 if the respondent is a student, 0 if a nonstudent.
Y is a categorical variable for the user's income, with eight possible values.
EDCN ("education") takes one of six education values, ranging from 1 for primary to 6 for a master's degree or above.
Overuser = 1 if the respondent answered "sometimes," "every time," or "most of the time" to 5 or more of Young's proposed questions to assess Internet addiction. This is a soft version of Young's criteria for classifying user addiction.
4. The variables *User, Overuser,* and *Exp* are complementary and must be considered jointly. There is no "nonuser overuser" or "experienced nonuser."

Table 4.C.1
Regression Sample and Subsamples and Number of Observations

	Users		Nonusers	
	#	%	#	%
All	976	100.0	964	100.0
Urban	786	80.5	824	85.5
Urban males	575	58.9	436	45.2
Urban males < 35 yrs. old	546	55.9	158	16.4
Urban male nonstudents	356	36.5	377	39.1
Urban male students	219	22.4	59	6.1
Urban females	211	21.6	388	40.2
Urban female students	103	10.6	69	7.2
Rural	190	19.5	140	14.5

Table 4.C.2
Coefficient, T-statistic, and Probability of No Effect on Life Goal (LG) Achievement: LG1, Learn More Knowledge

Independent Variable	All	Urban							Rural
		All Urban	Male	UM < 35	Female	UMNotS	Male st.	Female st.	
Urban	0.129								
	1.825								
	.06839								
Male	–0.009	–0.033							0.129
	–0.174	–0.576							0.819
	.86214	.56481							.4145
Student	0.290	0.314	0.352	0.394	0.224				0.163
	3.218	3.198	2.753	2.838	1.397				0.714
	.00134**	.00144**	.006150**	.00482**	.163554				.4763
NumLGs	–0.011	–0.010	–0.012	–0.015	–0.005	–0.000	–0.023	–0.026	–0.018
	–2.033	–1.682	–1.555	–1.850	–0.539	–0.033	–2.246	–1.870	–1.123
	.04241*	.09309•	.120698	.06526•	.590273	.9740	.02596*	.0640•	.2635
Import1	0.098	0.120	0.155	0.151	0.058	0.074	0.280	0.026	–0.042
	1.882	2.177	2.160	1.920	0.655	0.735	2.834	0.193	–0.282
	.06023•	.02981*	.031314*	.05569•	.513267	.4628	.00514**	.8474	.7787
LNAGE	–0.133	–0.095	–0.053	0.745	–0.205	–0.110	0.484	–0.551	–0.305
	–1.534	–1.043	–0.454	2.907	–1.362	–0.682	0.954	–1.115	–1.080
	.12551	.29720	.649978	.00389**	.174206	.4961	.34151	.2673	.2822
EDCN	0.000	–0.016	–0.053	–0.149	0.055	–0.030	–0.124	0.037	0.104
	0.013	–0.587	–1.507	–3.293	1.313	–0.561	–1.670	0.371	1.428
	.98954	.55722	.132632	.00110**	.190183	.5753	.09672•	.7116	.1557

Y	0.058	0.046	0.071	0.026	–0.006	0.084	–0.051	0.173	0.146
	2.579	1.905	2.233	0.703	–0.163	2.182	–0.724	1.669	2.521
	.01007*	.05714•	.026079*	.48272	.870494	.0301*	.47023	.0979•	.0129*
User	0.149	0.190	0.196	0.278	0.218	–0.103	0.320	0.465	–0.043
	1.475	1.769	1.413	1.936	1.189	–0.472	1.707	1.868	–0.149
	.14047	.07736•	.158347	.05372•	.235292	.6374	.08954•	.0644•	.8819
Exp	–0.008	–0.007	–0.002	–0.016	–0.022	0.027	–0.017	–0.039	–0.022
	–0.720	–0.585	–0.171	–1.093	–0.938	1.212	–0.902	–1.211	–0.680
	.47199	.55867	.863920	.27533	.349135	.2267	.36809	.2284	.4979
Overuser	0.210	0.176	0.202	0.216	0.120	–0.085	0.433	0.239	0.457
	1.664	1.264	1.289	1.420	0.361	–0.324	2.384	0.554	1.457
	.09657•	.20665	.197971	.15663	.718444	.7463	.01818*	.5805	.1476
# Users:	450	368	256	244	112	114	142	65	82
# Nonusers:	405	350	180	96	170	138	42	56	55
R^2:	0.066	0.074	0.074	0.087	0.098	0.035	0.159	0.092	0.108

Table 4.C.3
Coefficient, T-statistic, and Probability of No Effect on Life Goal (LG) Achievement: LG2, Get Stable, High-Paying Job, Better Business Opportunities

Independent		Urban							
Variable	All	All Urban	Male	UM < 35	Female	UMNotS	Male st.	Female st.	Rural
Urban	–0.134								
	–1.373								
	.1702								
Male	0.060	0.020							0.263
	0.732	0.224							1.251
	.4646	.823							.21421
Student	0.257	0.225	–0.005	–0.157	0.855				0.380
	1.854	1.475	–0.026	–0.736	3.257				1.084
	.0642•	.141	.9793	.462	.0014**				.28104
NumLGs	–0.018	–0.011	–0.014	–0.001	–0.009	–0.011	–0.044	–0.022	–0.061
	–2.274	–1.305	–1.284	–0.079	–0.581	–0.985	–1.401	–0.699	–2.893
	.0234*	.192	.2002	.937	.5625	.32578	.172	.4910	.00474**
Import1	–0.028	–0.005	0.041	0.126	–0.125	0.051	–0.103	–0.612	–0.106
	–0.378	–0.062	0.405	1.055	–0.932	0.465	–0.357	–1.909	–0.539
	.7056	.950	.6861	.293	.3530	.64214	.724	.0682•	.59134
LNAGE	0.146	0.222	0.119	0.404	0.555	0.078	0.433	–1.088	–0.191
	1.111	1.553	0.632	1.114	2.383	0.388	0.286	–0.866	–0.549
	.2672	.121	.5277	.267	.0185*	.69854	.777	.3950	.58413
EDCN	0.016	0.026	0.057	0.060	–0.065	0.060	–0.131	0.032	–0.035
	0.433	0.653	1.111	0.968	–0.948	1.067	–0.598	0.132	–0.343
	.6653	.514	.2675	.334	.3446	.28684	.554	.8963	.73254

Y	0.162	0.150	0.100	0.038	0.290	0.109	–0.155	0.410	0.196
	5.562	4.720	2.603	0.784	5.079	2.660	–1.010	1.615	2.500
	.18e–08***	.16e–06***	.0097**	.434	.15e–06***	.00831**	.320	.1194	.01415*
User	–0.072	–0.154	–0.246	–0.042	0.231	–0.378	0.030	–0.485	0.151
	–0.442	–0.870	–1.195	–0.181	0.592	–1.681	0.050	–0.764	0.364
	.6589	.385	.2330	.857	.5550	.09393•	.960	.4523	.71694
Exp	–0.004	0.005	0.010	–0.006	–0.028	0.024	–0.020	0.006	–0.035
	–0.252	0.259	0.456	–0.248	–0.607	1.038	–0.317	0.078	–0.750
	.8012	.795	.6485	.804	.5450	.30026	.753	.9387	.45484
Overuser	0.235	–0.022	–0.027	–0.026	–	–0.397	0.460	–	0.786
	1.254	–0.099	–0.118	–0.111	–	–1.376	1.134	–	2.146
	.2105	.921	.9059	.912	–	.17008	.266	–	.03441*
# Users:	266	212	167	152	45	138	29	14	54
# Nonusers:	293	242	133	65	109	123	10	18	51
R^2:	0.092	0.096	0.081	0.050	0.194	0.087	0.143	0.344	0.186

Table 4.C.4

Coefficient, T-statistic, and Probability of No Effect on Life Goal (LG) Achievement: LG5, Keep Up to Date

Independent Variable	All	Urban							Rural
		All Urban	Male	UM < 35	Female	UMNotS	Male st.	Female st.	
Urban	0.224								
	2.666								
	.0079**								
Male	0.117	0.104							0.211
	1.842	1.546							1.071
	.0660•	.1228							.288
Student	–0.165	–0.137	–0.048	–0.167	–0.485				–0.325
	–1.526	–1.192	–0.347	–0.963	–2.189				–0.837
	.1274	.2338	.72916	.3365	.030128*				.405
NumLGs	0.007	0.005	0.005	0.009	0.009	0.011	0.003	–0.039	0.010
	1.059	0.774	0.580	0.963	0.735	1.264	0.175	–1.517	0.509
	.2901	.4392	.56243	.3367	.463737	.20737	.8619	.13985	.613
Import1	0.368	0.398	0.357	0.443	0.417	0.360	0.305	0.506	0.148
	6.103	6.216	4.457	3.982	3.782	4.083	1.746	1.997	0.804
	.88e–09***	.06e–09***	.12e–05***	.46e–05***	.000222***	.96e–05***	.0844•	.05494•	.424
LNAGE	–0.131	–0.131	0.067	–0.292	–0.537	0.254	–0.529	–3.085	0.190
	–1.390	–1.316	0.540	–0.912	–3.044	1.739	–0.753	–2.672	0.603
	.1651	.1887	.58954	.3628	.002745**	.08329•	.4532	.01207*	.548
EDCN	0.031	0.029	0.040	0.040	0.002	0.133	–0.054	0.298	0.127
	1.071	0.970	1.062	0.748	0.041	3.072	–0.505	1.589	1.249
	.2846	.3327	.28904	.4555	.967088	.00236**	.6151	.12244	.216

Y	0.007	0.000	-0.012	-0.026	0.000	-0.035	-0.085	-0.170	0.083
	0.299	0.003	-0.415	-0.614	0.002	-1.185	-0.696	-0.886	0.954
	.7654	.9977	.67856	.5397	.998257	.23732	.4881	.38258	.343
User	-0.097	-0.066	0.041	0.116	-0.381	0.178	-0.081	0.080	-0.050
	-0.764	-0.502	0.262	0.612	-1.330	0.988	-0.244	0.179	-0.115
	.4450	.6162	.79359	.5411	.185539	.32387	.8077	.85882	.909
Exp	-0.018	-0.017	-0.018	-0.017	0.008	-0.033	0.030	-0.013	-0.060
	-1.322	-1.189	-1.159	-0.961	0.231	-1.921	0.871	-0.247	-1.117
	.1865	.2351	.24730	.3377	.817624	.05584•	.3864	.80626	.268
Overuser	-0.251	-0.286	-0.275	-0.324	-0.195	-0.437	0.120	-0.861	0.330
	-1.703	-1.782	-1.598	-1.735	-0.380	-2.208	0.353	-1.077	0.735
	.0892•	.0753•	.11094	.0842•	.704528	.02812*	.7250	.28989	.464
# Users:	261	226	188	171	38	115	73	20	35
# Nonusers:	341	294	168	46	126	147	21	19	47
R^2:	0.096	0.092	0.074	0.093	0.188	0.135	0.088	0.440	0.205

Table 4.C.5

Coefficient, T-statistic, and Probability of No Effect on Life Goal (LG) Achievement: LG9, Improve the Physical Health of Myself or My Family

Independent Variable	All	Urban							Rural
		All Urban	Male	UM < 35	Female	UMNotS	Male st.	Female st.	
Urban	0.037								
	0.462								
	.64424								
Male	–0.052	–0.060							0.049
	–0.887	–0.978							0.269
	.37528	.328390							.78868
Student	–0.003	0.064	0.191	0.156	–0.064				–0.362
	–0.028	0.537	1.166	0.739	–0.348				–1.105
	.97741	.591387	.244573	.4611	.72778				.27175
NumLGs	–0.006	–0.003	–0.008	–0.009	0.008	–0.006	–0.009	–0.042	–0.022
	–0.855	–0.472	–0.891	–0.753	0.671	–0.606	–0.393	–1.446	–1.127
	.39290	.636960	.373389	.4523	.50295	.5449	.695	.1572	.26253
Import1	0.181	0.229	0.228	0.307	0.207	0.230	0.202	0.464	–0.160
	3.203	3.853	2.804	2.558	2.369	2.589	0.898	2.057	–0.897
	.00142**	.000129***	.005316**	.0113*	.01857*	.0101*	.372	.0472*	.37172
LNAGE	–0.068	–0.026	–0.039	0.281	–0.008	0.109	–0.198	–0.208	–0.235
	–0.763	–0.268	–0.302	0.778	–0.058	0.746	–0.165	–0.190	–0.921
	.44580	.788970	.763067	.4378	.95369	.4562	.870	.8506	.35910
EDCN	–0.055	–0.053	–0.086	–0.141	–0.012	–0.033	–0.194	–0.119	–0.058
	–1.979	–1.840	–2.117	–2.330	–0.291	–0.710	–1.132	–0.621	–0.618
	.04824*	.066173•	.034917*	.0209*	.77131	.4783	.262	.5389	.53831

Y	0.025	0.036	0.071	0.034	–0.004	0.054	0.188	0.278	–0.017
	1.129	1.482	2.054	0.615	–0.133	1.518	1.002	1.372	–0.249
	.25911	.138893	.040672*	.5390	.89408	.1302	.320	.1787	.80375
User	–0.175	–0.125	–0.130	–0.190	–0.085	–0.297	0.201	0.243	–0.405
	–1.156	–0.756	–0.620	–0.820	–0.306	–1.139	0.515	0.585	–0.986
	.24824	.450006	.535368	.4133	.75997	.2558	.609	.5622	.32640
Exp	0.002	–0.003	0.008	0.007	–0.034	0.039	–0.042	–0.041	0.034
	0.104	–0.184	0.361	0.273	–1.022	1.366	–0.898	–0.857	0.676
	.91702	.853813	.718205	.7850	.30795	.1730	.373	.3971	.50049
Overuser	–0.018	0.006	–0.001	–0.015		0.106	–0.392		0.014
	–0.090	0.026	–0.003	–0.052		0.332	–0.754		0.036
	.92792	.979569	.997985	.9586		.7404	.454		.97154
# Users:	212	177	129	123	48	75	54	23	35
# Nonusers:	531	455	238	70	217	218	20	20	76
R^2:	0.046	0.054	0.053	0.082	0.075	0.048	0.152	0.258	0.077

Table 4.C.6
Coefficient, T-statistic, and Probability of No Effect on Life Goal (LG) Achievement: LG10, Improve the Mental Health of Myself or My Family

Independent		Urban							
Variable	All	All Urban	Male	UM < 35	Female	UMNotS	Male st.	Female st.	Rural
Urban	0.040								
	0.414								
	.6793								
Male	–0.011	–0.082							0.340
	–0.149	–1.043							1.668
	.8814	.2975							.099961•
Student	–0.069	0.029	0.101	0.029	–0.084				–0.607
	–0.515	0.197	0.498	0.112	–0.393				–1.597
	.6069	.8437	.61893	.911	.694888				.115139
NumLGs	–0.015	–0.012	–0.012	–0.026	–0.011	–0.001	–0.049	–0.041	–0.036
	–1.803	–1.292	–0.918	–1.608	–0.809	–0.076	–1.743	–1.234	–1.628
	.0721•	.1970	.35951	.110	.419924	.9392	.0881•	.2291	.108209
Import1	0.132	0.181	0.153	0.137	0.225	0.191	–0.060	0.437	–0.224
	1.862	2.401	1.459	0.912	2.074	1.596	–0.252	1.624	–1.068
	.0632•	.0168*	.14596	.364	.039715*	.1124	.8024	.1175	.289398
LNAGE	–0.183	–0.075	–0.031	0.076	–0.197	0.043	–0.416	–2.837	–0.718
	–1.661	–0.634	–0.189	0.158	–1.088	0.232	–0.262	–1.716	–2.377
	.0974•	.5262	.85003	.875	.278369	.8167	.7947	.0991•	.020341*
EDCN	–0.004	–0.006	0.008	–0.039	–0.030	0.018	0.061	0.289	0.024
	–0.118	–0.146	0.153	–0.485	–0.536	0.292	0.264	1.114	0.216
	.9057	.8838	.87868	.629	.592422	.7703	.7933	.2762	.829439

Y	0.024	0.028	0.052	–0.005	–0.000	0.056	–0.037	0.154	–0.028
	0.885	0.937	1.200	–0.078	–0.012	1.209	–0.179	0.710	–0.355
	.3767	.3492	.23121	.938	.990811	.2283	.8589	.4846	.723879
User	–0.308	–0.126	–0.188	–0.244	–0.004	–0.366	0.035	0.174	–0.923
	–1.749	–0.636	–0.715	–0.879	–0.012	–1.090	0.075	0.350	–2.122
	.0809•	.5254	.47543	.381	.990604	.2773	.9405	.7295	.037594*
Exp	0.015	–0.000	0.012	0.017	–0.027	0.037	–0.030	–0.042	0.066
	0.705	–0.011	0.376	0.519	–0.685	0.982	–0.509	–0.708	1.133
	.4811	.9913	.70712	.605	.494157	.3275	.6134	.4857	.261402
Overuser	0.416	0.147	0.183	0.138		0.391	–0.176		0.765
	2.087	0.533	0.614	0.441		1.027	–0.346		2.137
	.0374*	.5944	.53998	.660		.3058	.7305		.036273*
# Users:	143	113	83	81	30	45	38	15	30
# Nonusers:	333	286	152	51	134	135	17	17	47
R^2:	0.043	0.034	0.030	0.050	0.055	0.040	0.084	0.318	0.268

Table 4.C.7
Coefficient, T-statistic, and Probability of No Effect on Life Goal (LG) Achievement: LG14, Keep in Touch with Friends and Family Who Don't Live Nearby

Independent		Urban							
Variable	All	All Urban	Male	UM < 35	Female	UMNotS	Male st.	Female st.	Rural
Urban	0.050								
	0.750								
	.45352								
Male	0.003	0.007							–0.042
	0.064	0.125							–0.318
	.94917	.90062							.75128
Student	–0.116	–0.029	0.025	–0.018	–0.153				–0.357
	–1.233	–0.283	0.189	–0.116	–0.896				–1.496
	.21804	.77707	.85058	.907559	.3713				.13715
NumLGs	–0.018	–0.016	–0.022	–0.031	–0.006	–0.018	–0.031	–0.022	–0.019
	–3.009	–2.509	–2.804	–3.541	–0.529	–1.828	–2.150	–1.137	–1.247
	.00271**	.01238*	.00531**	.000488***	.5972	.0688•	.03422*	.2598	.21448
Import1	0.382	0.428	0.449	0.452	0.401	0.465	0.383	0.315	0.170
	7.305	7.493	6.381	5.139	4.068	5.619	2.655	1.492	1.301
	.14e–13***	.39e–13***	.42e–1***	.15e–07***	.46e–05***	.91e–08***	.00935**	.1406	.19568
LNAGE	–0.240	–0.235	–0.164	–0.186	–0.357	–0.105	–0.101	–1.080	–0.084
	–2.939	–2.719	–1.442	–0.718	–2.559	–0.726	–0.180	–1.183	–0.334
	.00339**	.00675**	.15020	.473733	.0111*	.4687	.85785	.2411	.73928
EDCN	–0.006	–0.012	–0.019	–0.010	–0.015	–0.009	–0.038	0.021	–0.007
	–0.224	–0.460	–0.564	–0.213	–0.328	–0.217	–0.396	0.141	–0.110
	.82266	.64602	.57307	.831898	.7432	.8285	.69334	.8883	.91265

Y	0.004	0.011	0.013	–0.003	0.010	0.015	–0.040	0.096	0.017
	0.182	0.491	0.448	–0.078	0.236	0.503	–0.318	0.652	0.284
	.85537	.62362	.65427	.938081	.8133	.6151	.75151	.5168	.77652
User	0.196	0.182	0.072	0.091	0.429	0.056	0.101	0.628	0.421
	1.696	1.422	0.467	0.550	1.801	0.277	0.346	1.658	1.374
	.09029•	.15564	.64085	.582644	.0730•	.7820	.72979	.1021	.17175
Exp	–0.026	–0.018	–0.002	–0.003	–0.048	0.006	–0.013	–0.034	–0.067
	–1.968	–1.233	–0.138	–0.168	–1.675	0.270	–0.380	–0.738	–2.068
	.04944*	.21819	.89044	.866997	.0952•	.7870	.70484	.4631	.04058*
Overuser	–0.015	0.081	0.067	0.070	0.269	–0.013	0.146	0.229	0.020
	–0.115	0.529	0.402	0.434	0.714	–0.061	0.498	0.476	0.063
	.90872	.59704	.68821	.664726	.4760	.9516	.61974	.6355	.94986
# Users:	341	266	131	173	85	106	75	49	75
# Nonusers:	417	350	139	54	161	164	25	25	67
R^2:	0.088	0.108	0.126	0.160	0.109	0.124	0.147	0.119	0.105

Table 4.C.8

Coefficient, T-statistic, and Probability of No Effect on Life Goal (LG) Achievement: LG15, Leisure, Entertainment

Independent		Urban							
Variable	All	All Urban	Male	UM < 35	Female	UMNotS	Male st.	Female st.	Rural
Urban	0.088								
	1.161								
	.24604								
Male	0.177	0.204							0.030
	3.157	3.450							0.169
	.00167**	.000601***							.8660
Student	–0.177	–0.206	–0.185	–0.269	–0.317				–0.167
	–1.995	–2.158	–1.529	–1.846	–1.987				–0.592
	.04640*	.031336*	.1272	.065979•	.048343*				.5557
NumLGs	–0.013	–0.009	–0.013	–0.011	–0.003	–0.008	–0.025	0.003	–0.026
	–2.301	–1.520	–1.760	–1.297	–0.273	–0.816	–1.851	0.200	–1.372
	.02171*	.129050	.0791•	.195875	.785264	.415	.06661•	.841994	.1739
Import1	0.407	0.455	0.500	0.443	0.346	0.551	0.386	0.642	0.109
	7.451	7.886	6.915	5.130	3.537	6.470	2.840	4.122	0.624
	.86e–13***	.58e–14***	.02e–11***	.59e–07***	.000508***	.16e–10***	.00531**	.000112***	.5341
LNAGE	–0.111	–0.116	–0.063	–0.110	–0.280	–0.212	0.354	–0.940	–0.277
	–1.351	–1.360	–0.575	–0.453	–1.995	–1.532	0.630	–1.742	–0.833
	.17710	.174390	.5658	.651250	.047519*	.127	.53012	.086303•	.4074
EDCN	0.008	0.012	0.023	0.057	–0.011	0.006	–0.001	0.162	–0.016
	0.337	0.470	0.678	1.320	–0.248	0.136	–0.016	1.513	–0.174
	.73656	.638608	.4984	.187809	.804709	.892	.98753	.135234	.8619

Y	–0.028	–0.029	–0.019	–0.039	–0.063	0.006	–0.227	0.057	–0.061
	–1.253	–1.249	–0.650	–0.973	–1.573	0.188	–2.109	0.536	–0.675
	.21081	.212079	.5159	.331482	.117301	.851	.03701*	.593688	.5017
User	0.179	0.168	0.118	0.290	0.283	–0.172	0.335	0.513	0.016
	1.686	1.487	0.839	1.905	1.431	–0.911	1.441	2.028	0.044
	.09228•	.137588	.4017	.057922•	.154112	.363	.15222	.046743*	.9646
Exp	–0.021	–0.022	–0.016	–0.033	–0.036	0.001	–0.020	–0.073	0.014
	–1.803	–1.717	–1.087	–2.084	–1.522	0.059	–0.809	–2.524	0.364
	.07179•	.086529•	.2779	.038074*	.129707	.953	.42040	.014126*	.7171
Overuser	0.045	0.109	0.061	0.021	0.609	0.403	–0.045	0.470	–0.202
	0.353	0.791	0.405	0.135	1.599	1.606	–0.222	1.241	–0.547
	.72431	.429298	.6855	.892395	.111457	.110	.82461	.219224	.5857
# Users:	388	319	236	224	83	131	105	47	69
# Nonusers:	294	268	150	52	118	127	23	25	26
R^2:	0.110	0.132	0.130	0.126	0.131	0.157	0.165	0.331	0.074

Table 4.C.9

Coefficient, T-statistic, and Probability of No Effect on Life Goal (LG) Achievement: LG17, Relax, Relieve Tension

Independent		Urban							
Variable	All	All Urban	Male	UM < 35	Female	UMNotS	Male st.	Female st.	Rural
Urban	0.131								
	1.256								
	.2099								
Male	0.072	0.030							0.280
	0.844	0.318							1.375
	.3990	.7505							.17381
Student	0.078	0.078	0.112	0.201	0.020				–0.196
	0.581	0.538	0.624	1.018	0.081				–0.515
	.5616	.5907	.533083	.3096	.9359				.60843
NumLGs	0.003	0.006	–0.004	–0.007	0.031	0.002	–0.014	0.015	0.005
	0.393	0.659	–0.365	–0.640	1.933	0.145	–0.881	0.589	0.228
	.6945	.5103	.715455	.5227	.0557•	.88453	.38058	.558	.82051
Import1	0.162	0.197	0.213	0.280	0.107	0.054	0.441	0.213	0.020
	2.037	2.280	1.986	2.477	0.709	0.361	3.006	0.859	0.092
	.0422*	.0232*	.048120*	.0140*	.4799	.71883	.0034**	.394	.92713
LNAGE	–0.319	–0.318	–0.374	–0.279	–0.295	–0.398	0.169	–0.430	–0.503
	–2.240	–2.069	–1.845	–0.814	–1.230	–1.379	0.265	–0.551	–1.288
	.0256*	.0393*	.066099•	.4166	.2212	.16975	.79179	.584	.20235
EDCN	0.034	–0.013	–0.003	–0.027	–0.052	–0.002	–0.056	–0.034	0.356
	0.896	–0.321	–0.050	–0.455	–0.779	–0.032	–0.557	–0.204	3.147
	.3708	.7480	.960063	.6492	.4374	.97426	.57872	.839	.00246**

Y	0.035	0.036	0.040	0.063	0.059	0.050	–0.082	0.020	–0.046
	1.031	0.979	0.888	1.139	0.862	0.947	–0.643	0.117	–0.499
	.3033	.3281	.375535	.2560	.3903	.34520	.52177	.908	.61964
User	0.273	0.373	0.191	0.184	0.775	0.045	0.177	0.689	–0.209
	1.795	2.250	0.925	0.891	2.419	0.140	0.614	1.389	–0.534
	.0733.	.0250*	.355820	.3741	.0172*	.88909	.5405	.171	.59536
Exp	–0.027	–0.026	–0.016	–0.024	–0.060	0.001	–0.024	–0.037	–0.046
	–1.643	–1.428	–0.779	–1.142	–1.537	0.049	–0.789	–0.616	–1.010
	.1011	.1542	.436508	.2547	.1271	.96126	.4318	.541	.31603
Overuser	0.010	0.050	0.028	0.027	0.379	0.087	–0.055	0.142	–0.037
	0.066	0.306	0.152	0.150	0.968	0.308	–0.238	0.296	–0.103
	.9476	.7597	.879438	.8808	.3352	.75884	.8125	.768	.91800
# Users:	295	247	193	190	54	109	84	35	48
# Nonusers:	179	149	79	46	70	57	22	23	30
R^2:	0.058	0.063	0.049	0.047	0.143	0.035	0.136	0.111	0.219

5 Problematic Internet Use among Internet Café Users in China

Wei Shang, Xuemei Jiang, Jianbin Hao, and Xiaoguang Yang

Abstract

Problematic Internet use (PIU), defined as "excessive use or addictive tendencies toward the Internet" (Czincz and Hechanova 2009), is an issue of global importance, particularly among adolescents. The Chinese media often portray Internet cafés as places where young people only play online games and waste time. This chapter reviews the incidence of PIU among Internet café users in China. A distinction is made between Internet overuse and users with addiction tendencies. It finds that of the 976 users surveyed, 2.2 percent could be defined as Internet "addicts," and another 16 percent display some signs of overuse. Males between 18 and 25 years old, and self-identifying as coming from a rural area, are most likely to display signs of PIU. There are significant differences between Internet addicts, overusers, and common users. Overusers start to use the Internet or Internet cafés at a younger age; they also visit more cafés, spend more time there, prefer to use Internet cafés located near them, play more games, and believe that the option to use the Internet café overnight is an important feature. Willingness to pay for Internet café services does not vary much between problematic Internet users and ordinary users. Nevertheless, "addicted" users show greater willingness to visit Internet cafés more often should the price of services come down. This suggests that subsidies lowering the price to encourage more use among low-income people would also induce problematic users to spend even more time in Internet cafés. However, limiting overnight Internet café use while increasing government subsidies for Internet cafés in rural areas or those servicing low-income users could increase information and communication technology penetration without encouraging problematic Internet use.

Background

In China, as Internet penetration has increased, public concern about adolescents' obsession with Internet browsing and online games has also grown. Parents see Internet cafés as incubators of Internet addiction by adolescents and a major factor contributing to a perceived loss of control over their children.[1]

In response to public outcry, a member of the Eleventh National People's Congress (2010) proposed that all Internet cafés be shut down to prevent Internet addiction among adolescents. Café operators retorted in their own defense that Internet cafés are only places for young people to get together and socialize after school or work, and therefore provide a function similar to that of karaoke bars.

Young (1996) was one of the first to propose that Internet addiction be considered a mental health disorder, and in her 1998 paper, she proposed an eight-item questionnaire to diagnose Internet addiction. According to Young, time spent on the Internet is one of the most direct indicators of Internet addiction, and spending between 40 and 80 hours per week on the Internet is considered to be overuse (Young 2004). Internet addiction is considered harmful because it leads to or is highly correlated with little or no social life, poor school performance, and online affairs (Kubey, Lavin, and Barrows 2001; Young 2004).

Problematic Internet use (PIU) is defined as "an inability to control one's use of the Internet" (Billieux and Van der Linden 2012, p. 24). It is associated with low satisfaction with life (Wang et al. 2008) and psychological factors such as shyness, defined as the fear of meeting people and discomfort in the presence of others (Chak and Leung 2004), and loneliness (Morahan-Martin and Schumacher 2000). It may or may not be linked to other psychiatric disorders (Beard and Wolf 2001; Shapira et al. 2003).

This chapter reviews existing research related to PIU and analyzes the results of a survey of Internet café users in China to determine the presence and levels of Internet "addiction" and overuse. Policy implications for Internet café regulation are proposed in the last part of the chapter.

Research Questions

Excessive Internet use is not necessarily a sign of addiction. Griffiths, for example, found only two addicted subjects out of five cases of excessive Internet use (Griffiths 2000). Overuse, problematic Internet use, and excessive Internet use are more frequently identified among users than is addiction. The Wang et al. (2011) research on 12,446 high school Internet users found that 12.2 percent were problematic Internet users. Whang, Lee, and Chang (2003) conducted research on 13,588 Internet users and determined that 3.5 percent could be considered Internet addicts (IAs) and 18.4 percent possible Internet addicts. Identifying different degrees of PIU is therefore an important first step to diagnosing and treating the condition.

The characteristics and causes of Internet addiction are also important research issues. According to Brenner (1997), Internet addiction or problematic Internet use is often found among young male users. Besides social demographic characteristics of IAs, Armstrong, Phillips, and Saling (2000) found low self-esteem to be a predictor of Internet addiction. Kim and Kim (2010) provide more information on predictors of Internet game addiction. Using a decision tree model, they found several causative factors, including gender, type of school, number of siblings, economic status, religion, time spent alone, gaming place, payment to Internet café, frequency and duration of visits, parents' ability to use Internet, occupation (mother), trust (father), expectations regarding adolescent's study (mother), supervising (both parents), and rearing attitude (both parents). Odaci's (2011) research on college students found a negative relationship between a student's self-perception of academic efficacy and PIU. Although most existing research targeted college or high school students in various countries, the findings may serve as the basis for research into Internet addiction among Internet café users in China.

Several diagnostic measures of Internet addiction exist, and a growing body of research reveals the causes and consequences of problematic Internet use. However, research on the incidence of overuse among China's Internet café users is limited. The present research aims to help fill this gap. Three research questions are addressed: (1) What is the extent of problematic Internet use in Internet cafés in China? (2) What are the demographic characteristics of problematic Internet users? and (3) What Internet café regulation measures may alleviate problematic Internet use, especially among adolescents?

Indicators

Young's (1996) criteria for screening Internet addiction are based on those established in the *Diagnostic and Statistical Manual of Mental Disorders*, 4th edition (*DSM–IV*), to identify persons affected by pathological gambling. She proposed that persons who answered "yes" to five or more of the following questions be classified as addicted:

1. Do you feel preoccupied with the Internet (think about previous online activity or anticipate next online session)?
2. Do you feel the need to use the Internet with increasing amounts of time in order to achieve satisfaction?
3. Have you repeatedly made unsuccessful efforts to control, cut back, or stop Internet use?
4. Do you feel restless, moody, depressed, or irritable when attempting to cut down or stop Internet use?

5. Do you stay online longer than originally intended?

6. Have you jeopardized or risked the loss of a significant relationship, job, educational, or career opportunity because of the Internet?

7. Have you lied to family members, therapist, or others to conceal the extent of your involvement with the Internet?

8. Do you use the Internet as a way of escaping from problems or relieving a dysphoric mood (e.g., feelings of hopelessness, guilt, anxiety, or depression)?

Beard and Wolf (2001) noted that the first five questions are qualitatively different from the last three. A person might answer "yes" to these first five questions without impairing his or her ability to function. Beard and Wolf illustrate this point using as an example a young mother overly preoccupied with her new baby (question 1), who feels a need to be constantly near her newborn (question 2), has repeatedly but unsuccessfully tried not to obsess over caring for her child (question 3), feels restless or moody on account of her excessive concern (question 4), and spends more time near the baby than she feels is necessary (question 5).

Answering "yes" to the last three questions, however, would suggest that a user's ability to cope with the demands of daily life was being impaired (feelings of depression, helplessness, anxiety, escapism) or that his or her interactions with others were being affected (lying, underperformance at school or work, damage to a significant relationship). Beard and Wolf (2001) in general object to the use of the term *addiction* and prefer a less theoretically contentious term such as *problematic Internet use*. They propose that a better diagnosis of the underlying pathology would be achieved by modifying the original criteria to acknowledge the observed qualitative differences in the questions used so that a person be considered affected by the disorder only if he or she answered "yes" to all of the first five questions and to at least one of the last three.

To assess the extent to which Internet café users are affected by addiction or overuse, our questionnaire in China included Young's eight-question screening tool.[2] We used the translation of these eight questions introduced by Cao et al. (2007). Two levels of problematic Internet use are considered, according to the user's degree of Internet dependency:

- A respondent is considered an *Internet overuser* if he or she answers "usually," "most times," "sometimes," or "rarely" to all of the first five questions and at least one of the last three. This is a broad definition of overuse that would classify as overusers persons whose risk of having PIU affect their lives is small.[3]
- A respondent is considered an *Internet "addict"* if he or she answers "usually" or "most times" to all of the first five questions and at least one of the last three. This criterion is

similar to the one proposed by Beard and Wolf (2001), except that these authors had "yes" or "no" as possible answers to each question, whereas we allow a five-scale answer and consider "usually" and "most times" as a "yes."

In addition to Young's eight Internet addiction diagnostic questions, our questionnaire contains four other sections designed to investigate: (1) Internet use, (2) Internet café use, (3) user objectives, and (4) user demographic features. The third category, user objectives, is analyzed in detail in the previous chapter on China (chapter 4).

The focus in this chapter is on questions appearing in the first, second, and fourth parts of the questionnaire. The first section contains four questions addressing when and where a user first used the Internet and computer and his or her most frequent (preferred and/or most visited) Internet access venues (i.e., school, home, Internet cafés, etc.). The second section comprises fifteen questions about what kind of Internet café users usually visit, how much they are willing to pay for the service, their usage patterns, the activities they usually perform in Internet cafés, and their motivation for using an Internet café. With regard to their willingness to pay, a question about how much they are paying now and two questions about how much more or less they would likely use the café if the price were to go down or up were included to ascertain users' valuation of Internet café services. The fourth section of the questionnaire includes demographic questions about respondents' gender, age, education, occupation, and income.

Findings

Problematic Internet Use

Three groups of users are identified: normal users, overusers, and "addicted" users. The percentages of each group in our user sample are as follows:

	#	%	Cumulative %
Addicted	22	2.2	2.2
Overusers	155	15.9	18.1
Normal	799	81.9	100
Total	976	100.0	

Overall, the proportion of IAs is low (2.2 percent). Most cybercafé users can be classified as normal users (i.e., they do not display characteristics of overuse or addiction).

Table 5.1
Problematic Internet Use (PIU): Recent Estimates for Korea and China

	Students (%)	All (%)	Basic features of sample	Measure of PIU used
Whang, Lee, and Chang (2003)		3.5	7,878 respondents to online survey Mean age 26.7 years, range 20–40 58% male, 42% female	Modified Korean version of Young (1998)'s 20-question Internet addiction test
Cao et al. (2007)	2.4		2,620 from 4 high schools in Changsha City Ages 12–18, average 15.2 years 54% male, 46% female	Young 8-item questionnaire using Beard and Wolf (2001) criteria
Kim et al. (2010)	21.8		853 Korean junior high school students 2008 survey 45% male, 55% female	20-item addiction questionnaire by Korea Agency for Digital Opportunity and Promotion. % given is "high risk" users
Wang et al. (2011)	12.2		12,446 high school student Internet users in Guandong Province Mean age 15.6 years, range 10–23 47% male, 52% female	Young (1998)'s 20-question Internet addiction test
Our estimate (2010 survey)				
Modified Young criteria	6.3	4.2	**Students** subsample: 189 middle & high school student PAV users; Average age 17.7 years, range 12–25; 72% male, 28% female. **All** user sample: 976 PAV users; Average age 23 years; 73% male, 27% female	8-item Young questionnaire, using either Young (1998) or Beard and Wolf (2001) criteria, modified so that "usually" or "most times" = "yes"
Modified Beard and Wolf criteria[a]	3.2	2.2		

[a]Modified Beard and Wolf criteria: All of the first five of Young's questions and at least one of the last three marked as "usually" or "most times."

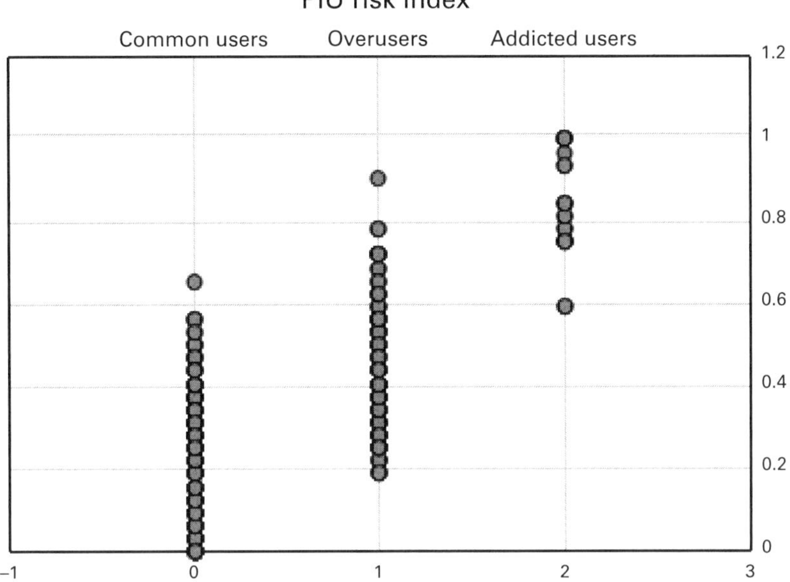

Figure 5.1
Scatter chart of PIU risk index by user type.

We also considered an Internet addiction group of special interest from a public policy perspective: high school students. Cao et al. (2007) estimated that 2.4 percent of high school students from four schools in Changsha City could be classified as addicted to the Internet. Using the same questionnaire and criteria, we arrived at an estimate of 3.2 percent "addicts" in a subsample of 189 middle and high school student users of Internet cafés. Other estimates (shown in table 5.1) are higher. These estimates are not fully comparable. There is consensus that overuse is associated with health and behavioral problems, but there is no agreement on how to define or measure "addiction" or "overuse."

We also calculated a PIU risk index by treating all eight questions as equally important and normalizing its value to lie between 0 and 1. This essentially follows Young's criteria but disregards Beard and Wolf's distinction between the first five and the last three questions. The PIU risk index lets us get an appreciation of how much at risk of problematic Internet use a user may be.

This PIU index is highly correlated with PIU types. The Pearson correlation coefficient is 0.760 and is significant at the level 0.01. As shown in the scatter chart of PIU types and PIU risk index (figure 5.1), the normal users and addicted users are quite

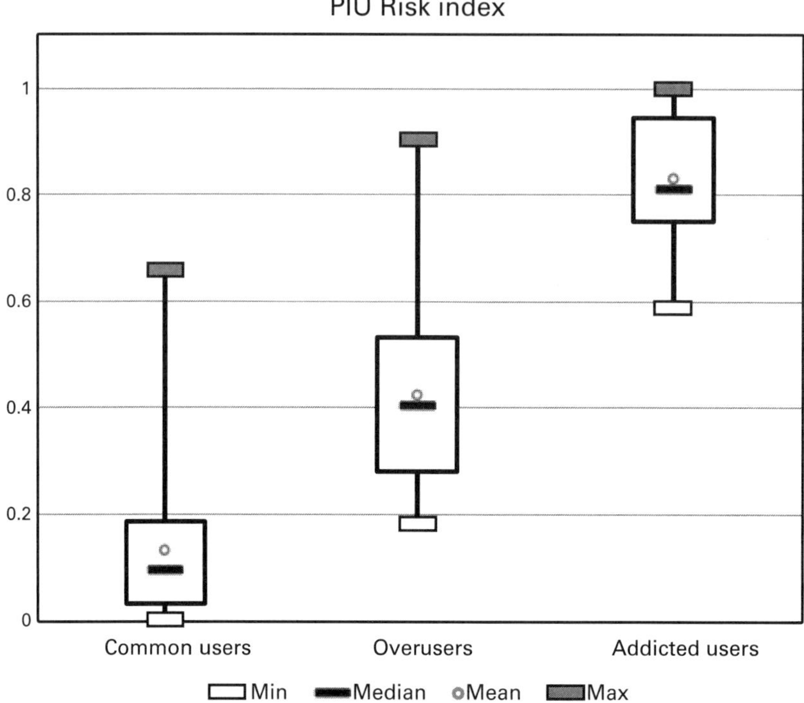

Figure 5.2
Boxplot of PIU risk index by user type.

separate in terms of the value of the PIU risk index. There are some outliers in the separation of normal users and overusers, as shown in the boxplot in figure 5.2.

User Demographics

PIU types are significantly correlated with gender, age, and rural/urban residency status but not with education, income, or different professions (table 5.2). Male rural residents ages 18 to 25 are the most likely to be at risk of PIU.

Male users are more likely than females to be Internet addicted or overusers. Among all survey respondents, using Beard and Wolf's (2001) criteria, 2.5 percent of male users may be classified as IAs and 17.4 percent as Internet overusers. Among female users, only 1.5 percent may be classified as addicted and 11.7 percent as overusers. The correlation between gender and PIU type is significant at 0.05 level.

Age and PIU risk index are significantly correlated at 0.05 level. The Pearson correlation coefficient is –0.078, which means younger people have a higher tendency toward PIU. When users are grouped into the following age categories—under 18, between 18

Table 5.2
Internet Use and Demographic Features

		Level of Internet Use			
		Normal (%)	Overuse (%)	Addict (%)	Count
Gender	Male	80.0	17.4	2.5	569
	Female	86.8	11.7	1.5	230
Age	< 18	84.4	13.5	2.1	96
	18–25	80.2	17.5	2.3	698
	> 25	86.8	11.0	2.2	182
Residency	Urban	83.7	14.2	2.0	786
	Rural	74.2	22.6	3.2	190
Education	Under high school	83.4	14.0	2.5	157
	High school & junior college	81.9	15.6	2.5	570
	College and above	80.7	17.7	1.6	249
Income	< 1,500 yuan/month	80.9	16.8	2.2	624
	> 1,500 yuan/month	83.5	14.2	2.3	352
Student status	Nonstudents	84.4	13.3	2.3	557
	Students	78.5	19.3	2.1	419

and 25, and over 25—users between the ages of 18 and 25 have a higher ratio of addiction and overuse than the other two age groups.

Internet addiction and overuse among rural residents are 3.2 and 22.6 percent, respectively, higher than for urban users, indicating that rural users are more likely to be Internet addicted or overusers than urban users. The correlation between rural/urban and PIU type is significant at level 0.01.

The highest incidence of Internet addiction (2.8 percent) is found among junior college-educated people; all other groups are below the average Internet addiction ratio (i.e., 2.2 percent in our research). The highest Internet overuse ratio (18 percent) is found among college graduates, followed by 16.2 percent of the high school group. PIU type is not correlated at statistically significant levels with education but is instead highly correlated with age and rural/urban status. This is reasonable in China. Education is age determined, and most rural people have not completed high school because compulsory education in China includes only primary and middle school. Furthermore, when rural students get into college, their *hukou* (residence) classification is changed from their village to the city where the college is located; thus, most of the students who come from rural areas will consider themselves urban residents.

Table 5.3
Internet Start Age and Internet Café Start Age

	Common and Overusers	Addicted		Sum of Squares	df	Mean Square	F	Sig.
Internet start age	15.30	12.95	Between groups	118.700	1	118.700	4.224	.040
			Within groups	27368.799	974	28.099		
			Total	27487.499	975			
Café start age	16.03	13.64	Between groups	122.710	1	122.710	4.582	.033
			Within groups	26084.487	974	26.781		
			Total	26207.197	975			
Yrs of Internet use	7.28	8.73	Between groups	45.246	1	45.246	4.668	.031
			Within groups	9441.307	974	9.693		
			Total	9486.553	975			
Yrs of café use	6.56	8.05	Between groups	47.735	1	47.735	5.163	.023
			Within groups	9004.510	974	9.245		
			Total	9052.245	975			

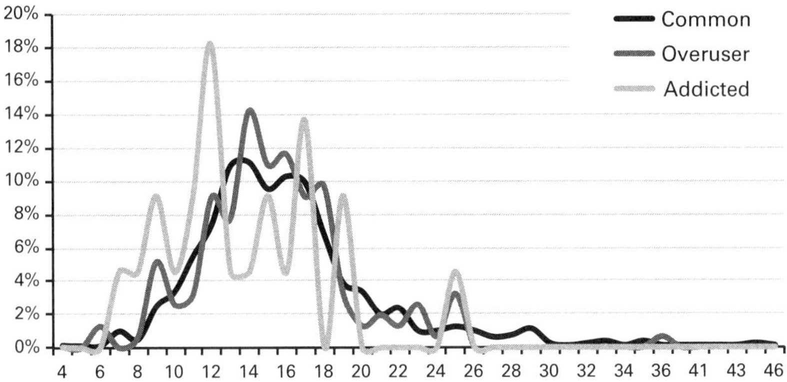

Figure 5.3
Age at which Internet café use starts for different PIU user types.

Among all survey respondents, 42.9 percent were students. When we distinguish between students and nonstudents, the correlation with PIU types surfaces. Nineteen percent of student users overuse the Internet. The correlation between student and PIU type is significant at level 0.05.

Internet Café Use

We found significant variations among user types (i.e., common user, overuser, and addicted) with respect to the age that respondents started to use the Internet, the age that respondents started to use Internet cafés, and the number and frequency of visits to cafés.

Starting Age Respondents classified as IAs started using the Internet and Internet cafés at a younger age than other user types and have therefore been using the Internet and Internet cafés for longer and have visited more cafés than nonaddicts (table 5.3).

The percentage of users of different ages grouped by PIU types is shown in figure 5.3. The X axis shows users' age and the Y axis the corresponding percentages in the sample population. Internet overusers and common users started using Internet cafés at a similar age—on average, when they were 15 to 16 years old. Addicted users, however, started using cafés earlier, on average when they were 12 to 13 years old. The age at which users started to use the Internet correlates strongly with the age they started using Internet cafés and thus follows a similar pattern.

Internet Café Use Patterns The majority of common users and overusers have visited one to five Internet cafés in the past year. In contrast, most addicted users have visited

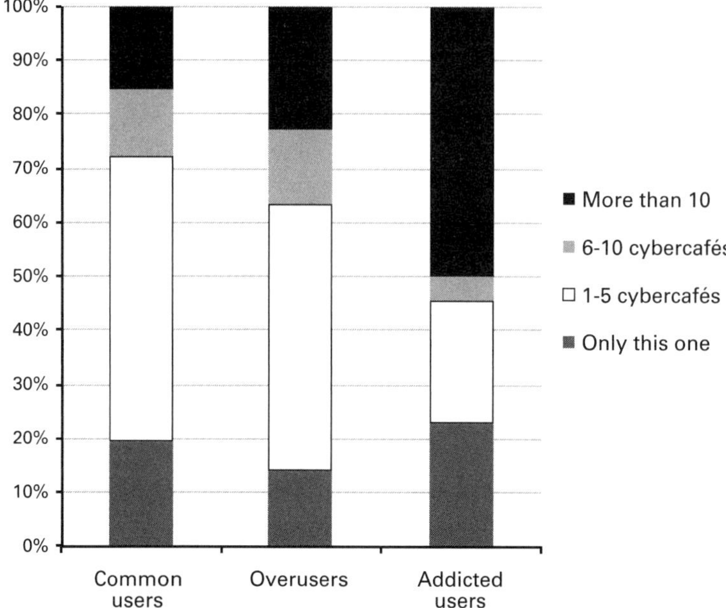

Figure 5.4
Number of Internet cafés visited in past 12 months, by PIU user type.

more than ten Internet cafés during this period. Overusers and addicted users visit more Internet cafés than common users (see figure 5.4).

Addicted users and overusers visit Internet cafés more frequently than common users (figure 5.5). Forty-five percent of addicted users visit an Internet café every day or almost every day. In general, overusers stay longer at each Internet café visit than common users; however, addicted users do not report staying longer per visit than the other two groups (figure 5.6). The average time spent per visit is about the same for all users, but addicted users and overusers spend more total time in Internet cafés because they go there more frequently than common users. Addicted users and overusers also tend to use more than one place of access than common users (table 5.4).

Willingness to Pay for Using Internet Cafés

No significant difference was found across the PIU user types between what users pay on average for using Internet cafés and the price they are willing to pay. Significant differences were, however, observed when the possible impact of price changes is considered. Specifically, the likelihood of increased use of Internet cafés should there be a reduction in price is most pronounced among respondents identified as IAs (see table

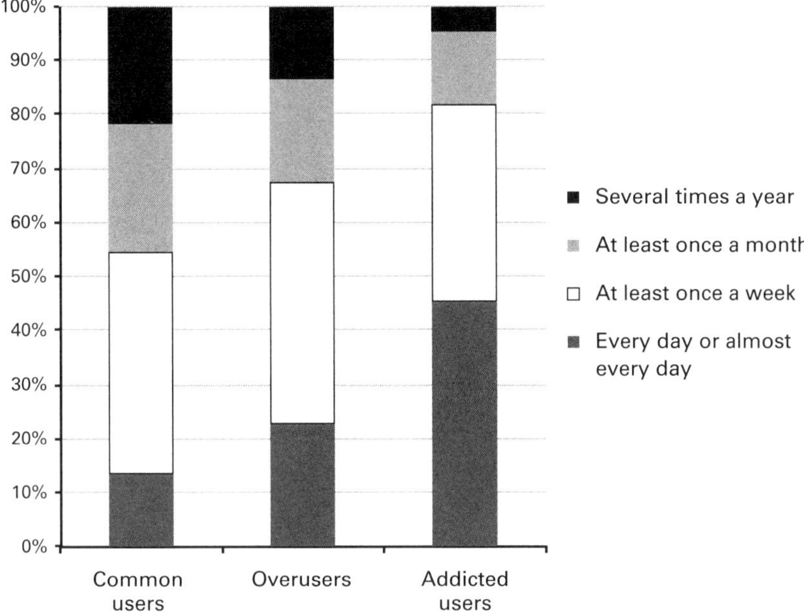

Figure 5.5
Frequency of Internet café visits, by PIU user type.

5.5). Common users appear to be the least affected by both price increases and decreases. The addicted group, in contrast, exhibits a more significant response to price changes. When the price of cybercafé use increases, more of the addicted users will visit less often, compared with the other two PIU types, and when price decreases, a relatively larger number of addicted users expect to visit cybercafés more often.

User Behavior

Use of videogames is the most significant activity correlated with Internet addiction (figure 5.7). The possibility of staying overnight is the most significant Internet café factor correlated with Internet addiction (table 5.6).

Gaming Activities at Internet Cafés Ten common Internet activities were considered: email, chatting, Internet surfing, blogging, social networking, watching movies or TV, gaming, listening to or downloading music, news reading, and online shopping. Gaming shows a strong correlation with PIU types. Addicted users show the highest ratio of game playing among Internet activities examined: more than 70 percent of respondents identified as IAs said that they played games "every time" or "most times"

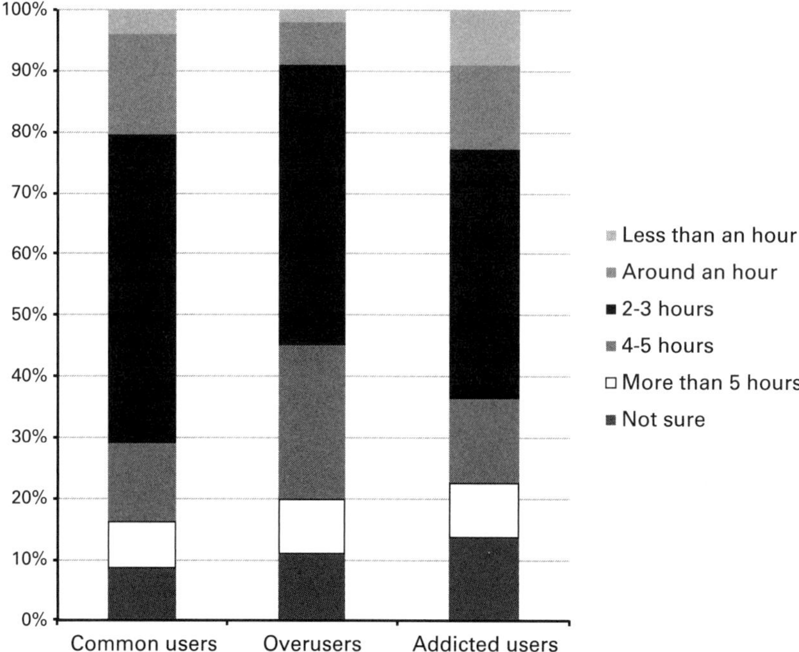

Figure 5.6
Duration of Internet café visits, by PIU user type.

they visited an Internet café. Respondents who overuse the Internet also displayed high frequency of game playing in Internet cafés: approximately 60 percent said that they played games "every time" or "most times" (figure 5.7).

Factors That Determine Choice of Internet Café Among the factors influencing users' use of Internet cafés, café environment, Rural/Urban status, availability of food and beverage service, and the possibility of staying overnight are significantly related with PIU types (tables 5.6 and 5.7).

The possibility of staying overnight at the Internet café had the most significant and highest coefficient in determining which Internet café to patronize. In particular, a high number of respondents identified by the survey as IAs considered this to be a "very important" factor in deciding which Internet café to frequent. Also important is the availability of food and beverages at the Internet café (tables 5.6 and 5.7). The possibility of staying overnight with food and beverage service allows Internet addicts to indulge in gaming or other things at an Internet café.

Table 5.4
Predominant Place of Access of Internet Café Users and of Problematic Internet Users

	All users		Overusers and addicted	
Predominant Access Venue Used	#	%	#	%
No predominant place	82	8.4	11	6.4
Users with only one predominant access place				
Cybercafé	289	29.6	47	27.2
School	99	10.1	21	12.1
Home	130	13.3	18	10.4
Office	25	2.6	2	1.2
Friend's house	8			
Library	3			
Mobile phone	34	3.5	6	3.5
Other venue	1			
Subtotal	589	60.3	94	54.3
Users with two predominat places (only two)				
Cybercafé and home	28	2.9	8	4.6
Cybercafé and mobile	107	11.0	23	13.3
Cybercafé and school	9	0.9	5	2.9
Cybercafé and office	10	1.0	4	2.3
Cybercafé and friend's house	2			
Home and school	8	0.8	1	0.6
Home and office	11			
Home and friend's house				
Home and mobile	48	4.9	10	5.8
School and mobile	15	1.5	2	1.2
Other combinations of two predominant places	21			
Subtotal	259	26.5	53	30.6
Users with three or more predominant places	46	4.7	15	8.7
All users	976	100.0	173	100.0

Table 5.5
Demand Change According to Internet Café Price Change

Price Change	Self-reported Expected Demand Response	PIU Type Common (%)	Overuser (%)	Addicted (%)	Total (%)
Increase	Stop visiting	8.5	8.4	9.1	8.5
	Come less often	58.6	69.0	81.8	60.8
	No change	32.9	22.6	9.1	30.7
	All respondents	100.0	100.0	100.0	100.0
Decrease	No change	60.0	45.8	27.3	57.0
	Come more often	40.0	54.2	72.7	43.0
	All respondents	100.0	100.0	100.0	100.0

Table 5.6
Correlation of PIU Types with Café Features

Is This Vital When You Decide to Spend Money in a Café?

	Spearman's rho	Correlation Coefficient	Sig. (2-tailed)	N
1	Café environment	−.077*	.018	945
2	Internet speed	.010	.761	949
3	Computer hardware and software	.002	.954	932
4	Residency of respondent (rural/urban)	−.071*	.031	918
5	Price	.058	.078	926
6	Service attitude	−.026	.433	921
7	Safety	−.058	.080	908
8	Food and beverage service	.096**	.004	900
9	Possibility of staying overnight	.131**	.000	899

Conclusions and Policy Implications

Our survey results confirmed most of the existing literature and reports. However, interesting results relating to users' willingness to pay to use Internet cafés and the factors they considered most important in deciding which café to patronize drew our attention and suggest practical policy recommendations for regulating Internet cafés in China.

First, the addiction ratio of our sample is 2.2 percent, which is slightly lower than the 2.4 percent reported by Cao et al. (2007). The addicted group's demographic

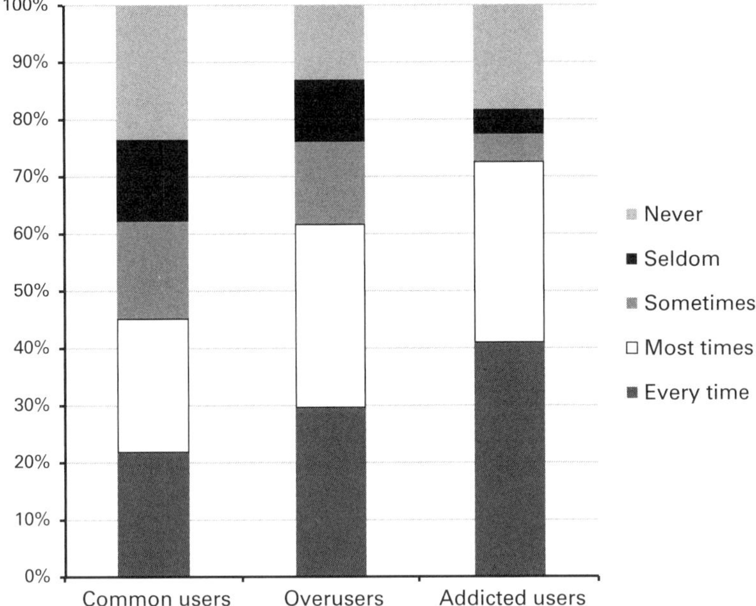

Figure 5.7
Frequency with which different PIU-type respondents play games when visiting cafés.

characteristics—young males—coincide with previous research and common media portrayals. However, our research reveals that rural residents are more likely to be addicts or overusers than urban residents. This may be because of a lack of diverse entertainment in rural areas or because some of the rural respondents are working in urban areas in places distant from their families.

Second, the addiction symptom is accompanied by intense Internet use and is associated with game playing. Internet-addicted people tend to visit more Internet cafés more frequently; they prefer cafés close to their home or workplace, and they tend to use various venues to access the Internet. They prefer Internet cafés that offer overnight services. Internet-addicted users are also more affected by decreases in Internet café fees—in other words, money is still a constraint for them to be more deeply immersed in the Internet.

What are the implications of our findings for Internet café regulation in China? On the one hand, opening more Internet cafés at low prices in remote areas may boost ICT penetration in currently underserved rural communities. On the other hand, cheap Internet café service and loose regulation may make it easier for users at risk of PIU to use the Internet in ways that harm them.

Table 5.7
Importance of Possibility of Staying Overnight and Food and Beverage Service, by PIU Type

		PIU Type					
		Common		Overuser		Addicted	
		#	%	#	%	#	%
Possibility of staying overnight	Not important at all	264	33	29	19	6	27
	Unimportant	47	6	13	8	–	–
	Less important	41	5	11	7	1	5
	Neutral	262	33	52	34	3	14
	Important	45	6	14	9	–	–
	Rather important	47	6	13	8	2	9
	Very important	93	12	23	15	10	45
Food and beverage service	Not important at all	176	22	27	17	3	14
	Unimportant	51	6	7	5	–	–
	Less important	63	8	8	5	1	5
	Neutral	267	33	56	36	6	27
	Important	68	9	17	11	1	5
	Rather important	70	9	16	10	1	5
	Very important	104	13	24	15	10	45

Two practical measures may be considered. One is to limit overnight service, a measure that has already been adopted by some local governments. Together with the restriction of overnight service, the provision of printing and other ICT support services (e.g., computer data storage) should also be allowed and even encouraged to promote greater instrumental use of Internet cafés. Another possible measure to explore is to encourage Internet café operators to change their pricing policy to offer lower rates to users who use fewer than three hours, which is what most common users do. Also, to encourage low-income and rural people to access the Internet without indulging in gaming, the government could offer them free coupons for two hours of Internet use a day.

Because of the complex situation of low Internet penetration and problematic Internet use by some users, it is difficult to design appropriate regulations governing Internet cafés. By understanding the situation and users' behavior, we can begin to develop policies that are more reasonable and effective.

Notes

1. Sample reports appear below. (Note: websites listed are in Chinese only.)

Parents advocate drawing a map of bad Internet cafés of Wu Han city.	Jing Chu web: Jing Tian Jin newspaper	http://hb.qq.com/a/20120223/001059.htm
Pupils indulged in Internet cafés; parents are nail-biting.	Shang Rao Night Press	http://www.srzc.com/news/srxw/a/2012/0215/183427.html
Parents abhor the gathering of adolescents at Internet cafés during winter vacation.	CNWEST	http://news.cnwest.com/content/2012-01/09/content_5829839.htm

2. Details of survey procedures and implementation are presented in chapter 4, appendix 4.A.
3. The definition of overuse in this chapter differs from the one used in chapter 4. Overuse is used here to identify *potential* persons at risk. Overuse in chapter 4 is a control independent variable in regressions and is defined as any user who responds "usually," "most times," or "sometimes" to five or more of Young's eight questions.

Overusers in present chapter (including addicts)	177
Regression overusers in chapter 4 (including addicts)	104
Coincidences	88
Users classified as overusers here but not in chapter 4 regressions	89
Users classified as overusers in previous chapter but not here	16

References

American Psychiatric Association. 1994. *Diagnostic and Statistical Manual of Mental Disorders*, 4th ed. Washington, DC: American Psychiatric Association.

Armstrong, Lynette, James G. Phillips, and Lauren L. Saling. 2000. Potential Determinants of Heavier Internet Usage. *International Journal of Human-Computer Studies* 53 (4): 537–550.

Beard, Keith W., and Eve M. Wolf. 2001. Modification in the Proposed Diagnostic Criteria for Internet Addiction. *Cyberpsychology & Behavior* 4: 377–383.

Billieux, Joël, and Martial Van der Linden. 2012. Problematic Use of the Internet and Self-Regulation: A Review of Early Studies. *The Open Addiction Journal* 5 (Suppl. 1: M4): 24–29.

Brenner, Viktor. 1997. Psychology of Computer Use: XLVII. Parameters of Internet Use, Abuse and Addiction: The First 90 Days of the Internet Usage Survey. *Psychological Reports* 80:879–882.

Cao, Fenglin, Su Linyan, Liu TieQiao, and Gao Xueping. 2007. The Relationship Between Impulsivity and Internet Addiction in a Sample of Chinese Adolescents. *European Psychiatry* 22: 466–471.

Chak, Katherine, and Louis Leung. 2004. Shyness and Locus of Control as Predictors of Internet Addiction and Internet Use. *Cyberpsychology & Behavior* 7 (5): 559–570.

Czincz, Jennifer, and Regina Hechanova. 2009. Internet Addiction: Debating the Diagnosis. *Journal of Technology in Human Services* 27 (4): 257–272.

Griffiths, Mark. 2000. Does Internet and Computer 'Addiction' Exist? Some Case Study Evidence. *Cyberpsychology & Behavior* 3 (2): 211–218.

Kim, Ki Soo, and Kyung Hee Kim. 2010. A Prediction Model for Internet Game Addiction in Adolescents: Using a Decision Tree Analysis. *Journal of Korean Academy of Nursing* 40 (3): 378–388.

Kim, Yeonsoo, Jin Young Park, Sung Byuk Kim, In-Kyung Jung, Yun Sook Lim, and Jung-Hyun Kim. 2010. The Effects of Internet Addiction on the Lifestyle and Dietary Behavior of Korean Adolescents. *Nutrition Research and Practice* 4 (1): 51–57.

Kubey, Robert W., Martin J. Lavin, and John R. Barrows. 2001. Internet Use and Collegiate Academic Performance Decrements: Early Findings. *Journal of Communication* 51 (2): 366–382.

Morahan-Martin, Janet, and Phyllis Schumacher. 2000. Incidence and Correlates of Pathological Internet Use Among College Students. *Computers in Human Behavior* 16 (1): 13–29.

Odaci, Hatice. 2011. Academic Self-Efficacy and Academic Procrastination as Predictors of Problematic Internet Use in University Students. *Computers & Education* 57 (1): 1109–1113.

Shapira, Nathan A., Mary C. Lessig, Toby D. Goldsmith, Steven T. Szabo, Martin Lazoritz, Mark S. Gold, and Dan J. Stein. 2003. Problematic Internet Use: Proposed Classification and Diagnostic Criteria. *Depression and Anxiety* 17 (4): 207–216.

Wang, Edward Shih-Tse, Shui Lian Chen Lily, Julia Ying-Chao Lin, and Michael Chih-Hung Wang. 2008. The Relationship Between Leisure Satisfaction and Life Satisfaction of Adolescents Concerning Online Games. *Adolescence* 43 (169): 177–184.

Wang, Hui, Xiolan Zhou, Ciyong Lu, Jie Wu, Xueqing Deng, and Lingyao Hong. 2011. Problematic Internet Use in High School Students in Guangdong Province, China. *PLoS ONE* 6 (5).

Whang, Leo Sang-Min, Sujin Lee, and Geunyoung Chang. 2003. Internet Over-Users' Psychological Profiles: A Behavior Sampling Analysis on Internet Addiction. *Cyberpsychology & Behavior* 6 (2): 143–150.

Young, Kimberly S. 1996. Psychology of Computer Use: XL. Addictive Use of the Internet: A Case That Breaks the Stereotype. *Psychological Reports* 79 (3): 899–902.

Young, Kimberly S. 1998. Internet Addiction: The Emergence of a New Clinical Disorder. *Cyberpsychology & Behavior* 1 (3): 237–244.

Young, Kimberly S. 2004. Internet Addiction: A New Clinical Phenomenon and Its Consequences. *American Behavioral Scientist* 48 (4): 402–415.

6 The Contribution of Five *Télécentres Communautaires Polyvalents* to Cameroon's Rural Secondary Education

Sylvie Siyam Siwe, Laurent Aristide Eyinga Eyinga, Avis Momeni, Olga Balbine Tsafack Nguekeng, Abiodun Jagun, Ramata Molo Thioune, and Francisco J. Proenza

Abstract

In a bid to address weaknesses in its education system, in 2005 the Government of Cameroon adopted a strategy that introduced information technology into the school curriculum and established multipurpose community telecenters (*télécentres communautaires polyvalents* [TCPs]) to help overcome shortcomings such as a lack of educational materials in rural communities. In this study, we examine the self-reported academic performance of secondary school students interviewed in five of the thirty-four TCPs set up to date. We find that students who study hard and are motivated to learn generally acquire Internet skills in the TCPs. Among mid- and upper secondary students, the evidence further suggests that, beyond study effort, having access to the Internet gives students a performance edge. Nevertheless, being motivated to learn and spending long hours studying remain keys to academic success and outweigh any advantage that access to the Internet or computers may confer. Furthermore, there is some evidence suggesting that spending too much time at a TCP may thwart academic achievement. The government is to be commended for taking the initiative, but it is disappointing that so few TCPs have managed to fully function over a sustained period of time.

Introduction

Cameroon has a population of about 20 million people, of whom 47 percent live in rural areas. The country ranked 150th in human development in United Nations Development Program's (2013) *Human Development Report 2012*. About 40 percent of the population falls below the national poverty line (United Nations Development Program 2013).

The main weaknesses of the country's educational system are unequal access to education for girls and the poor, substandard learning and working conditions, inadequate distribution of teachers, and a shortage of textbooks and essential materials (Comité Technique d'Élaboration de la Stratégie Sectorielle de l'Éducation 2006). A major thrust of the education sector strategy is to "improve the quality and relevance of education provided" (Comité Technique d'Élaboration de la Stratégie Sectorielle de l'Éducation 2006, p. 92) by, among other initiatives, promoting access to modern information and communication technology (ICT) within the school system.

This strategy will be difficult to implement. Mobile cellular teledensity has been rising fast, reaching 60 percent in 2012, but only about 4 percent of the population uses the Internet (International Telecommunications Union 2012). ICT services are still relatively expensive and virtually inaccessible in rural areas. Most students complain of not having access to a computer despite having computer courses in their program. In 2011, only about 7.4 percent of all households had computers (International Telecommunications Union 2012), and this proportion is much lower in rural communities.

The government has sought to improve people's access to telecommunications services and the Internet, in part, through a program to set up multi-purpose community telecenters (TCPs) in rural areas (Ministry of Posts and Telecommunications 2005).[1] To date, thirty-four TCPs have been established (Ministry of Posts and Telecommunications 2008).

According to the program manager at Ministry of Posts and Telecommunications (MINPOSTEL), TCPs could help improve the performance of teachers by providing access to digital resources and allowing exchanges with other institutions around the world. The professional literature supports this view (Karsenti et al. 2005; Laferrière 1999; Lebrun 2007) and suggests that Internet access can broaden the range of subject and course materials available to students and teachers. This can be especially important for rural schools. According to Tchamabe (2009), a TCP may impart efficiency to an educational system by enhancing learning experiences, facilitating the acquisition of basic skills, and building the capacity of teachers.

In practice, learners use ICT to review lessons, access tests of other institutions and those of previous years, and prepare presentations (Tchamabe 2009). Perreault (2003) found that sharing of educational materials through websites and intranets was commonplace among students. Van Oel's (2007) study of schools in twenty-five European countries observed positive impacts on group and collaborative work, hours of study after school, creativity, interpersonal skills, innovation, motivation, and self-confidence. Desgent and Forcier (2004) also note that ICT has helped significantly to increase the proportion of girls who pass their courses.

The impact of ICT on educational outcomes is difficult to demonstrate (van Oel 2007) because it is not easy to isolate the impact of technology from that of other factors. Having access to ICT in schools does not automatically ensure a positive impact on student performance (Attenoukon 2011), and perceptions of impact are unlikely to be uniform among teachers or students, nor will they be unaffected by differences in context.

To our knowledge, no previous study has tried to assess the impact of computers and the Internet, accessible through Cameroon's TCPs, on the academic performance of rural secondary students. This study seeks to help fill this gap.

Methodology

Selection of the TCPs

Our first task was to select suitable centers. To be able to detect impacts on education, a TCP had to have: (1) reliable Internet access; (2) reliable equipment and energy supply; (3) been in operation for at least three years; (4) a significant number of students and teachers as customers (or, as a proxy indicator, a large proportion of young people age 25 or less as customers); and (5) initiatives in place to support education, with some services specifically designed for students and teachers.

Among Cameroon's thirty-four functional TCPs, only eighteen were found to have access to the Internet. Equipment rollout follows a stepwise progression, and connection to the Internet through Very Small Aperture Terminal (VSAT) or fiber optics by Cameroon Telecommunications (CAMTEL) is usually the last step. The managers of the eighteen TCPs that had connectivity were invited to a focus group meeting. Eleven responded and, of these, five reported experiencing frequent power cuts lasting longer than three days. (A sixth center was removed from the list because it had been in operation less than three years.) Thus, of Cameroon's thirty-four TCPs in place, only five—Bangang, Ambam, Makenene, Bankim, and Jakiri[2]—met the five criteria deemed essential for the conduct of this study (table 6.1).

Data Collection

Complete data on 1,015 students were collected over a one-month period (November 8 to December 8, 2010).[3] All secondary school students using each of the TCPs during this period were surveyed. All respondents agreed to cooperate. The interviewers chosen were local residents and employees of the TCP who were known to the respondents, which facilitated data collection.

The student questionnaire gathered basic demographic information about each student's school performance in the past three years, their level of computer and Internet literacy and previous training, the frequency of visits and activities engaged in while visiting the TCP, basic demographic features and school-related variables, and a final

Table 6.1
Basic Features of Five TCPs Studied, as Assessed during Selection and Subsequently Verified during Field Research

	TCP1	TCP2	TCP3	TCP4	TCP5
Year established	2006	2005	2005	2006	2005
% of users ≤ 25 years	55%	75%	65%	75%	55%
Education services	Training contract with school	Training	Training	Training	Training
Number of computers	10	9	4	6	10
Functionality of computers[a]	63%	100%	100%	45%	63%
Energy availability[b]	–	79%	93%	67%	93%
Internet connection[c]	[d]	Good	Good	Good	Fair

[a]Computers in operation as % of computers installed.
[b]Days with power as % of days the center is open for service.
[c]Possible grades: None, Poor, Acceptable, Fair, Good.
[d]TCP1 is connected through fiber optics. Its Internet connection was not functioning when our survey was conducted but was restored a few days later.

section on personal objectives and direct inquiries regarding the perceived impact of the TCP.

Cameroon's official languages are English and French, the latter being more widely used. The majority of students in the sample (750) are taught in French, but some, especially those interviewed in Jakiri, are taught in English (150) and some in bilingual schools (114). Survey interviews were conducted in French at Bangang, Ambam, Makenene, and Bankim, and in English at Jakiri.

Self-Assessed Performance, Hours of Study, and Student Motivation

Students were asked to assess whether their academic achievement over the past three years had declined, remained stable, or improved. This is not an objective measure of school performance: it is a self-assessment requiring memory recall over a three-year period and is subject to error. The student's response may also be biased toward his or her most recent school performance experience (i.e., over the last year as opposed to over the past three years) and tends to have an upward optimistic bias (Pearson, Ross, and Dawes 1992).

In practice, student responses may have an overall upward bias. Only about 13 percent estimated their three-year performance as declining, about half (53 percent) as stable, and about a third as improving. With slight variations, this pattern holds regardless of education level or gender (table 6.2).

Table 6.2
Self-assessed Academic Performance in Last 3 Years, by Gender and School Level

	Male		Female		All Students	
School Level	#	%	#	%	#	%
Lower level						
Falling	16	8.0	24	13.6	40	10.6
Stable	121	60.5	101	57.4	222	59.0
Rising	63	31.5	51	29.0	114	30.3
Subtotal	200	100.0	176	100.0	376	100.0
Mid-level						
Falling	42	16.9	26	14.7	68	16.0
Stable	121	48.8	84	47.5	205	48.2
Rising	85	34.3	67	37.9	152	35.8
Subtotal	248	100.0	177	100.0	425	100.0
Upper level						
Falling	13	11.4	10	10.0	23	10.7
Stable	55	48.2	57	57.0	112	52.3
Rising	46	40.4	33	33.0	79	36.9
Subtotal	114	100.0	100	100.0	214	100.0
All secondary						
Falling	71	12.6	60	13.2	131	12.9
Stable	297	52.8	242	53.4	539	53.1
Rising	194	34.5	151	33.3	345	34.0
All	562	100.0	453	100.0	1015	100.0
%	55.4		44.6		100.0	

To assess, indirectly, the reliability of the school performance measure, we examined its correlation with two variables known to be positively correlated with school performance: the student's motivation (Broussard 2002; Fyans and Maehr 1987; Zimmerman 1990) and hours of study (Duckworth and Seligman 2005; Stinebrickner and Stinebrickner 2007).

Although an imperfect measure, self-assessments of school performance over the past three years appear to reflect the school performance of the students in our sample fairly accurately. When students were asked whether "acquiring knowledge to succeed in school" was one of their goals, nearly all (979) said yes. When they were next asked to rate the importance they attached to this goal, their responses were more telling: 44 percent marked "very," 32 percent "medium," and 1.5 percent "weak." Table 6.3 shows the number of students who identified acquiring knowledge to succeed in school as a

Table 6.3
Self-assessed Academic Performance in Last 3 Years, by Gender, School Level, and Whether "Acquiring Knowledge to Succeed in School" Is a Very Important Goal

	Male		Female		All Students	
School Level	#	% Yes	#	% Yes	#	% Yes
Lower level						
Falling	9	56.3	15	62.5	24	60.0
Stable	70	57.9	63	62.4	133	59.9
Rising	40	63.5	37	72.5	77	67.5
Subtotal	119	59.5	115	65.3	234	62.2
Mid-level						
Falling	22	52.4	12	46.2	34	50.0
Stable	73	60.3	50	59.5	123	60.0
Rising	62	72.9	56	83.6	118	77.6
Subtotal	157	63.3	118	66.7	275	64.7
Upper level						
Falling	8	61.5	4	40.0	12	52.2
Stable	27	49.1	25	43.9	52	46.4
Rising	33	71.7	30	90.9	63	79.7
Subtotal	68	59.6	59	59.0	127	59.3
All levels						
Falling	39	54.9	31	51.7	70	53.4
Stable	170	57.2	138	57.0	308	57.1
Rising	135	69.6	123	81.5	258	74.8
All students	344	61.2	292	64.5	636	62.7

very important goal, distributed according to their self-assessment of performance. Considering the three secondary school levels jointly, students who identified "acquiring knowledge…" as a very important goal represent 53 percent of those with falling performance, 57 percent with stable performance, and 75 percent with rising performance. This correlation holds for both genders and for the three secondary school levels considered.

Hours of study are also positively correlated with self-performance assessments in our sample. For every school level, and for males and females alike, those with a "rising" performance rating also reported spending the most time studying outside the classroom, while those who self-reported "falling" performance studied the least (table 6.4).

Table 6.4
Hours of Study per Week by Gender, School Level, and Self-Assessed Academic Performance in Last 3 Years

	Male			Female			All Students		
School Level	% < 3	% 3–5	% ≥ 5	% < 3	% 3–5	% ≥ 5	% < 3	% 3–5	% ≥ 5
Lower level									
Falling	62.5	18.8	18.8	37.5	29.2	33.3	47.5	25.0	27.5
Stable	24.8	47.9	27.3	26.7	39.6	33.7	25.7	44.1	30.2
Rising	27.0	31.7	41.3	21.6	31.4	47.1	24.6	31.6	43.9
Mid-level									
Falling	31.0	52.4	16.7	38.5	53.8	7.7	33.8	52.9	13.2
Stable	10.7	61.2	27.3	22.6	42.9	34.5	15.6	53.7	30.2
Rising	8.2	45.9	45.9	11.9	32.8	55.2	9.9	40.1	50.0
Upper level									
Falling	23.1	38.5	38.5	20.0	60.0	20.0	21.7	47.8	30.4
Stable	7.3	52.7	40.0	14.0	66.7	17.5	10.7	59.8	28.6
Rising	0.0	50.0	50.0	0.0	51.5	48.5	0.0	50.6	49.4
All levels									
Falling	36.6	42.3	21.1	35.0	45.0	20.0	35.9	43.5	20.6
Stable	15.8	54.2	29.6	22.3	47.1	30.2	18.7	51.0	29.9
Rising	12.4	42.3	45.4	12.6	36.4	51.0	12.5	39.7	47.8

Findings

The TCPs

The five TCPs chosen for study are located in Bangang, Ambam, Makenene, Bankim, and Jakiri. At all five sites, the TCP is the only point of access to the Internet. The TCPs are located in rural areas, generally in the regional urban center or the administrative seat of local government. Two are located in the local post office. Each TCP is equipped with telephones (two to five), copiers (one or two), fax machine (one), computers (four to ten), modem (one), VCR (one), printers (two to four), and scanners (one or two), and has enough hardware to meet the needs of (student) users. Installed software programs, free or proprietary, are mainly word processing, spreadsheets, and, to a lesser extent, translation software. The TCP typically offers the following services: training in the use of computers and the Internet, telephony, office stationery, faxing, photocopying, and video editing. A summary profile of each TCP is given in table 6.1.

TCP management is under the control of a management committee—usually chaired by the mayor and comprising an administrative authority, a representative of the decentralized government services, a traditional authority, and a representative of the civil society—that is responsible for setting prices for services, analyzing and adopting the annual action plan proposed by the manager, and monitoring and controlling the management of the TCP. This committee reports to the MINPOSTEL. TCP managers are relatively young (27–44 years old) men or women who hold at least a *baccalauréat* (final secondary education degree) and have received government training in TCP management.

The average number of customers varies from twenty to thirty per day and is constantly increasing, particularly in response to communication campaigns organized by managers. Users ages 25 and under represent at least 55 percent of TCP clients.

The computers in the five TCPs studied were in good working order at the time of our survey. Basic maintenance is provided by managers; for major breakdowns, the TCPs rely on experts from out of town. Operational challenges faced by TCP managers include lack of local service support, connectivity problems, equipment failure, and frequent power cuts.

TCP Student User Profile

Of our total sample, 55 percent are males and 45 percent are females. The gender distribution across the five TCPs is fairly even, except in TCP3 (where males account for two-thirds of interviewees) and, to a lesser extent, TCP5 (table 6.5). All ages from 10 years old up are represented, but two-thirds of the sample are 16 or older (table 6.6), and fewer than 4 percent are younger than 12.

Cameroon's secondary education lasts about seven years and may be divided into three stages: lower level (four or five years) leading to the BECP/CAP exam, mid-level (after the BEPC/CAP) and leading to the *Probatoire* exam; and upper level, when students have obtained the *Probatoire* diploma and are in their final year of secondary school.[4] Generally, fewer students are found in the upper level, which lasts only about a year. In our sample, one in five students is in this group; the majority is in the mid (42 percent) and lower (37 percent) levels (table 6.6). There are, however, more lower than middle secondary students in TCPs 1, 2, and 4, whereas the reverse is true in TCPs 3 and 5 (table 6.5).

The most striking differences are in the digital skills of interviewees. Ninety-nine percent of the students in TCP2 were computer literate, and 92 percent had Internet skills. At the other extreme, in TCP3, which has only four computers (table 6.1), only 29 percent of the students were computer literate, and only 25 percent had Internet skills.

Table 6.5
Distribution of Students Interviewed, by Center, School Level, Three-Year Self-Assessed Performance, and Computer Literacy

	TCP1		TCP2		TCP3		TCP4		TCP5		All TCPs	
School Level	#	%	#	%	#	%	#	%	#	%	#	%
Gender												
Male	102	51.3	91	46.4	144	67.6	102	51.3	123	59.1	562	55.4
Female	97	48.7	105	53.6	69	32.4	97	48.7	85	40.9	453	44.6
Age												
< 12	4	2.0	4	2.0	4	1.9	15	7.5	10	4.8	37	3.6
12–15	63	31.7	60	30.6	77	36.2	51	25.6	44	21.2	295	29.1
≥ 16	130	65.3	129	65.8	132	62.0	134	67.3	153	73.6	678	66.8
Secondary school level												
Lower	87	43.7	117	59.7	57	26.8	78	39.2	37	17.8	376	37.0
Mid	65	32.7	76	38.8	115	54.0	73	36.7	96	46.2	425	41.9
Upper	47	23.6	3	1.5	41	19.2	48	24.1	75	36.1	214	21.1
School performance												
Falling	32	16.1	16	8.2	22	10.3	19	9.5	42	20.2	131	12.9
Stable	131	65.8	95	48.5	120	56.3	103	51.8	90	43.3	539	53.1
Rising	36	18.1	85	43.4	71	33.3	77	38.7	76	36.5	345	34.0
Computer literacy	122	61.3	194	99.0	61	28.6	175	87.9	150	72.1	702	69.2
Home computer	56	28.1	57	29.1	47	22.1	45	22.6	56	26.9	261	25.7
Internet skills	75	37.7	181	92.3	53	24.9	121	60.8	123	59.1	553	54.5
Interviewees	199		196		213		199		208		1015	

Table 6.6
Distribution of Students, by School Level, Age, and Gender

	Male		Female		All Students	
Age	#	%	#	%	#	%
Lower level						
< 12	21	10.5	14	8.0	35	9.3
12–15	94	47.0	89	50.6	183	48.7
≥ 16	85	42.5	73	41.5	158	42.0
Subtotal	200	100.0	176	100.0	376	100.0
Mid-level						
< 12	2	0.8	–	–	2	0.5
12–15	65	26.2	39	22.0	104	24.5
≥ 16	181	73.0	138	78.0	319	75.1
Subtotal	248	100.0	177	100.0	425	100.0
Upper level						
< 12	–	–	–	–	–	–
12–15	4	3.5	5	5.0	9	4.2
≥ 16	110	96.5	95	95.0	205	95.8
Subtotal	114	100.0	100	100.0	214	100.0
All secondary by school level						
Lower level	200	35.6	176	38.9	376	37.0
Mid-level	248	44.1	177	39.1	425	41.9
Upper level	114	20.3	100	22.1	214	21.1
All secondary by age						
< 12	23	4.1	14	3.1	37	3.6
12–15	163	29.0	133	29.4	296	29.2
≥ 16	376	66.9	306	67.5	682	67.2
All	562	100.0	453	100.0	1015	100.0
%	55.4		44.6		100.0	

Notes: Lower level: Lower than or equal to BEPC/CAP. Mid-level: Between BEPC/CAP and *Probatoire*/BP. Upper level: *Probatoire*/BP or higher.

Have TCPs Helped Students Improve Their School Performance?

TCPs appear to have helped some students improve their school performance. A larger proportion of rising performers than stable performers access the Internet and make use of word processing, view and download textbooks, and prepare schoolwork; and a greater proportion of stable performers carry out these activities compared with falling performers. TCPs have also helped a greater proportion of rising performers become more confident and better informed than is the case for the other two groups (table 6.7).

Students were also asked to identify, from among four options, the primary means they use to improve their school performance: the TCP, studying in groups, approaching and working with teachers, and consulting books (table 6.8). The most popular response (40 percent) was approaching and working with teachers. The TCP was ranked second and chosen by 28 percent of the students. Studying in groups and consulting books tied for third place and were chosen in each case by 15 percent of the students.

Table 6.7
Most Popular Activities and School-Related Activities of Students, by Self-Assessed School Performance

	Falling	Stable	Rising
	131	539	345
Number in Group	%	%	%
Most popular TCP activities[a]			
Photocopying	64.9	68.1	77.1
Internet access	40.5	46.8	63.2
Word processing	35.9	34.0	41.7
Printing	28.2	29.9	31.3
Telephone	26.0	27.1	28.7
School-related activities[b]			
Viewing/getting textbooks	20.6	24.9	34.2
Preparing for exams, homework, etc.	67.2	68.3	76.2
Communicating with teachers	10.3	13.0	8.3
Has the TCP helped you become:			
More confident?	51.1	60.9	71.0
Better informed?	58.0	70.1	78.0

[a]Each student was asked to select three TCP activities (see full list in table 6.8).
[b]School-related activities students engage in when visiting the TCP.

Table 6.8
TCP Use by Secondary Students—All Performance Levels

	Male	562	Female	453	All	1015
TCP Use	#	%	#	%	# obs.	%
Are you computer literate?	372	66.2	330	72.8	486	47.9
Do you have a computer at home?	162	28.8	99	21.9	261	25.7
Do you know how to use the Internet?	301	53.6	252	55.6	553	54.5
How often do you visit the TCP?						
Once a week	361	64.2	310	68.4	671	66.1
Two or three times a week	158	28.1	107	23.6	265	26.1
More than three times a week	29	5.2	28	6.2	57	5.6
How long do you stay when you visit the TCP?						
At most one hour per day	345	61.4	286	63.1	631	62.2
Two to three hours per day	172	30.6	126	27.8	298	29.4
More than three hours per day	43	7.7	41	9.1	84	8.3
Services most frequently used[a]						
Telephone	133	23.7	146	32.2	279	27.5
Telecopy/fax	15	2.7	10	2.2	25	2.5
Internet access	290	51.6	233	51.4	523	51.5
Payment services	7	1.2	5	1.1	12	1.2
Photocopying	395	70.3	323	71.3	718	70.7
Word processing	228	40.6	146	32.2	374	36.8
Data processing	64	11.4	30	6.6	94	9.3
Printing	178	31.7	128	28.3	306	30.1
Money transfer	9	1.6	5	1.1	14	1.4
Onsite training	14	2.5	12	2.6	26	2.6
Search for jobs or internships	14	2.5	10	2.2	24	2.4
Distance learning	10	1.8	3	0.7	13	1.3
Cultural events	6	1.1	6	1.3	12	1.2
Space rentals	2	0.4	2	0.4	4	0.4
School-related activities most frequently engaged in when using Internet at TCP[b]						
View/get textbooks	153	27.2	126	27.8	279	27.5
Pay the school	6	1.1	11	2.4	17	1.7
Communicate with teachers	33	5.9	27	6.0	60	5.9
Prepare for exams, presentations, and homework	396	70.5	323	71.3	719	70.8
Learn foreign languages and cultures	100	17.8	66	14.6	166	16.4

Table 6.8 (continued)

TCP Use	Male #	562 %	Female #	453 %	All # obs.	1015 %
Register abroad	13	2.3	11	2.4	24	2.4
Other	96	17.1	75	16.6	171	16.8
Has the TCP helped you become more self-confident?	357	63.5	283	62.5	640	63.1
Has the TCP helped you become better informed?	400	71.2	323	71.3	723	71.2
What is the primary means by which you try to improve your school performance?						
The TCP	140	24.9	150	33.1	290	28.6
Studying in groups	96	17.1	58	12.8	154	15.2
Approaching & working with teachers	247	44.0	163	36.0	410	40.4
Consulting books	74	13.2	79	17.4	153	15.1
Other	5	0.9	3	0.7	8	0.8

[a]Students were asked to list the three services they used most frequently.
[b]Students were asked to list their three most frequent school-related activities.

Training in Computer and Internet Use Nearly 60 percent of all students learn how to use computers at school (table 6.9). TCPs provide an important complementary computer training service, especially if we consider those who learn from TCP organized training (17 percent) and those who teach themselves how to use computers while visiting the TCP (11 percent). TCP organized training is for a fee. Some students learn computers at private institutions, probably while on vacation visiting city relatives. Home training is nonexistent.

Because TCPs are the only place of Internet connection in many localities, they play a critical role in teaching students to use the Internet (table 6.10). TCP-provided training and self-training at the TCP, respectively, account for 51 percent and 17 percent of students who have Internet skills. Private training institutions play a secondary but important training role (19 percent), particularly for older female students. According to TCP managers, this training probably takes place during school holidays in private institutions located in other cities. A few local schools apparently also provide some Internet training to older students (6 percent).

Computer Skills and School Performance Three-quarters of secondary students have computer skills, and nearly two-thirds (63 percent) know how to use the Internet. Nearly

Table 6.9

Computer Literate Students, by Age, Gender, and Venue or Way They Learned to Use Computers

	Male		Female		All Students	
Age	#	%	#	%	#	%
Computer literate < 12 with full data						
School	9	47.4	5	55.6	14	50.0
Private institution	4	21.1	–	–	4	14.3
TCP	4	21.1	1	11.1	5	17.9
Self-taught	–	–	1	11.1	1	3.6
Home	–	–	–	–	–	–
Other	2	10.5	2	22.2	4	14.3
Subtotal	19	100.0	9	100.0	28	100.0
Computer literate 12–15 with full data						
School	51	54.8	52	55.9	103	55.4
Private institution	10	10.8	13	14.0	23	12.4
TCP	14	15.1	19	20.4	33	17.7
Self-taught	18	19.4	9	9.7	27	14.5
Home	–	–	–	–	–	–
Other	–	–	–	–	–	–
Subtotal	93	100.0	93	100.0	186	100.0
Computer literate ≥ 16 with full data						
School	149	57.3	134	58.8	283	58.0
Private institution	30	11.5	29	12.7	59	12.1
TCP	42	16.2	42	18.4	84	17.2
Self-taught	33	12.7	14	6.1	47	9.6
Home	–	–	–	–	–	–
Other	6	2.3	9	3.9	15	3.1
Subtotal	260	100.0	228	100.0	488	100.0
All ages (with data)						
School	209	56.2	191	57.9	400	57.0
Private institution	44	11.8	42	12.7	86	12.3
TCP	60	16.1	62	18.8	122	17.4
Self-taught	51	13.7	24	7.3	75	10.7
Home	–	–	–	–	–	–
Other	8	2.2	11	3.3	19	2.7
Subtotal	372	100.0	330	100.0	702	100.0

Table 6.10
Students Who Know How to Use the Internet, by Age, Gender, and Venue or Way They Learned to Use It

	Male		Female		All Students	
Age	#	%	#	%	#	%
Know Internet < 12 with full data						
School	–	–	–	–	–	–
Private institution	–	–	–	–	–	–
TCP	5	50.0	5	100.0	10	66.7
Self-taught	5	50.0	–	–	5	33.3
Home	–	–	–	–	–	–
Other	–	–	–	–	–	–
Subtotal	10	100.0	5	100.0	15	100.0
Know Internet 12–15 with full data						
School	8	11.6	4	5.9	12	8.8
Private institution	10	14.5	16	23.5	26	19.0
TCP	38	55.1	37	54.4	75	54.7
Self-taught	10	14.5	9	13.2	19	13.9
Home	–	–	–	–	–	–
Other	3	4.3	2	2.9	5	3.6
Subtotal	69	100.0	68	100.0	137	100.0
Know Internet ≥ 16 with full data						
School	14	6.3	10	5.6	24	6.0
Private institution	32	14.4	46	25.7	78	19.5
TCP	109	49.1	89	49.7	198	49.4
Self-taught	52	23.4	21	11.7	73	18.2
Home	–	–	–	–	–	–
Other	15	6.8	13	7.3	28	7.0
Subtotal	222	100.0	179	100.0	401	100.0
All ages						
School	22	7.3	14	5.6	36	6.5
Private institution	42	14.0	62	24.6	104	18.8
TCP	152	50.5	131	52.0	283	51.2
Self-taught	67	22.3	30	11.9	97	17.5
Home	–	–	–	–	–	–
Other	18	6.0	15	6.0	33	6.0
Subtotal	301	100.0	252	100.0	553	100.0
%	54.4		45.6		100.0	

one-third (28 percent) of the students interviewed have computers at home.[5] Tables 6.11 and 6.12 show the differences in self-assessed school performance depending on whether the respondents had computers and Internet skills. A higher proportion of students with rising performance had computer skills (75 percent) than did those with stable (66 percent) or falling (66 percent) performance.

Computer skills are practically a requirement for Internet use. Of the 553 students who said they had computer skills, 96 percent indicated they also knew how to use the Internet.

Better-Performing, Hard-Working Students Use the Internet for School Purposes

A greater proportion of rising performers, i.e., 63 percent, use the Internet access service provided by the TCP, compared to only 47 percent of stable and 41 percent of falling

Table 6.11

Self-assessed Academic Performance in Last 3 Years, by Gender, School Level, and Whether Student Is Computer Literate

	Male		Female		All Students	
School Level	#	% Yes	#	% Yes	#	% Yes
Lower level						
Falling	11	68.8	14	58.3	25	62.5
Stable	79	65.3	80	79.2	159	71.6
Rising	43	68.3	38	74.5	81	71.1
Subtotal	133	66.5	132	75.0	265	70.5
Mid-level						
Falling	26	61.9	17	65.4	43	63.2
Stable	67	55.4	57	67.9	124	60.5
Rising	63	74.1	50	74.6	113	74.3
Subtotal	156	62.9	124	70.1	280	65.9
Upper level						
Falling	10	76.9	8	80.0	18	78.3
Stable	35	63.6	40	70.2	75	67.0
Rising	38	82.6	26	78.8	64	81.0
Subtotal	83	72.8	74	74.0	157	73.4
All school levels						
Falling	47	66.2	39	65.0	86	65.6
Stable	181	60.9	177	73.1	358	66.4
Rising	144	74.2	114	75.5	258	74.8
All students	372	66.2	330	72.8	702	69.2

performers. A higher proportion of students with rising performance had Internet skills (63 percent) than did stable performers (51 percent; table 6.12), and the latter proportion is higher than among students with falling performance (44 percent). This performance advantage is more pronounced at the mid and upper secondary school levels (table 6.12).

Use of the Internet seems to account for the performance difference. Except for activities that do not require use of the Internet, such as word processing, printing, and photocopying, a larger proportion of students with Internet skills than those without use the TCPs for school-related activities. The TCPs also seem to help students overcome the scarcity of textbooks that is common in Cameroon's rural communities (table 6.13).

About 40 percent of students who know how to use the Internet go to TCPs to view or download school-related materials (table 6.14).

Students who lack Internet skills visit TCPs less frequently, and their visits are shorter. Few of them access the Internet (24 percent) compared with students who are comfortable with the technology (75 percent; table 6.13).

Students who do not know how to use the Internet may have a stellar academic record, and those who are familiar with the technology can falter, but the Internet does seem to give students an edge. Rising performers account for 39 percent of those who know the technology but only 28 percent of those who do not (table 6.15). This correlation between rising performance and Internet skills was observed in four of the five TCPs studied. The exception is TCP1, where the proportion of rising performers among users who have Internet skills is only 14.7 percent, compared with 20.2 percent among those who do not. Notice that TCP1 has relatively few rising performers—only 18 percent—compared with 34 to 43 percent for the other four TCPs.

Knowing how to use the Internet is also correlated with the amount of time students spend studying after school (table 6.16). Among students who spend less than three hours a day studying, the proportion who is Internet savvy is 27 percent, compared with 50 percent among those who study three to five hours and 76 percent among those who study more than five hours a day. This correlation holds for all effort and secondary school levels.

Is There an Internet Advantage? Does knowing how to use the Internet confer a school performance advantage beyond the effect of a student's study effort?

To test this hypothesis, we estimated separate models, one for each of the three secondary school levels. Our focus is on the probability that a student is a rising performer, a dichotomous dependent variable that takes a value of 1 if the student self-assessed his

Table 6.12

Self-Assessed Academic Performance, by Gender, School Level, and Whether Student Knows How to Use the Internet

School Level & Performance Group	Male			Female			All Students		
	Do Not Know	Know How to Use	% who know	Do Not Know	Know How to Use	% Who Know	Do Not Know	Know How to Use	% Who Know
Lower level									
Falling	11	5	31.3	17	7	29.2	28	12	30.0
Stable	59	62	51.2	42	59	58.4	101	121	54.5
Rising	33	30	47.6	24	27	52.9	57	57	50.0
Subtotal	103	97	48.5	83	93	52.8	186	190	50.5
Mid-level									
Falling	21	21	50.0	15	11	42.3	36	32	47.1
Stable	73	48	39.7	42	42	50.0	115	90	43.9
Rising	29	56	65.9	24	43	64.2	53	99	65.1
Subtotal	123	125	50.4	81	96	54.2	204	221	52.0
Upper level									
Falling	6	7	53.8	3	7	70.0	9	14	60.9
Stable	22	33	60.0	24	33	57.9	46	66	58.9
Rising	7	39	84.8	10	23	69.7	17	62	78.5
Subtotal	35	79	69.3	37	63	63.0	72	142	66.4
All school levels									
Falling	38	33	46.5	35	25	41.7	73	58	44.3
Stable	154	143	48.1	108	134	55.4	262	277	51.4
Rising	69	125	64.4	58	93	61.6	127	218	63.2
All students	261	301	53.6	201	252	55.6	462	553	54.5

Table 6.13
Popular Activities and School-Related Activities and TCP Effect on Confidence, by Whether Student Knows How to Use the Internet

	Knows How to Use Internet?	
	Yes	No
Number in Group	553	462
Most popular TCP activities[a]		
Photocopying	50	69
Internet access	75	24
Word processing	31	44
Printing	20	42
Telephone	33	21
School-related activities[b]		
View/get textbooks	40	12
Prepare for exams, homework, etc.	84	55
Communicate with teachers	8	3
Has the TCP helped you become:		
More confident?	83	40
Better informed?	90	49

[a]Students were asked to select the three activities they engaged in most frequently when visiting the TCP.
[b]School-related activities students engaged in when visiting the TCP.

or her performance as rising, and zero otherwise. We posit that this probability may be determined by a student's gender, age, motivation (i.e., whether the student considers learning a very important goal), computer skills, Internet skills, hours of study, and hours of TCP use. The substantial differences in academic requirements justify separate models by secondary school level, and we include four dummy variables in each model to capture differences from attending one or another venue. The results are presented in tables 6.17a through 6.17c.

Gender has no apparent effect on the probability of rising performance at any level. Age also does not make much difference, except at the lower level. Perhaps being a student 16 years or older at this level reflects performance limitations that are not otherwise captured.

Attending a particular TCP makes a positive and significant difference for lower level students interviewed in TCP5 and for mid-level students interviewed in TCP3 and TCP4. Underlying these differences are localized factors about which we have little information.

Table 6.14
TCP Use for School Purposes, According to Whether Student Knows How to Use the Internet, and Self-Assessed Performance in Past Three Years—All Secondary Levels

Performance and Response Options to: "What are the school-related activities you engage in when using the TCP?"	Knows How to Use Internet?					
	Yes		No		All Students	
	#	%	#	%	#	%
Falling	58	100.0	73	100.0	131	100.0
View/get textbooks	24	41.4	3	4.1	27	20.6
Communicate with teachers	4	6.9	2	2.7	6	4.6
Prepare for exams, presentations, and homework	48	82.8	40	54.8	88	67.2
Learn foreign language and cultures	20	34.5	2	2.7	22	16.8
Stable	277	100.0	262	100.0	539	100.0
View/get textbooks	98	35.4	36	13.7	134	24.9
Communicate with teachers	28	10.1	8	3.1	36	6.7
Prepare for exams, presentations, and homework	225	81.2	143	54.6	368	68.3
Learn foreign language and cultures	73	26.4	7	2.7	80	14.8
Rising	218	100.0	127	100.0	345	100.0
View/get textbooks	100	45.9	18	14.2	118	34.2
Communicate with teachers	14	6.4	4	3.1	18	5.2
Prepare for exams, presentations, and homework	193	88.5	70	55.1	263	76.2
Learn foreign language and cultures	61	28.0	3	2.4	64	18.6
All performance levels	553	100.0	462	100.0	1015	100.0
View/get textbooks	222	40.1	57	12.3	279	27.5
Communicate with teachers	46	8.3	14	3.0	60	5.9
Prepare for exams, presentations, and homework	466	84.3	253	54.8	719	70.8
Learn foreign language and cultures	154	27.8	12	2.6	166	16.4

A clear determinant of rising school performance is the number of hours a student spends studying outside the classroom. The corresponding coefficient is statistically significant in all three models. Another important factor is being motivated to learn, with statistically significant coefficients in the mid- and upper level models.

Knowing how to use computers has a positive sign in all three models, but is not statistically significant perhaps because of insufficient variability within the sample.

Having Internet skills makes a statistically significant difference in the mid- and upper level models. In the lower level, such skills seem to produce a negative effect,

Table 6.15
Internet Knowledge Status, School Performance, Frequency of TCP Use, and Gender

Internet Status and Frequency of TCP use	Male		Female		All	
	#	%	#	%	#	%
Do not know how to use Internet	261		201		462	
By performance						
Falling	38	14.6	35	17.4	73	15.8
Stable	154	59.0	108	53.7	262	56.7
Rising	69	26.4	58	28.9	127	27.5
How often do you visit the TCP?						
Once a week	195	74.7	159	79.1	354	76.6
Two or three times a week	48	18.4	34	16.9	82	17.7
More than three times a week	10	3.8	3	1.5	13	2.8
How long do you stay when you visit the TCP?						
At most one hour per day	203	77.8	159	79.1	362	78.4
Two to three hours per day	50	19.2	37	18.4	87	18.8
More than three hours per day	7	2.7	5	2.5	12	2.6
Know how to use Internet	301		252		553	
By performance						
Falling	33	11.0	25	9.9	58	10.5
Stable	143	47.5	134	53.2	277	50.1
Rising	125	41.5	93	36.9	218	39.4
How often do you visit the TCP?						
Once a week	166	55.1	151	59.9	317	57.3
Two or three times a week	110	36.5	73	29.0	183	33.1
More than three times a week	19	6.3	25	9.9	44	8.0
How long do you stay when you visit the TCP?						
At most one hour per day	142	47.2	127	50.4	269	48.6
Two to three hours per day	122	40.5	89	35.3	211	38.2
More than three hours per day	36	12.0	36	14.3	72	13.0

Table 6.16
Proportion of Students Who Know How to Use Internet, for Given Combinations of Study Hours, School Level, and School Performance

	Hours of Study (per Week)		
	< 3 hrs (%)	3–5 hrs (%)	> 5 hrs (%)
Lower level			
Falling	5.3	40.0	63.6
Stable	31.6	49.0	82.1
Rising	14.3	30.6	84.0
All lower level	22.1	43.8	81.3
Mid-level			
Falling	39.1	47.2	66.7
Stable	21.9	38.2	64.5
Rising	46.7	50.8	80.3
All mid-level	32.9	43.5	72.8
Upper level			
Falling	20.0	72.7	71.4
Stable	41.7	59.7	62.5
Rising	–	77.5	79.5
All upper level	35.3	66.9	71.8
All students			
Falling	23.4	50.9	66.7
Stable	29.7	47.3	71.4
Rising	25.6	53.3	81.2
All students	27.2	49.5	75.6

although the negative coefficient is significant only at a 12 percent probability level. It makes sense that upper and mid-level students should benefit: it is at higher educational levels that texts and assignments are most advanced yet accessible from the Internet. Also, perhaps younger students, even if they "know how to use the Internet," have not yet developed the skills to use it effectively for school purposes.

There is some indication that spending too much time at the TCP could be counterproductive: the coefficients for spending three hours or more per visit are negative in all three models. This result is statistically significant only in the mid level model (table 6.17b). For mid-level students, spending two to three hours in the TCP has a negative and statistically significant effect, and spending more than three hours will further diminish students' prospects of a rising performance.

Table 6.17a

Lower Level Secondary: Logistic Regression of Probability That a Student Will Have a Rising Performance

	Estimate	Std. Error	Z Value	Pr(>|z|)	
Intercept	–1.424	0.5719	–2.491	0.013	**
Gender	0.144	0.2386	0.604	0.546	
Age (12–15)	–0.403	0.4138	–0.973	0.330	
Age (≥ 16)	–0.816	0.4320	–1.889	0.059	*
TCP2	0.640	0.4994	1.281	0.200	
TCP3	0.447	0.4312	1.036	0.300	
TCP4	0.584	0.4424	1.320	0.187	
TCP5	1.396	0.4647	3.004	0.003	***
Computer literate	–0.124	0.3386	–0.366	0.715	
Motivated	0.290	0.2946	0.984	0.325	
Internet skills	–0.506	0.3286	–1.539	0.124	
TCP use (two to three hrs/visit)	0.362	0.3111	1.165	0.244	
TCP use (> three hrs/visit)	–0.186	0.4990	–0.373	0.709	
Hours of study	0.515	0.2173	2.368	0.018	**
McFadden Pseudo R^2		0.05989			

Note: Statistical significance levels: * $\alpha = .1$; ** $\alpha = .05$; *** $\alpha = .01$; **** $\alpha = .001$.

These findings are for the most part confirmed when we consider the three school levels jointly, using the upper level as the basis in the logistic regression and including dummy variables to account for the differences between the performance of upper and lower level students and of upper and mid level students (table 6.17d).[6]

To better grasp these results, we focus on upper secondary school students for which our model in table 6.17c exhibits the highest McFadden pseudo R-squared of 0.19 and, accordingly, best explains the observed variability. Consider the odds ratio, that is, the probability that a student's performance is rising divided by the probability that it is not.[7] The odds ratio of an upper secondary student is estimated to more than double (i.e., increase 2.27 times) if the student has Internet skills, more than double (i.e., increase 2.43 times) for every significant change in hours of study outside the classroom (e.g., from less than 3 hours to 3–5, or from 3–5 to 5 and more), and will be multiplied nearly fivefold (by 4.9) if the student regards learning to be a very important goal. Although not with statistical significance, the model also suggests that upper secondary students that spend more than three hours during each visit to the TCP, the odds ratio of a rising performance could be cut by about half (i.e., multiplied by 0.45).

Table 6.17b

Mid-Level Secondary: Logistic Regression of Probability That a Student Will Have a Rising Performance

	Estimate	Std. Error	Z Value	Pr(>|z|)	
Intercept	–1.779	1.5470	–1.150	0.250	
Gender	–0.133	0.2234	–0.596	0.551	
Age (12–15)	0.933	1.4964	0.623	0.533	
Age (≥ 16)	–0.656	1.4825	–0.443	0.658	
TCP2	0.389	0.5049	0.771	0.440	
TCP3	0.762	0.4345	1.754	0.079	*
TCP4	0.864	0.4488	1.924	0.054	*
TCP5	0.220	0.4286	0.513	0.608	
Computer literate	0.313	0.3202	0.977	0.328	
Motivated	0.630	0.2587	2.436	0.015	**
Internet skills	0.586	0.2878	2.036	0.042	**
TCP use (two to three hrs/visit)	–0.536	0.2565	–2.089	0.037	**
TCP use (> three hrs/visit)	–0.630	0.4549	–1.385	0.166	
Hours of study	0.603	0.1946	3.098	0.002	***
McFadden Pseudo R^2		0.097115			

Note: Statistical significance levels: * α = .1; ** α = .05; *** α = .01; **** α = .001.

Table 6.17c

Upper Level Secondary: Logistic Regression of Probability That a Student Will Have a Rising Performance

	Estimate	Std. Error	Z Value	Pr(>|z|)	
Intercept	–5.565	1.4137	–3.937	0.000	****
Gender	0.251	0.3370	0.744	0.457	
Age (12–15)	–	–	–	–	
Age (≥ 16)	1.716	1.2071	1.422	0.155	
TCP2	–1.076	1.4308	–0.752	0.452	
TCP3	0.321	0.57796	0.555	0.579	
TCP4	0.671	0.5260	1.276	0.202	
TCP5	–0.162	0.4994	–0.325	0.745	
Computer literate	0.549	0.4370	1.257	0.209	
Motivated	1.590	0.3750	4.239	0.000	****
Internet skills	0.823	0.3986	2.064	0.039	**
TCP use (two to three hrs/visit)	–0.088	0.3666	–0.241	0.809	
TCP use (> three hrs/visit)	–0.793	0.5964	–1.329	0.184	
Hours of study	0.887	0.2955	3.002	0.003	***
McFadden Pseudo R^2		0.18785			

Note: Statistical significance levels: * α = .1; ** α = .05; *** α = .01; **** α = .001.

Table 6.17d
All Secondary Levels: Logistic Regression of Probability That a Student Will Have a Rising Performance

	Estimate	Std. Error	Z Value	Pr(>|z|)	
Intercept	–1.508	0.5010	–3.010	0.003	***
Gender	0.049	0.1421	0.344	0.731	
Age (12–15)	–0.796	0.3822	–2.082	0.037	**
Age (≥ 16)	–0.812	0.3868	–2.099	0.036	**
Difference between upper and lower-level students	–0.207	0.2383	–0.867	0.386	
Difference between upper and mid-level students	0.007	0.1946	0.036	0.971	
TCP2	0.174	0.3055	0.570	0.568	
TCP3	0.499	0.2593	1.923	0.054	*
TCP4	0.727	0.2570	2.830	0.005	***
TCP5	0.463	0.2513	1.841	0.066	*
Computer literate	0.193	0.2000	0.967	0.334	
Motivated	0.616	0.1621	3.804	0.000	****
Internet skills	0.254	0.1805	1.407	0.159	
TCP use (two to three hrs/visit)	–0.183	0.1646	–1.114	0.265	
TCP use (> three hrs/visit)	–0.518	0.2766	–1.871	0.061	*
Hours of study	0.566	0.1245	4.542	0.000	****
McFadden Pseudo R^2		0.0671			

Note: Statistical significance levels: * $\alpha = .1$; ** $\alpha = .05$; *** $\alpha = .01$; **** $\alpha = .001$.

Conclusions and Recommendations

The experience of secondary students who visit these five rural TCPs lends credence to the premise under which these facilities were established, namely, that student access to computers and the Internet can make a positive difference in their academic performance. Students who study hard and are motivated to learn generally find a way to acquire Internet skills in these TCPs. The technology may be appreciated for reasons unrelated to school (e.g., recreation), but rising performers tend to make more intensive use of the Internet for school-related purposes (e.g., school research, downloading textbooks), suggesting that one reason they use the technology is for its value as a learning tool. The evidence also suggests that at the mid and upper secondary levels, having access to the Internet gives students a performance edge beyond that associated with their study habits.

Having a desire to learn and spending long hours studying remain keys to academic success. The effect on school performance of these two critical variables far outweighs any advantage conferred by access to the Internet. Furthermore, spending too much time at a TCP may thwart academic achievement. School administrators and officials should be aware of these possible negative implications of excessive TCP use. This is not a call for strict rules regarding TCP use but a warning for government and school officials, parents, and students of the importance of self-regulation in academic success.

The Government of Cameroon is to be commended for its TCP initiative, but it is disheartening to see how limited the program's reach has been to date. Of the thirty-four TCPs that have been installed, we were able to find only six operating sustainably. The nation's ambitious objective of using TCPs to expand educational opportunities will have to wait until the challenges of expanding electricity and connectivity to rural communities are overcome.

The slow pace of rural deployment of telecenters in developing countries presents a quasi-experimental opportunity for researchers to compare the effects of introducing a new technology into previously unconnected rural settings. Future research in this area should consider robust measures of academic performance (e.g., student performance records) and comparisons of school performance between communities, some with TCP access and others without.

Notes

1. During an interview, the Minister of Posts and Telecommunications (2008) announced the ambitious goal of installing 2,000 telecenters by 2015.

2. This study does not aim to evaluate the performance of individual TCPs or compare differences in student performance according to which TCP they attend. We consider how these differences might affect school performance, but we mask the identity of individual TCPs by referring to them according to an arbitrarily assigned number from 1 through 5.

3. In Cameroon, the school year runs from September 1 to June 30.

4. During these seven years, students have to pass three exams to obtain an official diploma.

After the first four or five years of study, students take an official national examination that leads to the BEPC (*Brevet d'études du premier cycle*) or the CAP (*Certificat d'aptitudes professionnelles*). The BEPC is optional, and a student can continue secondary schooling even if he or she fails to obtain this diploma. The CAP is a technical diploma that qualifies the student for a job as a technician.

The second or middle stage lasts up to one year, at the end of which all students must pass the *Probatoire* examination or obtain a BP (*Brevet professionnel*). Students can't continue their secondary studies without the *Probatoire* diploma.

The last exam is taken about a year later, at the end of secondary education, and leads to the *Baccalauréat* diploma, which qualifies the student to pursue university studies.

5. This is consistent with ITU figures for 2011, indicating that 7.4 percent of Cameroon's households have computers at home (International Telecommunications Union, 2012). Rich families have three members on average and low-income families more than six (Republic of Cameroon 2009). Assuming five persons per household and one computer per family, ITU's 7.4 percent figure over the entire population is equivalent to 37 percent of households having computers.

6. When we consider the three secondary levels together (table 6.17d) age differences gain importance, with older students performing better than younger students, study hours and motivation coefficients remain highly significant determinants of school performance, and the negative impact on school performance of spending more than three hours on each visit to the TCP is perceptible and statistically significant. The coefficients of computer and Internet skills are positive but not very significant because these regressions include lower level students in the estimating sample.

We also ran a separate model jointly considering upper and mid-level students but excluding lower level students. The results are similar to those shown in tables 6.17b and 6.17c. The coefficients for "Internet skills," "Motivated," and "Study time" are all positive and statistically significant, and the coefficients for spending two hours or more per visit to the TCP are negative and significant.

7. The odds ratio is obtained by applying the natural logarithm exponential function to the coefficient estimates in tables 6.17a through tables 6.17d (Fox and Weisberg 2011).

References

Attenoukon, Serge Armel. 2011. *Technologies de l'information et de la communication (TIC) et rendement académique en contexte universitaire béninois: Cas des apprenants en Droit de l'Université d'Abomey-Calavi.* PhD diss., Université de Montréal. https://papyrus.bib.umontreal.ca/xmlui/bitstream/handle/1866/5139/Attenoukon_Serge_A_2011_these.pdf;jsessionid=29EA8BB8CF8ECC1A818E451AC4ECCBF5?sequence=2/.

Broussard, Sheri Coates. 2002. *The Relationship between Classroom Motivation and Academic Achievement in First and Third Graders.* MSc thesis, Louisiana State University and Agricultural and Mechanical College. http://etd.lsu.edu/docs/available/etd-1107102-185505/unrestricted/Broussard_thesis.pdf.

Comité Technique d'Élaboration de la Stratégie Sectorielle de l'Éducation. 2006. *Draft du document de stratégie sectorielle de l'Éducation.* Republic of Cameroon: Ministère de l'Éducation de Base (MINEDUB), Ministère des Enseignements Secondaires (MINESEC), Ministère de l'Emploi et de la Formation Professionnelle (MINEFOP), Ministère d'Enseignement Supérieur (MINESUP). UNESCO. http://unesdoc.unesco.org/images/0014/001497/149764f.pdf.

Desgent, Colette, and Céline Forcier. 2004. *Impacts des TIC sur la réussite et la persévérance.* Gatineau: Collège de l'Outaouais. January. http://www.cdc.qc.ca/parea/desgent_outaouais_2004_rapport_PAREA.pdf.

Duckworth, Angela L., and Martin E. P. Seligman. 2005. Self-Discipline Outdoes IQ in Predicting Academic Performance of Adolescents. *Psychological Science* 16 (12): 939–944.

Fox, John, and Sanford Weisberg. 2011. *An R Companion to Applied Regression. 2nd ed.*Los Angeles: Sage.

Fyans, Leslie J., and Martin L. Maehr. 1987. Sources of Student Achievement: Student Motivation, School Context and Family Background. Paper presented at the 95th annual convention of the American Psychological Association, August 28–September 1.

International Telecommunications Union. 2012. Statistics webpage. http://www.itu.int/en/ITU-D/Statistics/Pages/stat/default.aspx?utm_source=twitterfeed&utm_medium=twitter/.

Karsenti, Thierry, Sophie Goyer, Stéphane Villeneuve, and Carole Raby. 2005. *L'impact des technologies de l'information et de la communication sur la réussite éducative des garçons à risque de milieux défavorisés.* Montréal: Centre de recherche interuniversitaire sur la formation et la profession enseignante (CRIFPE). December. http://www.frqsc.gouv.qc.ca/upload/editeur/rapport-Karsenti_avec_annexe_1_a_11.pdf.

Laferrière, Thérèse. 1999. *Avantages des technologies de l'information et des communications (TIC) pour l'enseignement et l'apprentissage dans les classes de la maternelle à la fin du secondaire.* Paper prepared for Rescol Industrie Canada. http://desette.free.fr/pdf/avantages.pdf.

Lebrun, Marcel. 2007. *Théories et méthodes pédagogiques pour enseigner et apprendre: Quelle place pour les TIC dans l'éducation?* Brussels: De Boeck.

Ministry of Posts and Telecommunications. 2005. *Stratégie sectorielle du domaine des télécommunications et TIC.* October. Yaoundé, Cameroon: Author. http://www.share4dev.info/telecentreskb/documents/4586.pdf

Ministry of Posts and Telecommunications. 2008. *Performances des P&T* 4 (August–October). Yaoundé, Cameroon: Author. http://www.minpostel.gov.cm/images/stories/documents/publications/Performancesdespettnum4.pdf.

Pearson, Robert W., Michael Ross, and Robyn M. Dawes. 1992. Personal Recall and the Limits of Retrospective Questions in Surveys. In *Questions about Questions: Inquiries into the Cognitive Bases of Surveys*, ed. Judith M. Tamur, 65–91. New York: Russell Sage.

Perreault, Nicole. 2003. Rôle et impacts des TIC sur l'enseignement et l'apprentissage au collégial. *Pédagogie collégiale* 16 (3): 3–10. http://www.imf.org/external/pubs/ft/scr/2010/cr10257.pdf

Republic of Cameroon. 2009. *Growth and Employment Strategy Paper: Reference Framework for Government Action over the Period 2010–2020.* IMF Country Report No. 10/257. Washington, DC: International Monetary Fund.

Stinebrickner, Todd R., and Ralph Stinebrickner. 2007. *The Causal Effect of Studying on Academic Performance*. NBER Working Paper No. 13341. Cambridge, MA: National Bureau of Economic Research. http://www.nber.org/papers/w13341.pdf.

Tchamabe, Marcelline Djeumeni. 2009. *L'impact des TIC sur les apprentissages scolaires en Afrique. Une étude comparée auprès d'établissements secondaires du Cameroun*. http://www.resatice.org/jour2009/communications/com-m-djeumeni-tchamabe.pdf.

United Nations Development Program. 2013. *Human Development Report 2012 – The Rise of the South: Human Progress in a Diverse World*. New York: Author. http://hdr.undp.org/sites/default/files/reports/14/hdr2013_en_complete.pdf.

van Oel, Bert Jaap. 2007. *Study of the Impact of ICT in Primary Schools (STEPS), Part 5: Analysis of the Good Practices and Case Studies*. Study commissioned by the European Commission, Directorate General Education and Culture. Public Services Contract no. EACEA/2007/4013. http://eacea.ec.europa.eu/llp/studies/documents/study_impact_technology_primary_school/5_case_studies_report_steps_en.pdf.

Zimmerman, Barry J. 1990. Self-Regulated Learning and Academic Achievement: An Overview. *Educational Psychologist* 25 (1): 3–17.

II Facilitating Inclusion and Enabling the Buildup of Social Capital

7 The Appropriation of Computer and Internet Access by Low-Income Urban Youth in Argentina

Sebastián Benítez Larghi, Carolina Aguerre, Marina Laura Calamari, Ariel Fontecoba, Marina Moguillansky, Jimena Orchuela, and Jimena Ponce de León

Abstract

Our research in Buenos Aires sought to understand the ways in which youth from low-income sectors use new technologies in their daily lives and the significance they attribute to them. We focused on technology accessed at three different types of venues located in the county of La Matanza: (1) a community initiative run by a local grassroots organization, (2) an information and communication technology (ICT) training and access center run by an organization with the support of the Government of Argentina, and (3) a cybercafé. The research is centered on the practices of low-income youth in these venues and explores the modes of appropriation of ICT that contribute to changes (positive or negative) in terms of employability, education, socialization, and participation in the political realm.

The research was conducted through direct observation of venues, in-depth interviews of users in public access venues, and surveys of users and nonusers. The main finding of our study is that public access venues and community centers that support public access through ICT training contribute to the social inclusion of youth in poor urban environments. Community ICT training centers (CITCs), such as the two considered in this study, satisfy training needs that are not met by market-oriented institutions or formal schooling. Cybercafés are spaces of sociability and contact where the main activities are centered on communication and entertainment over the Internet.

Given the central role of cybercafés in providing Internet access to low-income sectors, special attention should be paid to the observed decline of these facilities in marginal neighborhoods as well as nationwide. We recommend the promotion of participation by women and consider it important to disseminate information about cybercafé activities and the significance of these spaces among youth in order to strengthen links with the school environment. We suggest establishing training centers in marginalized communities, where the data reveal high rates of alienation among young people. Finally, we recommend reproducing the PC Refurbishment and Repair Workshop implemented by the La Matanza MTD center, as we have been able to appreciate how this type of initiative can help young people improve their immediate job prospects.

Introduction

How can low-income populations access information and communication technology (ICT) and acquire the necessary skills to use it? How and why do they use it? How important are computers and the Internet in their daily lives? These questions must be considered when evaluating the potential impact of any public policy, yet little research has addressed them.

The present chapter seeks answers, focusing on the plight of urban, low-income youth in Argentina and on the significance of public access to ICT in their daily lives. In a context in which the first-order "digital divide" (Camacho 2005; Warschauer 2003) is still significant and "digital poverty" (Barrantes 2007) results in an unequal distribution of knowledge and computer skills, our study focuses on the strategies subjects develop for the appropriation (Thompson 1998) of ICT in various computer and Internet public access venues and support spaces.

We compared three different public access support models and examined the contribution of each in terms of the socioeconomic development of the social groups in question. We selected three different cases located in the municipality of La Matanza, a section of a densely populated county of the same name situated on the outskirts of the City of Buenos Aires that has one of the highest poverty rates in the country. These cases were: (1) a privately operated, for-profit center or cybercafé; (2) a grassroots initiative self-managed by a community group, the Unemployed Workers Movement (MTD) of La Matanza; and (3) an ICT Training and Access Center (CEA)[1] sponsored and financed through a state program and organized by a community association, the Cirujas Civic Association. All three are situated within the context of poverty and urban marginality that has a specific excluding impact on low-income youth.

Strictly speaking, only the cybercafé qualifies as a public access venue (PAV). We consider the CEA and MTD venues to be community ICT training centers (CITCs) devoted primarily to ICT training, although the MTD center also provides free public access to its computers outside of class time. We have sought to determine the contribution (Ramirez 2007), positive or negative, of each of these three types of centers to low-income urban youth in La Matanza with respect to the following aspects of their daily lives: sociability, education, and employment.

Our research reveals that these three types of center contribute, in unequal and varying ways, to the social inclusion of low-income youth. Beyond indicating that the various spaces play a role in the incorporation and socialization of ICT, the main findings of our study relate to the differences among the three types of centers.

On the one hand, the community- and state-sponsored spaces (i.e., the CITCs) emphasize computer skills training, responding to a demand that neither the market nor schools can fully satisfy. They also contribute to creating a demand for ICT use among sectors of the population that previously had none, for lack of contact with and awareness of the possibilities the technology offers. These community spaces are valued by youth because they provide an accessible way to respond to the social demands and requirements of work life and contemporary education. Also, the CITCs provide guidance in the potential uses of computers and the Internet. These social spaces offer a relaxed environment that mitigates the fear and anxiety that computer use generates in low-income sectors and facilitate the channeling and realization of young people's expectations regarding ICT.

The cybercafé, on the other hand, aside from providing a space for social contact, also facilitates self-directed learning and provides an environment where youngsters can put into practice the skills learned in the CITCs. Internet communications are among the most highly valued activities of low-income urban youth in La Matanza.

We present our findings in the following order. We begin by explaining our research strategy and the methodological tools used. We then describe the socioeconomic context, the current conditions of access in the area studied, and, in particular, the situation of youth in La Matanza. In the third section, we present the main features of the three venues studied, and we compare how technology is appropriated in each of these spaces in terms of training, socialization, work, civic participation, and gender. The chapter concludes with recommendations for the design of policies and programs dedicated to the social inclusion of youth.

Methodology

Given the exploratory nature of our research, and keeping in mind that we sought to understand the significance of ICT in public access and ICT training spaces for low-income youth, we employed a predominantly qualitative methodological strategy designed to capture the perspective and voice of subjects.

Our study consisted of two sequential phases. The first exploratory phase was devoted to establishing contact with the centers: we carried out observations of the various spaces as well as a series of preliminary interviews. In the second phase, we developed a systematic comparison of the three types of space by conducting semistructured interviews with users of the various spaces and nonusers of the Internet. This qualitative research allowed us to evaluate the question of public access to ICT from the subjective perspective of the youth, observing the importance assigned to the technologies and their daily use in the centers. The systematic comparison of the case studies enabled us to establish the similarities and differences between the ways the three venues facilitated technology appropriation. With respect to research techniques, we used nonparticipant observation and qualitative interviews with a semistructured script designed to facilitate comparisons between cases. We surveyed residents in the zone of influence of the three centers studied to systematize the findings of the qualitative analysis. Given the limited reach of the two CITCs, we did not find any of their users in this survey, which is therefore representative only of home users, cybercafé users, and nonusers. Accordingly, we have not incorporated these results into the analysis except in specific instances when data from the survey are used to support observations based on the qualitative analysis.[2]

The nonparticipant observations were carried out on different days and times at the three selected venues. The observations concentrated on the following aspects: infrastructure and activities, user types, and user practices. These observations allowed us to form an overall impression of the day-to-day dynamics of these spaces and of their users' practices, interactions, preferences, and tendencies while there. The study was therefore able to go into more depth with respect to the uses of ICT rather than relying exclusively on the reports provided by the subjects.

The semistructured interviews sought to evaluate the practices and meanings that youth assign to the use of ICT in public spaces. We conducted forty interviews with young users and nonusers of the spaces, both men and women, between the ages of 15 and 39. The questionnaire was structured to enable comparisons between the various centers with respect to motives, education, socialization, work, and political involvement. The interviews were processed using ATLAS.ti software (http://www.atlasti.com/index.html). Table 7.1 shows the distribution of the interviews among supervisors (employees or instructors), users, and nonusers.

The Context

After experiencing one of the worst economic, political, and social crises in its history (1998–2004), Argentina is currently undergoing a period of sustained economic growth. The social fabric of the country is slowly being reconstructed. While the epicenter of the crisis occurred in 2002, it is estimated that 50 percent of the population lived in poverty for almost eight years while the unemployment rate rose to a record 22 percent.[3] Since then, economic growth and a series of inclusive policies have led to improvement in employment indexes and a reduction of poverty. Unemployment among youth has fallen significantly over the past decade, from 36 percent in 2002 to

Table 7.1
Distribution of Semistructured Interviews, by Gender and Age

		Cybercafé		MTD Center		Cirujas CEA		
		F	M	F	M	F	M	Subtotal
Supervisors		–	2	1	1	2	–	6
	Age							
Users	≤ 19	1	4	–	3	2	–	10
	20–29	2	2	4	4	2	–	14
	30–39	1	–	3	2	2	–	8
Nonusers	≤ 19	–	–	2	–	–	–	2
	20–29	1	–	1	–	–	–	2
	30–39	–	–	1	–	–	–	1
Subtotal		5	8	12	10	8	–	43

18 percent in 2013, which is still high, especially when compared with the overall national unemployment rate of 6.7 percent.[4] However, inequalities persist, and job insecurity, informal employment, and inflation are the main issues currently facing inhabitants of the most vulnerable areas, such as that of our study.

Since 2009, telecommunications have been at the center of the Argentine political scene, with several government initiatives aimed at increasing competition in the sector and universalizing access to ICT. These include the Law on Audiovisual Communication Services (*Ley de Servicios de Comunicación Audiovisual*), the Connecting Equality Program (*Programa Conectar-Igualdad*, which aims to provide netbooks to all public secondary school students), and the "MyPC"[5] and "Argentina Connected"[6] programs, designed to ensure computer and Internet access in the most underprivileged areas.

Our study was conducted in La Matanza County in the province of Buenos Aires, the most populated county in the metropolitan area surrounding the City of Buenos Aires. Despite the fact that La Matanza is located within a global megacity, it is one of the most neglected places in the Metropolitan Area of Buenos Aires (MABA). According to the latest census (National Institute of Statistics and Censuses 2010), the county has 1,772,130 inhabitants. In 2006, 72 percent of the people of La Matanza were living below the poverty line, and 20 percent were unemployed. The indexes were likely worse among youth (Universidad Nacional de La Matanza 2006). With economic growth and recent social policies, these indicators have most likely improved, but La Matanza remains marked by decades of poverty, structural unemployment, and social exclusion.

Argentina has also experienced a phenomenon that has become common in several Western societies: the presence of *ni-nis* (*ni estudia ni trabaja*), or "neither-nors," youth who neither study nor work. The number of young people nationwide with no formal secondary education now stands at 550,000, and 20 percent of youth between the ages of 14 and 24 (approximately 1.2 million people) neither study nor work.[7] There are no specific data on this particular segment of the population in La Matanza, but we estimate that the prevalence of "neither-nors" in this area is likely significant given that adolescents between ages 15 and 19 represent 8.1 percent of the total population of the municipality,[8] and, as we will see below, several of the subjects we interviewed are "neither-nors" or were at some point in their lives.

In Argentina, access to computers and the Internet is unevenly distributed according to socioeconomic level, proximity to major cities, gender, and age. The highest access to these services is concentrated among the upper and middle classes, youth ages 12 to 34, males, and residents of the Buenos Aires Metropolitan Area (SistemaNacional de Consumos Culturales 2008). The districts of Laferrere and González Catán in La Matanza, where our studies took place, exhibit a minimal presence of ICT, with fewer than 10 percent of homes having computers (SistemaNacional de Consumos Culturales 2008). Bear in mind that these data quickly become outdated and that the current percentage of homes with computers is likely higher.[9] With respect to the use of cybercafés, young men are the most frequent consumers (Finquelievich and Prince 2007). In 2008, the use of cybercafés in Argentina began to decline, in part, because of lower technology costs, increased connectivity through cell phones, and Wi-Fi (D'Alessio 2010; Soriano 2010).[10]

In summary, our study was conducted in a context marked by poverty, unemployment, and barriers in accessing ICT that especially affect youth, many of whom neither study nor work in formal settings.

Characterization of the Three Case Studies

Table 7.2 sums up the main characteristics of the centers studied. Only one space, the cybercafé, qualifies as a PAV that is readily available to service the demand of the general public for computer and Internet access. The other two venues are CITCs. The Cirujas CEA provides computer training only, and the MTD center, in addition to training, provides free public access to computers only when these are not being used for courses. In light of this restriction, members of the general public and members of the organization do not regularly frequent the site for computer or Internet use.

Table 7.2
Main Characteristics of Venues Studied

	Cybercafé	MTD Center	Cirujas CEA
# computers	16	8	8
# computers with Internet	16	8	1
Hours of operation	12 P.M.–10 P.M. daily	9 A.M.–7 P.M. daily	Hours vary according to the courses offered
Users per week (approx.)	150	40	30
Type of connection	Broadband	Broadband	Connection through cell phone technology
ICT services	Internet access, printing, burning CDs	Basic computer and computer repair courses, printing, occasional access to computers and Internet	Basic computer courses; currently does not offer free access to computers and Internet
Funding	Privately run (hourly rates)	Early financing came from an NGO (Fundación Equidad); today it is self-financed (MTD)	State funds for startup, after which the organization must, in theory, be self-financed
Role of supervisors	Customer service, computer upkeep, charging customers, assisting and supporting customers on request	Teaching and supervision of activities, customer support during free access time	Teaching
Rules of use	Open use, no rules	Training and supervised use during free time; use of social networking sites and chat is allowed during the last hour, but games are prohibited	Games are prohibited
Publicity and promotion	None: the storefront is indication of its presence	Through personal networks of members of the organization	Through social networks of members of the organization
Other activities	None	Bakery, sewing and clothing design workshop, preschool	State- and NGO-run programs, adult literacy and microcredits

Unemployed Workers Movement of La Matanza

The La Juanita Cooperative run by the La Matanza MTD is located in the Gregorio Laferrere neighborhood in La Matanza County. The national MTD emerged in the mid-1990s out of a series of protests against unemployment and hunger. Originally, it was one of the most important organizations in the incipient social movement of unemployed Argentinian workers known as *piqueteros*, who blocked routes and organized protests in order to get their message across. However, when the state began to distribute plans and social subsidies to calm protests, the MTD viewed the subsidies as attempts at government control.[11] The La Matanza MTD was the only unemployed workers' group that decided not to accept the subsidies, opting instead for a strategy of regional and community work along with the self-management of independent and cooperative entrepreneurial ventures. This caused a significant reduction in its social base, but the movement managed to create a bakery, a sewing and clothing design workshop, and a preschool. While the MTD's background places it within an "anarcho-syndicalist" and leftist tradition (Svampa and Pereyra 2004), since 2007, it has formed part of the Coalición Cívica, a centrist political party.[12]

Within this context of self-management, in early 2006, the center added a computer room and began offering public Internet access and courses in PC use, Internet navigation, and computer repair and refurbishment. These activities were initiated through the center's ties to the *Fundación Equidad* (Foundation for Equality),[13] which donated computers to the cooperative so they could offer local residents courses on basic PC use. One of the principal members of the MTD received training in computer use and PC refurbishing from the Foundation. The initial funding and training provided by the Foundation laid the groundwork for the development of the courses offered by the cooperative, which are now offered independently thanks to donations from private businesses and revenues generated by the sale of refurbished PCs and other MTD ventures, such as the bakery and the textiles workshop.

The computer room has eight computers networked together, with Wi-Fi Internet access provided by a local business that rebroadcasts the signal received from other providers through homemade antennae. The cooperative offers several courses (including PC Use, Computer Repair and Refurbishment, and Internet Use) as well as a Computer Repair and Refurbishment Workshop, providing services to local residents and functioning at the same time as a source of employment and work experience for youth who have taken the courses. In addition, when the room is not being used for courses, local residents have free access to the computers and Internet. This activity is secondary; the courses and computer refurbishment take priority.

The MTD sends a clear message regarding the use of ICT: while educational, work-related, and communications uses are encouraged, games are not permitted, and as a general rule, minors are not allowed in the room without adult supervision.

We identified two main types of users of the MTD center. The first group consists of young men who take the repair and refurbishment course to acquire job skills. The second comprises young women and adults who visit the center in their free time to learn to use computers. The gender difference in the composition of course participants is consistent with the organization's intent, namely, to encourage women to learn how to use computers and men to learn how to repair them.

Cybercafé

The cybercafé chosen for this study is located two blocks from the La Matanza MTD center, and is one of the few remaining cybercafés in the neighborhood.[14] It was inaugurated in 2003, and, after closing for a period of time (2006–2008), it was reopened by the same owner at its current location. It is a rectangular space with tinted glass windows that make it difficult to see in from the outside and vice versa. It has sixteen computers that are on average three years old. The computers are installed side by side and separated by white panels that give users a certain degree of privacy. The cybercafé currently does not use Internet content filters because, according to the owner, they were blocking some very popular pages. In addition to computer and Internet access (US$0.70/hour), the cybercafé offers printing services (US$0.12 per printed page).

Given that the neighborhood, La Juanita, is relatively peripheral within the district of Laferrere, only local residents frequent the cybercafé. The users are mostly young men; few women visit the place. Within the cybercafé, the space is used in two different ways with respect to activities carried out and the duration of sessions. The predominant users are adolescent males who visit more than three times a week and stay for one to five hours each time, interacting with friends, chatting, using online social networks, and playing online games. A second group of users, primarily young women and adults, make brief visits (maximum one hour) less than three times a week and with concrete goals such as searching for specific information or checking email.

With respect to the clear gender difference in the profiles of cybercafé users, we offer the following explanation. The aesthetics and spatial layout of the cybercafé suggest that one of the targeted segments of the public are young men who want to look at pornography—an activity that is also facilitated by the absence of filters. While we were unable to confirm through our interviews whether this was a generalized practice or a business strategy of this particular cybercafé (the owner assured us that he personally blocked access to pornographic sites), our observations confirmed that in the owner's absence, at least two young men accessed sites of this type. It is reasonable to assume that the combination of these factors generates an environment perceived as risky by young women, who therefore choose to limit the time they spend there.

ICT Training and Access Center, Cirujas Civic Association

The Cirujas Civic Association was founded in 1996 and since 2001 has been based in González Catán in La Matanza County. With support from the National Agricultural Technology Institute (*Instituto Nacional de Tecnologías Agropecuarias* [INTA]), the association created a center for sharing experiences in an effort to improve agricultural capabilities for work in local gardens. The association's activities have been reinforced and diversified through different state- and NGO-sponsored initiatives supporting commercial ventures, youth issues, citizenship building, adult literacy, and microcredit programs. Although the association has no explicit political affiliation, it is clearly tied to and supportive of the reigning political party, which acknowledges Peronism as its main ideological influence and whose policies are left of center.

In mid-2010, the community organization formed ICT Training and Access Center No. 157 (*Centro de Enseñanza y Acceso Informático*) under the MyPC Program, which aims to foster digital inclusion among low-income people by granting resources to help regional organizations establish community technology training and access centers. The program provides them with the latest technology and finances the necessary modifications to the facilities, training in how to run the space, and the cost of Internet access for one year. For its part, the organization agrees to habilitate the space appropriately, meet specific service standards, offer training to the public, and guarantee that the Cirujas CEA will remain open for at least three years, in return for which it is allowed to charge user fees.

The Cirujas CEA currently has eight new computers that run on open source software developed under the MyPC Program. It offers computer skills training courses, citing among its objectives digital inclusion and job placement skills. However, the center currently does not have Internet access because this would require covering the cost of laying the cable (not currently available in the area) for service installation. For this reason, only the main terminal has an Internet connection via cell phone. This situation undoubtedly affects the services offered by the Cirujas CEA. Drawbacks include not only a lack of connectivity and appropriation of the most empowering aspects of the network, but a contribution to the image of Internet use as having potentially negative effects. Nevertheless, those running the space indicate that this is a temporary problem that will soon be resolved given that one of their objectives is precisely the provision of Internet access to their users.

With regard to the profile of the Cirujas CEA users, most were adolescent or adult women. There were also some adolescent and adult men, but they were in the minority and almost exclusively members of the association who were participating in the microcredit program.

Numerical Significance of the Three Venue Types

It is difficult to ascertain how common these three different types of venue are, but it is clear that cybercafés are the most prevalent. Gomez (2009) estimates that in 2008, Argentina had around 18,500 cybercafés, 1,300 community and public libraries, and 491 community telecenters with Internet access.

Gomez's (2009) survey covered telecenters that provided public access and are run on a not-for-profit basis by either nongovernmental organizations (NGOs) or government agencies. Strictly speaking, CITCs such as the Cirujas CEA and the MTD center are not PAVs and should not have been counted as telecenters by Gomez. In practice, CITCs share common features with telecenters: they are usually run by NGOs or government, and one of their aims is to increase access to ICT by low-income people. Because of these similarities, CITCs are likely to be counted as telecenters in formal surveys such as Gomez's (2009).

More recent data from the National Survey on Access and Use of Information Technology and Communication show that by the end of 2011, about 58 percent of the urban population used computers, primarily at home (76 percent), but also at work (42 percent), Internet cafés (19 percent), educational institutions (16 percent), someone else's home (13 percent), or other community spaces such as CITCs (about 2 percent) (National Institute of Statistics and Censuses 2012).

Youth Appropriation of ICT in Each Type of Venue

In this section, we review the activities of youth and their use of ICT in different types of venues in an attempt to understand the significance of these practices in terms of education, socialization, employment, and civic involvement.

The concept of *appropriation* (Thompson 1998) is key. By appropriation, we are referring to the material and symbolic processes of interpreting and assigning meaning to a specific cultural artifact by a given social group, emphasizing the ability of subjects to connect this process with their objectives. The cultural artifacts—in this case, ICT and the centers used to access or learn how to use ICT—are appropriated insofar as they are *socially significant* for a group in relation to their particular symbolic universe—in other words, the subjective needs of the group (Winocur 2007). The process of appropriation varies according to social class, gender, generation, and personal experience. From this it follows that studying the motivations and strategies of skills acquisition, as well as the question of gender, is paramount.

Based on an understanding of technology as a process of appropriation between subject and object that involves multiple types of mediation, we believe that it is possible to evaluate the contribution of CITCs to the daily life of low-income urban youth. In this interrelationship between the potential offered by ICT and the universe of practices and representations inhabited by low-income youth, it is possible to estimate the impact of public access to new technologies on the socioeconomic development of these groups.

Motives

In general terms, users frequent these venues to use computers and navigate the Internet. Other reasons why youth visit these spaces include: to acquiring computer skills (training), meet with friends (socialization), improve their prospects for employment (work), and, in some cases, carry out formal online procedures or participate in an organization (participation). These motivations are emphasized and articulated in different ways by the users of each type of venue given that the characteristics of each space encourage certain uses and inhibit others.

The majority of venue users interviewed do not have a computer at home, or if they do, they do not have Internet access, so their primary motive for visiting these spaces is to use the Internet. However, it is important to analyze the basis of the demand for connectivity among these users and the motivations behind their computer and Internet use.

Cybercafé users state that they frequent the space mainly in search of entertainment: they go there to meet their friends and participate in online games. "I began coming here in order to play, because we don't have a computer at home" (Jonathan, 17, cybercafé user). In our observations of this space, we noted that the majority of users were young men, and they spent most of their time playing online. Even when they have a computer or Internet at home, they are attracted to the cybercafé as a place to meet friends and play online games: "I used to have Internet at home, but I came here to hang out because it was boring staying at home alone. I would come here with the guys, we'd have a Coke and then I'd go home" (Gustavo, 21, cybercafé user). In this sense, our data confirm the specialized literature on the subject, which identifies cybercafés as "the new corner" (Bouille 2008), the meeting space of choice for youth from low-income sectors. Along with the presence of their friends is the fact that the cybercafé computers are specially equipped for online gaming.

At the MTD center, in contrast, the main motivation of the young people who use the space is to learn computer use and repair. In other words, they go there to take computer courses, generally with the idea of improving their job skills and employment prospects. For the men, the computer refurbishment and repair courses provide them with some marketable job skills. For the women, the courses on PC and Internet use qualify them for potential jobs as secretaries. For adult women and women with children, they are also a way of finding some leisure time and understanding what their children do on the computer.

As for the Cirujas CEA, the venue does not offer public access to computers and the Internet. Currently, all of its users are students, whose main motivation for frequenting the space is to participate in formal training in computer use. According to those interviewed, computer skills are essential in getting jobs, and this is why they visit the space.

Training/Education

The spaces analyzed differ in their contribution to training youth in ICT use: teaching is the central objective of the state and community spaces but a secondary function of the cybercafés. Indeed, one of the key aspects of the MTD center and Cirujas CEA experiences is the educational project framed within a social project aimed at collective transformation.

The courses offered at the MTD center and Cirujas CEA aim to satisfy the need for training and computer skills that is not met by schools. Moreover, these spaces attract segments of the population that have never come into contact with ICT, thereby helping to resolve not only the issue of access but also the absence of demand.[15] In both cases, the users feel that the classes take place in a friendly and comfortable environment that is fostered by the instructors. This relaxed setting enables novice users to overcome their initial fears more quickly and naturally. Several students compare their experiences, which they rate as positive, with those of other courses in which they had difficulties:

> *It didn't go well because the teacher would walk out, he would leave, and it was a course I was paying for. I realized that it was useless. It's different here. You call them and they come and explain things, and then they explain them again. That's good. Maybe that's why I failed. There, the important thing was to pay, pay, pay. It didn't matter whether or not you learned. I got discouraged and I left.* (Liliana, 32, Cirujas CEA user)

In observing the MTD center and Cirujas CEA courses, we noted that the instructors used a variety of strategies designed to encourage comprehension and the practical application of course content. One recurring pedagogical strategy consisted of establishing analogies between computer and Internet functions and other aspects of students' daily lives. In this sense, the role of the instructors was extremely relevant. The strong social sense behind their actions encouraged more favorable attitudes toward participating and helping those with fewer computer skills:

It's very satisfying to see them progressing. Some suddenly begin to try other things. They excel. They begin to work in computer repairs. (Daniel, MTD center instructor)

The friendly ambiance of the classes translates user comfort into positive results and a good rapport with the instructors. In the interviews we carried out, all the students mentioned their confidence in the space and acknowledged it as an essential element in their learning experience. This finding is consistent with the assertion that computer-related learning is based on the availability of the instrument and its use, in terms of personal experience, beyond the influence of resources offered in specialized courses (Sey and Fellows 2009). While we observed that a significant amount of self-learning and learning-by-doing occurs in the cybercafés, what we found in the CITCs are valuable nontechnical factors, such as the comfort level of the youth and the extent of their interaction with instructors, which should be taken into consideration when evaluating those spaces' impact on learning.

In particular, at the Cirujas CEA, classes are given at scheduled times, although the actual delivery is quite informal. The flexibility observed at the beginning contrasts with the systematic approach in other aspects of the classes. On the one hand, we observed that the instructor assumes a position of authority; on the other hand, the users-students bring their notes to class and complement them with specially designed notebooks. The teaching method used in the workshops was similar to that used in a traditional and formal education situation. The syllabus covered a broad spectrum of functionalities of the PC, beginning with hardware and ending with a discussion of design elements, including the use of a word processor, spreadsheet, and basic Internet tools. One of the main contributions of the training in CITCs is that the instructors motivate users to continue their studies by reinforcing the objectives students aim to achieve through the courses and boosting their confidence in their learning abilities. As a result, many students decide to begin or resume their formal studies.

When he first came here, he knew a little about using computers, but nothing about how to fix them. So I showed him. One day he hugged me and gave me a kiss.... "What happened?"... "I enrolled in university." "What are you studying?" I thought he was going to say economics or something like that, right? But he said, "Systems engineering."... I felt like crying. (Freddy, 31, MTD center user and instructor)

One of the most notable contributions of the MyPC initiative with respect to education and training is reflected in the experience of Ana, a Cirujas CEA member and instructor. Thanks to this project, she has not only improved her computer skills and living conditions, but she found a space for her concerns and her desire for social participation (see box 7.1).

To sum up, in both the MTD center and the Cirujas CEA, the acquisition of computer skills, along with the motivation imparted by the proactive atmosphere of the community space, influences and reinforces new users' expectations. Despite being profit-driven and communication-oriented, the cybercafé also allows its users to acquire computer skills. In fact, according to the survey (figure 7.1), the cybercafé was ranked by almost half the users (49 percent) as the most important place for learning Internet

Box 7.1
Ana

Ana is a young single mother from González Catán. After dropping out of high school, and thus leaving the space she shared with her peer group, she maintained her contact with the Cirujas Civic Association. She has been a member since she was fourteen, when she began accompanying her mother, a community educator, to the Association.

In this context, Ana received education and support and found her vocation. In the mornings, she works as an educator for the *Programa Envión* (Ministry of Social Welfare, Province of Buenos Aires), which provides integration and social support services for children, adolescents, and youth in at-risk social situations (e.g., homelessness, facing criminal charges, in situations of poverty, excluded from the school system, etc.). Ana divides her afternoons between promoting the Good Faith Bank (*Banco de la Buena Fe*), coordinating the Cirujas venue, and giving computer workshops in the new CEA. With reference to the latter, she evaluates the motivation for learning and distinguishes it from the issue of access: "If a person wants to learn, but they don't have Internet or anything, that doesn't mean they don't have the same potential as someone else. What does make a big difference is having access to a computer."

She has had a computer at home for only a year, but now she can't imagine not having one: "It's hard. It would be like not having a phone. It's my life. Because you get so used to technology and then when it's not there, it feels like you're missing something.... It's like being alone in the middle of nowhere."

Despite the fact that she does not yet consider it a reliable source of income, Ana explains that her political education and access to information were completely transformed by Internet access. Being a member of the community space enables her to do what she wants and loves to do in the present: "I love teaching computer skills, interacting with people, being in this place. I find a certain calm." Her role as instructor has allowed her to interact with many people from other CEAs, including instructors and government officials. She has gained a significant place within the hierarchy of the Association, and this has increased her expectations for the future. In addition to her ongoing work managing projects in the Association, she plans to finish high school and continue her computer education.

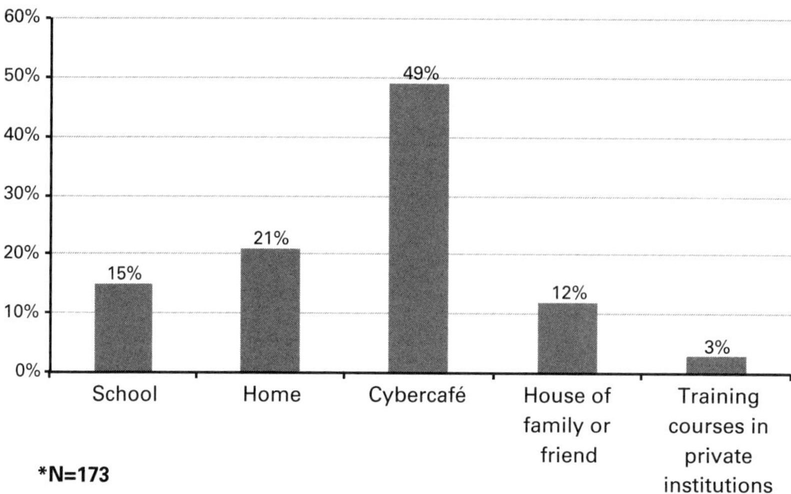

Figure 7.1
Most important place for learning how to use the Internet.

skills and the second most important place, after school, for learning computer skills (30 and 35 percent, respectively).

Although it does not have specific resources for training users in computer use, the cybercafé is a place for self-learning or learning with friends or (to a lesser degree) with the help of supervisors and a place to practice knowledge acquired at school or in the CITCs. In this sense, our study confirms what the literature indicates with respect to the computer training component in cybercafés. As Best (2010) points out, despite the fact that teaching computer skills is not part of their mission, cybercafés do potentially form part of the mechanism in learning to use computers. In the absence of instructors or teachers, users consult each other, particularly their friends and, when necessary, the supervisor, when they encounter difficulties in performing certain activities on the computer. As a result, the acquisition of skills in the cybercafé depends on the autodidactic capacity of each individual, the help users offer each other, and the good will of supervisors.

On the computer you learn more when you're on your own and start trying things. Fiddling with the computer you have the potential of running into problems and figuring out how to solve them. That's the difference between taking a course and messing around on the computer yourself. (Amanda, 27, cybercafé user)

With respect to the connection with school, the three venues studied are complementary to formal education channels in terms of training in computer use. Often schools encourage the use of computers and the Internet. When students do not have access to ICT at home, youth go to the public spaces to complete their school tasks.

I also use the computer to get information, to do schoolwork, for help with things I don't know. At school, they tell us to look for information online in order to do our homework. It he lps for school, for homework, and when you don't understand something. (Jonathan, 17, cybercafé user)

School demands also generate strategies for cooperation among family members, particularly when students are too young to go to the cybercafé or when the students are women, in which case their younger brothers are given the task of looking for information online so that the women can complete their schoolwork. In addition, in families with older parents where the generation gap is evident, youth will often look for online information for their parents:

Sometimes I look for information for my mom online since she doesn't know anything about the Internet and she's studying.... (Marina, 22, cybercafé user)

This case evokes the role of "informal infomediary" fulfilled by some of the members of these groups. *Infomediaries* (information intermediaries) are trusted third-party providers of information advice or services (Dalton, Beck, and Huckfeldt 1998; Deephouse and Heugens 2009)—in this case, seeking information online, computer use, and so on. We consider these users to be "informal infomediaries" for the people close to them (e.g., relatives and friends), given that they already possess knowledge of computer use, as opposed to the "formal infomediaries" who offer training at the CITCs (Cirujas CEA and MTD center).

Another motive for visiting the CITCs is school demands. According to the instructors and supervisors, youth often visit these centers rather than the cybercafé to seek information online for school assignments.

Teachers tell them to look online but they don't know that the students don't have Internet. It's a problem in area schools. So they come here and they can ask what to do to get the information. The cybercafé is more structured. The supervisor looks at you funny or tries to charge you extra. (Daniel, 38, MTD center instructor)

To sum up, training is an explicit goal for youth who visit the MTD center and the Cirujas CEA, but it is also an implicit need, imposed and proposed by the interactions generated in all of the venues considered, including the cybercafé. The subjects express the importance of the ambiance and didactic resources for training, highlighting the potential of spaces that generate self-confidence through concrete practice and accepting, in exchange, the informalities of the process in the community- and state-sponsored spaces.

Socialization

Most of the technological knowledge and skills acquired by youth in the various public access spaces are related to communications. The majority of uses and the time devoted to them, especially in the cybercafé but also in the MTD center, involve communications purposes enabled through a variety of platforms and computer programs, such as chat, Messenger, Facebook, online games, Fotolog, and, to a lesser extent, email (again, games are not allowed in the MTD center). Subjects interviewed observed that online contacts occupy an increasing amount of space in their lives while the use of these tools by relatives and friends produces a "contagion effect."

Interviewer: Marta, did you encourage her to get Facebook?

Marta: Yes, yes. If I don't get her to do things ... she never would. I told her, I have Facebook and I have a ton of friends ... we bumped into some girls the other day by chance, I looked for them and they were friends of mine....

Angela: And so I thought, "this is good." It's great for keeping in touch. (Marta and Angela, 34 and 36, MTD center users)

In this way, new technologies are integrated into the daily lives of youth as an additional (and increasingly important) medium for communication with relatives and friends, one that sometimes supplements and sometimes complements cell phones. The lower costs and the possibility of being available most of the time tilt preferences from phones to electronic means.

This trend is especially significant among young immigrants from neighboring countries for whom electronic communication is a vital necessity: ICT is socially essential for them because it enables them to communicate with friends and relatives:

To communicate with my family in Bolivia, I use Messenger and especially video chat because it is cheaper than talking by phone. Calling Bolivia costs $0.75 per minute. I have five minutes to talk to my whole family. On the other hand, I can contact my brother by Internet and my mother and my daughter. I can talk with all of them. I can be two hours. Now I can tell them about my life. I can show them photos. We can talk more about everything. (Freddy, 31, MTD center user and instructor)

This need to be connected makes these technological practices meaningful in the lives of youth from low-income sectors. The majority of those we interviewed mentioned that they had made new friendships online—interestingly enough, one of the most frequent mechanisms is through online games that allow real-time dialogue with remote players. This new type of friendship, not necessarily based on face-to-face encounters (although electronically mediated contacts do occasionally lead to in-person meetings), allows youth to transcend the territorial limitations of their neighborhoods. For instance, thanks to these types of contacts, many of those we interviewed had traveled to other cities; hence, the value that some give to these contacts and the generalized perception of the importance of having Internet access.

Q: Do you think that if you didn't have a computer you would lose touch with some people?

A: Yes, with schoolmates from high school who live far away or people I know who live in other places. I wouldn't have any way of talking with them. (Jonathan, 17, cybercafé user)

This communications potential is one of users' primary motives for accessing ICT in the three types of centers studied. The possibility of communicating with others appears to be essential, as a way of staying connected to the world and keeping up with modern advances. The general perception of users is that a lack of connectivity would result in exclusion.

The best thing about the computer and Internet is that you're not disconnected from the world, you're not outside of technology, of the advances in the world. (Eugenia, 39, MTD center user)

When it comes to the social aspect, the cybercafé has a particular impact. The main motivation of young men in visiting the cybercafé is that, beyond providing access to ICT, it has become an essential place for meeting and socializing in their daily lives. As an example, we present a brief story of one of the café's most frequent users in box 7.2.

The cybercafé fulfills a social function quite apart from the advantages of ICT access. In fact, even when they have Internet at home, youth find that the cybercafé functions as a place to meet their friends and take a step back from their problems. Peer groups and friendships play a key role in the appropriation of ICT by youth. It is friends who prompt their initial use, who help them and share knowledge with their peers. ICT is mainly used for communicating between friends and forging new friendships. Friendship is undoubtedly an integral part of the daily lives of youth, and the meaningfulness of ICT is based on this.

Employment

Work is a major concern for youth from low-income sectors, who face a difficult situation characterized by high unemployment rates and the challenges of acquiring initial job experience. Within the social imaginary of youth, knowledge and skills related to the use of ICT are essential for breaking into the job market.

Knowing how to use a PC is always useful. For whatever job, they ask if you have computer skills, just in case. Even for a street-sweeping job they ask for computer skills. I don't know, maybe they ask about a computerized machine… a computerized broom. (Alejandro, cybercafé user)

By offering ICT training and employment counseling, community- and state-sponsored spaces stimulate the expectation of economic progress in youth.

Box 7.2
Gabriel

Gabriel, 21, has lived in the La Juanita neighborhood since he was born. He completed high school but has never managed to hold on to a steady job. He worked at a metal factory, was unemployed for a year—a true "neither-nor"—and now helps out at the cybercafé. He has a computer at home, but the Internet was disconnected a few months ago because the local business that transmitted the signal closed. His main motivation for going to the cybercafé is to spend time with his friends. The most positive memory he has of the space is connected with the death of his father: "My dad had died and my friends brought me to the cybercafé.... I hadn't been here for a long time. It was good to be here because at home I was bored, I was sad. Here, I'm with people. I spend a while here and I clear my head a bit."

Gabriel's interaction with computers isn't limited to a specific period or activity; rather, it is spread out throughout the day. With games, Messenger, and Facebook all open, Gabriel steps out to chat or drink mate or soda with friends on the sidewalk. Gabriel is proud of having made many friendships and met many girls through these programs. People from nearby cities as well as other provinces and countries form part of an extensive network of contacts established via Internet that have allowed him to travel, experience other realities, and forge weak but significant bonds.

When asked if he could have met these people without the Internet, he answers:

"No; without a computer, no. It's not possible. A computer without Internet is like having... ears and not being able to hear...."

Thanks to experience acquired at home and in the cybercafé, Gabriel acknowledges that his computer skills have improved:

"I used to feel like a chimp, looking for the letters, but now I can look somewhere else while I type.... I can talk to the guy next to me and write at the same time. And write well."

In the MTD's La Juanita cooperative, the supervisors suggest that the main objective in offering computer courses is to provide useful training for the job market, which will improve job possibilities for youth and help the organization become independent by generating its own earnings:

One of the most important objectives is that the kids can put something together themselves and begin to become independent. They have to begin to find their own way, and it's important. I hope that many cooperative ventures come out of this training experience. (Mónica, 40, MTD supervisor)

The Repair and Refurbishment Workshop offers a work option to former students of the cooperative. The majority of the current workshop participants took the computer classes offered and can therefore apply the knowledge they learned in a profitable venture that also gives them work experience. The Workshop refurbishes and/or repairs donated computers that are then sold at low prices to interested area residents (often the students themselves). The youth who participate in the Workshop receive 80 percent of the proceeds from sales of refurbished computers while the remaining 20 percent goes to the cooperative. Therefore, in addition to work experience, youth have the opportunity to buy their own computers. Indeed, students who are unable to pay cash can earn a computer by performing tasks in the cooperative.[16] In some cases, this exchange has become a way of incorporating new members into the movement, with youth who take the courses making a commitment to become instructors or computer technicians.

The exchange takes place when the kids help others to narrow the digital divide. You say to them: "Look, you're doing this, helping the other kids, giving them the same possibilities you were given here," and they like that. They love it. (Facundo, 38, MTD supervisor)

These youth get evident satisfaction from helping others who need training or who want to get their first computer:

What I like about coming here is putting computers together and donating them. I really like helping. (Martín, 19, former student and current instructor at the MTD center)

Undoubtedly, this reflects attempts by movement leaders to instill values of solidarity and cooperative education among youth. Many of the youth who exhibit a greater commitment to these activities tend to approach the space with specific interests in ICT and hope to find employment the center. In other cases, taking computer courses through the MTD center allows students to forge work-related contacts with small businesses and/or foundations where they can find a job or continue their training. The majority are youth who neither study nor work, those defined as "neither-nors"; thanks to their participation in the space, they are able to find jobs or are inspired to resume their studies.

One day an acquaintance calls me and says, "You train kids. I need someone to work here. I'll teach them the Internet part." So I said, I have kid so-and-so. We brought him over there. They took him on for a one-week trial period and now it's been like three months that he's working with him. (Mónica, 40, MTD center supervisor)

Perhaps Freddy's story best illustrates the role of the MTD center in transforming the life of a member, not only in terms of employment (see box 7.3).

In short, the MTD center seems to operate as an intermediary that expands the social capital of youth, offering them a network of contacts that tend to form a "virtuous circle," including training, access to PCs and the Internet, and the possibility of getting a job.

Box 7.3
Freddy

Freddy is from Bolivia. He completed high school there and began his university studies, but he had to drop out when his father died. In 2005, he decided to emigrate to Argentina in hopes of improving his economic situation. Attracted by an offer of work in a clandestine sewing workshop, he found himself in a risky situation of forced labor, exploitation, and continuous threats by his employers to hand him over to the police. Thanks to an MTD poster, he approached members who helped him distance himself from this exploitative situation. He began to work at the cooperative as a tailor, and there he found out that the space also offered free computer courses. He took several courses and learned to use, repair, and refurbish computers. At the same time, he began to go to cybercafés to practice his skills, and there he learned to navigate the Internet.

After a while, the coordinator of the computer workshop at La Juanita helped him get a scholarship from the Fundación Equidad to take an advanced computer course on the condition that he would return to the cooperative to share what he had learned. Since then Freddy has taught several computer courses at La Juanita as a way to repay the education and support he obtained there for free. He is especially eager to promote the courses among his fellow Bolivians, to help them get better jobs and give them tools to avoid exploitation. Thanks to the education he received at the MTD, Freddy now has a stable job in a computer supply store. He earns a decent salary (around US$800 a month), which he supplements by giving classes at several institutions and doing odd jobs in computer maintenance and repair. He has a computer and broadband Internet at home, allowing him, among other things, to download programs that he uses for work and to communicate with his relatives in Bolivia. He has also used the Internet to take online courses and learn various computer programs.

With respect to the state-sponsored center (i.e., the Cirujas CEA), the expectations of those attending the courses are entirely associated with improving their employability. Several of those interviewed expressed the belief that acquiring computer knowledge is a step on the path toward getting their first job or a more skilled job: "I think that studying can help me for work because now for everything you need to have studied computers" (Ileana, 18, Cirujas CEA student).

With respect to the cybercafé, employment is less important for several reasons. First of all, the space does not provide training and does not have the goal of improving employability among its users. Additionally, cybercafé users are mainly youth who in many cases are not yet seeking jobs because they are still school age. Among the slightly older users and those who already work, we note that they do not use computers at their workplace probably because the social sector in question often ends up in informal and low-skilled jobs. In any case, and despite the fact that computers are not part of their daily work environment, the cybercafé users expressed beliefs regarding the utility, speed, and time-saving advantage of having a computer in the workplace.

Like the other subjects interviewed, cybercafé users believe computer and Internet knowledge are indispensable for competing in today's job market. The users of all three types of spaces state that despite the centrality of the relationship between ICT and jobs, they do not look for work online. This is due in part to a certain distrust of putting their personal data online[17] and a fear of being deceived,[18] as well as, at least in part, the fact that they feel they are more likely to find a job through traditional channels.

As indicated by a variety of studies (Gonzáles-Rodrigo and Saíz-Gonzáles 2008; Granovetter 2005; Kuhn and Skuterud 2004) and based on our own research, we can conclude that the online search for employment does not appear to be effective, and getting a job largely depends on having the right contacts. This experience, shared by all social classes, is strongly rooted in low-income sectors. For this reason, mass education practices and practices dedicated to obtaining employment are not observed in the cybercafé. Similarly, our survey respondents did not ascribe high significance to the impact of accessing ICT on their employment prospects.

Indeed, ICT does not have a major impact on places where no daily need for it exists and where it is not socially meaningful. Therefore, the contribution of the cybercafé is not so much toward obtaining employment or improving income as toward generating "significant ties" (Boase et al. 2006), which, although nominally weak, are perceived by users as potentially beneficial in terms of future employment.

However, in the MTD center, and currently to a lesser degree in the Cirujas CEA, social imaginaries, expectations, and reality appear to converge more effectively. The MTD center's PC Repair and Refurbishment Workshop and the courses offered address the desires and anxieties of its users by offering a concrete space for processing and fulfilling them and achieve employment-related results by reinforcing the expectations and capabilities of youth, offering them immediate job prospects, increasing their confidence in seeking future jobs, and strengthening their interest in education.

Gender

While in Europe and the United States the digital divide with respect to gender has narrowed over the past several years, in Latin America and particularly in Argentina, it remains an issue.[19] Women continue to face challenges in terms of access to and training in computers and the Internet.

Of the three venues studied, the cybercafé was a predominantly male space, due to both the profile of its users and the primary purpose and activities of the space. At the Cirujas CEA, women were in the majority, whereas at the MTD center, the gender profile appeared to be more balanced. Participation of women in the CITCs is consistent with their high level of involvement in grassroots organizations. In low-income sectors, particularly during periods of high unemployment, women assume the responsibility of guaranteeing the material welfare of families, taking on not only traditionally "female" tasks (e.g., organizing community groups linked to daily needs, such as soup kitchens and preschools) but also "male" tasks, such as the production and management of income. Meanwhile, the men take refuge in private space, shamed by the lack of employment and thrown off balance by the loss of their traditional role of principal provider (Svampa and Pereyra 2004).

It's very hard for men to do what for women is quite natural. When we start to need things, if our children need something, we dive in, not only in economic terms but also as part of an overall struggle. I know many women who are married and their husbands have a hard time understanding. They say, "Why are you wasting your time?" (Karina, 42, Cirujas CEA supervisor)

In this context, compared to the discouraging and intimidating atmosphere we observed in the cybercafé, the CITCs offer a safe place for women to develop their computer skills. Several women interviewed stated that having access to a potential source of education means building a path to their first job or more highly skilled jobs. However, a CITC is not considered merely a functional space for training and acquiring technical skills: in our interviews, it was repeatedly cited as a place for personal development.

I want to be able to work. At home, my husband's salary is not enough. I mean, it's enough for the basics, but not for other things, expanding the house, building a room for my daughter. (Isabel, 31, Cirujas CEA user)

Furthermore, in interpreting the meaning of these motivations in daily life, we observed that both younger and older women see these courses as an opportunity to obtain some independence from their husbands and their role as mothers. Acquiring technological proficiency is considered an essential step in embarking on paths that represent an alternative to domestic chores. Thus, they often experience their participation in the courses as "time and space for me"—in other words, an autonomous environment where they as women, rather than as wives or mothers, are the protagonists and recipients of potential benefits.

It depends on my time. If the girls are with their father, I don't have to be the serious mother and I do other things. I go out, I go to shows and that sort of thing. I am with my music and the technology, phone and computer. I don't know, perhaps an artist comes. Yesterday, for instance, I went to the cybercafé to look and there were tickets for Bon Jovi. (Laura, 27, MTD center user)

A more profound meaning of the experience with technology emerges, particularly among women, as these venues come to be regarded as spaces for self-realization, sharing, and personal growth. This perspective is not as common among male users, although men also experience affective and solidarity bonds, even in the cybercafé.

Given the characteristics of the case studies, it is not surprising that for women who wish to use technology, the cybercafé is merely a transitional space where they carry out specific tasks that require little time and commitment to their surroundings. Nor is it remarkable that they visit cybercafés infrequently and not for long, whereas they enjoy visibility and prominence in the community and state spaces.

What is characteristic and different in the way women appropriate these spaces is that they use them as a bridge to other things: to access the job market, for example (something shared by the men), but also—and herein lies the principal difference—to achieve an enriched dialogue with their children and families. When their children have computer skills and they do not, they feel left out of their children's experience, and this is a key factor in their motivation. The narratives of the women we interviewed revealed a unique symbolic and cultural universe in their relationship with technology and public space in general.

Conclusions and Recommendations

Public spaces are the main access venues to ICT for youth from urban, low-income sectors in a context in which poverty is reinforced through a lack of supply and demand for ICT access. As indicated in the literature, the digital divide and digital poverty stem from social, economic, and cultural divisions and poverty perpetuated through deep inequalities.

Public access and support spaces for ICT are appropriated by youth as a response to this deficiency. While cybercafés are the main access point for Internet use and enable subjects to overcome the first-order digital divide, community training spaces (such as the MTD center and Cirujas CEA) address the second-order digital divide by allowing users to acquire technological skills.

CICTs are appropriated differently by youth from low-income sectors, producing distinct results in terms of sociability, expectations with regard to work and education, increased self-esteem and confidence, and desire for independence (table 7.3). In their own ways and with varying degrees of success, the different venues function, based on subjects' appropriation of them, as mechanisms for the social integration of youth from low-income sectors. These youth are not digital natives but rather digital immigrants who learn to use technologies through CITCs; their experience is shaped by a context of digital poverty with many insufficiencies: lack of available services, insufficient economic resources, and lack of cognitive abilities.

Table 7.3
Summary Comparison of the Venues Studied

	Private PAV (Cybercafé)	Community (MTD Center)	State/Community (Cirujas CEA)
User profile	Mostly male adolescents with wide-ranging and extended periods of use. Women visit less frequently and stay only briefly to perform specific and concrete tasks.	Youth and adults, both male and female. Men take repair courses and women learn to use PCs.	Mostly women (both younger and older) taking introductory computer courses.
User Motives	To meet with friends, play online, access the Internet.	To learn to use a computer and the Internet, and computer repair (a trade).	To learn to use a computer.
Training/ education	Not offered; this is a space for first contact with ICT and practicing skills.	Central function. Different courses are offered, with job prospects and practical guidance.	Central function. Formal computer courses are offered.
Work	Not the main purpose, but in gaining familiarity with computers, users increase their confidence in employability.	Courses oriented to job prospects within and outside the MTD. The MTD generates work contacts and improves users' confidence in employability.	Courses improve users' job skills and their confidence in employability.
Socialization	Primary function. Youth make new friends in the cybercafé and via the Internet.	Forges social bonds and allows communications uses of the Internet.	Not a significant aspect, although one of the motivations for the students is to learn to use the computer to communicate.
Citizen participation	The space is occasionally used to complete online forms and procedures.	Users develop a commitment to the organization.	ICT is seen as an opportunity for personal expression.
Gender	The characteristics and guidance turn this into a predominantly male space that resists the integration of women.	User profile is heterogeneous; the space is friendly and safe for women.	The nature of the organization and the course schedule contribute to generating a predominantly female space valued as a safe place for women.

The type of space influences the spectrum of users who regularly frequent it to use ICT, particularly with respect to age and gender. The cybercafé is clearly a male space (particularly for young men between the ages of 17 and 25), confirming what is indicated in the literature, whereas the Cirujas CEA is predominantly a space of young and adult women (ranging in age from 15 to 40). The MTD center user group is more heterogeneous with respect to age and gender: it comprises men and women, young and old. We did observe a specific distribution by gender and age according to the type of course: men preferred PC repair and refurbishment courses (hardware), whereas women preferred computer and Internet user courses (software), replicating in the information age the division of roles that accompanied the gendered organization of work in the "Ford Motor Company" era. The cybercafé users have, on average, more computer and Internet skills and experience than those who frequent the MTD center or Cirujas CEA, who are generally engaging in their first interactions with computers. In terms of impact, the influence of the state and community spaces is restricted in territorial terms; although their results are qualitatively relevant, they affect only a limited number of users and therefore do not have a noticeable effect in quantitative terms.

The greatest contrast among the three CITCs is in their primary function: the central goal of the community- and state-sponsored spaces (MTD center and Cirujas CEA) is to provide computer training, whereas the cybercafé's is to provide access to the latest-generation technology, specifically designed for communications and games-related commercial use. In correlation with these distinctive characteristics, we observed that the motives of users of the different spaces were also distinct. Those who visit the cybercafé do so to play online games or communicate with friends, whereas those who go to the state and community spaces do so primarily to acquire computer skills. Returning to the discussion on digital poverty (Barrantes 2007), we can conclude that cybercafés essentially supply connectivity, whereas the MTD center and the Cirujas CEA address issues of demand, lack of skills, and information capital. Some of the people who frequented the CITCs had never before had contact with computers and seemingly had no immediate reason to incorporate them into their daily lives. The difference between the pedagogical objectives of the CITCs, in contrast with the multiple uses enabled by the cybercafé, is related to the type of activities engaged in by the users in the respective spaces.

Based on the results of our research, we propose that the following recommendations be kept in mind by those developing public policies aimed at improving the extent and efficiency of each type of venue.

Cybercafés

Given the central role of cybercafés in providing Internet access for low-income sectors, special attention should be paid to the confirmed decrease of these spaces in outlying neighborhoods and indeed nationwide (D'Alessio 2010; Soriano 2010). Because not all homes have ICT access, as the number of cybercafés dwindles, the number of young nonusers will rise. As we have seen, cybercafés fulfill a social function as a meeting and support place for young males who, if these venues disappeared, would spend most of their time on the street, where risks and vulnerability are higher. Likewise, the social capital of the young cybercafé users would be diminished because many of their contacts outside the physical limits of their neighborhoods would be lost.

Nevertheless, improved state regulation of these spaces is necessary, especially with regard to controlling content available to children, given that the use of filters currently appears to depend on the owners. Finally, we believe it is important to promote the activities and significance of these spaces to youth in such a way as to strengthen their ties to the school environment. To this end, we suggest that the data from our study and similar studies be used as input in the training of teachers who are being prepared for "one-on-one" instruction in schools. Through an understanding of youth activities in cybercafés, prejudices can be overcome, and the two spaces can work together more effectively.

Community Spaces: Self-Managed or State-Supported

Based on our research, we wish to emphasize the results obtained by the CITCs managed by grassroots organizations. Spaces such as the MTD center and Cirujas CEA are well placed to meet the demands of a significant portion of low-income sectors that place high value on acquiring technological skills. If spaces like these were replicated by the hundreds, they would have a significant impact in terms of training on young men and women who have been marginalized from the education system and job market as adults because of their lack of contact with and knowledge of ICT. These spaces are managed by organizations that are focused on meeting the day-to-day needs of their members and manage to inscribe social significance to ICT access. By promoting an atmosphere of trust and mutual assistance, the CITCs enable participants to overcome the fears and anxieties generated by the social imperatives of using a computer and being connected. Both the MTD center and the Cirujas CEA manage to reinforce the educational and occupational expectations of users who, depending on the stage they are at in their lives, see access to ICT as an opportunity to gain autonomy and independence, either from their parents (in the case of younger users) or from domestic life and the role of wife and mother (in the case of young women).

Based on these results, we recommend that new research be carried out in order to numerically evaluate the impact of training on users and determine how to reproduce the experience of the CEA of the Cirujas Civic Association and the even more specific and unique case of the La Matanza MTD center on a large-scale basis throughout the country and in other countries. We believe that this would strengthen the promotion of these state initiatives, providing, as in the MyPC Program, the technology and funds required to run these CITCs without necessarily imposing management by the state. It has been shown that the greater the involvement and responsibility of the grassroots organization, the greater its members' commitment to and appropriation of the space.

Additionally, we suggest establishing these spaces in the most marginalized areas, where data reveal high rates of disconnection. It should be noted that this recommendation is being followed to some degree by the evaluation team of the MyPC Program as well as the designers of the Argentina Connected Plan, under the authority of the Ministry of Federal Planning, which anticipates establishing so-called Knowledge Access Hubs (*Núcleos de Acceso al Conocimiento* [NAC]) in areas with low ICT availability.

With respect to the unmet needs that must be addressed, these spaces must have adequate facilities dedicated exclusively to ICT access. Likewise, time for free Internet access should be increased beyond the training courses. In this sense, it is vital that in the absence of private providers, the state guarantee the necessary connectivity for these organizations.

With respect to the details of each of these spaces, we recommend introducing the MTD center's PC Refurbishment and Repair Workshop to the Cirujas CEA. We have seen how this initiative fulfills the desire of youth to improve their immediate job prospects; it could have an even greater impact if young women were encouraged to participate as well.

Likewise, we suggest that both spaces adjust their teaching methods and course content, which are generally strictly technical and practical, to increase their relevance to the daily activities of users, given that users are more effective and eager in their appropriation of knowledge when it is meaningful and useful to them in their daily lives.

Although home connectivity and the use of smart phones are steadily increasing, it is important not to lose sight of the social functions of the various PAVs and support centers for low-income people in general and youngsters in particular. Not all youth worldwide are digital natives, and not all of them are able to integrate ICT into their daily lives with the same ease. Different contexts, backgrounds, experiences, and sociocultural profiles, unequal distribution of capital—all affect the process of ICT appropriation. Among middle- and upper class youth, the integration of ICT unfolds in a natural and individual way in their home, school, university, and work environments. For low-income youth, in contrast, overcoming the fears and anxieties that ICT generates often depends on collective spaces that are appropriated by youth as part of their personal strategy to remain socially connected.

Notes

1. CEA stands for *Centro de Enseñanza y Acceso a la Informática*, which roughly translates as ICT Training and Access Center.

2. The survey was conducted using door-to-door interviews and covered 300 residents in the zone of influence of the selected venues. The sample included minimum quotas for age, gender, and type of user (home user and public-space user and nonuser).

3. *Source:* Instituto Nacional de Estadística y Censos (INDEC) http://www.indec.mecon.ar/nuevaweb/cuadros/74/grafpobreza2.xls.

4. Official data available at http://www.indec.mecon.ar. Data for 2013 was obtained from: http://www.argentina.ar/temas/pais/20023-crecio-el-empleo-joven-en-el-pais and http://www.argentina.ar/temas/economia-y-negocios/27448-la-tasa-de-desempleo-se-ubico-en-66-en-2013.

5. The MyPC Program (*Programa MiPC*) aims to reduce the digital divide in two ways: (1) making computers and information technologies available at a reduced cost at sales centers in different parts of the country, and (2) creating ICT Training and Access Centers (CEAs). Our study focuses on one of the CEAs created in La Matanza in September 2010.

6. The Argentina Connected Program (*Programa Argentina Conectada*), created by Telecommunications decree 1552/2010, proposes the expansion of broadband throughout the country in order to connect ten million homes by 2015. *Source*: http://www.argentina.ar/_es/pais/C5142-plan-nacional-de-telecomunicaciones-argentina-conectada.php.

7. *Source:* http://alainet.org/active/38978&lang=es.

8. *Source:* http://www.hcdiputadosba.gov.ar/osl/actividades%5Cencuentros_descentralizados%5C3%20seccion%5Cmidde%5COSL_Midde%20local_La%20Matanza%20v2.pdf.

9. According to our fieldwork findings, there appear to be significantly more computers in homes. Of those interviewed, around 50 percent reported having a computer at home, although because of the shortage of providers in the area, only a few had Internet access. This tendency is consistent with the rise in the number of broadband connections observed in Buenos Aires province: a 16.4 percent increase between December 2009 and December 2010. *Source:* http://www.indec.mecon.ar/nuevaweb/cuadros/14/Internet_03_11.pdf.

10. Whereas in 2006, 49 percent of users surveyed reported accessing the Internet from a cybercafé, in 2008, this figure fell to 22 percent and in 2009 to only 14 percent (D'Alessio 2010).

11. See http://volunteers.uwcrcn.no/movimiento-de-trabajadores-desocupados-de-la-matanza-buenos-aires-argentina/.

12. In 2007, the leader of the MTD, Héctor "Toty" Flores, was elected as a national representative of the party.

13. Fundación Equidad (www.equidad.org) is a nonprofit organization dedicated to "providing services and technology to promote equal opportunities, social integration, and care for the environment." In partnership with other civil society organizations and several businesses, it backs various initiatives to refurbish computers, provide support and cooperation for research on the access and use of ICT, and create community access centers.

14. Several subjects interviewed made reference to a decline in business in the area's cybercafés. This observation coincides with the trends reflected in the current statistics on the topic (see Soriano 2010).

15. As Barrantes (2007) points out, in the contexts of digital poverty, one of the challenges in promoting the use of ICT is an absence of demand among a population who, never having used a computer, find no reason to learn to use one.

16. *"About a year ago, we bought a computer here, refurbished at La Juanita"* (Mercedes, MTD student). *"I've had a computer for two months. I earned it by working here and they gave it to me"* (Vanina, MTD student).

17. *"You have to be crazy to look for work online. It scares me. I don't like it. I don't even put personal data in my e-mails. I have my first name there but not my last name"* (Nélida, cybercafé user).

18. *"A friend of mine was looking for work on the Internet. It was supposedly to be a waitress but it was far from that. I prefer to go where my friends tell me. They were working in San Justo and they told me they needed girls. I went and applied"* (Ileana, Cirujas CEA student).

19. In Latin America, the BRIDGE Report on Gender and Development (Gurumurthy 2004), the Women's Networking Support Program (PARM) of the Association for Progressive Communications (APC), and initiatives such as GenderIT.org and GEM, demonstrate how first- and second-order effects of the digital divide are present precisely because they are related to other variables with respect to inequality, such as education and socioeconomic levels.

References

Barrantes, Roxana. 2007. Analysis of ICT Demand: What Is Digital Poverty and How to Measure It? In *Digital Poverty: Latin American and Caribbean Perspectives*, ed. Hernán Galperín and Judith Mariscal, 29–53. Lima: DIRSI-IDRC.

Best, Michael L. 2010. Connecting In Real Space: How People Share Knowledge and Technologies in Cybercafés. Paper presented at the 19th AMIC (Asian Media Information and Communication Centre) Annual Conference, Singapore. http://www.globalimpactstudy.org/wp-content/uploads/2010/10/amic.final_.1.1.pdf.

Boase, Jeffrey, John B. Horrigan, Barry Wellman, and Lee Rainie. 2006. *The Strength of Internet Ties*. Washington, DC: Pew Internet and American Life Project.

Bouille, Julieta. 2008. Cibercafés o la nueva esquina: Usos y apropiaciones de internet en jóvenes de sectores populares urbanos. In *Ciberculturas juveniles. Los jóvenes, sus prácticas y representaciones en la era de Internet*, ed. Marcelo Urresti. Buenos Aires: La Crujía Ediciones.

Camacho, Kemly. 2005. La brecha digital. In *Palabras en juego: Enfoques Multiculturales sobre las Sociedades de la Información*, coordinated by Alain Ambrosi, Valérie Peugeot, and Daniel Pimienta. Paris: C & F Édition.

D'Alessio, I. R. O. L. 2010. *Internet en la Argentina*. Buenos Aires. http://www.dalessio.com.ar/xpublico/archivos/1346_I_13_Libro_Internet_sintesis.pdf.

Dalton, Russell J., Paul A. Beck, and Robert Huckfeldt. 1998. Partisan Cues and the Media: Information Flows in the 1992 Presidential Election. *American Political Science Review* 92 (1): 111–126.

Deephouse, David L., and Pursey P. M. A. R. Heugens. 2009. Linking Social Issues to Organizational Impact: The Role of Infomediaries and the Infomediary Process. *Journal of Business Ethics* 86 (4): 541–553.

Finquelievich, Susana, and Alejandro Prince. 2007. *El (involuntario) rol social de los cibercafés*. Buenos Aires: Editorial Dunken. http://www.oei.es/tic/rolcibercafes.pdf.

Gomez, Ricardo. 2009. *Measuring Global Public Access to ICT: Landscape Summary Reports from 25 Countries Around the World*. CIS Working Paper No. 7. Seattle: Technology & Social Change Group (TASCHA) (formerly the Center for Information & Society [CIS]), University of Washington Information School. https://digital.lib.washington.edu/researchworks/bitstream/handle/1773/16292/TASCHA_Gomez_MeasuringPublicAccess_2009.pdf.

Gonzáles-Rodrigo, Elena, and Jorge Saíz-Gonzáles. 2008. ¿Quién busca trabajo en Internet? In *TIC y trabajo: hacia nuevos sistemas organizativos, nuevas estructuras ocupacionales y salariales, y nuevos mecanismos de intermediación*. Universitat Oberta de Catalunya (UOC) Papers 6: 40–49. http://www.uoc.edu/uocpapers/6/dt/esp/dossier_tic_y_trabajo.pdf.

Granovetter, Mark S. 2005. The Impact of Social Structure on Economic Outcomes. *Journal of Economic Perspectives* 19 (1): 33–50.

Gurumurthy, Anita. 2004. *Gender and ICTs: Overview Report*. Brighton, UK: BRIDGE, Institute of Development Studies.

Kuhn, Peter, and Mikal Skuterud. 2004. Internet Job Search and Unemployment Durations. *American Economic Review* 94 (1): 218–232.

National Institute of Statistics and Censuses (Argentina). 2010. *Argentina Population and Housing Census 2010*. Buenos Aires, Argentina: Author. http://www.censo2010.indec.gov.ar/.

National Institute of Statistics and Censuses (Argentina). 2012. National Survey on Access and Use of Information Technology and Communication (*Encuesta Nacional sobre Acceso y Uso de Tecnologías de la Información y la Comunicación [ENTIC]*). Buenos Aires, Argentina: INDEC.

Ramirez, Ricardo. 2007. Appreciating the Contribution of Broadband ICT with Rural and Remote Communities: Stepping Stones Toward an Alternative Paradigm. *Information Society* 23 (2): 85–94.

Sey, Araba, and Michelle Fellows. 2009. *Literature Review on the Impact of Public Access to Information and Communication Technologies*. CIS Working Paper No. 6. Seattle: Technology & Social Change Group (TASCHA) (formerly the Center for Information &Society [CIS]), University of Washington Information School. http://library.globalimpactstudy.org/sites/default/files/docs/CIS-WorkingPaperNo6.pdf.

SistemaNacional de Consumos Culturales. 2008. *Informe N° 4/Marzo 2008*. Buenos Aires: Author.

Soriano, Fernando. 2010. El ciber pasó de moda y hoy sobrevive con el mail 'al paso'. *Clarín*, December 18. http://www.clarin.com/sociedad/ciber-paso-moda-sobrevive-mail_0_392960807.html.

Svampa, Maristella, and Sebastián Pereyra. 2004. *Entre la ruta y el barrio*. Buenos Aires: Biblos.

Thompson, John. 1998. *Los media y la modernidad*. Barcelona: Ediciones Paidós Ibérica.

Universidad Nacional de La Matanza. 2006. Proyecto: Seguimiento de la situación social en el Municipio de La Matanza 2004–2005. http://observatoriosocial.unlam.edu.ar/descargas/6_seguimiento_lamatanza.pdf.

Warschauer, Mark. 2003. *Technology and Social Inclusion: Rethinking the Digital Divide*. Cambridge, MA: MIT Press.

Winocur, Rosalía. 2007. La apropiación de la computadora e Internet en los sectores populares urbanos. *Versión* 19: 191–216.

8 Impact of Public Access to Computers and the Internet on the Connectedness of Rural Malaysians

Nor Aziah Alias, Marhaini Mohd Noor, Francisco J. Proenza, Haziah Jamaludin, Izaham Shah Ismail, and Sulaiman Hashim

Abstract

This chapter reports the findings of research conducted in 2010 on the connectedness of rural Malaysians who accessed computers and the Internet through the rural Internet centers (RICs) established by the Malaysian government in 2000 and 2003. We examine the impact of the RICs on users' sense of social connectedness, defined as the feeling of belongingness and being linked and related to a network, community, or group that one trusts and interacts with. Our study's findings give credence to the RIC initiative. Users use RIC facilities and services to connect with family, friends, and acquaintances, with new people external to their social circle, and (albeit to a much lesser degree) with government. Users perceive a heightened sense of connectedness and feel that this connectedness has had a positive impact in their lives. There appears to be room to expand the impact of RIC telecenters so that they foster greater collaboration and help nurture the development of positive social capital. Some of the possibilities for expanding impact are identified.

Introduction

Malaysia has a population of 29.3 million (UNDP 2013, 195) and is one of a few developing economies that have been growing rapidly since the 1970s. Malaysia has a high human development ranking—62nd among the 187 countries considered by UNDP (2014) and a relatively high GDP per capita (estimated as $21,824 PPP in 2013 by UNDP (2014). The Government of Malaysia envisages the country's transformation into a knowledge-based society through many initiatives, including programs based on information and communication technology (ICT).

As of 2013, 67 of every 100 inhabitants were Internet users (ITU 2013). The broadband household penetration rate was 62.3 percent in 2011 (MOSTI 2011). Internet subscribers are concentrated in Kuala Lumpur and in the surrounding state of Selangor (comScore 2010). Connectivity is much lower in the rest of the country. Internet use is also constrained by a low level of computer ownership, which is "estimated to be as high as 88 percent in urban areas, but no more than 12 percent in the rural areas" (Gomez 2009, 71). The access challenge in Malaysia is essentially the provision of service to rural communities where an estimated 26 percent of the country's population lives (UNDP 2014).

Malaysia's telecenter project is one of the government's key initiatives to bridge the rural–urban digital divide through free shared access to computers and the Internet. The connectivity needs of rural residents are being addressed in part through the telecenter program, which established forty-two telecenters from 2000 to 2003. However, the financial sustainability of rural telecenters is often challenged (Proenza 2001) and this is as true in Malaysia as elsewhere (Ibrahim, Yasin, and Dahalin 2010). It is therefore important to ascertain whether government sponsorship of telecenters is worthwhile, by asking whether telecenters are making a positive impact on people's lives. The focus of this chapter is on whether the rural Internet center (RIC) program has fostered connectedness among telecenter users—i.e., whether RIC use increases users' sense of being linked and related to other persons or to the community.

The Malaysian government has many public access support programs, of which the most ambitious is the Universal Service Provision (USP) Program that includes the Community Broadband Library Project and the Community Broadband Center Project initiated by the Malaysian Communications and Multimedia Commission. The USP Program started in 2007 with 44 district libraries equipped with broadband; by December 2009 it had reached 859 libraries (Abu Bakar 2010). The Community Broadband Center Project, funded with USP resources, was launched in 2008 with 73 centers. The number of community broadband telecenters is still growing as more USP providers are getting involved. The Ministry of Rural and Regional Development's Infodesa project began in 2001 with six telecenters and by 2009 reported a total of 242. Individual states also sponsor their own separate public access programs. Not all of these access points are fully operational.

Our study focused on RICs for three reasons. First, unlike district libraries which are often found in relatively large towns, RICs are located in rural and often isolated communities; only in the last three years have broadband library initiatives been aggressively pursued in smaller rural communities. Second, RICs are run by the post offices following a homogeneous and well-defined approach, which is not always the case for other programs. Third and most important, RICs are the longest running rural access program, and the passing of time is needed before their impact can be perceived and appreciated.

Connectedness matters for the individual as well as for society. An extensive literature points to a strong association between connectedness and positive outcomes in personal health and well-being (Barber and Schluterman 2008; Berkman et al. 2000; Cockshaw and Shochet 2007; Markham et al. 2010; Sadlo 2005). "Happy people have richer social networks than unhappy people, and social connectedness contributes to a lack of disability as we age" (Seligman 2011, 206). Social connectedness is also a building block of social capital. When members of a socially connected group establish trusting relationships, they often find ways to cooperate in joint activities that are beyond the possibilities of individual members (Larsson 2007; Pretty 2003). As the technology has become ubiquitous in developed countries, group action using the Internet has become commonplace, and impacts online and local communities (Rainie, Purcell, and Smith 2011).

Rural Internet Centers in Malaysia

Malaysia's rural Internet centers (RICs) or Pusat Internet Desa (PID) have been in operation since 2000. The Ministry of Information, Communication and Culture is in charge of the RIC project. As of 2010, forty-two RICs were in operation, each with its own website and network of members. Each RIC is hosted by the local post office and managed by two staff, and provides ICT training and services to members of the community at minimal cost. RICs also run entrepreneurial and other community activities and programs. Table 8.1 lists the number and geographical location of the RICs in the rural areas of Malaysia's thirteen states.

RICs have an average of three to four desktop computers, but we found one RIC with ten computers. When user demand exceeds computer availability, users are limited to one hour per session. RIC users comprise adolescents, school leavers, housewives, entrepreneurs, and senior citizens. The managers describe the majority of their RIC users as students and job seekers. They also report more female users (45–80 percent) than males: women prefer to use the RICs, where they feel safer and more comfortable than in cybercafés. Most of the senior citizens who frequent the RICs are men.

Hours of operation of the RICs are 8 A.M. to 5 P.M., Monday through Friday. RICs are busiest in mid-morning and late afternoon after school. Most adults visit in the morning, and students and women age 25 to 35 in the afternoon. Our data showed a steady stream of users throughout the day: those who come in for training sessions in the morning, adults in the mid-morning and afternoon, and school-age youths in the late afternoon. Unless training is in session, the RIC managers interviewed reported an average of twenty to thirty regular users per week, with a few registering as many as

Table 8.1
Number of Rural Internet Centers (RICs) in Malaysia, by State

State	#	Rural Internet center sites
Sabah	3	Tenom, Kota Belud, Kota Marudu
Sarawak	4	Mukah, Betong, Bau, Song
Perlis	1	Simpang Empat
Kedah	4	Bukit Kayu Hitam, Yan, Kuala Nerang, Kupang
Pulau Pinang	2	Tasek Glugor, Balik Pulau
Perak	5	Selama, Kuala Kurau, Langkap, Tanjung Malim, Parit
Selangor	6	Beranang, Sungai Pelek, Rasa, Hulu Langat, Tanjung Sepat, Sungai Air Tawar
Negri Sembilan	3	Kota, Lenggeng, Bandar Seri Jempol
Melaka	1	Tanjung Kling
Johor	6	Bandar Tenggara, Bandar Penawar, Labis, Pagoh, Sungai Mati, Sri Medan
Pahang	3	Sungai Koyan, Bukit Goh, Bandar Tun Razak
Trengganu	2	Besut, Marang
Kelantan	2	Kuala Krai, Kuala Balah
Total	42	

Source: http://www.pid.net.my/ (site no longer accessible)

fifty to sixty per week. This represents an average of four to six users per day. RIC use appears to fluctuate during the year. A higher number of users was recorded during school breaks and after major national examinations. By and large, RIC usage peaks at the end of the year when school leavers (those who have completed high school and are entering post-secondary education) come in to be trained, and declines during the rainy season (December to February) when rains and floods deter RIC users.

Local context, culture, politics, and community support are strong determinants of RIC activities and outcomes (Alias et al. 2010). RICs situated in communities that have other public access options such as cybercafés and broadband centers tend to cater to mature users who are not comfortable with the youth-dominated culture of the other venues mentioned. For instance, a 63-year-old male interviewed at one of the Malaysian RICs commented that the community broadband center was too noisy for him. Most RIC managers respond to the local clientele, providing services and developing activities that fit the needs and characteristics of the users. Community users influence RIC managers' personal development: managers from the same community tend to be socially connected to users. Managers say they develop their skills and ICT expertise in response to local needs.

According to a ministry official interviewed, sustaining and developing the RICs has been challenging. Maintenance of the centers and the status of the managers hired on a contract basis are frequent problems. Other concerns include the status and ownership of the RICs. Though initiated as government agencies, RICs have been allowed to grow and evolve almost independently. Other than the paychecks of the managers, there has been sporadic support from the ministry in the form of new computers and upgrades of old ones.

Methodology

The concept of connectedness has been studied in various fields, including psychology (Baumeister and Leary 1995; Russell, Norman, and Heckler 2004; Yoon and Lee 2010), sociology (Romero et al. 2003), higher education (Glaser and Bingham 2009; Terrell, Snyder, and Dringus 2009), teacher education (Daves and Roberts 2010), and communication (Gray and Dennis 2010; Wei and Lo 2006). It has been used to study varied social phenomena such as voter turnout (Timpone 1998), adolescent behavior (Karcher 2001; Markham et al. 2010; Taylor-Seehafer, Jakobvitz, and Steiker 2008), and the academic success of visually impaired undergraduates (Scott 2009). This breadth of research has led to differences in the definition of the concept of connectedness and in the indicators used to measure it (Barber and Schluterman 2008).

The Concept of Connectedness in the Context of RIC Use

We define social connectedness as *the feeling of belongingness, being linked to and related to a network, community, or group that one trusts and interacts with*. This definition is consistent with Baumeister and Leary's view (1995) of the need to belong as a fundamental human motivation, and with self-determination theory's *relatedness need*, "a psychological necessity that involves having positive interpersonal interactions and trusting relationships" (Moller, Deci, and Elliott 2010, 754).

By this definition, does access to computers and the Internet enhance RIC users' sense of connectedness?

We considered social connectedness among RIC users with regard to user engagement and sense of belonging or relatedness (figure 8.1). RICs provide access to computers and the Internet; user participation or engagement is a necessary intermediate step. Engagement can manifest through greater knowledge of what is happening beyond a person's immediate situation and in public institutions affecting them, and through greater interaction with a community with which the user identifies and with people who are emotionally linked to them. The sense of belonging or relatedness is what we

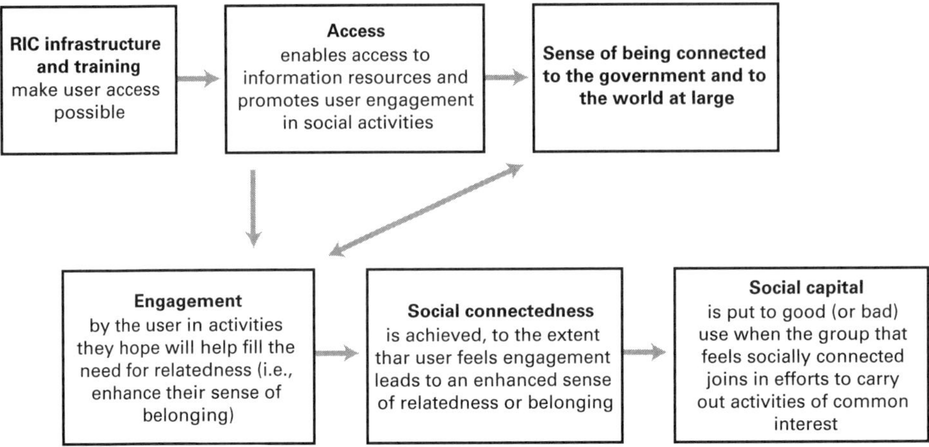

Figure 8.1
A framework of connectedness among Malaysian RIC users.

here refer to as social connectedness. Social connections normally begin with loose contacts between people; but even these weak ties are frequently a source of valuable practical information (Boase et al. 2006; Granovetter 1973,).

We also examined the extent to which RIC users reported a sense of being connected to government. Connectedness with government or even to the world at large may occur, but tends to be less immediate and personal. Connectedness with government does not fulfill the sense of belonging or the "relatedness need" described by Baumeister and Leary (1995) and by Moller, Deci, and Elliot (2010).

Figure 8.2 depicts various levels of social connectedness that may be achieved through RIC use. Lower levels in the pyramid are more readily achievable than higher levels. They are not necessarily less useful, but higher levels require greater trust between participants and involve complex coordination efforts; i.e., they require social capital. Users also exhibit varying levels of RIC utilization and ICT literacy, thus limiting the extent to which RIC users may reach higher levels. This study focuses on the three lower levels.

Population, Sampling, and Research Instrument

The research sites were selected from among the forty-two RICs in Malaysia, with at least one RIC from each of the thirteen Malaysian states. The respondents were rural people, both men and women, who frequented the RICs on randomly selected days. They were of various ages and occupations, and held various family responsibilities.

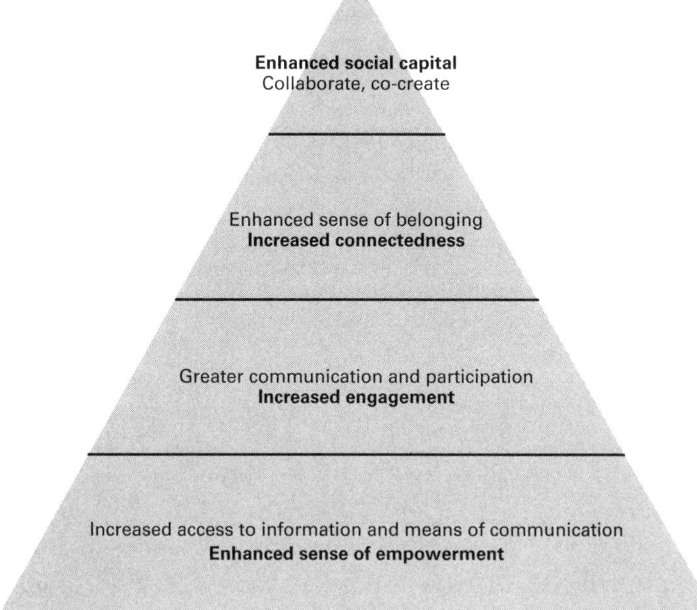

Figure 8.2
Typology of RIC users' connectedness possibilities.

RIC user perceptions were used to measure connectedness.[1] A twenty-five-item online questionnaire was developed to gauge the perceived impact on connectedness. Scales used include a five-point Likert scale, a numeric scale, and semantic differential scales (e.g., "No involvement" to "Extremely involved"). The user survey was hosted at www.surveymonkey.com.

RIC managers were invited to assist with data collection, and fifteen managers who agreed to participate were paid based on the number of RIC users responding to the questionnaires. Participating managers were keen to get every RIC visitor to fill out the questionnaire. They were given six weeks to help users by directing them to the survey website.

Three hundred and thirty-one users who came to the fifteen RICs on randomly selected days participated in the survey, and 299 users completed the survey. Most respondents had basic ICT skills. The majority (63 percent) were female. Thirty-seven managers and assistant managers also responded to a separate survey on their views of the RIC. Survey data were complemented with face-to-face interviews at the RICs with eighteen users and ten managers and assistant managers.

Findings

We first present a brief profile of RIC users and examine the activities and objectives in which users engage when they visit the RIC. We then assess the extent to which RIC users perceived an enhancement in their social connectedness on the basis of self-reported increases in: (1) sense of empowerment related to increased access to information through the RIC, and (2) user engagement, e.g., increased communication with family and friends and with other social entities such as nongovernmental or charity organizations. We conclude with an overall assessment of perceived impact on RIC users' lives in a variety of spheres, including connectedness.

Profile of RIC Users

A total of 331 users responded to our online survey on connectedness, with 299 complete responses (table 8.2). About 20 percent of survey respondents (61 observations) visited an RIC every day; the majority (170 respondents, 57 percent of our sample) visited less often but at least once a week. We consider these two groups to be "frequent RIC visitors" (232 observations; see table 8.2). The remaining 22 percent comprised RIC users who visited infrequently: "when there is training," "when my Internet connection is down," "when there is a program or meeting," "whenever I accompany my child," or "when I feel the need to increase my knowledge."

Most RIC users do not own computers, nor do they have Internet access at home. Mohd Noor (2013) found that nearly 60 percent of the 199 RIC users she surveyed reported that the RIC was the place they most frequently used to access the Internet (table 8.3). Our own field observations suggest that most young RIC users do not have Internet-connected computers in their homes, and that it is primarily older users who have their own PCs or laptops. The latter, however, still visit the centers, mainly for ICT support and training. One user interviewed described her experience thus: *"Before I learned of the RIC, I had no idea how to use the Internet and I really did not know about the advances in the outside world."*

The survey conducted by Shah Alam and Abdullah (2009) of cybercafés in two Malaysian cities, Melaka and Sarawak, exhibited considerable gender and age imbalance: 80 percent of respondents were male, and fewer than 1 percent of the interviewees were over 40 years old. The situation is quite different in the RICs. Most of our RIC survey respondents (63 percent) were female, and most of the frequent RIC users were young. Users age 50 and over account for about 5 percent of survey respondents (table 8.2).

Table 8.2
RIC User Survey Respondents: All Users, Frequent Users and Infrequent Users, by Age and Gender

	Male		Female		All	
Age groups	#	%	#	%	#	%
All RIC users						
< 13 yrs	3	2.7	6	3.2	9	3.0
13–17 yrs	9	8.1	27	14.4	36	12.0
18–24 yrs	37	33.3	90	47.9	127	42.5
25–35 yrs	37	33.3	39	20.7	76	25.4
36–50 yrs	16	14.4	20	10.6	36	12.0
> 50 yrs	9	8.1	6	3.2	15	5.0
Total	111	100.0	188	100.0	299	100.0
%	37.1		62.9		100.0	
Frequent users[a]						
< 13 yrs	3	3.5	3	2.0	6	2.6
13–17 yrs	5	5.9	22	15.0	27	11.6
18–24 yrs	30	35.3	70	47.6	100	43.1
25–35 yrs	27	31.8	34	23.1	61	26.3
36–50 yrs	13	15.3	14	9.5	27	11.6
> 50 yrs	7	8.2	4	2.7	11	4.7
Total	85	100.0	147	100.0	232	100.0
%	36.6		63.4		100.0	
Infrequent users*						
< 13 yrs	0	0.0	3	7.5	3	4.5
13–17 yrs	4	14.8	5	12.5	9	13.4
18–24 yrs	8	29.6	18	45.0	26	38.8
25–35 yrs	10	37.0	6	15.0	16	23.9
36–50 yrs	3	11.1	6	15.0	9	13.4
> 50 yrs	2	7.4	2	5.0	4	6.0
Total	27	100.0	40	100.0	67	100.0
%	40.3		59.7		100.0	

*Frequent users were defined as those who used the RIC at least once a week, infrequent users as those who did so less frequently.

Table 8.3
Distribution of Survey Respondents by Age and Place Most Frequently Used to Access the Internet

Place most frequently used to access the Internet	Age (years)				Total	
	< 20	20–30	31–50	> 50	#	%
Home	6	8	1	–	15	7.5
Work	–	10	4	–	14	7.0
House of friend or family	1	–	1	–	2	1.0
School/college	11	3	–	1	15	7.5
Cybercafé	15	7	–	–	22	11.1
Public library	8	–	–	–	8	4.0
RIC	52	45	13	7	117	58.8
Mobile	2	–	2	–	4	2.0
Do not know	–	1	1	–	2	1.0
Total	95	74	22	8	199	100.0

Source: Separate online survey of RIC users conducted by Mohd Noor, 2013.

Many RIC managers and assistant managers were female, which helped attract women and older users to the RIC. Women feel more comfortable in a welcoming environment and older adults need frequent support that may not be readily available in youth-dominated cybercafés. Women were also less apprehensive or shy when trained by RIC managers, many of whom often worked beyond regular hours to answer users' questions and provide online help.

User Activities and Objectives

Users were highly involved in activities such as using MS Office applications (61 percent) and browsing the Internet (58 percent). A fair percentage read online news, used email, and engaged in social networking and chats. Nearly 50 percent of users attended training sessions at the RICs (table 8.4).

Compared to young users (up to 24 years old), a higher proportion of mature users (24 and older) engaged in reading news online, attended training sessions, and used government services (table 8.4).

Survey respondents were presented with a list of 18 possible objectives for using the RIC and asked to select those they identified as their own objectives (table 8.5). On average, users identified 11–12 objectives for using the RIC. The most popular one, chosen by 89 percent of users, was to upgrade their skills using computers and the Internet. Other popular objectives were: becoming better informed (76 percent),

Table 8.4
Number and % of Users Engaged in Various Activities either Always or Frequently, for All Users and by Gender and Age Group

Activity	Male		Female		Young (≤ 24)		Mature (≥ 25)		All	
	#	%	#	%	#	%	#	%	#	%
Use MS Office applications	71	64.0	111	59.0	91	52.9	91	71.7	182	60.9
Browse the Internet	73	65.8	99	52.7	87	50.6	85	66.9	172	57.5
Access and read online news	54	48.6	56	29.8	31	18.0	79	62.2	110	36.8
Use email	61	55.0	83	44.1	71	41.3	73	57.5	144	48.2
Social networking (Facebook, Friendster, etc.)	62	55.9	85	45.2	76	44.2	71	55.9	147	49.2
Attend training session	48	43.2	97	51.6	75	43.6	70	55.1	145	48.5
Chat via YM, Facebook	62	55.9	86	45.7	79	45.9	69	54.3	148	49.5
Browse government website or portal	46	41.4	50	26.6	38	22.1	58	45.7	96	32.1
Use online government services	36	32.4	50	26.6	31	18.0	55	43.3	86	28.8
Seek help from RIC personnel in preparing document	39	35.1	61	32.4	47	27.3	53	41.7	100	33.4
Access NGO website / hobby or interest group	32	28.8	37	19.7	22	12.8	47	37.0	69	23.1
Listen to andor download music	32	28.8	37	19.7	36	20.9	33	26.0	69	23.1
Write blogs	19	17.1	33	17.6	21	12.2	31	24.4	52	17.4
Buy stuff online	17	15.3	30	16.0	17	9.9	30	23.6	47	15.7
Watch video online	25	22.5	31	16.5	31	18.0	25	19.7	56	18.7
Average # of activities rated "Always or frequently"	6.8		5.7		5.1		7.3		5.3	
# of respondents with at least one "Always or frequently" response	100		166		147		119		258	
Max # of respondents (% denominator)	111		188		172		127		299	

Table 8.5
Objectives for Using RIC, by Gender and Age Group

	Male		Female		Young (≤ 24)		Mature (≥ 25)		All	
Activity	#	%	#	%	#	%	#	%	#	%
Improve my ability to use the computer and the Internet (for any purpose)	86	86.0	159	90.3	133	85.3	112	93.3	245	88.8
Become better informed with latest news and information	77	77.0	134	76.1	113	72.4	98	81.7	211	76.4
Keep in touch/communicate with family, friends and acquaintances using the Internet (e.g., via email, chat, Facebook, etc.)	74	74.0	129	73.3	111	71.2	92	76.7	203	73.6
Meet friends, socialize, and make new friends at the RIC	64	64.0	125	71.0	105	67.3	84	70.0	189	68.5
Make new friends and/or find a mate or partner through the Internet	60	60.0	123	69.9	105	67.3	78	65.0	183	66.3
Have fun—play games, download music, watch video clips, relieve tension, go online for no particular reason, just for fun or pastime	63	63.0	112	63.6	111	71.2	64	53.3	175	63.4
Complete task, work or research online	67	67.0	102	58.0	88	56.4	81	67.5	169	61.2
Improve skills related to my job (or get a new or better job)	61	61.0	106	60.2	86	55.1	81	67.5	167	60.5
Improve my academic performance in school	54	54.0	108	61.4	106	67.9	56	46.7	162	58.7
Get more info on better products or services for myself and my family (for health, travel, etc.)	65	65.0	99	56.3	79	50.6	85	70.8	164	59.4
Get more and better government services (get info, communicate with officials/ agencies, transact with government online)	59	59.0	98	55.7	78	50.0	79	65.8	157	56.9
Find a job (new job, different job)	52	52.0	90	51.1	73	46.8	69	57.5	142	51.4

Develop my interest/hobby and my social/ charity work	47	47.0	86	48.9	61	39.1	72	60.0	133	48.2
Develop and maintain my own site or blog	42	42.0	89	50.6	75	48.1	56	46.7	131	47.5
Artistic or literary realization (write a book, poetry, music, computer art, etc.)	39	39.0	78	44.3	63	40.4	54	45.0	117	42.4
Improve performance of my own business or farm (e.g., advertise products, identify new market and new customers, etc.)	42	42.0	71	40.3	50	32.1	63	52.5	113	40.9
Contribute regularly to blogs that interest me or my family	40	40.0	75	42.6	64	41.0	51	42.5	115	41.7
Conduct business online	43	43.0	62	35.2	47	30.1	58	48.3	105	38.0
Support political or social causes that I find worthwhile (in part or solely through online groups, blogs or discussions)	40	40.0	64	36.4	51	32.7	53	44.2	104	37.7
Average # of objectives	11.6		11.7		11.1		12.4		11.7	
# users in category who chose at least 1 goal	100		176		156		120		276	

keeping in touch with family and friends (74 percent), meeting friends at the center (69 percent), socializing at the center (68 percent), and looking online for new friends or a life partner (66 percent).

There were no major differences in the objectives of male and female users. Women were more prone to visit the RIC to make friends online (70 percent) than men (60 percent; table 8.5), and more women (51 percent) than men (42 percent) maintained their own website or blog. A higher proportion of women (61 percent) than men (54 percent) visited the RIC to improve their academic performance, yet 67 percent of male users but only 58 percent of female users selected completing a task, work or research online as one of their objectives in using the RIC.

Differences in objectives by age were more pronounced (table 8.5). Among young people (under 24), having a good time and playing games (71 percent) and improving school performance (68 percent) were more popular than among mature users (53 and 47 percent, respectively), whereas using the RIC to improve the performance of their own business was more important among mature users (52 percent) than among young people (32 percent). Older users were less inclined to use the Internet to stay in touch. A 38-year-old male user interviewed preferred to use his telephone when communicating with family members and close friends. To him, hearing the other person's voice was more personal and meaningful.

To summarize, when users visit an RIC they engage in a variety of activities for different purposes. Connecting with family and friends figures prominently among their activities and objectives.

Empowerment through Access

About 79 percent of respondents felt empowered by the RICs (table 8.6a). They felt the RIC had made it easier for them to find out what was happening in the community (77 percent), in the country (82 percent), and among family and friends (74 percent), and to get information on their children's education (70 percent; table 8.6a). They also found it easier to use email to communicate with family and friends (81 percent). Fewer users felt the effect of the RIC on other activities, such as getting information on products (57 percent), advertising their own products (45 percent), or conducting transactions with government (52 percent).

There were no major differences between frequent and infrequent users in the perceived empowerment that the appearance of the RIC may have brought about (table 8.6b). The exception perhaps is that a greater proportion of frequent users (55 percent) than of infrequent users (43 percent) reported that the RIC made it easier for them to pay their bills.

Table 8.6a

Perceptions of Empowerment through Information Facilitated by the RIC: All Users

	Agree or Strongly Agree		Neutral*		Disagree or Strongly Disagree	
Type of Empowerment Perceived	#	%	#	%	#	%
Compared to before the RIC, it is now relatively easy to:						
Get information about what is happening in my community	231	77.3	64	21.4	4	1.3
Get information about what is happening in my country	245	81.9	53	17.7	1	0.3
Get information about what is happening to my family and friends	221	73.9	73	24.4	4	1.3
Get information about entertainment	199	66.6	93	31.1	7	2.3
Get information about the price and availability of products I consume	171	57.2	120	40.1	8	2.7
Pay bills	158	52.8	132	44.1	9	3.0
Advertise my product or business	136	45.5	153	51.2	8	2.7
Get information about my education / children's education	210	70.2	85	28.4	4	1.3
Conduct government-related transactions without leaving my village	160	53.5	130	43.5	8	2.7
Use the computer to type letters and stuff	251	83.9	48	16.1	–	–
Find information on employment opportunities	221	73.9	78	26.1	–	–
Apply for jobs / apply for university placement	224	74.9	75	25.1	–	–
Use email to communicate with my family and friends	243	81.3	54	18.1	2	0.7
Compared to before the RIC, I feel more empowered now	235	78.6	63	21.1	1	0.3

Note: Percentages are calculated in reference to the total number of respondents in the sample (299).

*Includes blank responses.

Table 8.6b

Perceptions of Empowerment through Information Facilitated by the RIC: Infrequent and Frequent Users

Type of Empowerment Perceived	Agree or Strongly Agree #	Agree or Strongly Agree %	Neutral[a] #	Neutral[a] %	Disagree or Strongly Disagree #	Disagree or Strongly Disagree %
Frequent users[b]						
Compared to before the RIC, it is now relatively easy to:						
Get information about what is happening in my community	181	77.7	48	20.6	3	1.3
Get information about what is happening in my country	189	81.1	43	18.5	–	–
Get information about what is happening to my family and friends	171	73.4	57	24.5	4	1.7
Get information about entertainment	151	64.8	77	33.0	4	1.7
Get information about the price and availability of products I consume	131	56.2	95	40.8	6	2.6
Pay bills	128	54.9	96	41.2	8	3.4
Advertise my product or business	106	45.5	118	50.6	7	3.0
Get information about my education / children's education	159	68.2	70	30.0	3	1.3
Conduct government-related transactions without leaving my village	122	52.4	103	44.2	7	3.0
Use the computer to type letters and stuff	193	82.8	39	16.7	–	–
Find information on employment opportunities	169	72.5	63	27.0	–	–
Apply for jobs / apply for university placement	174	74.7	58	24.9	–	–
Use email to communicate with my family and friends	185	79.4	45	19.3	2	0.9
Compared to before the RIC, I feel more empowered now	180	77.3	51	21.9	1	0.4
Sample size, frequent users (used to calculate %)	233		233		233	
Infrequent users[b]						
Compared to before the RIC, it is now relatively easy to:						
Get information about what is happening in my community	50	74.6	16	23.9	1	1.5
Get information about what is happening in my country	56	83.6	10	14.9	1	1.5

Table 8.6b (continued)

Type of Empowerment Perceived	Agree or Strongly Agree		Neutral[a]		Disagree or Strongly Disagree	
	#	%	#	%	#	%
Get information about what is happening to my family and friends	50	74.6	16	23.9	–	–
Get information about entertainment	47	70.1	17	25.4	3	4.5
Get information about the price and availability of products I consume	39	58.2	26	38.8	2	3.0
Pay bills	29	43.3	37	55.2	1	1.5
Advertise my product or business	30	44.8	35	52.2	1	1.5
Get information about my education / children's education	50	74.6	16	23.9	1	1.5
Conduct government-related transactions without leaving my village	37	55.2	28	41.8	1	1.5
Use the computer to type letters and stuff	58	86.6	9	13.4	–	–
Find information on employment opportunities	52	77.6	15	22.4	–	–
Apply for jobs / apply for university placement	50	74.6	17	25.4	–	–
Use email to communicate with my family and friends	58	86.6	9	13.4	–	–
Compared to before the RIC, I feel more empowered now	54	80.6	13	19.4	–	–
Sample size, infrequent users (used to calculate %)	67		67		67	

[a]Includes blank responses.

[b]Frequent users were defined as those who used the RIC every day or at least once a week, infrequent users as those who did so less frequently.

A large majority of users (82 percent) used the RIC for communication purposes. Seventy-nine percent felt that use of the RIC had increased their communication with family, 83 percent indicated that their communication with distant friends had increased, and 74 percent felt they now had a wider social network (table 8.7).

Social Engagement

Survey respondents were asked to rate, on a scale of 0 (none) to 6 (extremely), their level of involvement in an online club, society, or community, their awareness of the activities of family members and friends living far away, and their acquaintance with relevant NGOs or groups (table 8.8). The majority of users had a moderate level of

Table 8.7
Use of RIC for Communication Purposes in Last 12 Months and Respondents' Perception of RIC Impact on Communications

	All		Frequent*		Infrequent*	
	#	%	#	%	#	%
Use of RIC for communication purposes						
Total possible in-group respondents	299		232		67	
Used RIC for communications in last 12 months	244	81.6	195	84.1	50	74.6
Perceived impact						
Communication with family increased	192	78.7	152	77.9	40	80.0
Communication with distant friends increased	202	82.8	160	82.1	42	84.0
Now have a wider social network	180	73.8	144	73.8	35	70.0

*Frequent users were defined as those who used the RIC every day or at least once a week, infrequent users as those who did so less frequently.

engagement. Awareness of the activities of distant friends was rated at an average of 3.4, the activities of family members at 3.2, for those of NGOs at 2.4. Only 15 percent of users indicated no engagement at all in clubs, and even fewer reported no awareness of the activities of family members (7 percent) or friends (4 percent) living far away (table 8.8).

Connectedness

In face-to-face interviews, users frequently mentioned the ease of getting information as a way of staying connected. Some users described it as being "connected to the world, the latest news and advances," and felt this information prevented their being marginalized and "left out." Some saw the increase in information as a way to be connected to "external information," and to events and occurrences outside their own community. "Connecting beyond borders" and "boundless connectedness" were other expressions used. These phrases denote ubiquity, allowing rural people to stay connected to anybody, anywhere, at any time. They also suggest that users feel they are "an informed person" when they are connected to the world, thanks to the RIC: "Having access to the latest information and advances makes me a more knowledgeable person." These responses indicate that people perceive an increased empowerment through access to information and resources (lower level in figure 8.2).

RIC users were also developing and strengthening ties with people beyond their immediate community. Some were connected to others through email and social

Table 8.8
Social Engagement of RIC Users in Select Spheres

	Not at all		1–3[a]		4–6[a]	
To What Extent Are You:	#	%	#	%	#	%
All RIC users						
Involved in an online club, society, or other online community?	47	15.7	113	37.8	60	20.1
Aware of the activities carried out by family members who live far away?	20	6.7	102	34.1	102	34.1
Aware of the activities carried out by friends who live far away?	13	4.3	102	34.1	102	34.1
Acquainted with relevant NGOs or groups (MERCY, consumer groups, WWF, etc.) via Internet use at the RIC?	48	16.1	102	34.1	70	23.4
Number of observations used to calculate %	299		299		299	
Frequent users[b]						
Involved in an online club, society, or other online community?	37	15.9	91	39.2	47	20.3
Aware of the activities carried out by family members who live far away?	16	6.9	87	37.5	87	37.5
Aware of the activities carried out by friends who live far away?	10	4.3	84	36.2	84	36.2
Acquainted with relevant NGOs or groups via Internet use at the RIC?	36	15.5	83	35.8	56	24.1
Sample size, frequent users (used to calculate %)	232		232		232	
Infrequent users[b]						
Involved in an online club, society, or other online community?	10	14.9	24	35.8	12	17.9
Aware of the activities carried out by family members who live far away?	4	6.0	17	25.4	17	25.4
Aware of the activities carried out by friends who live far away?	3	4.5	19	28.4	19	28.4
Acquainted with relevant NGOs or groups via Internet use at the RIC?	12	17.9	20	29.9	14	20.9
Sample size, infrequent users (used to calculate %)	67		67		67	

[a]Survey respondents were asked to rate the extent of their involvement on a scale of 0 (not at all) to 6 (extremely).

[b]Frequent users were defined as those who used the RIC every day or at least once a week, infrequent users as those who did so less frequently.

networks. A user reported that his access to ICT via the RIC "enables me to make online social friends for the purpose of exchanging opinions on selected topics." Several users reported that thanks to the RIC, they had reconnected with long-lost friends and old friends. They also felt "close to friends." A number of users mentioned being connected to business associates and peers, resulting in a wider business network and providing potential for their ventures to thrive.

Some felt greater social awareness as a result of online and offline activities at the RIC. A post office worker, for example, spent his lunch hour connecting to various social groups and nongovernmental organizations. An older adult viewed his RIC visits as enhancing his sense of community: he felt he was "a part of the community." A young university student continued to visit the RIC even after completing her ICT training. She described the RIC as a place where she and the friends she made at the center "hold our reunion." Another user said of the RIC, "There were very few PCs but I made new friends."

We also talked with users regarding their use of Government 2.0 tools such as the Prime Minister's Facebook page. A user who was the village head saw the importance of having a Facebook account in order to stay connected to the State Minister, who maintains an active Facebook account through which he divulges information to his subordinates. But most users expect authenticity of responses and active input. One user contended that he chose not to be a part of the network because "it is not the Prime Minister who posts or replies to our posts; his staff does that."

Our findings from face-to-face interviews are corroborated by the survey data. About 40 percent of users feel a moderate degree of connection with others in their social network (marked as 1–3 on a scale of 0–6), and 27 percent marked 4–6, indicating a relatively high degree of connection with their network (table 8.9). Over a third of respondents (38 percent) were fairly engaged (marked 4–6), contributing ideas by leaving comments, sending messages, or chatting through online social networks. Contributing to other people's blogs was less frequent, probably because fewer people operate blogs. There were no major differences between frequent and infrequent users.

The sense of connection to community leaders is more limited. Quite a few respondents (12 percent) did not feel connected to community leaders, and fewer than 20 percent felt significantly connected to them (i.e., marked 4–6) (table 8.9). Of those using the RICs to communicate, a small percentage (16 percent) reported accessing the Prime Minister's Facebook page and/or the State Minister's Facebook page (8 percent), or followed the Prime Minister on Twitter (4 percent). Although presently limited, there appears to be the potential to generate an added sense of connectedness between the citizenry and political leaders.

Table 8.9
RIC User Perceptions of Connectedness

	Not at all		1–3[a]		4–6[a]	
To What Extent Do You:	#	%	#	%	#	%
All RIC users						
Feel you can share ideas and expertise with others in your social network?	17	5.7	115	38.5	88	29.4
Feel you are part of the social network to which you belong?	19	6.4	121	40.5	80	26.8
Feel connected to the community leaders through access to an informal network?	37	12.4	124	41.5	59	19.7
Feel connected when you are aware of the plans and activities of family and friends who live far away?	13	4.3	112	37.5	95	31.8
Contribute ideas by commenting/writing in others' blogs?	56	18.7	101	33.8	63	21.1
Contribute (e.g., leave comments, send messages, chat) to an online social network?	18	6.0	91	30.4	111	37.1
Number of observations used to calculate %	299		299		299	
Frequent users[b]						
Feel you can share ideas and expertise with others in your social network?	13	5.6	95	40.9	67	28.9
Feel you are part of the social network to which you belong?	16	6.9	96	41.4	63	27.2
Feel connected to the community leaders through access to an informal network?	28	12.1	102	44.0	45	19.4
Feel connected when you are aware of plans and activities of family and friends who live far away?	11	4.7	90	38.8	74	31.9
Contribute ideas by commenting/writing in others' blogs?	41	17.7	84	36.2	50	21.6
Contribute (e.g., leave comments, send messages, chat) to an online social network?	14	6.0	73	31.5	88	37.9
Sample size, frequent users (used to calculate %)	232		232		232	
Infrequent users[b]						
Feel you can share ideas and expertise with others in your social network?	4	6.0	21	31.3	21	31.3
Feel you are part of the social network to which you belong?	3	4.5	26	38.8	17	25.4
Feel connected to the community leaders through access to an informal network?	9	13.4	24	35.8	13	19.4
Feel connected when you are aware of plans and activities of family and friends who live far away?	2	3.0	23	34.3	21	31.3
Contribute ideas by commenting/writing in others' blogs?	15	22.4	19	28.4	12	17.9

Table 8.9 (continued)

	Not at all		1–3[a]		4–6[a]	
To What Extent Do You:	#	%	#	%	#	%
Contribute (e.g., leave comments, send messages, chat) to an online social network?	4	6.0	20	29.9	22	32.8
Sample size, infrequent users (used to calculate %)	67		67		67	

[a]Survey respondents were asked to rate the extent of their involvement on a scale of 0 (not at all) to 6 (extremely).

[b]Frequent users were defined as those who used the RIC every day or at least once a week, infrequent users as those who did so less frequently.

Impact

RIC use may or may not impact various aspects of people's lives, including their knowledge and education, access to resources, communication with family and friends, contact with new people, access to government information and services, leisure, hobbies, health, and business (tables 8.10a–8.10d). A remarkably high percentage of users perceived that RIC use had a positive impact (strongly or somewhat positive) on the following aspects (table 8.10a): knowledge and education (96 percent), access to resources (90 percent), communication with family and friends (88 percent), and meeting new people (81 percent); the last three of these four categories being closely linked to an enhanced sense of connectedness. A lower proportion of RIC users perceived a positive but lesser impact on business or income (57 percent) or sending or receiving money (55 percent).

Few respondents reported instances of negative impact. The greatest incidence of negative impact was among frequent users in relation to meeting new people (12 percent; table 8.10b). Females apparently were slightly more frequently affected adversely (3 percent compared with 2 percent for males; table 8.10c). These trends appear to be unrelated to age (table 8.10d).

Conclusions and Recommendations

Many RIC users address the manager as *cikgu*, or "teacher," and some regard the manager as indispensable. Users' open-ended responses revealed numerous requests to keep the employment of managers, who were described as "knowledgeable and friendly." The personality of the manager also contributes to users' willingness to frequent the RIC. Several housewives interviewed expressed their fondness for the manager, whom they visit regularly to acquire information on courses or events that they can attend

Table 8.10a
Perceived Impact of RIC Use on Users: All Respondents

	Positive Impact									
	Strongly		Somewhat		Strongly Or Somewhat Positive		No Impact*		Somewhat or Very Negative	
All Respondents	#	%	#	%	#	%	#	%	#	%
Knowledge and education	206	68.9	80	26.8	286	95.7	10	3.3	3	1.0
Access to resources and skills needed for jobs and personal tasks	178	59.5	91	30.4	269	90.0	30	10.0	–	–
Maintaining communication with family and friends	177	59.2	86	28.8	263	88.0	35	11.7	1	0.3
Meeting new people (online or offline)	136	45.5	106	35.5	242	80.9	49	16.4	8	2.7
Other leisure activities	120	40.1	114	38.1	234	78.3	64	21.4	1	0.3
Access to government information and services	124	41.5	104	34.8	228	76.3	71	23.7	–	–
Pursuit of interest, hobby or charity work	121	40.5	106	35.5	227	75.9	71	23.7	1	0.3
Health	112	37.5	111	37.1	223	74.6	73	24.4	3	1.0
Business/income	86	28.8	84	28.1	170	56.9	128	42.8	1	0.3
Sending and receiving money	87	29.1	76	25.4	163	54.5	132	44.1	4	1.3

*Includes blank responses.

Table 8.10b
Perceived Impact of RIC Use on Frequent and Infrequent Users

	Positive Impact									
	Strongly		Somewhat		Strongly or Somewhat Positive		No Impact[a]		Somewhat or Very Negative	
	#	%	#	%	#	%	#	%	#	%
Frequent users[b]										
Knowledge and education	161	69.4	60	25.9	221	95.3	8	3.4	3	4.5
Access to resources and skills needed for jobs and personal tasks	144	62.1	66	28.4	210	90.5	22	9.5	–	–

Table 8.10b (continued)

	Positive Impact									
	Strongly		Somewhat		Strongly or Somewhat Positive		No Impact[a]		Somewhat or Very Negative	
	#	%	#	%	#	%	#	%	#	%
Maintaining communication with family and friends	137	59.1	69	29.7	206	88.8	25	10.8	1	1.5
Meeting new people (online or offline)	105	45.3	80	34.5	185	79.7	39	16.8	8	11.9
Other leisure activities	93	40.1	87	37.5	180	77.6	51	22.0	1	1.5
Access to government information and services	97	41.8	81	34.9	178	76.7	54	23.3	–	–
Pursuit of interest, hobby or charity work	94	40.5	80	34.5	174	75.0	57	24.6	1	1.5
Health	90	38.8	85	36.6	175	75.4	54	23.3	3	4.5
Business/income	74	31.9	63	27.2	137	59.1	95	40.9	–	–
Sending and receiving money	72	31.0	59	25.4	131	56.5	98	42.2	3	4.5
Sample size, frequent users (used to calculate %)	232									
Infrequent users[b]										
Knowledge and education	44	65.7	21	31.3	65	97.0	2	3.0	–	–
Access to resources and skills needed for jobs and personal tasks	33	49.3	26	38.8	59	88.1	8	11.9	–	–
Maintaining communication with family and friends	39	58.2	17	25.4	56	83.6	11	16.4	–	–
Meeting new people (online or offline)	30	44.8	26	38.8	56	83.6	11	16.4	–	–
Other leisure activities	26	38.8	27	40.3	53	79.1	14	20.9	–	–
Access to government information and services	26	38.8	23	34.3	49	73.1	18	26.9	–	–
Pursuit of interest, hobby or charity work	26	38.8	25	37.3	51	76.1	16	23.9	–	–
Health	21	31.3	26	38.8	47	70.1	20	29.9	–	–
Business/income	11	16.4	20	29.9	31	46.3	35	52.2	1	1.5
Sending and receiving money	14	20.9	17	25.4	31	46.3	35	52.2	1	1.5
Sample size, infrequent users (used to calculate %)	67									

[a]Includes blank responses.

[b]Frequent users were defined as those who used the RIC every day or at least once a week, infrequent users as those who did so less frequently.

Table 8.10c
Perceived Impact of RIC Use on Users, by Gender

	Positive impact									
	Strongly		Somewhat		Strongly or Somewhat Positive		No Impact*		Somewhat or Very Negative	
User Category	#	%	#	%	#	%	#	%	#	%
Male (111 observations)										
Knowledge and education	69	62.2	37	33.3	106	95.5	4	3.6	1	0.9
Access to resources and skills needed for jobs and personal tasks	60	54.1	41	36.9	101	91.0	10	9.0	–	–
Maintaining communication with family and friends	68	61.3	26	23.4	94	84.7	17	15.3	–	–
Meeting new people (online or offline)	49	44.1	36	32.4	85	76.6	24	21.6	2	1.8
Other leisure activities	43	38.7	46	41.4	89	80.2	22	19.8	–	–
Access to government information and services	45	40.5	44	39.6	89	80.2	22	19.8	–	–
Pursuit of interest, hobby or charity work	46	41.4	44	39.6	90	81.1	21	18.9	–	–
Health	41	36.9	47	42.3	88	79.3	21	18.9	2	1.8
Business/income	32	28.8	31	27.9	63	56.8	48	43.2	–	–
Sending and receiving money	33	29.7	29	26.1	62	55.9	48	43.2	1	0.9
Female (188 observations)										
Knowledge and education	137	72.9	43	22.9	180	95.7	6	3.2	2	1.1
Access to resources and skills needed for jobs and personal tasks	118	62.8	50	26.6	168	89.4	20	10.6	–	–
Maintaining communication with family and friends	109	58.0	60	31.9	169	89.9	18	9.6	1	0.5
Meeting new people (online or offline)	87	46.3	70	37.2	157	83.5	25	13.3	6	3.2
Other leisure activities	77	41.0	68	36.2	145	77.1	42	22.3	1	0.5
Access to government information and services	79	42.0	60	31.9	139	73.9	49	26.1	–	–
Pursuit of interest, hobby or charity work	75	39.9	62	33.0	137	72.9	50	26.6	1	0.5
Health	71	37.8	64	34.0	135	71.8	52	27.7	1	0.5
Business/income	54	28.7	53	28.2	107	56.9	80	42.6	1	0.5
Sending and receiving money	54	28.7	47	25.0	101	53.7	84	44.7	3	1.6

*Includes blank responses.

Table 8.10d
Perceived Impact of RIC Use on Users, by Age

	Positive impact									
	Strongly		Somewhat		Strongly or Somewhat Positive		No Impact*		Somewhat or Very Negative	
User Category	#	%	#	%	#	%	#	%	#	%
Young (≤ 24 years old; 172 observations)										
Knowledge and education	118	68.6	44	25.6	162	94.2	7	4.1	3	1.7
Access to resources and skills needed for jobs and personal tasks	99	57.6	53	30.8	152	88.4	20	11.6	–	–
Maintaining communication with family and friends	106	61.6	46	26.7	152	88.4	19	11.0	1	0.6
Meeting new people (online or offline)	74	43.0	63	36.6	137	79.7	30	17.4	5	2.9
Other leisure activities	66	38.4	69	40.1	135	78.5	36	20.9	1	0.6
Access to government information and services	63	36.6	60	34.9	123	71.5	49	28.5	–	–
Pursuit of interest, hobby or charity work	65	37.8	64	37.2	129	75.0	42	24.4	1	0.6
Health	56	32.6	66	38.4	122	70.9	47	27.3	3	1.7
Business/income	40	23.3	37	21.5	77	44.8	95	55.2	–	–
Sending and receiving money	43	25.0	44	25.6	87	50.6	83	48.3	2	1.2
Mature (≥ 25 years old; 127 observations)										
Knowledge and education	88	69.3	36	28.3	124	97.6	3	2.4	–	–
Access to resources and skills needed for jobs and personal tasks	79	62.2	38	29.9	117	92.1	10	7.9	–	–
Maintaining communication with family and friends	71	55.9	40	31.5	111	87.4	16	12.6	–	–
Meeting new people (online or offline)	62	48.8	43	33.9	105	82.7	19	15.0	3	2.4
Other leisure activities	54	42.5	45	35.4	99	78.0	28	22.0	–	–
Access to government information and services	61	48.0	44	34.6	105	82.7	22	17.3	–	–

Table 8.10d (continued)

	Positive impact									
	Strongly		Somewhat		Strongly or Somewhat Positive		No Impact*		Somewhat or Very Negative	
User Category	#	%	#	%	#	%	#	%	#	%
Pursuit of interest, hobby or charity work	56	44.1	42	33.1	98	77.2	29	22.8	–	–
Health	56	44.1	45	35.4	101	79.5	26	20.5	–	–
Business/income	46	36.2	47	37.0	93	73.2	33	26.0	1	0.8
Sending and receiving money	44	34.6	32	25.2	76	59.8	49	38.6	2	1.6

*Includes blank responses.

together. Such connectedness is priceless; it promotes trust and civic engagement, thus generating social capital within the community.

According to Warschauer (2003), marginalized groups are more successful at acquiring Internet-related skills and literacy when they merge to participate in a community-based project; e.g., when they use computing and other resources to address a neighborhood problem or participate in a group activity. The evidence gathered in this study suggests that RIC users are being impacted at a low level of connectedness. Most users do not seem to have reached the higher levels of collaborating or co-creating depicted by the upper levels of figure 8.2.

We found some evidence of collaborative user engagement, specifically in Marang, where the RIC functions largely as an entrepreneurial center. Users are actively involved in the social entrepreneurs' club, an initiative launched in 2008 with assistance from a consulting firm hired by the ministry to aid in setting it up. In principle all RICs have their own social entrepreneurs' club, whose objective is to encourage entrepreneurship and foster socialization and cooperation between rural entrepreneurs. The club also aims to support the creation of business opportunities and networks among community members. For the club to function as a social and business connector, the RIC manager is expected to play a major role in encouraging participation. The manager of the Marang RIC is engaged in running the entrepreneurs' club: he plans workshops, mini trade shows and carnivals, and secures the resources needed to realize these activities. Users meet at the RIC to discuss and seek assistance from the manager, as well as from other entrepreneurs and visiting government officials. Marang RIC users have successfully marketed their products online through the web page kuspidmarang.

blogspot.com. The venture requires a good knowledge of the Internet, email, and web publishing. Accordingly, users engaged in this activity tend to be more proficient in the use of ICT, and use ICT tools to stay connected not only with family and friends but with business associates.

Various factors account for the moderate levels of connectedness observed. Some are operational in nature (1–3 below), while others (4, 5) are linked to human and social constraints:

1. *Hours of operation* RICs usually keep the same hours as post offices, which means in practice that they are not open at night or on weekends. These limited operating hours may hinder greater engagement. Users working in government offices, for instance, are unable to access the RIC on weekdays. School-going youths come in after school and normally have only a few hours before the RIC closes at 5 P.M.
2. *Limited space and equipment* RICs have on average three or four computers and some of the larger RICs have only eight workstations. To give access to more users, individual sessions are limited to one hour. A total of 181 open-ended comments were received from users participating in the survey, 91 of which specifically stated the need for more computers in the RICs. As one user commented, "I have to squeeze in between and share the computer."
3. *Restrictions* Some managers restrict synchronous communication tools such as chatting or instant messaging. As a result, users have to rely on asynchronous communication applications such as email, which usually means that they do not get an immediate response but have to return to check their email account later on.
4. *User skill level* Some users have yet to reach a level of IT competence that would allow them to use the technology more collaboratively or productively.
5. *User objectives* Some users may not need to use the RIC for communication purposes, either because they have their own computer and Internet connection at home or because they prefer to use other modes of communication such as mobiles.

Our findings give credence to the RIC initiative. The impact of telecenters on people's lives is positive and their sense of connectedness is enhanced by telecenter use. There also appears to be room to expand the impact of RIC telecenters so that they foster greater collaboration and help nurture the development of positive social capital. To that end, we recommend that the Malaysian government look for ways to address the limitations listed above. We also recommend that a thorough assessment of the costs and benefits of the social entrepreneurs' club initiative throughout the RIC system be conducted, and that the feasibility of expanding the initiative to engage users from other Malaysian telecenter programs be examined.

Note

1. Initially we intended to use RIC nonusers as comparators, but only a few nonusers were willing to participate in the research. Those nonusers who were interviewed tended to give positive evaluations of ICT and RIC utilization.

References

Bakar, Abu. Dato' Raslin Bin. 2010. *Annual Report to Conference of Directors of National Libraries in Asia and Oceania (CDNL-AO) 2010*. Malaysia: National Library of Malaysia. http://www.cdnl.info/2010/CDNL_2010_-_country_report_MALAYSIA.pdf.

Alias, Nor Aziah, Haziah Jamaludin, Sulaiman Hashim, Izaham Shah Ismail, and Norisah Suhaili. 2010. Theories of Change and Evaluation of Malaysian Rural Internet Centers. Paper presented at The ICTD 2010 Conference, London, December 13–16.

Barber, Brian K., and Julie Mikles Schluterman. 2008. Connectedness in the Lives of Children and Adolescents: A Call for Greater Conceptual Clarity. *Journal of Adolescent Health* 43: 209–216.

Baumeister, Roy F., and Mark R. Leary. 1995. The Need to Belong: Desire for Interpersonal Attachments as a Fundamental Human Motivation. *Psychological Bulletin* 117: 497–529.

Berkman, Lisa F., Thomas Glass, Ian Brissette, and Teresa E. Seeman. 2000. From Social Integration to Health: Durkheim in the New Millennium. *Social Science & Medicine* 51: 843–856.

Boase, Jeffrey, John B. Horrigan, Barry Wellman, and Lee Rainie. 2006. *The Strength of Internet Ties*. Washington, DC: Pew Internet and American Life Project.

Cockshaw, Wendell D., and Ian M. Shochet. 2007. Organisational Connectedness and Well-being. In *Proceedings of the 42nd Annual Australian Psychological Society Conference 2007*, 83–87. Brisbane. http://eprints.qut.edu.au/13156/1/13156.pdf.

comScore Inc. 2010. Malaysian Internet Usage Driven Primarily by People in Central Region. Press release issued October 7. http://www.comscore.com/Insights/Press_Releases/2010/10/comScore_Expands_Segmentation_Capabilities_in_Malaysia.

Daves, David P., and Jalynn G. Roberts. 2010. Online Teacher Education Programs: Social Connectedness and the Learning Experience. *Journal of Instructional Pedagogies* 4: 1–9.

Glaser, Hollis F., and Shereen Bingham. 2009. Students' Perceptions of their Connectedness in the Community College Basic Public Speaking Course. *Journal of the Scholarship of Teaching and Learning* 9 (2): 57–69.

Gomez, Ricardo. 2009. *Measuring Global Public Access to ICT: Landscape Summary Reports from 25 Countries Around the World*. CIS Working Paper No. 7. Seattle: Technology & Social Change Group (TASCHA) (formerly the Center for Information & Society [CIS]), University of Washington Information School. https://digital.lib.washington.edu/researchworks/bitstream/handle/1773/16292/TASCHA_Gomez_MeasuringPublicAccess_2009.pdf.

Granovetter, Mark S. 1973. The Strength of Weak Ties. *American Journal of Sociology* 78 (6): 1360–1380.

Gray, David, and Donald Dennis. 2010. Audience Satisfaction with Television Drama: A Conceptual Model. Australian and New Zealand Marketing Academy Conference, November 29–December 1, 2010. Christchurch, New Zealand: University of Canterbury.

Ibrahim, Huda, Azman Yasin, and Zulkhairi Md Dahalin. 2010. Financial Sustainability Issues in Malaysia's Telecenters. *Computer and Information Science* 3 (2): 235–240.

International Telecommunications Union (ITU). 2013. Statistics webpage. Geneva: ITU. http://www.itu.int/en/ITU-D/Statistics/Pages/stat/default.aspx?utm_source=twitterfeed&utm_medium=twitter/.

Karcher, Michael J. 2001. The Hemingway Measure of Adolescent Connectedness: Validation Studies. Paper presented at the 109th American Psychological Association Conference, San Francisco, CA, August 24–28.

Larsson, Andreas C. 2007. Banking on Social Capital: Towards Social Connectedness in Distributed Engineering Design Teams. *Design Studies* 28: 605–622.

Malaysian Ministry of Science. Technology and Innovation (MOSTI). 2011. *ICT Indicator*. http://nitc.mosti.gov.my/nitc_beta/images/stories/ictindicator/SampleICTIndicatorBooklet1.pdf.

Markham, Christine M., Donna Lormand, Kari M. Gloppen, Melissa F. Peskin, Belinda Flores, and Barbara Low, and the Lawrence Duane House. 2010. Connectedness as a Predictor of Sexual and Reproductive Health Outcomes for Youth. *Journal of Adolescent Health* 46 (3S): S23–S41.

Noor, Mohd. Marhaini. 2013. Evaluating the Contribution of Community Informatics to Rural Development: The Case of Malaysia's Rural Internet Centres. PhD diss. University of Southern Queensland, Toowoomba, Australia.

Moller, Arlen C., Edward L. Deci, and Andrew J. Elliot. 2010. Person-Level Relatedness and the Incremental Value of Relating. *Personality and Social Psychology Bulletin* 36 (6): 754–767.

Pretty, Jules. 2003. Social Capital and Connectedness: Issues and Implications for Agriculture, Rural Development and Natural Resource Management in ACP Countries. CTA Working Document Number 8032, February. Wageningen, The Netherlands: ACP-EU Technical Centre for Agricultural and Rural Cooperation (CTA).

Proenza, Francisco J. 2001. Telecenter Sustainability: Myths and Opportunities. *Journal of Development Communication* 12 (2): 94–109.

Rainie, Lee, Kristen Purcell, and Aaron Smith. 2011. *The Social Side of the Internet*. Washington, DC: Pew Internet and American Life Project.

Romero, Natalia, Joy van Baren, Panos Markopoulos, Boris de Ruyter, and Wijnand IJsselsteijn. 2003. Addressing Interpersonal Communication Needs through Ubiquitous Connectivity: Home and Away. *Lecture Notes in Computer Science* 2875: 419–429.

Russell, Cristel A., Andrew T. Norman, and Susan E. Heckler. 2004. The Consumption of Television Programming: Development and Validation of the Connectedness Scale. *Journal of Consumer Research* 31: 150–161.

Sadlo, Melissa Catherine. 2005. *Effects of Communication Mode on Connectedness and Subjective Well-Being. Thesis for Graduate Diploma of Psychology*. Melbourne, Australia: Deakin University; http://www.deakin.edu.au/research/acqol/publications/resources/thesis-sadlo-m.pdf.

Scott, Ricky. 2009. *Undergraduate Educational Experiences: The Academic Success of College Students with Blindness and Visual Impairments. PhD diss.* Raleigh, NC: North Carolina State University; http://repository.lib.ncsu.edu/ir/bitstream/1840.16/3692/1/etd.pdf.

Seligman, Martin. 2001. *Flourish*. New York: Free Press.

Shah Alam, Syed, and Zaini Abdullah. 2009. Cyber Café Usage in Malaysia: An Exploratory Study. *Journal of Internet Banking and Commerce* 14 (1).

Taylor-Seehafer, Margaret, Deborah Jakobvitz, and Lori Holleran Steiker. 2008. Patterns of Attachment Organization, Social Connectedness, and Substance Use in a Sample of Older Homeless Adolescents: Preliminary Findings. *Family & Community Health* 31 (1S): S81–S88.

Terrell, Steven R., Martha M. Snyder, and Laurie P. Dringus. 2009. The Development, Validation, and Application of the Doctoral Student. *Internet and Higher Education* 12 (2): 112–116.

Timpone, Richard J. 1998. Structure, Behaviour and Voter Turnout in the United States. *American Political Science Review* 92 (1): 145–158.

United Nations Development Program (UNDP). 2014. *Human Development Report 2014 —Sustaining Human Progress: Reducing Vulnerabilities and Building Resilience*. New York: UNDP. http://hdr.undp.org/sites/default/files/hdr14-report-en-1.pdf.

Warschauer, Mark. 2003. *Technology and Social Inclusion: Rethinking the Digital Divide*. Cambridge, MA: MIT Press.

Wei, Ran, and Ven-Hwei Lo. 2006. Staying Connected while On the Move: Cell Phone Use and Social Connectedness. *New Media & Society* 8 (1): 53–72.

Yoon, Eunju, and Richard M. Lee. 2010. Importance of Social Connectedness as a Moderator in Korean Immigrants' Subjective Well-Being. *Asian American Journal of Psychology* 1 (2): 93–105.

9

The Capacity-Enhancing Power of ICT: The Case of Rural Community-Based Organizations in the Peruvian Andes

Jorge Bossio, Juan Fernando Bossio, and Laura León
with the collaboration of María Alejandra Campos and Gabriela Perona

Abstract

This study examined the impact on the organizational capacity of nine grassroots organizations (*organizaciones sociales de base* [OSBs]) located in a rural district of Peru's Andean region, Daniel Hernández (Tayacaja province, Huancavelica department), associated with the use of computers and the Internet from public access venues (PAVs), such as telecenters and *cabinas públicas* (i.e., cybercafés).

PAVs help make communication processes more effective and facilitate meetings and coordination, especially with external agents. PAVs have greater impact on OSBs when they are linked to the organization's objectives and goals and when actors who facilitate information flows between the OSB and external agents use the Internet to search for funding opportunities. PAVs can also become public spaces where members meet and coordinate activities.

PAVs may help strengthen the capacity of OSBs, but their limitations should be taken into account by programs that deploy information and communication technology (ICT) in rural areas. To be specific, some organizational skills are more likely to be impacted by ICT (e.g., those related to inter-institutional links, leadership, infrastructure, and external communications) than others (e.g., supervision and monitoring and evaluating plan implementation).

The study's recommendations are directed toward public and private organizations that seek to foster a more productive use of technology by OSBs. First, programs should focus on developing those capacities that are most impacted by PAVs, such as leadership, networking, and financial management. Second, given that youths tend to adopt technology most readily, their participation in grassroots organizations should be encouraged. Third, the promotion of PAVs as part of universal Internet access initiatives should consider including OSBs, not just individuals, as part of their goals. In parallel, projects should promote OSBs' use of PAVs as a management tool. Finally, public agencies should ensure that PAVs are socially inclusive and discourage all forms of discrimination.

Introduction

Around the world, community-based organizations (CBOs) are part— the most important part—of the social capital of the poor (Schildermann 2002). CBOs form around common interests, generally to satisfy members' basic needs, such as food security and health (Serna Purizaca, 2005).

Research on ICT use by CBOs tends to focus on the impact of ICT on the beneficiaries of the CBO; there has been little study of the impact of ICT on the CBOs themselves, particularly in rural areas. The closest analysis of ICT impact on CBOs occurs in the telecenter literature (Sey and Fellows 2009). As some researchers note, the greater impact of ICT may be on the CBO itself (Amariles et al. 2006; Brainard and Brinkerhoff 2004; Voida 2011).

This study was carried out in late 2010 in nine CBOs in the Daniel Hernández district of the Peruvian highlands. It assesses change in the organizational capacities due to the availability of PAVs, specifically in a series of organizational capacities adapted from the analytical framework developed by Lusthaus et al. (2002). Analysis of the evidence is also guided by the concept of technology as a tool for capacity amplification (Toyama 2011), given that both individual and organizational capacities can be amplified by the use of Internet public access points.

Context

Peru has experienced a decade of continuous economic growth, but the unequal distribution of this growth has increased the gap between rich and poor, especially between the rural and urban populations. While poverty rates have dropped nationwide, rural areas have not benefited equally. The district of Daniel Hernández, which was chosen for the fieldwork for this study, is in the province of Tayacaja, in the department of Huancavelica. In this rural district in the Peruvian highlands, poverty rates are high, and in recent history, the population has suffered from the violence of armed groups (Instituto Nacional de Estadística e Informática 2008).

The district has shown signs of a resurgence of CBOs in recent years. There has also been a significant increase in the penetration of information technologies, especially mobile telephony and the Internet, in the district's urban area. In 2003, with support from the New Zealand Aid Programme (the New Zealand government's international aid and development program managed by the Ministry of Foreign Affairs and Trade), the first Internet PAV was installed in the district of Daniel Hernández.

Community-Based Organizations in Peru

CBOs are important in rural areas, in part, because of their role as intermediaries between the rural population and external agents (Diez 1997; Trivelli, Escobal, and Revesz 2009). In the countryside, these organizations complement the work of families, particularly in activities that require collective action, such as coordination with external agents and authorities, commercialization, technical assistance, and microcredit (Diez 2000). CBOs resemble cooperatives in that they are formed by people who benefit from the organization, but they differ in that they are not necessarily commercial entities.

Serna Purizaca (2005) classifies Peruvian CBOs into three generations. The first were founded in the 1960s in an effort to meet basic needs such as the installation of water or sewer service. The second arose in the 1990s in response to the economic crisis, as a survival strategy to satisfy basic food needs. These were mainly women's organizations, such as community kitchens or mothers' clubs associated with the province-wide Glass of Milk (*Vaso de Leche*) program. The third generation is oriented toward production and takes an entrepreneurial approach, seeking access to resources such as credit or technical assistance. These three types of organizations currently operate in Peru in different areas and to different degrees.

The Study Area

Huancavelica is a department in the central highlands of Peru, on the western side of the Andes Mountains, between 3,660 and 5,328 meters above sea level. The region is extremely rugged, with high mountains, deep ravines, and intermountain valleys. According to the 2007 National Census, the population growth rate in the department is 1.2 percent per year, and it currently has a population of 471,720 people.

Tayacaja is the second most densely populated province in the department, with 107,470 inhabitants, 10,060 of whom live in Daniel Hernández (Instituto Nacional de Estadística e Informática 2010).

The district covers an area of 106 square kilometers. The urban center is Mariscal Castilla, situated 3,280 meters above sea level. The district also contains two smaller towns, Mashuayllo and Marcopata, as well as the farming communities of Atocc and San Cristóbal de Huaylacucho.

Daniel Hernández falls into the poorest quintile of Peru's 1,836 districts. Its population is predominantly rural (60 percent), and about 79 percent fall below the poverty line. Life expectancy at birth is 71.13 years, and the illiteracy rate is 80 percent (Instituto Nacional de Estadística e Informática 2010; United Nations Development Programme 2010). The district of Daniel Hernández borders the district of Pampas, the provincial capital, and the two districts' urban areas are currently undergoing a process of integration.

The district's recent history has been marked by violence. During the 1980s and 1990s, Peru suffered the most violent internal conflict it had seen since the country declared independence in 1821. The violence was concentrated in the most vulnerable areas in the interior, with high rates of poverty and exclusion. The Truth and Reconciliation Commission (*Comisión de la Verdad y Reconciliación* [CVR]) reported that Huancavelica is the department with the fourth highest number of deaths and disappearances as a result of the conflict. Most affected was the neighboring department of Ayacucho, which had the highest numbers of deaths and disappearances—40 percent of the 70,000 victims estimated by the Truth and Reconciliation Commission (Comisión de la Verdad y Reconciliación 2003). Daniel Hernández became a refuge for families and individuals displaced by the internal violence during those years.

Access to Information and Communication Technology

Internet use has increased among Peru's urban population, from 46 percent in 2007 to 58 percent in 2013. Internet access is far more limited in rural areas, although it also increased from 7 percent in 2007 to 8 percent in 2013 (Instituto Nacional de Estadística e Informática 2013). To address rural access limitations, in the late 1990s, development agencies and the government launched rural telecenter projects (Bossio and Sotomayor 2010), as happened in Daniel Hernández.

According to official figures (Ministerio de Transportes y Comunicaciones 2011), wideband connection density in the Huancavelica region is 0.28 connections per 100 inhabitants. There are telecenters, or public and municipal Internet booths, in the area as a result of development programs implemented there. Between 2002 and 2006, Peru's *Instituto Nacional de Investigación y Capacitación de Telecomunicaciones* (INICTEL) implemented the pilot Rural Information and Communication Technology Establishments (*Establecimientos Rurales de Tecnologías de la Información y Comunicación* [ERTIC]) project in ten districts in the provinces of Huancavelica and Tayacaja. The project funded the establishment of a telecenter in each district, all of them managed by municipal governments (Bustamante, Burneo, and Alvarado 2009).

In the specific case of the Daniel Hernández district, New Zealand's Unitec Institute of Technology implemented a telecenter project in 2003 that gave the municipality management control over the center operations and provided training to some district residents in computer and Internet use. For many years, this telecenter has been the only Internet PAV in the district, although in the neighboring town of Pampas, just two kilometers from Daniel Hernández, there are 15 to 20 privately owned PAVs.

From the beginning, the telecenter in Daniel Hernández has served the public, but because it is in the only Internet access venue in the district, service has focused on providing facilities for computer courses at the nearby Mariscal Cáceres School. During school hours (8 A.M. to 4 P.M.), the telecenter is used almost exclusively by the school.

(This may have changed in late 2010, when Mariscal Cáceres School was expected to open a computer laboratory.) Because of the difficulty of gaining access to the Daniel Hernández telecenter, local CBOs chose to use the PAVs in Pampas. Members of the organizations indicated that they prefer to use PAVs that belong to or are managed by members of the association, because this is the only way to ensure they receive the support they need to use the computers and services efficiently.

In the case of the Salqui Cooperative and the Aromatic Herb Producers' Association, a PAV was installed at places where each of these CBOs usually hold their meetings.

We teach them to create their own email. The president already has an email address. He has difficulties, but he is using the computer. (Janet, manager of the Salqui cooperative)

Computers are not the most widespread means of communication in the area. Mobile telephone companies have begun to invest in the infrastructure necessary to serve rural markets. There are currently 125,000 mobile lines in Huancavelica, representing 26 percent penetration, although Huancavelica remains the Peruvian region with the lowest mobile telephone density (Ministerio de Transportes y Comunicaciones 2011). Daniel Hernández (along with Pampas, Pazos, and Acraquia) was one of the first districts in the province to have mobile telephone service, beginning in 2006 (Organismo Supervisor de Inversión Privada en Telecomunicaciones 2013). However, coverage is limited to the district's main towns, particularly those in the valley and close to the city of Pampas.

Organizations Studied

In the district of Daniel Hernández, we identified thirteen CBOs divided into four categories depending on their purpose: assistance to people displaced by violence, survival, education, and production and commercialization. For research purposes, we worked with nine of them. Table 9.1 shows the main characteristics of the organizations studied.

Displacement-Focused Organizations Two organizations focusing on displacement issues were included in the study. These are the oldest of the organizations studied. Both were formed in response to the government-sponsored process of recognition of victims. The members of both organizations are extremely poor; they come from the most depressed areas of Huancavelica or Ayacucho. They have no homes, property, or family to help them. The organizations assist with the registration and recognition of persons who qualify as having been affected by violence according to the criteria established by the National Reparations Council (*Consejo Nacional de Reparaciones*).

Table 9.1
Summary of Characteristics of the Community-Based Organizations (CBOs) Studied

Organization	Type/ Objective	Established	# of Members	Main PAVs Used	PAV Use Frequency and Type	Assistance Received for Skill Building and Use of PAVs
ADESNORTAY	Assistance to displaced persons	2003	90	Telecenter of the municipality of Daniel Hernández	Occasional. Organizational purposes: tracking registration of victims, etc.	Training in Daniel Hernández telecenter
ADAVIP	Assistance to displaced persons	2002	200	Does not use	None	None
Sarita Colonia	Survival	2008	25	Does not use	None	None
Glass of Milk Mothers' Club (*Club de Madres del Vaso de Leche*)	Survival	2005	44 cttees, 1,700 bene-ficiaries	Does not use	None	None
APAFA	Education	2005	400	Does not use	None	None
Huancavelica Student Council (*Consejo de Estudiantes—Huancavélica*)	Education	2006	5 members of the leadership board and 160 students	Uses the university Internet since it was installed 2 years ago. Before that, used the Daniel Hernández telecenter	Email	Trained by the school as part of systems education
Aromatic Herb Producers' Association (*Asociación de Productores de Hierbas Aromáticas*)	Productive	2003	30	Uses PAV that operates in secretary's home	Obtaining funds for projects and contacts with businesses	President and secretary trained by INICTEL-UNI in 2002
APROLEDH	Productive	2004	60	Does not use	None	None
Salqui Cooperative (*Cooperativa Salqui*)	Productive	2006	150	Manager of Salqui owns a PAV	Former manager uses Internet regularly to seek project funding	Both the current and former managers learned to use the Internet in their post-secondary studies

The Association of Displaced People of Northeastern Tayacaja (*Asociación de desplazados del Nor-Oriente de Tayacaj* [ADESNORTAY]) was created in 2003, the year the telecenter was set up in Daniel Hernández. The group has used the center since it opened, with assistance from the operator of the telecenter and the project sponsored by New Zealand's Unitec Institute of Technology, receiving training in the use of the computers. The local government that took office in 2007, however, withdrew the support the organization had previously received. The telecenter eliminated its evening hours, seriously affecting the organization, because all the members worked during the day and could only use the telecenter in the evening. The members of the organization now use the private PAVs in the city of Pampas.

[With] the former mayor we would stay until ten at night; sometimes the mayor himself would come and congratulate the ladies. The new mayor has marginalized us in every way—he doesn't even let us use the auditorium. (ADESNORTAY member)

The Association of Displaced People and Victims of Political Violence (*Asociación de desplazados y víctimas de la violencia política* [ADAVIP]) was established for the same reasons as ADESNORTAY. Its membership consists entirely of displaced people from Ayacucho. When it was formed in 2002, it had 230 members, but that number has gradually decreased because members have moved away or become discouraged by the lack of results. Unlike ADESNORTAY, this organization has not been successful in implementing projects and makes almost no use of ICT.

Survival-Focused Organizations Survival-focused organizations provide food and security to people who live in extreme poverty.

In Daniel Hernández, there are forty-four Glass of Milk (*Vaso de Leche*) committees. This program was established in 2005 in the province of Tayacaja. Despite their poverty, the committees, made up almost exclusively of women, constitute an important social nucleus. The literacy rate among the members is low: the leaders who do know how to read and write are the ones who maintain the relationship with program administrators (who are municipal government employees) and food suppliers.

Another survival-focused organization is the Sarita Colonia women's organization, a neighborhood organization that runs projects for its members with financing from the provincial government of Tayacaja. This organization was established recently and is implementing its first project, which addresses domestic violence. The organization's use of ICT is recent and limited mainly because of illiteracy and a lack of technological skills.

Since we are hernandinas we get help from the district municipality. Mr. Nicolás even wrote my last summary report. I can't write it myself. I don't know how to write,... and it's much worse in the case of my co-workers. (Meche, Sarita Colonia member)

To implement the project, they have used mobile telephones to report incidents of domestic violence. Here again the organization has the support of a representative of the municipal government who helps them prepare reports and find information.

Education-Focused Organizations Wherever there is a school in Peru, there is also an organization whose goal is to see that the students receive a good education. When the students are minors, the organization is the Parents' Association (*Asociación de Padres de Familia* [APAFA]); when the students are adults, the organization is the Student Center (*Centro de Estudiantes*) or Student Federation (*Federación de Estudiantes*). Both types of organizations exist in Daniel Hernández and were included in this study.

The Mariscal Cáceres Public School's Parents' Association was created in compliance with a law passed in 2006. It has successfully promoted projects such as the collective construction of a classroom for secondary school students and the construction of a greenhouse for agricultural technical education. The association has facilitated the purchase of computers for a school computer lab; there is, however, no evidence of any use of information technologies for the organization's own purposes, even though the group's leaders know how to use the Internet.

The Student Council of the Systems Engineering School was also studied. As a university organization, the Council's role is to contribute to university governance by participating in the School Councils and University Councils, which are administrative decision-making forums for all universities in Peru. To participate in those decisions, the Student Council must often make presentations to students about issues being discussed with authorities.

When we look for information, we always [check the] Internet lately to see how we are doing, or how to change, how to improve. (Student Council member)

One of the main problems these groups encounter is the difficulty of establishing a relationship with students who live in remote areas, because they lack both mobile telephony coverage and Internet access.

Communication among leaders generally takes place in person, and coordination is done by mobile telephone on weekdays, when all are in Daniel Hernández; on weekends they go to their homes, most of which are located far from the university in uncovered areas. They also communicate using chat and email, mainly through Hotmail accounts. Several students have laptops, and most learned to use the Internet in the municipal PAV in Daniel Hernández.

Producers' Associations Associations of producers are a recent development, promoted by the local and provincial governments to take advantage of economic resources made available by recent political and administrative decentralization. A significant number of productive associations have been established in Daniel Hernández in the past five years, but few have survived. Among the oldest, the study identified three that are currently in the process of growth and consolidation.

The Aromatic Herb Producers' Association (*Asociación de Productores de Hierbas Aromáticas*) was established approximately seven years ago and has more than thirty members throughout the province of Tayacaja. The organization's goal is to stockpile the herbs produced by members, process them, and sell them collectively. For several years the organization collected the output and sold it to small shops in Huancayo. However, thanks to increased access to communication, especially the Internet, the organization has been able to establish strategic partnerships with local government agencies and nongovernmental development organizations.

We use the Internet because our interest is to seek other markets to sell or export. (Yupanqui, Association member)

Through these contacts, the association has started projects to train farmers in production and in anticipation of a processing plant scheduled to open in the near future. The organization has increased its sales. Its main commercial partners are Sazón Lopesa and Agroindustrias Libia, both based in Huancayo.

Another local farm organization with a long history is the Association of Milk Producers of Daniel Hernández (*Asociación de Productores de Leche de Daniel Hernández* [APROLEDH]), which was founded approximately seven years ago as a collective initiative promoted by the municipal government of Daniel Hernández and by Logan Müller, a telecenter promoter who worked with the New Zealand Aid Programme. Although some members are familiar with Internet use, the organization does not use the Internet as a work tool. It does, however, use mobile telephones to organize meetings. This association has become stronger in recent years and recently merged with the newer Association of Milk Producers of the Province of Tayacaja (*Asociación de Productores de Leche de la Provincia de Tayacaja* [APROLET]), which includes about 150 producers and whose medium-range plan is to operate a new dairy processing plant that is being built in the district of Acraquia with funds from the provincial government.

The youngest producer organization is the Salqui Cooperative (*Cooperativa Salqui*), which includes farmers from various communities in Tayacaja. The goal is to increase the members' income through direct commercialization of products. Salqui was originally established in 2006 to respond to a call for bids for legume production from the Cooperation Fund for Social Development (*Fondo de Cooperación para el Desarrollo Social* [FONCODES]). When that project ended, the former manager of the cooperative sought new contracts on which the cooperative could bid. Part of the search for financing was done on Google and through direct searches on the websites of the *Fondo de las Américas* and the *Fondo Ítalo-Peruano*. The organization is currently receiving funds from the municipal government to build a processing plant. When the FONCODES project ended, the number of cooperative members dropped (from 400 to 150), but it is hoped that construction of the plant will create incentives and attract new members.

The Salqui Cooperative is the only organization studied that employs paid staff. The manager is a professional who became involved with the cooperative through the project for the production of legumes. When that project ended, he was hired by the cooperative. The manager provides the cooperative with office space in his home. A PAV also operates in that space from 9 A.M. to 7 P.M. on weekdays, allowing the association to use it as if it were the organization's headquarters. Association members can use the service for free and receive free assistance, whereas members of the public must pay for Internet or computer time at the same rate charged by other PAVs in the area.

Impact of Public Access on CBOs' Capacities

To analyze the impact of PAVs on organizational capacity, we used the framework described by Lusthaus et al. (2002) comprising eight areas of organizational capacity (table 9.2).

According to this approach, societies have a combination of capacities that affect the activities of individuals and organizations (Lusthaus et al. 2002). These capacities

Table 9.2
Organizational Capacity Areas Considered

Area	Description
Strategic leadership	Leadership, strategic planning, niche management
Organizational structure	Governance structure, operational structure
Human resources	Planning, staffing, developing, praising and rewarding, maintaining effective human resource relations
Financial management	Financial planning, financial accountability, financial statements and systems
Infrastructure	Facilities management, technology management
Management of programs and services	Planning, implementing, and monitoring programs and projects
Management of processes	Problem solving, decision making, communication, monitoring, and evaluation
Inter-institutional linkages	Planning, implementing, and monitoring networks and partnerships

Source: Lusthaus et al. (2002).

are related to available infrastructure, resources, and technology, and they enable individuals and organizations to reach different levels of performance.

Because grassroots organizations are small and often have a limited scope, we studied their functioning through a series of specific capacities related to the areas proposed by Lusthaus et al. (2002). This enabled us to assess the existence or nonexistence in each organization of each of the specific capacities listed in the assessment framework. Direct or indirect use of information technologies relating to the organizations' capacities was subsequently observed.

Public access to computers and the Internet has a different impact on different capacities. Appendix 9.A lists all of the capacities analyzed in this study and identifies cases where a notable impact that could reasonably be attributed to PAV use was observed, as well as cases where certain capacities exist in an organization but where PAVs have had no impact. Other capabilities identified by Lusthaus et al. (2002) but not detected in any of the organizations studied were not considered in the analysis.

According to Toyama (2011), ICT amplifies the productivity of individual and organizational capacities. The impact of ICT, therefore, depends on the existence and development of a specific capacity in an individual or organization, and it is greater in organizations with a higher degree of capacity development. In appendix 9.A, organizations with a larger number of capacities developed show evidence of a greater impact of ICT and PAVs, whereas organizations with few capacities show limited impact from PAVs. For example, ADESNORTAY, the Salqui Cooperative, and the Aromatic Herb Producers' Association have a larger number of capacities, whereas ADAVIP, APAFA, and the Glass of Milk Mothers' Club have fewer of the capacities assessed; it is therefore less likely to find an impact of PAVs on the latter organizations.

In appendix 9.B, which lists the capacities that existed in organizations but showed no impact from ICT and PAV use, we see that certain capacities exist in all or almost all of the organizations studied. These include the capacities necessary to bring the organization together around a vision and work plan; they have no connection with and would not be amplified by the use of ICT and PAVs because they are more directly related to the leader's credibility. Some capacities could potentially be impacted in the future depending on the development of others; one example is monitoring capacity. If there is no ICT-based operational management, monitoring will not be impacted by ICT; in other words, the latter capacity cannot exist without the former. Finally, some capacities are unlikely to be impacted by the use of ICT and PAVs in the medium term because they respond to social and community behaviors. This is the case with the capacity for assisting and showing solidarity with members of the organization.

Table 9.3
Impact on Specific Organizational Capacities in Eight Areas: Number of Capacities Considered, Number Strengthened, and Number of CBOs that had their Capacities Strengthened

	# of Capacities			
		Strengthened in at Least One CBO[b]		
Area	Considered[a]	#	%	# of CBOs with One or More Capacities Strengthened[b]
Strategic leadership (L)	24	12	50	5
Organizational structure (OS)	13	5	38	3
Human resources (HR)	9	4	44	4
Financial management (F)	8	5	63	5
Infrastructure (I)	6	4	67	5
Management of programs and services (PS)	10	4	40	4
Management of processes (P)	14	6	43	5
Inter-institutional linkages (Lk)	10	7	70	5

[a]The abbreviations in parentheses are labels linked to broadly defined capacity areas listed in the left-hand column. The full list of capacities considered appears in the tables in appendices 9.A (considered and impacted) and 9.B (considered but not impacted). Each of these appendices contains eight tables, one for each of the eight capacity areas listed here.
[b]Details in appendix 9.A.

It should be noted that community labor in Andean societies is known as *minka* and has been practiced by communities since the time of the Inca Empire.

Impact is most notable in the areas of inter-institutional linkages, financial management, and strategic leadership, and least notable in the areas of organizational structure and management of programs and services (table 9.3). Except in the case of financial management, PAVs have the most notable impact on capacities that involve linkages between the organization and its environment.

Despite having certain capacities, some organizations have not developed them using ICT and PAVs, whereas others have. For example, the *Capacity to search for new opportunities* exists in all organizations studied, but only four of the CBOs studied show an impact of ICT on that specific capacity (table 9.A.1). There could be potential for organizations to appropriate ICT to strengthen this specific capacity.

We have learned to use Internet, because it lets us access a considerable amount of information and knowledge; you inform yourself more quickly. (Montana, APAFA Treasurer)

Another interesting example is the *Capacity to distinguish between bias and evidence*, a capacity that was identified only in the Salqui Cooperative (table 9.A.7). The organization developed the capacity thanks to the use of ICT to obtain reliable information and develop partnerships with honest, responsible business partners. This specific capacity was not identified in the other organizations, which suggests that ICT cannot be expected to impact organizations in such a way that they strengthen capacities they did not previously have.

In the sections that follow we examine the impact observed on the CBOs in the various areas of the analytical model developed by Lusthaus et al. (2002) and highlight some key elements that affect PAV impact on CBOs.

PAVs as Meeting Places

Besides facilitating individual access to technologies, PAVs are also physical, public establishments where social groups can meet or which they can use as a point of reference. We have seen that the PAVs in Tayacaja have served some organizations as meeting places and/or institutional points of reference (a place to go to share information about the organization or about a member's participation). ADESNORTAY used the Daniel Hernández telecenter as a physical space to hold meetings; the center also served as a point of reference until the change in local government, which made decisions that restricted the group's use of the PAV.

The previous mayor, Fredy Ponce, supported us one hundred percent. The women would come here even at night, and they would have training sessions for us; but not the present mayor. He has shut us out. (ADESNORTAY member)

In the case of the herb producers and Salqui, the secretary of the herb producers' association and the manager of Salqui meet with members of their organizations in PAVs set up, respectively, in the secretary's brothers' home and the manager's home. These PAVs have become points of reference for the organizations and could help enhance members' Internet skills.

The impact of PAVs on CBOs is amplified when there is a direct relationship and close integration between the PAV and the organization and its goals and objectives. That is the case with Salqui and Hierbas Aromáticas, as well as with ADESNORTAY, which initially partnered with the municipal government's PAV. Although in all these cases the PAVs also serve the general public, the availability of the service strengthens the organizations.

This relationship between the PAVs and CBOs has fostered various organizational processes through advantages offered by use of and access to ICT. For example, ADESNORTAY was able to use the municipal PAV at a certain time of day (evening), the

Salqui farmers receive a discount and assistance at the PAV, and the members of Hierbas Aromáticas receive assistance in searching for information.

When PAV operators are sensitive to the organization's goals or belong to the organization, they help amplify capacities for use of and access to ICT. This is reflected in differences in members' perceptions of the way they are treated at the PAVs. Now that the members of ADESNORTAY do not have access to the telecenter, they have chosen to use a particular cybercafé because the owner is a member of the organization and the treatment of the organization's users is better. At other PAVs, they might encounter poor treatment rooted in discrimination against migrants and people who are illiterate.

The researchers gathered testimonials about the discrimination suffered by members, especially Quechua-speaking women migrants, in public Internet venues in Pampas. Representatives of Sarita Colonia and ADESNORTAY reported that several PAVs were costly and uncomfortable (the space was cramped and made it difficult for the women to work at the computer with another person), and did not give them assistance in using the computers.

Often you are not well received; sometimes they don't let you go in. For example, three or four of us come and they only let one or two enter the premises. (ADESNORTAY member)

They also said they suffered discrimination from PAV staff because they did not read or write well in Spanish. In the case of Sarita Colonia, the mistreatment was such that they decided not to use a particular PAV again.

Decentralization

When organizations have individual or group capacities related to access to information, recognize the need of members to have access to or use ICT, and their leadership is distributed, their capacities seem to be amplified by the PAVs to a greater extent than in organizations that operate in a centralized manner.

This is true of ADESNORTAY, which is characterized by its horizontal decision-making structure. At the organization's meetings, the leader acts more as a facilitator than a director. The same happens to a lesser extent in the productive organizations Salqui and Hierbas Aromáticas. In all three cases, the PAVs have had a significant impact on the capacities analyzed in practically all areas considered.

In our association, we could not work without learning the Internet. (Hierbas Aromáticas member)

In contrast, the Milk Producers' Association (*Asociación de Productores de Lácteos* [APL]), which has a centralized leadership style, had ICT access and skills, but the impact on the various capacities was not as great because there was less opportunity for collective decision making. The transfer of management of the milk processing plant in 2011 probably created new opportunities to increase the number of participants in managerial decisions.

Meanwhile, organizations with a distributed leadership style, such as the Parents' Association (*Asociación de Padres de Familia* [APAFA]) and Glass of Milk (*Vaso de Leche*) program, which have no need to develop individual leadership capacities, do not find ICT useful for their internal processes, although they have the necessary capacities. These organizations maintain a dependent relationship with their main partner—the school principal in the case of the APAFA and the municipal government in the case of the Glass of Milk program. This relationship implies a degree of technical assistance that makes it unnecessary for the leaders to develop capacities, including those related to PAV use, to enhance their management.

Planning

Even when several organizations have planning capacity, the PAV does not have an impact on their planning or organizational structure because some of the processes involved are mere formalities carried out to comply with requirements established by funding sources. In those cases, the information used to formulate the strategic plan is mainly local.

Any organization seeking outside funding must be formalized. That requires filing paperwork with the Public Registry (*Registros Públicos*), establishing the organization's hierarchical structure, and submitting its by-laws. None of the organizations studied has gone beyond the official requirements; all have limited themselves to the official format. Strategic planning documents, therefore, were a mere formality in all the organizations analyzed.

In the area of strategic planning, we have seen that the organizations whose nature is to address immediate problems, such as the Student Council and APAFA, are able to recognize and solve them efficiently by implementing short-term strategies. The information used to solve those problems is obtained directly, from observation of the context and from contact with the organization's members or beneficiaries. PAVs, therefore, have no real impact on obtaining relevant information for strategic planning.

The other organizations comply with the formality of having a work plan, but as noted earlier, those plans are not taken into consideration in decision-making. That is the case with the Salqui Cooperative: the candidates who run for leadership positions present plans during their campaign, but those plans do not guide their actions once they are elected.

Linkages with External Stakeholders

PAVs have a more notable impact on organizations that need to establish ties with a greater variety of outside institutions or stakeholders and where those linkages are not determined by pre-defined organizational structures.

This is especially true for producer organizations, which have to maintain ties with many nonmember stakeholders. Those linkages are more numerous and diverse than those of survival-focused organizations or the APAFA; the one exception being ADESNORTAY.

Hierbas Aromáticas and ADESNORTAY are the organizations on which use of PAVs and mobile telephones have had the greatest impact. This impact is related to capacities involving the development of inter-institutional linkages.

Before the phone arrived we would have to walk to his house. The person in charge of inviting would need to send a notice. With technology it is now easier to communicate. (Woman member of Hierbas Aromáticas)

In the case of Hierbas Aromáticas, the provincial government has facilitated the process of organizational integration and consolidation, as well as linkages with other sources of funding, such as the *Fondo Ítalo-Peruano*. The organization has taken advantage of that assistance, building its capacity to strengthen ties with markets, especially with distributors and processors in Huancayo (the largest big city) and Lima (Peru's capital and the main market for the association's products). Those contacts are maintained primarily by use of mobile telephones and, to a lesser extent, the Internet.

ADESNORTAY, meanwhile, is an organization of migrants from the highlands who frequently suffer discrimination and are considered ignorant by residents of the valley. Inter-institutional linkages constitute an important defense against this discrimination. Leaders of the organization acknowledged that the Daniel Hernández PAV was a key element in establishing those linkages because, from the outset, the organization used the PAV as a place to hold meetings, seek information, and establish contact with organizations of displaced people at the regional level, as well as with authorities responsible for keeping records of victims of violence and with aid and cooperation organizations.

In organizations with limited outside linkages, such as Sarita Colonia and ADAVIP, no impact from technology was observed. These organizations relate with others mainly through an intermediary—a provincial government staff member in the first case and a lawyer in the second case. Those intermediaries use the Internet and ICT but mainly in private spaces.

Coordination of Travel and Meetings

In general, mobile telephones are used more frequently than PAVs for long-distance coordination of visits or meetings. Even when some members of the organization have email, they may not use it daily, so it is more convenient to coordinate by mobile telephone. The impact of the use of ICT on organizational coordination is seen in the greater effectiveness of travel or other activities.

In the case of ADESNORTAY, visits from the registrar of displaced persons have been arranged ahead of time by email with the president of the organization, whose son checks email fairly regularly. However, when visits are planned without much advance notice, or when there is no prior coordination, the registrar calls the president of the association directly on his mobile phone one day before traveling to Tayacaja. In one way or another, this advance coordination has enabled the president to convene members who live in remote areas, and more victims are registered in a single visit.

ADAVIP, in contrast, coordinates with the lawyer only by mobile phone; its leaders have not appropriated the use of PAVs because of a lack of skills and lack of need. Unlike ADESNORTAY, ADAVIP has delegated coordination processes to authorities; therefore, its members have no need to learn to use ICT to enhance coordination.

Productive organizations also use ICT for coordination. One example is the Salqui Cooperative, where the manager uses mobile telephony from his office in Daniel Hernández to coordinate meetings with cooperative members in Salcabamba, a rural district in the province of Tayacaja situated four hours by bus from Pampas. Because of the poor quality of mobile coverage in the rural part of the district, this communication can only take place at night. With this advance coordination, all members attend the meeting with the manager.

Another example is that of the herb producers, who coordinate shipments of merchandise with clients in Lima and Huancayo via email and mobile phone. According to the leader of the organization, this advance coordination saves time because they no longer have to seek out their contacts after they arrive in the city; instead their contacts await them on the scheduled date.

Fundraising

Because they are poor residents of rural areas, the members of the CBOs studied are unable to make large contributions to their organizations' budgets. In the area of strategic leadership, an important capacity for the organizations studied is their ability to search and obtain funds to operate and invest.

Organizations that have pre-established sources of financing do not have the motivation to seek alternative sources. That is true of organizations that were created by the government and whose funding sources are provided by law (APAFA, Glass of Milk, and Student Council). The rest are forced to seek funds independently from other sources.

In this area the work of infomediaries can be crucial. In order to identify potential funding sources, organizations need a person who speaks Spanish well and knows how to use the Internet—two skills that most members do not possess.

We have not found PAVs having a direct impact this way, except in the specific case of the PAV operator in Daniel Hernández who helped ADESNORTAY search for information. Note that one member of the board of directors of ADESNORTAY also acts as an infomediary. Regarding other CBOs, the infomediaries hold positions in the local government or an NGO, where they have private Internet access. This is true of the Economic Manager of the Provincial Government of Tayacaja and the Salqui Cooperative's main infomediary, who has a computer with Internet access in his office, which he uses to help search for funding.

Internal Communication

In general, PAVs have an impact on the internal communication processes, both formal and informal, of the organizations studied. Following Andrade (2005), *formal communication* "occurs through official sources and/or channels of the organization," whereas *informal communication* "uses the non-official network of interpersonal relationships" (p. 15).

In nearly all the organizations studied, formal communication is done on paper and requires that the recipient sign a copy to certify that he or she has received the communiqué. The Student Center (*Centro de Estudiantes*) is an exception; they convene meetings and assemblies by making oral announcements during class hours and putting up posters on panels in hallways. The large number of students and the fact that they share a common space make those forms of communication more cost effective.

PAVs have an impact on formal communication because the communications are composed and printed in PAVs, and the PAV operators sometimes help the members of the organizations write letters and communiqués. The organizations' formal communications tend to be reinforced with the use of other media, especially radio, which ADESNORTAY, ADAVIP, and APL used for various reasons while the study was underway.

> *Now with technological progress and with globalization, we have to get up to speed, perhaps not one hundred percent, but at least some.* (ADESNORTAY member)

Informal communication in the organizations studied is done orally and in person. Even when leaders and some members are Internet users, they do not generally communicate by digital means, as most are only infrequent users. The exception, again, is the Student Center, whose members use Internet-based instant messaging (MSN Messenger). Young people have definitely appropriated technological tools; that is especially true of this group of systems engineering students.

Note the similarity between our findings and those of earlier studies of organizational communication in similar contexts. A study in Combayo (in Cajamarca, in Peru's northern highland) reported the importance of paper-based communication and the official status this confers in a society that is practically nonliterate (Bossio 2002). Meanwhile, an assessment of a project of information systems and telecenters in Huaral (Lima) found that the introduction of new technologies accelerated the informal, day-to-day communication of a farmers' organization and made it more efficient, whereas official communication continued to depend on paper and personal delivery because "the analysis shows that when urgency is more important than formality, the use of new technologies gains a foothold" (Bossio 2007).

In some cases (APL, Salqui, and Hierbas Aromáticas), mobile telephones are used for communication and coordination among members of the organization. In the case of APL, urgency is reported to be the motivation for this type of communication. It should be noted that of all the organizations observed, the members of APL are somewhat better off economically, and mobile telephony may be more accessible to them.

Confluence of Means

PAVs are only one of several means used by organizations to meet their objectives. The PAV plays a role at specific times, usually at the beginning or end of a communication process. Internal communication is still largely done face to face (in meetings, conversations in homes, assemblies, etc.). PAV-mediated communication processes generally involve someone outside the organization.

To illustrate the flow of communication, consider the example of a meeting of members of ADESNORTAY regarding an upcoming visit from the registrar of the Reparations Council. In this case, PAVs are used at the beginning and end of the flow, and communication is mainly face to face. The PAV serves to connect the organization with an outside agent. The registrar announces his intended arrival time in an email to the president and subsequently confirms by telephone (calling the leader's mobile phone). The email message must be read at the PAV by the president's son, who has the skills necessary for using email. The president must then inform all members of the registrar's arrival. Here, the means of communication traditionally used in rural areas of Peru—radio and word of mouth (or door to door)—come into play. These are the most efficient means for calling an urgent meeting; in other cases, this will be done via a printed communiqué delivered in person to each member.

The Role of Young People

Some CBOs whose members do not have Internet skills rely on their children or younger members of the organization, many of whom learned to use the Internet in PAVs.

We ourselves don't handle Internet too well, but our children often help us. (ADAVIP President)

Internet use in PAVs has increased in Pampas in recent years. Young people in the area have appropriated computer and Internet use, and it is common to see Internet booths occupied by children and adolescents who go after school to play games or communicate with friends using chat (Messenger) and social networks.

Sometimes my brothers and sisters, who are studying in school, do their homework and afterwards chat.... They have lots of stuff there in the Internet. (Sarita Colonia member)

Despite the Daniel Hernández telecenter's initial effort to train adults to use computers, most adults have not acquired those skills. Therefore, they turn to their children for help using the computers. In the case of ADESNORTAY, the president's son help him review his email account, which he uses to communicate with his main infomediary (the association secretary) and with the registrar of the National Reparations Council. In general, young people's participation in CBOs helps the groups take advantage of PAVs as a tool for organizational capacity building.

Conclusions and Recommendations for Public Policy

ICT is merely a tool that amplifies individual and organizational capacities in the direction of people's intentions (positive or negative) within the framework of the organization (Toyama, 2011). This concept rejects the idea that technology in itself is a cause of social transformation. ICT cannot take the place of capacities or people's good intentions, if those are not already in place. Technology will contribute more and with greater value when enhanced capacities and good intentions exist than in a context of lesser capacities or negative intentions.

Government agencies should take steps to ensure that the Internet becomes increasingly useful to CBOs. We offer four key recommendations:

1. Programs or projects for using ICT for development should include not only programs aimed at increasing the ability of organizations to use computers and the Internet but also capacity-building components aimed at strengthening the organizations, especially in areas where impact is most frequent, such as leadership, linkages, and financial management.

2. Greater participation by young people in community organizations should be promoted. Promotion of Internet access and PAV use is often aimed at children and young people because they appropriate ICT most easily. The participation of young people—who already use ICT—in CBOs strengthens the organizations' capabilities.

If ICT and PAVs are to have a greater impact on CBOs, therefore, ICT programs for development should create incentives for young people to participate in CBOs so they can contribute to the initial process of technology appropriation and subsequently to creating the critical mass needed for the program's sustainability. This promotion of participation should be suggested to the various stakeholders involved—first the CBO but also NGOs and government programs.

3. PAVs have more impact on CBOs when they are related to the organizations or have inclusive policies for their members. NGO or government development programs that include PAVs should go beyond providing universal individual Internet access and include CBOs as part of their goal. At the same time, programs and projects that work with CBOs—sponsored by NGOs or government agencies—should encourage the organizations to use PAVs (telecenters or public booths) as a management tool.

4. Public agencies that regulate the operation of PAVs should develop programs to make them more inclusive, especially those in which the government has more influence, such as telecenters. This means prohibiting all forms of discrimination and, especially, promoting inclusion through campaigns, contests, and other means.

References

Amariles, Fabiola, Olga Paz, Nathan Russell, and Nancy Johnson. 2006. The Impacts of Community Telecenters in Rural Colombia. *Journal of Community Informatics* 2 (3).

Andrade, Horacio. 2005. *Comunicación organizacional interna: procesos, disciplina y técnica*. Spain: Netbiblo.

Bossio, Juan Fernando. 2002. Flujos de información y comunicación en contextos rurales: Punto de partida para intervenciones en tecnologías de información y comunicación. In *Perú, el problema agrario en debate (SEPIA IX)*, ed. Manuel Pulgar Vidal, Eduardo Zegarra, and Jaime Urrutia, 662–687. Lima: Seminario Permanente de Investigación Agraria (SEPIA). http://www.sepia.org.pe/index.php?fp_cont=881

Bossio, Juan Fernando. 2007. Sostenibilidad de proyectos de desarrollo con nuevas tecnologías: el caso de la organización de regantes y su sistema de información en Huaral. *Journal of Community Informatics* 3 (3).

Bossio, Juan Fernando, and Katia Sotomayor. 2010. Acceso a información pública y TIC en Perú. In *Puntos de acceso público a Internet en América Latina*, ed. Melissa Arias, Kemly Camacho, and Adriana Sánchez, 103–118. San José, Costa Rica: Sula Vatsu.

Brainard, Lori A., and Jennifer M. Brinkerhoff. 2004. Lost in Cyberspace: Shedding Light on the Dark Matter of Grassroots Organizations. *Nonprofit and Voluntary Sector Quarterly* 33 (3S): S32–S53.

Bustamante, Roberto, Zulema Burneo, and Maicu Alvarado. 2009. Usos efectivos y necesidades de información para el desarrollo de estrategias apropiadas para proyectos TIC en el área rural. Consorcio de Investigación Económica y Social (CIES) and Centro Peruano de Estudios Sociales (CEPES). http://www.cies.org.pe/sites/default/files/investigaciones/usos-efectivos-y-nesecidades-de-informacion-para-el-desarrollo-de-estrategias-apropiadas.pdf.

Comisión de la Verdad y Reconciliación (CVR). 2003. Rostros y perfiles de la violencia. In Volume 1 of *Informe de la Comisión de la Verdad y Reconciliación*. Lima: Comisión de la Verdad y Reconciliación. http://www.derechos.org/nizkor/peru/libros/cv/i/3.html.

Diez, Alejandro. 1997. Diversidades, alternativas y ambigüedades: Instituciones, comportamientos y mentalidades en la sociedad rural. In *Perú, el problema agrario en debate (SEPIA VII)*, ed. Víctor Agreda, Alejandro Diez, and Manuel Glave, 247–326. Lima: Seminario Permanente de Investigación Agraria (SEPIA). www.sepia.org.pe/index.php?fp_cont=879/.

Diez, Alejandro. 2000. Reforma institucional. In *Desafíos del desarrollo rural en el Perú*, ed. Carolina Trivelli, Milton von Hesse, Alejandro Diez, and Laureano del Castillo. Lima: Consorcio de Investigación Económica y Social.

Instituto Nacional de Estadística e Informática. 2008. *Censos Nacionales 2007: XI de Población y VI de Vivienda: Perfil sociodemográfico del Perú*, 2nd ed. Lima: Author and United Nations Population Fund. http://www2.congreso.gob.pe/sicr/cendocbib/con4_uibd.nsf/2696B871FEEECEF305257BD00057B475/$FILE/Perfil_sociodemogr%C3%A1fico_del_Per%C3%BA.pdf.

Instituto Nacional de Estadística e Informática. 2010. *Mapa de Pobreza Provincial y Distrital 2009: El enfoque de la pobreza monetaria*. Lima: Author and United Nations Population Fund. http://www.unfpa.org.pe/publicaciones/publicacionesperu/INEI-Mapa-Pobreza-2009.pdf.

Instituto Nacional de Estadística e Informática. 2013. *Las tecnologías de información y comunicación en los hogares: Trimestre Enero-Febrero-Marzo*. Technical bulletin No. 6 (June) covering January—–March. Lima: Author. http://www.pcm.gob.pe/wp-content/uploads/2013/06/TIC-Oct-Ene-Mar-2013.pdf.

Lusthaus, Charles, Marie-Hélène Adrien, Gary Anderson, Fred Carden, and George Plinio Montalván. 2002. *Organizational Assessment: A Framework for Improving Performance*. Washington, DC: Inter-American Development Bank (IADB) and Ottawa, Canada: International Development Research Centre.

Ministerio de Transportes y Comunicaciones. Dirección General de Regulación y Asuntos Internacionales de Comunicaciones. 2011. *Estadísticas de servicios públicos de telecomunicaciones a nivel nacional*. Lima: Author. http://www.mtc.gob.pe/portal/comunicacion/politicas/estadisticas/Servicios%20P%C3%BAblicos%20de%20Telecom%20%20I%20Trim.%202011.pdf.

Organismo Supervisor de Inversión Privada en Telecomunicaciones. 2013. Indicadores de servicio móvil: Cobertura nacional por operador. Excel file available on Organismo Supervisor de Inversión Privada en Telecomunicaciones website. http://www.osiptel.gob.pe/WebsiteAjax/WebFormgeneral/sector/wfrm_Consulta_Informacion_Estadisticas.aspx?CodInfo=13478&CodSubCat=864&TituloInformacion=2.+Indicadores+del+Servicio+M%C3%B3vil&DescripcionInformacion/.

Schildermann, Theo. 2002. *Strengthening the Knowledge and Information Systems of the Urban Poor*. Report of DFID funded research. London: Department for International Development. http://www.ucl.ac.uk/dpu-projects/drivers_urb_change/urb_society/pdf_health_educ/ITDG_Schilderman_strenghthening_knowledge.pdf.

Serna Purizaca, Arnaldo. 2005. *Poder y participación en organizaciónes sociales de base*. Lima: Escuela para el Desarrollo.

Seye, Araba, and Michelle Fellows. 2009. *Literature Review on the Impact of Public Access to Information and Communication Technologies*. CIS Working Paper No. 6. Seattle: Technology & Social Change Group (formerly the Center for Information & Society), University of Washington Information School. http://library.globalimpactstudy.org/sites/default/files/docs/CIS-WorkingPaperNo6.pdf.

Toyama, Kentaro. 2011. Technology as Amplifier in International Development. In *Proceedings of the 2011 iConference* (iConference '11), 75–82. New York: Association for Computing Machinery.

Trivelli, Carolina, Javier Escobal, and Bruno Revesz. 2009. *Desarrollo rural en la sierra: Aportes para el debate*. Lima: Centro de Investigación y Promoción del Campesinado, Grupo de Análisis para el Desarrollo, Instituto de Estudios Peruanos, and Consorcio de Investigación Económica y Social. http://disde.minedu.gob.pe/xmlui/bitstream/handle/123456789/759/427.%20Desarrollo%20rural%20en%20la%20sierra%20aportes%20para%20el%20debate.pdf?sequence=1/.

United Nations Development Programme. 2010. *Informe sobre Desarrollo Humano Perú 2009: Por una densidad del Estado al servicio de la gente*. Vol. 1, *Las brechas en el territorio*. Lima: Author. http://www.pe.undp.org/content/peru/es/home/library/poverty/InformeDesarrolloHumano2009/.

Voida, Amy. 2011. Bridging Between Grassroots Movements and Nonprofit Organizations. Paper presented at the workshop on *HCI, Politics and the City: Engaging Grassroots Movement for Reflection and Action*. Vancouver: Conference on Human Factors in Computing Systems, May 7–8. http://amy.voida.com/wp-content/uploads/2013/04/grassrootsMovementsAndNonprofits-chi11.pdf.

Appendix 9.A Impacted Capacities by Points of Public Access to Internet

Abbreviations and Acronyms Used in the Tables

ADAVIP	*Asociación de desplazados y víctimas de la violencia política*—Association of Displaced People and Victims of Political Violence
ADES	ADESNORTAY, *Asociación de desplazados del Nor-Oriente de Tayacaja*—Association of Displaced People of Northeastern Tayacaja
APAFA	*Asociación de Padres de Familia*—Parents' Association
APL	APROLEDH, *Asociación de Productores de Lácteos*—Milk Producers' Association
CE	*Consejo de Estudiantes—Huancavélica*—Huancavélica Student Council
CS	*Cooperativa Salqui*—Salqui Cooperative
HA	*Asociación de Productores de Hierbas Aromáticas*—Aromatic Herb Producers' Association
SC	Sarita Colonia
VL	*Club de Madres del Vaso de Leche*—Glass of Milk Mothers' Club

Table 9.A.1
Impact of ICT and PAV Use on Strategic Leadership (SL)

	Support to Displaced		Survival		Education		Productive		
	ADES	ADAVIP	VL	SC	APAFA	CE	APL	CS	HA
Capacity to search for new opportunities	●	○	○	○	○	○	●	●	●
Capacity of other members to assume the leadership	●	○	○	○			●		●
Capacity to mobilize people around the organization	●	○	○	○	○			●	●
Capacity to carry out major projects	●	○		○	○	○	○	●	●
Leader's capacity to facilitate, moderate, and promote dialogue	●	○	○			○	○	●	○
Leader's motivation	●	○	○	○	○	○	●	○	○
Leader's capacity to inspire trust in the members of the organization	●	○	○	○	○	○	○	○	●
Capacity to formulate a work plan	●	○	○	○	○	●	○	○	○
Capacity to adapt to change	○	○					●	○	●
Leader's capacity to organize, enhance, and establish internal links	○	○	○		○	○	○	●	○
Capacity to gain support from the members	○	○	○	○	○	○	○	○	●
Organization's capacity to inspire trust in the community	○	○	○	○	○	○	○	●	○

● = observable impact, ○ = no impact

Table 9.A.2
Impact of ICT and PAV Use on Organizational Structure (OS)

	Support to Displaced		Survival		Education		Productive		
	ADES	ADAVIP	VL	SC	APAFA	CE	APL	CS	HA
Capacity to coordinate activities/functions	○	○	○		○	●		○	●
External political management capacity	○	○	○	○	○		○	○	●
Capacity to design a structure that allows the organization to achieve its objectives	○	○	○	○		○	○	○	●
Sufficiency of leaders (committees) to carry out the necessary work	●	○	○			○	○	○	○
Functional capacity to adapt to changes	○	○	○		○		○	○	●

● = observable impact, ○ = no impact

Table 9.A.3
Impact of ICT and PAV Use on Human Resources (HR)

	Support to Displaced		Survival		Education		Productive		
	ADES	ADAVIP	VL	SC	APAFA	CE	APL	CS	HA
Capacity to achieve individual goals	●	○	○	○	○		○	○	●
Capacity to create a suitable organizational environment	○	○	○			●	○	●	○
Capacity to improve skills, knowledge, and members' attitudes			○	○		○	○	○	●
Capacity to train new leaders	●	○	○	○		○	○	○	

● = observable impact, ○ = no impact

Table 9.A.4

Impact of ICT and PAV Use on Financial Management (F)

	Support to Displaced		Survival		Education		Productive		
	ADES	ADAVIP	VL	SC	APAFA	CE	APL	CS	HA
Capacity to seek financing	●	○		○	○		○	●	●
Capacity to obtain financing from available sources	●			●	○		○	○	●
Capacity to record financial information	○			●	○	●		○	
Capacity to generate financial and accounting reports	●		○	●	○	●			
Capacity to monitor performance and spending	○	○	○		○	●		○	○

● = observable impact, ○ = no impact

Table 9.A.5

Impact of ICT and PAV Use on Infrastructure (I)

	Support to Displaced		Survival		Education		Productive		
	ADES	ADAVIP	VL	SC	APAFA	CE	APL	CS	HA
Capacity to access information	●	○	○		○	●	●	●	●
Capacity to recognize the need to access/use ICT	●		○	○		●	●	●	●
Capacity to communicate (access to communication networks)	●		○	○	○	●		●	●
Capacity to provide adequate space	●						○	●	●

● = observable impact, ○ = no impact

Table 9.A.6
Impact of ICT and PAV Use on Management of Programs and Services (PS)

	Support to Displaced		Survival		Education		Productive		
	ADES	ADAVIP	VL	SC	APAFA	CE	APL	CS	HA
Capacity to plan projects	●	○		●	○	○	○	○	●
Capacity to generate reports	●		○	●	○	●	○	○	○
Capacity to link projects with organizational objectives	○	○		○	○	○	○	○	●
Capacity to meet deadlines	○			○		●	○	○	

● = observable impact, ○ = no impact

Table 9.A.7
Impact of ICT and PAV Use on Management of Processes (P)

	Support to Displaced		Survival		Education		Productive		
	ADES	ADAVIP	VL	SC	APAFA	CE	APL	CS	HA
Capacity to search for information that supports decisions	●	○				○	●	●	○
Capacity to communicate internally	○	○	○	○	○	●	○	●	○
Capacity to use effective means of communication	●	○	○	○	○	○	○	●	○
Capacity to distinguish between bias and evidence								●	
Capacity to make timely decisions	○					○	○	○	●
Capacity to access other members of the organization	○	○		○		○		●	○

● = observable impact, ○ = no impact

Table 9.A.8
Impact of ICT and PAV Use on Inter-institutional Linkages (Lk)

	Support to Displaced		Survival		Education		Productive		
	ADES	ADAVIP	VL	SC	APAFA	CE	APL	CS	HA
Capacity to seek opportunities for partnerships	●	○		○	○	●	○	●	●
Capacity to use electronic means	●			○	○	●	●	○	●
Capacity to establish partnerships with funding sources				○	○		○	●	●
Capacity to communicate needs and achievements to external publics				○	○		○	●	●
Capacity to obtain adequate support from allies	○	○	○	○	○	○	○	○	●
Capacity to search for people (contacts)	○	○		○	○		●	○	○
Capacity to maintain a network registry of external contacts			○				○	●	

● = observable impact, ○ = no impact

Appendix 9.B Existing Capabilities Not Impacted by Public Internet Access

Abbreviations and Acronyms Used in the Tables

ADAVIP	*Asociación de desplazados y víctimas de la violencia política*—Association of Displaced People and Victims of Political Violence
ADES	ADESNORTAY, *Asociación de desplazados del Nor-Oriente de Tayacaja*—Association of Displaced People of Northeastern Tayacaja
APAFA	*Asociación de Padres de Familia*—Parents' Association
APL	APROLEDH, *Asociación de Productores de Lácteos*—Milk Producers' Association
CE	*Consejo de Estudiantes—Huancavélica*—Huancavélica Student Council
CS	*Cooperativa Salqui*—Salqui Cooperative
HA	*Asociación de Productores de Hierbas Aromáticas*—Aromatic Herb Producers' Association
SC	Sarita Colonia
VL	*Club de Madres del Vaso de Leche*—Glass of Milk Mothers' Club

Table 9.B.1

Existing Capabilities Not Impacted by ICT and PAV Use: Strategic Leadership (SL)

	Support to Displaced		Survival		Education		Productive		
	ADES	ADAVIP	VL	SC	APAFA	CE	APL	CS	HA
Capacity of the leadership to achieve regarding the work plan	○	○	○	○	○	○	○	○	○
Leader's capacity to develop the organization's vision, advocate for it, and promote it	○	○	○		○	○	○	○	○
Capacity to carry out the work plan	○	○	○	○	○	○	○		○
Capacity to be cohesively behind the work plan	○	○	○		○	○	○	○	○
Recognition capacity	○	○				○	○	○	○
Capacity to create a plan that can be evaluated			○	○	○	○	○		
Capacity to create distributed leadership	○	○	○			○		○	
Leader's capacity to set goals, improve performance, and measure results			○		○		○	○	
Capacity to reformulate the work plan			○		○	○	○		
Capacity to generate suggestions	○						○	○	
Capacity of the members to suggest changes			○				○		
Capacity to value distributed leadership			○						

● = observable impact, ○ = no impact

Table 9.B.2
Existing Capabilities Not Impacted by ICT and PAV Use: Organizational Structure (OS)

	Support to Displaced		Survival		Education		Productive		
	ADES	ADAVIP	VL	SC	APAFA	CE	APL	CS	HA
Capacity to assess the organization's leadership	○	○	○	○	○	○	○	○	○
Capacity to define the roles of members	○	○	○	○	○	○	○	○	○
Clear hierarchy	○	○	○		○	○	○	○	○
Leadership capacity to identify the strengths of the organization	○	○	○				○	○	○
Decentralizing decision-making capacity	○	○	○			○		○	○
Capacity to structure work processes clearly and appropriately	○	○	○	○				○	○
Capacity to supervise the leadership/ management			○		○			○	○
Leadership capacity to create conditions to support change			○				○	○	

● = observable impact, ○ = no impact

Table 9.B.3
Existing Capabilities Not Impacted by ICT and PAV Use: Human Resources (HR)

	Support to Displaced		Survival		Education		Productive		
	ADES	ADAVIP	VL	SC	APAFA	CE	APL	CS	HA
Capacity to help and show solidarity with other members	○	○	○	○	○		○	○	○
Capacity to integrate members in a non-discriminatory way	○	○	○		○		○	○	
Capacity to select appropriate staff	○	○			○		○	○	
Capacity to introduce new members to the organization			○		○		○		
Capacity to provide incentives					○				

● = observable impact, ○ = no impact

Table 9.B.4
Existing Capabilities Not Impacted by ICT and PAV Use: Financial Management (F)

	Support to Displaced		Survival		Education		Productive		
	ADES	ADAVIP	VL	SC	APAFA	CE	APL	CS	HA
Capacity to provide operating expenses				○	○	○	○	○	○
Capacity to determine annual budget			○	○	○	○		○	○
Capacity to determine capital costs					○	○	○	○	

● = observable impact, ○ = no impact

Table 9.B.5
Existing Capabilities Not Impacted by ICT and PAV Use: Infrastructure (I)

	Support to Displaced		Survival		Education		Productive		
	ADES	ADAVIP	VL	SC	APAFA	CE	APL	CS	HA
Capacity to move/relocate	○	○	○	○	○	○	○	○	○
Capacity to maintain infrastructure					○		○	○	○

● = observable impact, ○ = no impact

Table 9.B.6
Existing Capabilities Not Impacted by ICT and PAV Use: Management of Programs and Services (PS)

	Support to Displaced		Survival		Education		Productive		
	ADES	ADAVIP	VL	SC	APAFA	CE	APL	CS	HA
Capacity to evaluate project results	○			○	○	○	○	○	○
Capacity to use and allocate resources	○			○	○	○	○	○	○
Capacity to establish appropriate program deadlines	○			○		○	○	○	○
Capacity to form teams	○			○	○	○		○	
Capacity to learn from mistakes							○	○	○
Capacity to conduct effective meetings							○		

● = observable impact, ○ = no impact

Table 9.B.7

Existing Capabilities Not Impacted by ICT and PAV Use: Management of Processes (P)

	Support to Displaced		Survival		Education		Productive		
	ADES	ADAVIP	VL	SC	APAFA	CE	APL	CS	HA
Capacity to diagnose problems	○	○	○	○	○	○	○	○	○
Capacity to adopt group decisions	○	○			○	○	○	○	○
Leadership capacity to communicate decisions to members	○	○	○			○	○	○	○
Leadership capacity to communicate progress and results to members	○	○	○			○	○	○	○
Capacity to determine degree of uncertainty (risk)	○					○	○	○	○
Capacity to evaluate the consequences of decisions	○					○	○	○	
Capacity to structure problems	○		○	○					
Capacity to evaluate alternative solutions	○			○			○		

● = observable impact, ○ = no impact

Table 9.B.8

Existing Capabilities Not Impacted by ICT and PAV Use: Inter-institutional Linkages (Lk)

	Support to Displaced		Survival		Education		Productive		
	ADES	ADAVIP	VL	SC	APAFA	CE	APL	CS	HA
Capacity to align institutional links with objectives			○		○	○	○	○	○
Capacity to enlist the volunteer services of nonmembers	○	○		○	○	○			○
Capacity to manage confidentiality and privacy of information	○	○	○				○		

● = observable impact, ○ = no impact

III Impact on Women

10 Women and Cybercafés in Uttar Pradesh

Nidhi Mehta and Balwant Singh Mehta

Abstract

The study was conducted in two mid-sized towns in India, namely, the Bhadohi and Ferozabad districts of Uttar Pradesh. We analyzed the outcome of structured in-depth interviews with 100 women users and 100 women nonusers of cybercafés. We identify the user profiles, usage patterns, and reasons for the low rate of cybercafé usage by women in northern India.

Our study reveals that cybercafé usage by women is most common among female students, followed by educated women from the upper socioeconomic class. They access information mostly relating to education, employment, and entertainment. Users usually go to cybercafés during the afternoon and evening when they are relatively free from other duties. Overall, we observed that few women use cybercafés, and those who do have many socioeconomic restrictions placed on on them; these obstacles are tied to social, cultural, structural (time, location, illiteracy), and environmental issues.

Women users, however, found cybercafés very useful. To close the gap between the value women perceive from cybercafé usage and actual usage, several suggestions can be made: (1) enhance literacy and awareness among women, (2) sensitize cybercafé operators to gender-specific issues and environment, (3) make content on gender issues available in local languages, (4) increase emphasis on English in schools, and (5) implement gender-specific welfare programs more thoroughly. These initiatives will not only enhance the sustainability of cybercafés but will provide wider Internet access to disadvantaged people in developing areas.

Introduction

Modern information and communication technologies (ICTs) such as computers and the Internet have the potential to benefit women in developing countries (Carter and Grieco 2000). Feminist theorists in particular have emphasized the ability of the Internet to provide a space for women, where they can breathe without facing the burden of social discrimination (Lawley 1993).

Internet access is far from reaching the entire population even in countries with high rates of Internet penetration (Warschauer 2003). In India, the low rates of personal computer ownership and the high costs of hardware and connectivity limit personal individual access to the Internet. As a result, shared access through cybercafés has mushroomed throughout India, and today such venues can be found even in smaller towns and some of the bigger villages. Of the 82 million Internet users in the country in 2011, around 37 percent (30 million) were living in towns of fewer than 500,000 people, which matches the population of the country's top eight metropolitan cities put together (29 million) (Internet and Mobile Association of India 2011). Some Indian women are benefiting from cybercafés, but use of these facilities by women is quite limited.

In a first survey conducted as part of this study, we interviewed thirty users at each of ten cybercafés (five located in Bhadohi and five in Firozabad) during their opening hours (10 A.M. to 10 P.M.) over three to four consecutive days. The overwhelming majority of users were men: of the 300 users surveyed, only nine (3 percent) were women. We also interviewed 200 nonusers among people outside and around each cybercafé during the daytime; of these, only eighteen (9 percent) were women.

Upon finding from this first survey that few women were users, the research team realized this was the most urgent social impact issue deserving scrutiny. Accordingly, we turned our attention to identifying the reasons underlying this form of gender exclusion from the technology by conducting a follow-up survey to address the following issues:

1. What are the main socioeconomic features of women users and nonusers of cybercafés?
2. What are the major barriers preventing greater use of cybercafés by women?
3. Are some cybercafés more successful in attracting women? If so, why?
4. Are there specific hours during the day when women prefer to visit cybercafés? If so, why?

Methodology

This complementary survey was conducted in the same two towns as the first survey, Bhadohi and Firozabad. We interviewed 173 additional women (91 users and 82 nonusers) to make a total sample of 100 each by using the snowball sampling method. To facilitate comparisons, users and nonusers were selected in equal proportion from similar categories of social group, occupation, education, and location.

Women cybercafé users interviewed during the first survey were revisited and helped us identify additional women users from similar localities (home), school, colleges, and offices. For nonusers, women users helped us to identify potential users among their family members, relatives, and friends with similar demographics. This way, in each locality, we were able to include nonusers with similar sociocultural backgrounds. To cover other female nonusers, we approached women members of the local governance body (*panchayat*)[1] and explained to them the purpose of our survey. They helped us to identify and approach other nonusers. As a result, we were able to include a wider geographical and socioeconomic sample of nonusers. One limitation of the study is that even among the users, many were infrequent users who had not visited a cybercafé in the previous six months.

Both quantitative and qualitative methods were used to collect data. Quantitative data were collected through two semistructured questionnaires (one for respondents and another for cybercafé owners/operators) and qualitative information through case studies and discussions with key stakeholders. The questionnaire collects demographic information and information about exposure and access to Internet at cybercafés. To explore the obstacles to cybercafé usage, the questionnaire also includes questions related to socioeconomic barriers.

Women in Indian Society

India is a vibrant country with many religions and beliefs. It also has diverse cultural and social norms in different parts of the country. Yet there are some commonalities across the country. For the most part, Indian society is a patriarchal one where men hold the positions of power and women are denied even basic rights (Dube 2001). Gender discrimination begins early in life, with many families celebrating the birth of a boy over that of a girl. This is reflected in India's high incidence of female infanticide and low male-female sex ratio (United Nations Children's Fund 2011). Subjectively, girls grow up with the sense that they are temporary members of the family and that expenditure on their upbringing and marriage is a burden (Vashista 1976).

Control of girl's sexual life (or denial thereof) is a central concern for many families. This places considerable restrictions on girls' mobility; they have few rights in the parental home and are expected to remain in the close custody of their male relatives. Many marriages are arranged by elder male family members, and the bride and groom often meet for the first time only at the wedding ceremony. After marriage, girls join their husband's family; the restrictions on their mobility continue in their husband's home, and depending on the custom, they may have to wear a veil in the presence of senior male members of the family (Robinson 2004).

Consistent with a patriarchal society, many Indian communities expect elder males to go out to earn for the sustenance of the family, whereas the women's sphere of work is the home and child care (Desai and Thakkar 2001). Although women's employment in teaching, finance, and other areas of the service sector is increasing, access to these fields is limited to educated women, usually from the higher socioeconomic strata.[2] Working women carry a double burden, with duties both within and outside the home; they often face considerable conflict and stress (Duraisamy and Duraisamy 1999). Women from lower socioeconomic strata end up working (if they work at all) in the informal sector, in low-skill activities in factories, construction sites, food processing units, small trade, and domestic labor.

The status of women has improved over time, with higher participation in education and formal employment, but large gender differences remain prevalent in Indian society, particularly in the northern part of the country (Mukhopadhyay and Tendulkar 2006).

Our study area, Uttar Pradesh, reflects the gender biases of a typical north Indian state. Bhadohi, a part of the Sant Ravidas Nagar district in eastern Uttar Pradesh, has an urban population of about 229,302; Firozabad, in western Uttar Pradesh, has an urban population of 833,169 (2011 Census).[3] Compared with other districts within the state, the districts in which these two towns are located have human development and gender development indices in the medium range. Literacy in Uttar Pradesh is quite imbalanced. In urban areas, 20 percent of men and 31 percent of women are illiterate; in rural areas, 24 percent of men and 47 percent of women are illiterate (Directorate of Census Operations 2013).

Findings

Demographic and Socioeconomic Factors

The profile of cybercafé users in our study reflects both the prevailing social gender norms and the recent changes taking place. The majority of female cybercafé users were young students who had completed higher secondary or tertiary education and belonged to what the government labels Upper Caste and Other Backward Class (OBC) (table 10.1). In general, users were younger and better educated than nonusers. Students were dominant among both users and nonusers (see table 10.1).

Cybercafé users are a relatively privileged group compared with the overall demographic of Uttar Pradesh, where OBCs account for 50 percent of the households, Scheduled Castes and Scheduled Tribes (ST/SC) for 25 percent, and upper social groups for 25 percent (Ministry of Statistics and Programme Implementation 2011). Highly educated

Table 10.1
Demographic Profile of Women Users and Nonusers Interviewed

Demographic Features		Users (#)	Nonusers (#)
Social group	Scheduled Caste	8	10
	Other Backward Class	43	46
	Upper Caste	49	44
	Total	100	100
Level of education completed	Primary	–	2
	Secondary	4	10
	Higher secondary	23	45
	Tertiary	73	43
	Total	100	100
Occupation	Working	12	20
	Unemployed	4	10
	Student	80	64
	Homemaker	4	6
	Total	100	100
Monthly household income (in Rs)*	≤ 7,500	25	25
	7,500–15,000	42	35
	15,000–30,000	29	36
	≥ 30,000	4	4
	Total	100	100
Age group	14–18	24	27
	19–25	72	61
	> 25	4	12
	Total	100	100
	Average age	20.2	21.6

*1 US$ = 45 Rs (rupees).

women from upper socioeconomic groups have started moving out and participating in formal employment. These women were using the Internet both in the workplace and at cybercafés. As one of them said,

I worked in a government office as an office assistant, and sent and received official and personal mails daily. Apart from mail, I also used to see information about education and employment opportunities available on different websites.

Another group of women, those who belong to families with lower socioeconomic status, have to work to survive. This group was employed in low-skilled jobs in factories and other small trading and had no interest in accessing the Internet at cybercafés. The third group comprises traditional upper class families, where women do not work outside the home but are involved full time in homemaking with its multiple roles, including housekeeping and caring for children and the elderly. Among our survey respondents, four women from this group visited cybercafés, but the others did not see the importance of the Internet in their life. As one of them said,

The whole day, I am too busy doing household work. By the time I am free from morning chores, the children come back from school. After having lunch I get two hours break in which I take rest. I am not interested in knowing about the Internet as it is of no use to me. Further, it can't help me in my household chores.

We identified an emerging new group of users who were accessing the Internet at home on their laptops and mobile phones. These users were from upper socioeconomic families and were few in number. One of them said,

I have my own laptop; whenever I need to email or download any information, I do it through my mobile. So I do not need to go to a cybercafé while I can access the Internet on the mobile.

Survey results show that, depending on their demographic profile, socioeconomic class, and occupation, different groups of users and nonusers exist in the communities. These women have different priorities in terms of their Internet use at cybercafés, as reflected in the frequency, time, and purpose of their visits.

Frequency and Time of Visits, and Departure Point

Social restrictions on women are still prevalent, a fact that is reflected in the frequency and time of their visits to cybercafés (table 10.2). For a number of reasons, women generally prefer to visit cybercafés in the afternoon and early evening. First, at those times, women have some freedom from household duties, and girls return from school. Second, family restrictions are relaxed during the day. Third, fewer males are present at cybercafés during the day, so women feel safer and feel they have some measure of privacy. (Female students noted that afternoon hours are the only time when they can avoid parental scrutiny and computer systems are also available.) Fourth, men are not at home in the afternoon, so women have the liberty of going out. Women travel to cybercafés from their homes and students from their schools/colleges.

Cybercafé Usage

Cybercafé usage involves some entertainment for most users. However, different groups of users use the Internet for other tasks as well. Young students visit cybercafés to access information related to their education and jobs (table 10.3). One girl said,

I have come to the cybercafé along with my friends to see my entrance examination result for bachelor of education. My friend and the venue operator helped me verify my results and search for colleges near our district, so I can pursue further counseling and admission.

Table 10.2
Frequency of Visits, Departure Point of Travel, Distance to Venue, and Time of Visit of Male and Female Users of Cybercafés

		Female	Male*
Frequency of visits to cybercafés	Daily	6	22
	Once a week	28	56
	Once a month	66	21
	Total	100	100
Departure point of travel to venue	Home	65	55
	Work	4	35
	School/university	29	10
	Other	2	1
	Total	100	100
Distance to venue	< 1 km	21	41
	1–2 km	31	25
	3–5 km	25	27
	> 5 km	7	7
	Do not know	16	–
	Total	100	100
Time of day	Morning	18	39
	Afternoon	27	18
	Evening	55	43
	Total	100	100
	N	(100)	(289)

*Data from first survey in which very few women were interviewed.

Table 10.3
Purpose for Visiting Cybercafés Selected by the 100 Women Users Interviewed

Purpose	# of Users
News	12
Other information	14
Government services	25
Employment and business opportunities	36
Entertainment	59
Education	88

Note: Users were able to select more than one purpose.

While working women accessed information related to their present jobs or to potential new jobs, more educated women from upper socioeconomic groups visited the cybercafé to download education-related information to help their children (table 10.3). One of them said,

My son got an assignment in which he had to collect information on all the planets of the solar system. To help him in completing his work I downloaded information on planets from the website at cybercafés.

Overall, women's network of family members, friends, colleagues, and Internet operators plays an important role in adoption of and learning about the Internet at cybercafés.

Besides Internet access, cybercafés provide a number of other products and services that attract women: for example, photocopying, scanning, faxing, computer training, mobile top-up cards, rail and air tickets, gift items, greeting cards, and food and beverages. One woman user said,

I go to cybercafés to purchase mobile recharge coupons, books for my kids, and gift items like toys, paintings, and greeting cards.

Women visiting cybercafés also get information about education, employment, and trading by interacting with cybercafé operators and Internet users.

Barriers

The study revealed that Internet users in towns fell into three groups: (1) a very small group of young girl students, (2) working women from upper socioeconomic classes, and (3) homemakers. As noted earlier, women face many socioeconomic hurdles in accessing the Internet at cybercafés. Using an open-ended question, we asked both users and nonusers about the three major barriers or challenges they faced in accessing the Internet at cybercafés. The qualitative responses were later coded into four major categories—social restriction, unfavorable environment at cybercafés, high cost, and infrastructure and capacity problems—and fourteen subcategories (table 10.4).

Social and Family Restrictions Social and family restrictions in the form of parental curfews or involvement in household duties emerged as the main barriers in accessing cybercafés (table 10.4). In towns, cybercafés are not considered suitable places for single girls because these places are popular for watching pornography. Parent-imposed curfews were mentioned as a barrier by 23 users and 50 nonusers; household chores by 20 users and 24 nonusers.

Table 10.4
Primary Barriers Preventing Women (Users and Nonusers) from Accessing Cybercafés More Frequently

		Users (#)	Nonusers (#)
Social and family restrictions	Parentally imposed curfews	23	50
	Household chores	20	24
Unfavorable environment at the cybercafés	Domination by male users	17	15
	Lack of toilet facilities	1	–
	Not enough space to sit properly	7	7
	Absence of female operators and instructors	2	7
	Inappropriate content on the desktop	3	–
High costs	Of Internet access at cybercafés	12	19
	Of transportation to cybercafés	4	8
Infrastructure and capacity problems	Inadequate transportation facilities	14	9
	Not enough computer stations	12	8
	No power backup during power failure	18	7
	Slow Internet speed	18	7
	Lack of English-language skills and financial problems	2	5
No response		18	27
Total (%)		100	100

Note: An open-ended question was used to ask both users and nonusers to name three major barriers or challenges to accessing the Internet at cybercafés. The qualitative responses were later coded into the four major categories and fourteen subcategories listed above.

One girl explained her curfew this way:

My retired father is totally against my accessing the Internet at cybercafés because he has heard that male users access pornography at these places.

Girls who visit cybercafés rapidly become the subject of gossip among townsfolk. As mentioned earlier, marriages are arranged by family members, usually through social networks of close relatives and friends. Therefore, parents impose curfews on their daughters in matters related to sex and public behavior.

Homemakers rarely get time away from their household chores. As one woman explained,

I spend my whole day in the kitchen, serving meals and tea to family members without any assistance. I am a graduate and want to access the Internet at cybercafés, but do not get free time from my household duties.

These restrictions were substantially higher among nonusers than among users (table 10.4).

Unfavorable Environment at the Cybercafé Because of the unfriendly environment and the predominance of male patrons, cybercafés are not considered suitable places for women (table 10.4). Sometimes male users watching pornographic material make derogatory comments to the female patrons. Thus, female users generally prefer to visit cybercafés with their colleagues/friends and family members. Some women users also stated that their male relatives either escort them or access information on their behalf. One of them said,

I go to the cybercafé along with my brother or father to access the Internet. The environment there is unfriendly, with a crowd of unemployed men. When these men see a girl alone, they make lewd comments or want to take undue advantage. Therefore, women and girls rarely visit cybercafés. Only if urgent, they go to a cybercafé, and then, too, with their male family members.

Other challenges to accessing the Internet at cybercafés mentioned by women users and nonusers were the lack of toilet facilities, the lack of space to sit, the absence of female operators and instructors, and inappropriate content left on the desktop by male users (table 10.4).

High Costs The high cost of Internet access and transportation was reported more frequently by nonusers than by users. Transportation costs inhibit nonusers and some users from using cybercafés (table 10.4). These costs are probably also responsible for the lower frequency of visits by women than by men (table 10.2). The survey found that the average transportation cost (20 rupees per trip) was twice that of cybercafé access cost (10 rupees per hour).

Infrastructure Barriers Infrastructure barriers were mentioned mainly by users but also by some nonusers. Specific issues include inadequate transportation facilities, insufficient number of workstations, no power backup during power outages, slow Internet speeds, lack of English-language skills, and financial constraints (table 10.4).

The women reported because long distances are involved (around one-third traveled more than three kilometers to the cybercafé), they must incur high transportation costs (table 10.2). Also, cybercafés often do not have enough computer stations available at busy times, and unreliable power further diminishes the experience. Women note having to wait too long or having to leave the premises without completing their business. One girl said,

I came here to upload an admission form; before I could mail it the electricity went off. I have been waiting here for half an hour, but in vain, and I do not know when the electricity will come on again.

A female college student noted,

I go to a cybercafé after attending college. Sometimes, due to unavailability of systems and frequent power failures, I have to wait for a long time. In such a situation, I call my mother and ask her if somebody is available at home to pick me up. If I am too late I skip Internet use on that day.

Slow Internet speed is another problem that is frequently cited, that requires users to wait for long periods to accomplish a few minutes of work.

The study also found that women who had not completed secondary education were unable to access the Internet at cybercafés because of their insufficient knowledge of English. One girl said,

I wanted to learn about computers and the Internet but could not fulfill my dream due to lack of English language. I did my secondary level education at a local government school in our local language, Hindi; in schools, teachers give less importance to the English language.

Conclusion and Recommendations

In much of Uttar Pradesh, most women are poor, their literacy rate is low, and their participation in the formal economy is limited. The social system is firmly entrenched and the society is conservative. Social norms generally restrict the movement of women outside the family or the immediate community. The environment at cybercafés is generally not considered female-friendly because these venues tend to be crowded with young men. Hence, women and their family members are not comfortable with the notion of women visiting cybercafés.

Women and girls in these mid-sized towns generally have little decision-making autonomy; they have little power within the household and little control over the use of financial resources. Among those who are able to leave their homes, working women and female students do so most often. Others rarely come out of their homes, do not talk to strangers, and are always chaperoned by male family members. When interacting with outsiders, male family members reply on their behalf. Illiterate women engaged in household activities generally felt that cybercafés were not useful to them and were not interested in taking part in the survey.

The great gender differences in small towns and rural areas in India appear to be echoed by women's Internet use in cybercafés. Although recent years have seen a rapid increase in affluence, literacy, and awareness among women in Indian towns and rural areas, many barriers still exist in traditional Indian society, limiting women's access to the Internet at cybercafés.

Survey respondents, operators, and other stakeholders made several recommendations for overcoming these barriers and improving Internet access at cybercafés:

1. *Awareness and capacity building* Survey results indicate that because of social restrictions and lack of English-language skills, women in towns are unaware of the importance of the Internet. There is an urgent need to give more emphasis to English language and computer training in primary and secondary schools, and to promote awareness about the usefulness of the Internet among women in smaller towns.

2. *Location and environment* The location, management, and design of the cybercafé should allay the concerns of women and their families. For instance, cybercafés could be run by women operators from the area, thereby giving them an independent source of income, economic power, and status as a role model for other women. Furthermore, operators, both male and female, should be sensitive to women's issues and create an environment that is comfortable for women. Some possibilities include designated women-only hours, computer screens facing the entrance, and cybercafé locations in parts of town where women feel comfortable. The availability of women-specific applications—for instance, those focusing on women's and children's health, job skills, and training programs—will also make cybercafés more relevant to women's lives.

3. *Access and infrastructure* Although there are many cybercafés, more needs to be done to address infrastructure problems such as lack of electricity, slow Internet connections, and insufficient access points. Therefore, for Internet usage to rise in smaller towns and rural areas, setting up core infrastructure is extremely important. The government should provide an adequate, reliable power supply and power facilities based on solar and other alternative energy sources. Unlike mobile telephony infrastructure, where companies are able to recover capital costs fairly quickly, broadband service providers are unable to do so. Realizing this, the Government of India has invested in initiatives such as the Common Service Centres and State Wide Area Network (SWAN) (Ministry of Information and Communication Technology, n.d.). Investments in core infrastructure such as setting up fiber optic connectivity through the SWAN are noteworthy, but such schemes are still absent in small towns and rural areas.

Notes

1. According to the 73rd and 74th amendments to India's constitution, 33 percent of local government representatives must be female.

2. The Government of India classifies the country's population into four main social groups: General Caste (GC), Other Backward Classes (OBC), Scheduled Castes (SC), and Scheduled Tribes (ST). The first two groups comprise higher socioeconomic strata, the latter two lower strata.

3. 2011 Census district population data available here: http://www.censusindia.gov.in/pca/default.aspx.

References

Carter, Chris, and Margaret Grieco. 2000. New Deals, No Wheels: Social Exclusion, Tele-Options and Electronic Ontology. *Urban Studies (Edinburgh, Scotland)* 37 (10): 1735–1748.

Desai, Neera, and Usha Thakkar. 2001. *Women in Indian Society*. New Delhi: National Book Trust.

Directorate of Census Operations. 2013. *Census of India 2011: Primary Census Abstract—Data Highlights Uttar Pradesh. Lucknow, Uttar Pradesh, India*. Uttar Pradesh: Government of India.

Dube, Leela. 2001. *Anthropological Explorations in Gender, Intersecting Fields*. New Delhi: SAGE Publications.

Duraisamy, Malathy, and P. Duraisamy. 1999. Women in the Professional and Technical Labour Market in India: Gender Discrimination in Education, Employment and Earnings. *Indian Journal of Labour Economics* 42 (4): 599–612.

Internet and Mobile Association of India. 2011. *Report on Internet in India (I-Cube) 2011*. New Delhi: Author. http://www.indiagovernance.gov.in/files/internet_usage.pdf.

Lawley, Elizabeth Lane. 1993. *Computers and the Communication of Gender*. http://www.itcs.com/elawley/gender.html.

Ministry of Information and Communication Technology. n.d. Department of Electronics and Information Technology website describing State Wide Area Network. Government of India. http://deity.gov.in/content/state-wide-area-network-swan/.

Ministry of Statistics and Programme Implementation. 2011. *Employment and Unemployment Survey, 2009–2010. National Sample Survey, 2009–10*. Government of India.

Mukhopadhyay, Swapna, and Suresh D. Tendulkar. 2006. *Gender Differences in Labour Force Participation in India: An Analysis of NSS Data*. Working Paper GN(III)/2006/WP2. New Delhi: Institute of Social Studies Trust (ISST). http://www.isst-india.org/PDF/Gender%20Network/Working%20paper/NSS%20paper.pdf.

Robinson, Rowena. 2004. *Sociology of Religion in India*. New Delhi: SAGE Publications.

United Nations Children's Fund. 2011. *The Situation of Children in India: A Profile*. New Delhi: Author. http://www.unicef.org/sitan/files/SitAn_India_May_2011.pdf.

Vashishta, B. K. 1976. *Encyclopedia of Women in India*. New Delhi: Praveen Encyclopedia Publications.

Warschauer, Mark. 2003. *Technology and Social Inclusion*. Cambridge, MA: MIT Press.

11 The Impact of Public Access to Telecenters: Social Appropriation of ICT by Chilean Women

Alejandra Phillippi and Patricia Peña

Abstract

This chapter reports the findings of a study in Chile that examined the impact on women of public access to computers and the Internet through the *Quiero Mi Barrio* telecenter network. Gender and culture variables are taken into consideration because these define forms of practical as well as symbolic meaning of a public community space such as the telecenter and of the Internet as a means of communication and information. The study highlights the importance of telecenters, given the limitations that cybercafés (the most common public access option) present to women. The analysis forms the basis for the following recommendations: the State should strengthen telecenters as spaces that attend to the needs and demands of women, encourage greater participation of women in the access to and beneficial use of technology, and foster the development of new models to develop women's digital skills and help them realize their aspirations and meet their everyday needs.

Introduction

What do poor urban Chilean women do in the telecenters set up under Chile's *Quiero Mi Barrio* ("I Love My Neighborhood") program? Are there differences in how women and men learn and use the information and communication technologies (ICTs) that can be accessed in these venues? What benefits are perceived by Chilean women who use computers and Internet in these centers?

This study presents part of the analysis and conclusions from an investigation conducted in Chile on the social impact associated with the implementation of the *Quiero Mi Barrio* (QMB) Telecenter Network (*Red de Telecentros Quiero Mi Barrio* [RQMB]) on a group of users and women nonusers living in conditions of socioeconomic vulnerability. The study focused on two telecenters: one located in a community (district) of the Chilean capital of Santiago (Metropolitan Region), and the other in San Fernando

(O'Higgins Region), a provincial city in a predominantly agricultural area 140 kilometers south of the capital.

The QMB program was implemented by the Ministry of Housing and Urban Development (*Ministerio de la Vivienda y Urbanismo* [MINVU]) between 2006 and 2009, during Michelle Bachelet's first Presidential administration (2006–2010).[1] Its purpose was to improve the infrastructure and quality of life in more than 200 vulnerable neighborhoods in Chile through a variety of social interventions. The addition of telecenters to the program was funded by the Sub-secretariat of Telecommunications (SUBTEL) in one of the final stages of the project. Launched in late 2009 and continuing into 2010 under the administration of President Sebastián Piñera, this particular implementation faced delays in its development and operational phases (some due to an earthquake on February 27, 2010). About 150 of these telecenters were installed in the neighborhoods targeted by the program.

The QMB program aims to work with vulnerable sectors of the population. Chilean women involved in this study live in working-class neighborhoods far from the civic and commercial centers of the city. In both the Metropolitan Region and the O'Higgins Region, these areas are characterized by medium-low and low socioeconomic levels, and their residents generally have minimum-wage incomes, basic levels of education, and precarious working conditions. Overcrowding is common and particularly evident in the cramped, poorly soundproofed apartment blocks posited as government-subsidized housing solutions, where resident families often lack privacy and peace. According to the testimonies of the women and men we interviewed in both neighborhoods, drug abuse, alcoholism, and delinquency are the main difficulties faced by people living in these settlements. Some of the residents have moved there from sectors of the city that have been eradicated, where social relationships were fraught with distrust and public spaces were thought of as dangerous places where bad habits are learned.

The *Quiero Mi Barrio* Telecenters

The objective of the telecenters belonging to the *Quiero Mi Barrio* Telecenter Network is "to achieve the social appropriation of ICT by people who live in the neighborhoods through 'meaningful use' of the available technology," where an objective of the strategic guidelines is "to watch for and observe why the telecenters installed in the country become part of the particular dynamics of the social, economic, and cultural order particular to each neighborhood" (Centro de Investigaciones de la Inclusión Digital and Sociedad del Conocimiento 2009, p. 4).

The centers are managed by the Neighborhood Development Councils, local volunteer administrative groups, with the support of a team of professionals from various universities who are responsible for area coordination of the network. The Research Center for Digital Inclusion and the Knowledge Society (Centro de Investigaciones de la Inclusión Digital and Sociedad del Conocimiento [CIISOC]) at *Universidad de la Frontera* (www.ufro.cl) has been charged with coordinating the project's execution in the southern part of the country; in the central regions, the responsible agencies are Universidad Central and the *Asociación de Telecentros Activos de Chile* (ATACH); and in the north, it is Universidad Arturo Prat. These coordinating entities are responsible for hiring the telecenter operators and making sure they take care of managing day-to-day operations and providing the services offered at the centers (using computers equipped with free software-based Ubuntu operating systems). The telecenters' strategy for economic sustainability has yet to be defined. In general, they do not charge for Internet access or computer training, but some request a volunteer cash contribution or charge below-market prices for their services.

The first of the two telecenters studied is located in the Villa San Francisco de Asís, a neighborhood in the Metropolitan Region of Santiago, Chile; the second is located in Villa San Hernán, in the City of San Fernando in the O'Higgins Region. Both neighborhoods are small (1,400 and 3,600 residents, respectively) and relatively young (San Francisco was built in 1980 and San Hernán in 1991). Developed as state-subsidized social housing projects, they consist of polygons of apartment blocks. The apartment units were assigned to families relocating from eradicated shantytowns in other communities and families who applied for housing subsidies in order to move out of relatives' homes where they lived as displaced "arrivals." In addition, San Hernán is located in a predominantly agricultural region that has lower development indicators than those in the capital.

These telecenters were selected for study because they had been in operation for a similar period of time. The following tables show some basic features of the two centers (table 11.1) and their users (table 11.2).

Gender, Cultural Appropriation, and Digital Literacy

Our study considers the gender perspective and its relation to ICT as a continuous dynamically evolving process that is constantly being redefined (Rodríguez Contreras 2011). It takes into account the contributions of communications, education, and cultural studies, that make us ask *what uses and appropriations* people make of various media and their contents, and requires us to consider the symbolic dimension of the process and the meaning and reassignments of meaning that people impose on their media consumption (Sunkel 2002, citing García Canclini 1999). In our case, technology and the telecenters are media and spaces that are incorporated into the lives of women and men in different ways.

Table 11.1
General Aspects of Telecenter Operations and Services

	San Francisco Telecenter	San Hernán Telecenter
Opened	January 2010	February 2010
Computers	9, all with Internet connection	8, 6 with Internet connection
Opening hours	Monday to Friday: 9 A.M. to 8 P.M. (without closing for lunch) Saturday: open for workshops and training only	Monday to Friday: 10 A.M. to 12 P.M. and 2 to 8 P.M. Saturday: 3 to 8 P.M. (for workshops and training only)
Users per week	200 (35 to 40 daily)	150 (30 daily)
Connectivity	Exclusive fiber optic (quality and speed of connection variable)	
Financing	QMB Program Resources—MINVU and SUBTEL (until 2012)	
Role of those in charge	Telecenter administration and management Opening and closing of the telecenter Cleaning and maintenance Supervision of operations and use of computers and Internet User support for those who request or require help Teaching of courses and training workshops	
Services	Free access to computers with Internet (with a box for volunteer contributions) Printing and photocopying (paid) Computer and Internet courses (free)	Access to computers with Internet: 300 Chilean pesos (approx. US$0.60) per hour
Rules of use	Basic rules of respect and sharing among users (particularly children). Pornography sites are blocked. 30-minute time limit on use, particularly at times of high demand. When children are doing homework, their access ends when they complete it	No time limit on use
Diffusion	Organization and operator member networks; word of mouth among neighborhood residents; signs on bulletin boards	Sign outside the telecenter; through organization and operator networks; word of mouth among neighborhood residents
Other activities	Telecenter operates in a community center where fundraising activities (for the improvement of the telecenter and community center) and community activities take place; for example, there is an oven to make bread to sell, and the facility is rented out for parties and bingos	Various fundraising activities

Table 11.2
Motivations, Assessments, and Gender of Telecenter Users

	San Francisco Telecenter	San Hernán Telecenter
User profiles	Mainly children (boys and girls) who go to do their homework. Also, young people and adults of both sexes. More adult women than adult men.	Mainly children (boys and girls) who go to do their homework. More adult women than adult men.
Motivation	For children and youth, the telecenter is a place to do homework and find entertainment. Adults frequent the telecenter mainly to check their email and use Facebook. They value the fact that the service is free. It is a peaceful place.	For children and youth, the telecenter is a place to do homework and find entertainment. Many parents leave their children at the telecenter because it is a safe place; they use it as a "babysitter." Adults frequent the telecenter mainly to check their email and use Facebook. They value the facts that it is affordable and close to their home or workplace.
Training	Free training is offered using the INTEL-Learn model, which covers basic user literacy for text software applications and Internet and email account use. Participants are evaluated based on development of a project that uses technology to meet a given user need.	Free training is offered in basic user literacy for text software applications, presentations, and Internet and email account use. A citizen journalism workshop was held for adults to create a news blog for the neighborhood.
Work	Work is associated with access to the telecenter and use of the Internet only in exceptional cases of unemployed people who come to send their résumé or to research job opportunities on line.	
Sociability	For some adults, the telecenter is a place where they can socialize and meet their neighbors.	A more impersonal environment is observed at this telecenter than at the one in San Francisco, and there is less exchange and interaction among users.
Gender	In the younger age group (children) there are no great gender differences. In contrast, more adult women than adult men tend to use the telecenters. The majority of the women go to check their email and look for information for their children's homework. Men go to the telecenter at the end of the workday, except for those who are unemployed. Their uses include downloading music or movies and watching videos on line.	

The gender perspective of the study considers that this "determines what it can expect, what is allowed and valued in a woman or a man in a given context" (United Nations Development Programme 2010). Also, the concept of appropriation used here is based on "learning by doing" and "learning by using," and it recognizes that people appropriate technology through different stages, including, for example, adoption, implementation, and reconfiguration (Bar, Pisani, and Weber 2007).

This chapter begins with a description of the methodology used; it then presents findings about the impacts, both positive and negative, of public access on male and female users and nonusers. We next focus on women, showing the impact that telecenters have on their lives and outlining women's role in better understanding the impact of their use of public access. We conclude with a discussion of public policy issues.

Methodology: Building the Categories from Daily Neighborhood Life

Understanding the ways that daily life changes or does not change as the women studied gain access to ICT through a telecenter requires an understanding of this group's sociocultural context and the variables that help determine the way these women appropriate the venue as well as access and use the Internet.

The study integrates quantitative and qualitative techniques using grounded theory methods; that is, constructing a theory inductively from data that are codified, comparatively analyzed, and relationally contextualized (Glaser and Strauss 1967; Strauss 1987; Strauss and Corbin 1998). Studies using this perspective emphasize looking for relevant information in various situations where what is being studied manifests itself, with constant examination for similarities and differences in the analysis of each sampled unit that is considered important to the research objective. Thus, everything done is based on the concepts that emerge as the study develops.

We worked from information and data gathered in both physical and social spaces to obtain information that would help identify the processes and situations produced by the implementation of telecenters in both neighborhoods. In a complementary manner, the gender perspective adopted in the study involved focusing on women users and nonusers of the public access centers; men were included for comparison.

We surveyed 295 men and women ages 18 and older from the two neighborhoods, regardless of whether they were users of the telecenter and whether they used computers and the Internet at other sites outside the telecenter (See table 11.A.1 in appendix 11.A). The survey was administered by two research assistants through in-person, face-to-face interviews on weekdays and weekends, in respondents' homes or at the telecenter or local community center. Participation was voluntary. The questions covered sociodemographic dimensions such as interviewee profiles, access to and use of the Internet in general, concepts and assessments associated with the Internet, access to and use of the telecenter, and assessments of the telecenter.

Once the initial results had been reviewed, profiles of the users and nonusers of the telecenters were constructed. Likewise, these initial data were used to create the first set of telecenter user profile categories according to two major criteria: frequency of visits to the telecenter and Internet use skill level. These criteria were used to classify the users into four categories:

Full-advanced: Uses the telecenter daily, is digitally literate, uses software, and knows how to search and use the Internet without help.

Full-novel: Uses the telecenter daily, is at an early stage of the digital literacy process, uses software, and searches and uses the Internet with help.

Sporadic-advanced: Uses the telecenter infrequently, is competent in software use, and knows how to search and use the Internet without help.

Sporadic-novel: Uses the telecenter infrequently and is beginning to use software and the Internet in general.

Interviews were then conducted based on these classifications until *theoretical saturation* was reached. At this point the investigator stops sampling the different groups in each category because the possible contribution of information is exhausted (Trinidad, Carrero Planes, and Soriano Miras 2006).

In parallel with the survey, the operators of the telecenters, directors of the Neighborhood Development Councils, and SUBTEL and MINVU consultants were also interviewed. They were asked about the implementation of the telecenters, their evaluation of the process in the short time that the program had been in operation, their perception and analysis of the impacts of the telecenters in the neighborhoods, and their perceptions of and opinions about the existence of a gender perspective in this process.

Survey respondents were invited to participate in five group conversation sessions with women and men from the two neighborhoods (table 11.A.2 in appendix 11.A) in order to contrast the results and better identify the profiles of the people who should be subsequently interviewed in depth. In the focus groups held at the San Francisco telecenter, fourteen women users, six women nonusers, and five men users participated. In the focus group held at the San Hernán telecenter, five women nonusers participated. These focus groups were held on weekdays and weekends, preferably in the afternoon, at community centers previously prepared by the organizations in charge. On average, each session had five to eight participants and lasted about fifty minutes. Topics discussed included the participants' neighborhood environment, daily routines, social practices, communication routines and practices, patterns of computer and Internet use (in general), and perceptions and assessments of the installation of the telecenter and Internet use in general.

As a final step, twenty-one people were interviewed in depth (table 11.A.3 in appendix 11.A). These conversations took place in the respondents' homes or at the telecenter and lasted about an hour and fifteen minutes. The topics of conversation were similar to those of the focus groups but more in depth through individual face to face exchanges.

Our findings are presented in the following sections.

The Impact of Two Telecenters in the Lives of Chilean Women

For a good portion of the residents of the neighborhoods served by RQMB, having a public access center for ICTs implies an opportunity to "get close" to something that until now has been beyond their reach mainly because of their socioeconomic conditions but also because of their lack of familiarity with the potential benefits of technology. By narrowing the gap between these women and digital technology, public Internet access makes what was "outside of my life" part of their daily routine.

It also implies that those who use these public access centers have access to technology that is otherwise beyond their reach (e.g., if they cannot afford to buy a computer or subscribe to Internet service). The telecenter constitutes one more form of access and one that adds value to the channels of media consumption they already use.

Impact Assessments from Users

Regardless of whether they are users, people have a certain familiarity with the Internet and generally perceive it as a "door opener." However, although the Internet is accessible to them in theory, taking advantage of it requires the development of certain abilities, as well as a space that is within the user's reach and forms part of their daily life.

Figure 11.1 summarizes the main assessments reported by survey respondents and how they perceived public access, the possibility of connectivity, and the impact of the telecenter. The figure reflects the convergences emerging in the interviews at both the San Francisco and San Hernán telecenters. No major differences are found in the assessments made. Emphasis is placed on the agreed-on information, which has been considered representative of tendencies.

The assessments have been articulated in two dimensions. The first is *positive impact* or *negative impact*, according to the respondent's perception of having a public Internet access center in their neighborhood. The second dimension depicts two large groups of

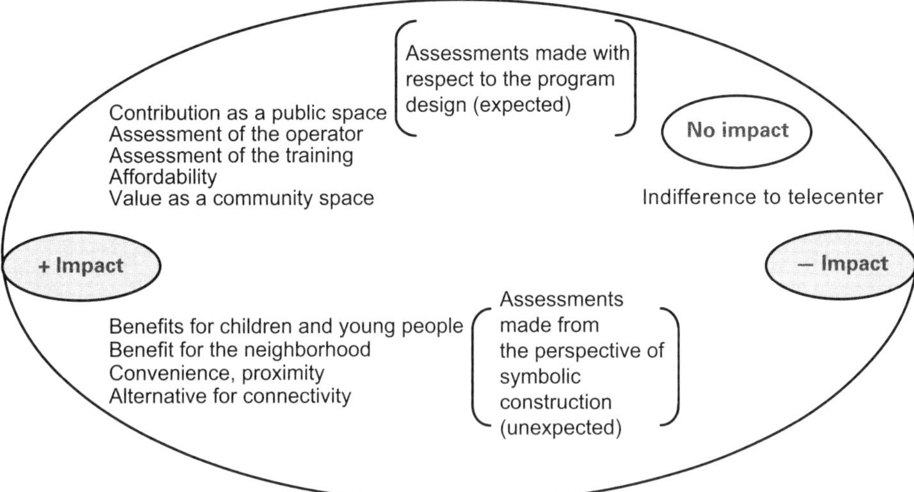

Figure 11.1
Assessments arising from analysis of the interviewees.

assessments: those that are *expected* because they are part of the design and conception of the program, and those that are *unexpected* and are observed as symbolic perceptions constructed by users and nonusers, both women and men.

Positive Impact: Expected Assessments What is the perception of the contribution made by having a public access space in the neighborhood? The general consensus among the twenty-one interviewees was that the telecenter is a positive addition to their neighborhoods and fifteen interviewees specifically associated this assessment with concrete benefits. Some commented that it should be considered a right to which they are entitled. Interviewees' appreciation is illustrated by the following statements (I = interviewer, R = respondent):

I: What effect has the telecenter had on the community?

R: There is more information for the people. (Woman user #5, full-novel user of the San Francisco telecenter)

R: Yes, first I thought that it was going to be for the school but later they explained that no, it was for everyone from the neighborhood.

I: What value does it have?

R: [It has] great value because people have a place to go to do their things, so that women stop doing other things and they can go and get connected. (Woman nonuser #2, San Hernán telecenter)

R: I think it's great that all people, that all kinds of people have the ability to go, get involved and learn, because one never has a limit to learning, there is always the right to learn and it's a benefit because it's free. (Man user #1, sporadic-novel user of the San Francisco telecenter)

Although it was not a requirement for selection, both telecenters studied are operated by women. Their duties include helping people use the computers so that novel users are able to overcome the "shame barrier," and acting as mediating agents in these processes as users require and request assistance. The appreciation for the center operator can be seen in the following comments by one of the interviewees:

I: How do you think community life has changed with the presence of the telecenter?

R: Yes, indeed it has changed a lot because not everyone has access to Internet here and people do not always have money to pay for the Internet. When they ask you for a fee in some venues, not everyone has the money or the resources.

I: Is that important?

R: Yes, because you can learn there. If you do not have a computer and you're embarrassed, you can learn there. There was once a lady who was learning and Karen [the operator] told her to do this or that...and I came here to learn.... (Woman user #2, sporadic-novel user of the San Francisco telecenter)

At least nine of the people interviewed expressed their appreciation for the digital literacy training offered by the telecenter, as indicated by the following comment:

R: Alone, yes, I chatted there. I learned how to use e-mail in the second course, to attach a file. I use the social networks and my e-mail every day. If I don't go to the telecenter I go to the Internet café or use my cell phone. (Woman user #10, sporadic-novel user of the San Hernán telecenter)

Free or low-cost access to computers connected to the Internet is considered an important contribution. The following statements reflect the sentiments of eight in-depth interviewees:

I: If the telecenter didn't exist, what would happen?

R: We'd have to go somewhere else...to a normal Internet café...and we'd have to spend more money, and that's something important here because an hour of surfing the Internet is much cheaper [here] than at an Internet café. (Man user #5, full-novel user of the San Hernán telecenter)

R: Well, the thing is that the benefit now is that the moms don't go downtown. Previously, I had to give my kid 500 pesos for the fare; now he does the work here, and with the 500 pesos I used to give him to go and come back, I have money left for a snack. The thing is that money is important in this neighborhood—I've seen it with the people, and that's the answer. I see how my son is here, and the youngest, I leave him here and later I come pick him up. (Woman nonuser #3, San Hernán telecenter)

In the focus groups of women users, there were manifestations of positive assessment of the telecenter as a community space where they run into neighbors and relatives. This aspect, however, was not mentioned by any of the people interviewed individually.

Positive Impact: Unexpected Assessments The unexpected assessment mentioned by the majority of the interviewees (sixteen of twenty-one) is that the most direct beneficiaries of the telecenter are the neighborhood children and youth.

I: How do you think the telecenter has changed the neighborhood?

R: For me, this has changed it in many ways because the children are learning more every day and it is good for them, they are more motivated, they behave better, and they can come in whenever they want.... (Woman user #4, sporadic-novel user of the San Francisco telecenter)

I: How did you feel when you saw the telecenter open with computers?

R: I felt like I was part owner—it's like something arrived at my house. I don't know if it will be a little complicated to explain it: it's that it's happiness, happiness because the children were going to have a way to do their homework. When my son was in grade school he had to go to the other side of the city to do his computer class homework, and he got home at two in the morning with me waiting at the door, because it was less dangerous back then.... (Woman user #11, sporadic-novel user of the San Hernán telecenter)

R: Now the children are part of an environment that didn't exist before. It gives them free access, and they have more opportunities to do their homework. (Man user #3, sporadic-advanced user of the San Francisco telecenter)

R: [It's] very important.

I: For whom?

R: For the neighborhood, for self-esteem, for the voice of the neighborhood, and, the most interesting, for the children because they are born next to their computer, and they took good advantage of the opening period because they didn't have to pay at all.... (Man user #4, full-novel user of the San Hernán telecenter)

Another perceived benefit is the recognition of the telecenter as a positive venue for everyone in the *villa* and a feeling of pride in being associated with the processes and changes to improve the appearance of the neighborhood. This was stated in one form or another by fourteen of the people interviewed in depth. The telecenter is seen as an initiative and a place that makes their *villa* stand out from others and adds to their quality of life.

R: Access to the Internet. I think the Quiero Mi Barrio program, more than the playgrounds and other changes, the best idea was installing a telecenter because the people can aspire to new levels. For example, if I have to do a "pre-u"[2] *and I don't have any money, I can do it on the Internet.* (Woman user #6, full-advanced user of the San Francisco telecenter)

I: Is it important that it continues to operate?

R: It's vital because point number one, it generates resources for the neighborhood, and two, it's a place to access culture because not every neighborhood has a telecenter.... (Woman user #10, sporadic-novel user of the San Hernán telecenter)

The telecenter is a PAV that does not involve spending money and in many cases is perceived as more comfortable and closer which means not wasting time going there. In addition, its facilities and equipment are apparently better than those at cybercafés or even of home Internet and computer setups, as mentioned by five people interviewed, including these two:

R: The thing is that I would like to take one of these [computers] home, because I have one at home with [Internet] connection and these seem easier to me than the one in my house because of the difference broadband makes. The one here is an LCD—I don't know, maybe that's the difference, and the keyboard is more comfortable. I like the ones here better. (Woman user #3, sporadic-novel user of the San Francisco telecenter)

I: Did your life change with the telecenter?

R: Yes, a lot. Before, I had to be looking around in other places because around here, in this area, there aren't any Internet cafés; the closest one is two neighborhoods away. I know that here I can come and be back one hour later; and so before, there were things I couldn't do, and I had to wait an hour or two to use a computer. (Man user #2, full-advanced user of the San Francisco telecenter)

The telecenter also provides an alternative to home connection (when available) and is generally used when there is no other way to access the Internet or when residential service is not available. Many respondents mentioned the telecenter as an alternative to paying a monthly fee to share some of their neighbors' Wi-Fi signal, an arrangement that, although illegal, is accepted in the community.

Three of the four users interviewed had a shared Internet connection at home. One commented:

R: Here there is a young man who provides Internet via Wi-Fi.

I: Is the connection constant or does it get interrupted sometimes?

R: It's paid Internet, and we pay for access. He has Telefónica, and he has the antenna put up and he shares it.

I: And when you don't have a connection?

R: I go to the telecenter. (Woman user #2, sporadic-novel user of the San Francisco telecenter)

Negative Impact or No Impact Four of the respondents—one man and one woman user, and one man and one woman nonuser—are indifferent to the telecenter. They do not perceive the space as contributing to their lives or bringing significant change to the neighborhood context, and they do not consider it a space that they can access. This can be understood as non-fulfillment of the program goal and is expressed in the following testimonials:

R: Aside from being bad?

I: Why do you say "bad"?

R: Bad, boring because there's nothing there; now that there's the telecenter, there are no pretty things that they do for the mothers. They [the young people] just lie there, partying until dawn. (Woman user #1, sporadic-advanced user of the San Francisco telecenter)

R: Of course I was left out, we were left out, yes, I am left out of the telecenter, also because imagine at night, everything is closed and you can't go in the gate.... (Man nonuser #1, San Francisco telecenter)

Access Differences by Gender

In addition to the positive assessment of the telecenter by both women and men, the results of the questionnaire reveal impacts differentiated by gender. The percentage of women users who connected to the Internet for the first time at the telecenter is 14 percent, versus 2 percent of men. The number of men who connect in other places is also greater, making the telecenter an additional option for connection for them. When asked about points of connection aside from the telecenter, 83 percent of the men but only 63 percent of the women said they knew of and had visited other venues.

Some of the women interviewed at the San Hernán telecenter mentioned having been to an Internet café at least once, usually to help with their children's homework, but this was not a regular occurrence. Two of them commented that such places are not welcoming and that they generate "suspicion" and impersonal treatment.

I: Have you been to an Internet café?

R: Yes, I have seen them. Once I went to one that is over there to do a homework assignment because this one was closed, but that was the only time.

I: Is it different from the telecenter?

R: The thing is, . . . here, it's more close to me or maybe it's closer to where I live, I think. . . . I don't know about the difference; the thing is that they helped me the same, and the information, and one starts to trust the person who works here more. . . . (Woman user #9, sporadic-novel user of the San Hernán telecenter)

R: It's that the telecenter is a study center and not a place to hide and download whatever you want. There is a big difference between an Internet café and a telecenter; they're not the same. (Woman user #10, sporadic-novel user of the San Hernán telecenter)

I: Do you go to cybercafés?

R: No, because they are dirty, dark, and cold, and the children make noise, and it is impossible to concentrate. (Woman user #8, full-advanced user of the San Hernán telecenter)

Women as Agents of Access "For Other People's Sake"

Observations made by the interviewees shed light on two important processes: first, the construction of gender as a *collective ideology* that gives weight to what "others expect or think of me," and second, a *self-construction* where each subject establishes his or her own personal attitude. These constructions are always linked to the role, or "imaginary," of what it is to be a woman or a man.

Even if both men and women make constructions, only women reported limiting their feelings when a man is placed in a position of power with respect to the woman, whether his relationship to her is partner or father. At least seven of the thirteen women interviewed mentioned this in their accounts, as expressed in the following interview excerpts:

R: Yes, I think that yes, women limit themselves more, they are more limited by the "what will they say." If you visited a certain page and your husband saw you and you closed the page, it could be because you have that mentality or a macho husband. (Woman user #5, full-novel user of the San Francisco telecenter)

R: My studies, yes, but it wasn't normal after I had my son because my other partner was very dominating and didn't let me finish, and that made me have a lot of problems because he wanted to do everything. . . .

The thing is that from a very young age I never had dreams . . . I had a very strict father who never said any good things about me, and, I don't know, I never . . . He always decided for me and never said anything to me. He cut my hair shorter like his, like a military cut; he liked to cut hair so he cut mine. (Woman user #2, sporadic-novel user of the San Francisco telecenter)

One of the open questions on the questionnaire was about people's goals and dreams and, specifically, how the Internet contributed to their achievement. The goals and dreams of the women interviewed were related to the well-being of the people close to them. Forty-four percent indicated that when asked about future goals or dreams they hope to achieve, the first thing they think of is "my children's studies" or "that my children have a better life." In contrast, only 23 percent of the men mentioned something similar as a first response, indicating that women are more concerned than men with the interests and welfare of others.

When describing their daily lives, including the feelings and the spaces they inhabit, thirteen of the women interviewed (two of whom work) made it clear that both dimensions are measured and truncated mainly by their domestic duties, which start with getting up in the morning and moving family life along with breakfast, continue with taking their children to school or kindergarten, and then dedicating themselves to cleaning activities and making lunch. Only once these activities are completed do they have free time to take a nap in order to get back to their chores and start others when the children come home. There are few distinctions made with respect to "weekend time," which according to media messages should be different from or involve fewer routine activities than the rest of the week. Only one of the women interviewed diverged from this pattern, and she lives alone.

In contrast, the men talk about timing in terms of their work schedules, which sometimes include long hours and weekend shifts. Only one of them reported less rigorous daily activity: the youngest man interviewed, he lives with his mother and works only sporadically.

For most in-depth interviewees (sixteen of twenty-one), both men and women, time off is scarce. Sunday is family time, but there is no equivalent during the rest of the week, and for three of the people interviewed, Sunday is just another working day. Also, part of the day on Sunday is dedicated to domestic work, cleaning, cooking, and "getting ready for the week." Only the woman living alone, who has a widow's pension, mentioned having leisure time.

Women's perception of the world is closely linked to their perception of the physical conditions of their neighborhood. Their perception of the city they live in, in contrast, is remote and has little prominence. Their symbolic view of the environment is confined to the boundaries of their homes. Of the seven interviewees linked to the San Francisco telecenter, only two mentioned participating in activities outside the neighborhood. In contrast, the women of San Hernán are more familiar with the spaces and services offered by the city in which they live. Even if both neighborhoods are parts of peripheral sectors of the city and the women's routines are confined to the physical space in which they live, it would seem that the distance between the neighborhood and the city center has a bearing on some of those routines. In the case of the Metropolitan Region, the marginalization of the neighborhood is aggravated by the size of the city and the limited resources and transportation options the women have to move about the city.

The men interviewed, particularly at the San Francisco telecenter, tended to be more connected to the Internet than the women in venues other than the telecenter. In general, they travel greater distances and move more freely throughout the city, for work or other reasons, which often allows them to find other options for Internet access and connectivity. It also implies that the men move within a physical space greater than the perimeter defined by their homes and that they inhabit less restricted spaces than the women do.

In the end, because they determine both the times at which users can access the Internet and how far they can go in their use of this resource, the dimensions of time and space influence men and women differently. Even when men and women are at the same physical distance from the access point, the telecenter has a greater positive impact on women because it puts something previously inaccessible within their reach.

Between "Literate Full-Advanced Users" and "Digital Illiterates"[3]

The following typology of women users serves as an aid in understanding the causes and contexts that condition women's perceptions of proximity to or distance from the telecenter and the Internet. Three stages can be detected in the perceptions of women interviewees:

1. Digitally literate, full-advanced users who consider themselves close to the telecenter and the Internet;
2. Full-novel users who are taking their first steps toward digital literacy; and
3. Nonusers who do not have the skills to use technology and whom we therefore call digitally illiterate. Their conceptions keep them distanced from the telecenter and digital technology.

Sporadic-advanced users and sporadic-novel users were not considered here because these women are outside the scope of the study—the former group because, being only occasional users of the telecenter, their processes of approaching technology are not related to the telecenter, and the latter group because these women, even if they have manifested an intention to learn computers or the Internet, have not consolidated the process in any verifiable way and are therefore grouped together with nonusers.

Digitally Literate Full-Advanced Users of the Telecenter Of the ten women users interviewed in depth, five fall into this category.

Two women (one from each telecenter) are intensive users of the telecenter and fairly advanced Internet users. They are more technologically experienced than the rest of the women and report having undergone digital literacy training processes prior to their arrival at the telecenter, which is why the telecenter's impact on them cannot be considered direct. They constitute a reference point for what may eventually be achieved by less experienced users.

For the other three women in this category, the Internet has an important place in their lives and routines, thanks to the connection they access at either the telecenter or another venue. They were offered the opportunity to become familiar with technology by someone close to them who introduced them to the Internet or provided them with access from their homes; in one case, the woman decided to buy a computer so that her children could do their homework at home. Even so, connectivity is frequently unstable. One of the women has an "illegal" Wi-Fi signal that a neighbor shares with (sells to) her, another does not always pay for service, and the third connects at a relative's house. In these cases, the telecenter provides an alternative that allows them to realize their high motivation to be connected.

Within their practices and patterns of Internet use, these three women describe purposes that have to do with online communication and sociability (social networking with friends, relatives, and acquaintances, particularly via Facebook, chat, and Messenger). To a lesser degree, they also start to develop website search routines of specific or favorite sites according to their motivations and preferences—for example, leisure, surfing the Web, or listening to music. This is reflected in the following quote from one of the women:

R: It's very relevant because the Internet changed my life and allowed me to contact my relatives who live outside of the country; together we use Facebook, Messenger, and Skype, and we also use the cameras. At home, I haven't been able to include my family as much because most of them work and aren't home during the day.

In my case, I am on the Internet for social reasons, both individual and family-related. With respect to the individual, I relate it with my own learning of many things. For example, I have bad handwriting, but the Internet has helped me to improve it by looking at methods to improve it. (Woman user #6, full-advanced user of the San Francisco telecenter)

The value of communication through the telecenter is vital for these women, and they even start to perceive more strategic or complex processes of appropriation, such as strengthening or innovating for their small business ventures (a mini-market, selling clothes, selling cosmetics). For one of the women users who manages a small neighborhood store, this process of appropriation of the various services and resources offered on the Web is evident. This does not mean that she has reached a higher level or greater depth with this type of use (e.g., filling out online applications for products or making payments and doing her banking online) because she still does not visualize this as an opportunity to do these particular things:

I: How relevant is the Internet in your daily life?

R: I think it's good for comparing product prices, for example, for my business. That's it, more than anything else, because your friends you just call once in a while, when you have time to connect. But that's it, really. Once in a while I look for addresses or telephone numbers to go somewhere, maybe find the closest bank.... And for my daughter's homework.... (Woman user #7, full-advanced user of the San Francisco telecenter)

The women who talk about their digital literacy processes have been guided or instructed by someone close to them, like a family member or friend, which tends to condition the *type of use* they make of the Internet (e.g., Google, Facebook, chat, or Messenger), *how they use it* (e.g., to contact former high school classmates or friends and relatives who live far away, or to accept and incorporate new contacts), and *what they use it for* (e.g., to download music, search for information, navigate popular websites). This fairly spontaneous process often goes unfinished, frequently continuing in an independent way through self-teaching by trial and error. One woman mentioned the support she received and what she learned thanks to the operator and a workshop held at the telecenter:

R: It's the possibility that I have to communicate with them. I have Facebook, I have Twitter, but I don't use it much because I find it very impersonal—it's like Messenger, unlike Facebook, where you can find out what's going on because you can see pictures and videos; and my Hotmail that I am always using and it's interesting because there are people who contact me in Santiago that I stopped seeing two years ago and there continues to be a respectful relationship there. (Woman user #8, full-advanced user of the San Hernán telecenter)

These five full-advanced users share their situations and the personal processes that have let them break out of their routines in the home and their exclusive role as mothers. Whether because they work outside the home, decided to open a small business, or made changes in their lives in response to a specific personal situation, they are now experiencing learning processes. These may include searching for other opportunities and challenges at a personal or family level, whether spontaneously or because they are "forced to"; however, all have as their objective helping their family get ahead and providing their children with better opportunities. They are very motivated women.

Full-Novel Users of the Telecenter: First Steps toward Digital Literacy In this group of users, we placed the five women interviewed in the two neighborhoods who identify as housewives or by some other activity. Their accounts evidence somewhat slower processes of approaching and appropriating technology, often through brief glimpses and opportunities to see "what the Internet's all about," how it works, and how it can serve or be useful to them.

They may have had their first contact with a computer or the Internet during one of their occasional visits to the telecenter or at the home of a relative or friend. They are starting to "discover." Their use is primarily focused on creating an email account, using Facebook, or doing a few searches with the help of someone else—perhaps the telecenter operator or a relative or friend who has more experience with technology.

In this group, digital literacy is also guided or mediated by someone close to the user, such as a relative or friend, a fact that determines *what* is used on the Internet, *how* it is used, and *for what* it is used. Unlike the other telecenter users, more specific reasons and motives appear for going to the telecenter more frequently.

I: You started to use the Internet because of your son, because you came to do homework with him. How often did you go to the telecenter?

R: They used to give him homework every three weeks; after that it was more frequent and this year as well. I went there to make photocopies for him or download information about something for him because there I could tell the woman in charge what I was looking for to download it [the information]. (Woman user #9, full-novel user of the San Hernán telecenter)

This process has been reinforced by the telecenter and supported by the help of the operator or by some training workshop. Two of these women had previous computer training, either during their studies in secondary school or another program, or from a course specifically taken outside the neighborhood, although many times they stopped practicing thereafter or did not update their training. This situation can be considered one of the obstacles to becoming a full-advanced user. Expectations related to greater "use-with-meaning" and an appropriation of technology are largely associated with continuing to learn or improving in their current activities.

Illiterate Nonusers of the Telecenter The four women in this group are distanced from both the telecenter and technology for a variety of reasons, ranging from their personal and family situation to situations that have to do with processes of "exclusion" associated with the way the telecenter operates in the neighborhood or with how they do not feel part of community and public projects or spaces.

Their assessments are associated with their expectations or imaginaries based on what they have heard and seen about the Internet and what you can do with it—or in their words, "what I would love to be able to do."

R: It's that sometimes talking with other people that have computers—for example, this boyfriend my daughter had used to be a teacher, and he always told me that he could teach me, that it wasn't hard because I used to say that it's not just sit down and plug in, and the thing is I have so many things on my mind and it could be just another thing to worry about; but maybe not because it might be another help; and the thing is that for example with the inventories I could go to the computer and see.

I: What stops you from trying to use it?

R: The thing is I haven't made the time. You have to be there at the time and concentrate, and it's a class that you go to take, and Jorge tells me that, "with one hour of me helping you, you're going to be able to do it alone and you can get on a computer and then you start to get on the computer and it will be easier for you, and you can do it yourself." (Woman nonuser #5, San Hernán telecenter)

The constructions that women make are rooted in the particular cultural ways in which they experience their lives and in general terms are expressed in visions rooted in roles that assign them responsibility for raising their children and taking care of their homes. The Internet is present in their accounts, but it is difficult for them to grasp how it is linked to their daily lives. It is easier to understand it as something that is useful to others, mainly their children.

Nevertheless, cell phone use is common among all of them, and they all refer to it as a medium and a technology that they have managed to incorporate into a good part of their communication routines. This technological device allows them to take the first step to digital literacy, and in some cases, it should be considered a means of initiation to and practice of digital technology. All cell phone users are full users; to become advanced users, they must overcome the same limitations they face in becoming advanced users of the Internet. Despite this, they have bridged the access gap because it is already established in their daily routines. What must happen for the telecenter to become established in the same way?

The greatest familiarity with ICT is observed in users who perceive the Internet as one more communication device. Intense users are rare. In these exceptional cases, when they can access a good broadband connection and have the opportunity to make frequent use of technology, they gradually accept the idea that the Internet "opens the doors to the world," and they are taken a little bit beyond their neighborhood limits. Even so, they recognize that they are not taking advantage of the full potential of ICT.

The Telecenter from the Perspective of the Woman's Role and Mediation of the Cultural Context

In discussing the positive impacts in depth, the categories expand, allowing the beneficiaries of those impacts to speak about their own assessments and perceptions. In this process, a marked difference emerges between the forms of impact represented by *expected* goals (e.g., those implicit in the design and implementation of the program) and those that are *unexpected* (i.e., expressed with respect to the symbolic construction that people make according to the meanings that access to and use of the telecenter represent for them). The forms of impact that describe meanings that intersect with daily life, convenience, and closeness become truly valued when the telecenter is installed within the space where respondents habitually circulate, eliminating the need to travel to another venue and apparently resolving the problems associated with "alternative" forms of connection, which are not always reliable because they depend on the payment or nonpayment of service and how many people share the signal. Thus, perceiving this benefit preferentially for the children corresponds to an age distance that they construct symbolically: it is closer for *them*, and they value it as something that helps them provide a better reality for their children.

Even if it is not possible to prove a negative impact as such, one of the meanings that emerged was the *indifference* of people who, although they could be users, appear not to value the presence of the telecenter in their neighborhood. Indifference is presented as an expression of "no impact" in light of limitations that emerge in perceptions of exclusion from symbolic constructions that the subjects can come to establish (perceptions that were not contemplated when the telecenter project was designed).

Nuances also emerge that differentiate the perceptions of impact depending on the gender of the subjects. Men and women construct the possibility of approaching a public access center and using digital media in different ways.

This is expressed by the concrete demands and necessities linked to women's role as mothers and/or housewives, giving form to the access to information and services in a public place like the telecenter. The motivations for use and the methods of searching for content are generally linked to tasks related to their children (e.g., homework) or to resources that are useful to them in the domestic arena of daily life (e.g., searching for recipes), and to a lesser extent to content related to personal care (generally associated with health problems and cosmetic care). Rarely is their participation associated with experiences of use and appropriation, as far as assigning it meaning as a space and a medium that facilitates the search for information associated with small business endeavors or their personal tastes and interests (e.g., handcrafts, fashion, and religion).

The dimensions of gender and culture define not only the forms of *practical consumption* (the *what for*) but also of *symbolic consumption* (the *what it means*) of a public community space like the telecenter and of the Internet as a network and medium of communication and information.

The categories proposed—from full-advanced user to nonuser, literate or illiterate—have to do with territorial distance, but they are also symbolic of how the telecenter is perceived and recognized as a personal space that allows the average woman from these neighborhoods to make "use-with-meaning" of the services and opportunities offered by the computers connected to the Internet.

Only to the extent that the telecenter is incorporated into the personal routines of these women, somewhere between the household chores and the vegetable market shopping, does it gain value and meaning as a step toward the ultimate goal of social appropriation of ICT, particularly with respect to the dreams, goals, and life objectives they hold for themselves and their families.

From the perspective of consumption, the social impact of public access to ICT is associated with the dimensions of the connectivity offered (close, convenient, and free), mainly for use as a communication device (Facebook is also a telephone) that is preferentially individual, as opposed to communal-collective, which presents another challenge.

The promise of technology, the image of the Internet as a window onto the world and the telecenter as "a door that opens up opportunities," acquires more importance when the woman, albeit living in a context of social, economic, and cultural vulnerability, has her own dreams, a few (small) concrete goals for her life and her family's life, or a more autonomous self-image—in other words, a woman who has her own personal motivations. Otherwise, her use remains subordinate to a use that merely supports "someone else's dream."

Thus, the role of ICT in the social inclusion of women takes on meaning in the consumption of that technology and of the space that facilitates its access (such as the telecenter) according to the symbolic value adopted by a *means* (not just a tool) that is offered from a *space* (a place) whose value is related to the *everyday life* in which it weaves the pattern of its own cloth. The accounts given by both men and women reveal a direct relationship between the respondents' symbolic worlds and the ways they put those worlds into practice through a "door opener" that makes technology possible in a space like the telecenter. The more elaborate the symbolic world, the more varied the practices achieved.

Recommendations

The positive impact of a telecenter and its digital literacy programs on the lives of women and their families can be much greater than on the lives of men partly because of the central role that women play within the family environment, but also because women initially are much more distanced from technology and public computer and Internet access centers than are men. For this reason, we propose the following recommendations.

1. Although in theory women and men can have equal access to cybercafés, in practice this does not happen. First, the social environment in cybercafés can sometimes be inhospitable for women; second, women, especially those living in poverty, need attention and assistance that go beyond mere physical access to technology. Hence, it is important that the State sponsor special access programs designed to service poor communities and meet the specific needs of women.

2. The *Quiero Mi Barrio* program and similar programs providing support to public access centers should dedicate special attention and resources to encouraging the participation of women and bringing them closer to the services and resources offered by the telecenters. The operators of the telecenters studied have played an important role in this regard, helping women approach and appropriate the technology. This role of the operators should be strengthened and even expanded through strategies that recognize the dynamics of women's social roles and everyday needs.

3. Digital literacy programs should embrace new models or paradigms that take into account the development of digital abilities and skills oriented toward the needs, expectations, and daily requirements of women in their different roles: for example, helping them support their children's studies and homework, attending to specific issues that concern them, and, above all, helping them realize their own dreams above and beyond their domestic duties.

Acknowledgments

The authors would like to express their gratitude for the support of the director of Chile's Sub-secretariat of Telecommunications (SUBTEL), the consultants at the universities responsible for implementation, and the directors and managers of the telecenters studied.

Notes

1. Michelle Bachelet was the first woman president of Chile. After her first presidential mandate, she served as head of the United Nations Entity for Gender Equality and the Empowerment of Women. She was subsequently elected to serve a second term (2014–2018) as president of Chile.

2. "Pre-u" stands for "pre-university," an educational opportunity to prepare for the university selection exam.

3. In Chile, it is common to refer to levels of literacy among people to describe their methods of use and appropriation of technology and public policies implemented to promote the use of technology are known as "Digital Literacy Processes."

References

Bar, François, Francis Pisani, and Matthew Weber. 2007. Mobile Technology Appropriation in a Distant Mirror: Baroque Infiltration, Creolization and Cannibalism. Paper prepared for discussion at Seminario sobre Desarrollo Económico, Desarrollo Social y Comunicaciones Móviles en América Latina, April 20–21. Buenos Aires: Fundación Telefónica. http://my.ss.sysu.edu.cn/wiki/download/attachments/147193964/Mobile+technology+appropriation+in+a+distant+mirror.pdf.

Centro de Investigaciones de la Inclusión Digital and Sociedad del Conocimiento. Universidad de la Frontera. 2009. MASTIC—Modelo de apropiación social de las tecnologías de información y comunicación para telecentros del programa Quiero Mi Barrio. Paper prepared for the Subsecretariat of Telecommunications. Santiago de Chile: Government of Chile.

García Canclini, Néstor. 1999. El consume cultural: una propuesta teórica. In *El Consumo Cultural en América Latina*, coordinated by Guillermo Sunkel. Bogotá: Convenio Andrés Bello.

Glaser, B., and Anselm L. Strauss 1967. *The Discovery of Grounded Theory: Strategies for Qualitative Research*. New York: Aldine Publishing.

Rodríguez Contreras, Amelia. 2011. Género y TIC. Hacia un nuevo modelo más equilibrado o la Sociedad de la Información a dos velocidades. PortalComunicación.com. http://www.portalcomunicacion.com/uploads/pdf/52_esp.pdf.

Strauss, Anselm L. 1987. *Qualitative Analysis for Social Scientists*. Cambridge, UK: Cambridge University Press.

Strauss, Anselm L., and Juliet M. Corbin. 1998. *Basics of Qualitative Research: Grounded Theory Procedures and Techniques*. London: SAGE Publications.

Sunkel, Guillermo. 2002. Una mirada otra. La cultura desde el consumo. In *Estudios y otras prácticas intelectuales latinoamericanas en cultura y poder*, coordinated by Daniel Mato, 287–294. Caracas: Consejo Latinoamericano de Ciencias Sociales and Universidad Central de Venezuela. http://www.globalcult.org.ve/pdf/Sunkel.pdf.

Trinidad, Antonio Requena, Virginia Carrero Planes, and María Soriano Miras Rosa. 2006. Teoría Fundamentada: 'Grounded Theory.' La construction de la teoría a través del análisis interpretacional. *Cuadernos Metodológicos* 37. Madrid: Centro de Investigaciones Sociológicas. http://www.uv.mx/mie/files/2012/10/LaConstrucciondelaTeoriadelAnalisiInterpretacional.pdf.

United Nations Development Programme. *Desarrollo Humano en Chile: Género: Los Desafíos de la Igualdad*. 2010. Santiago de Chile: Author. http://www.desarrollohumano.cl/informe-2010/PNUD_LIBRO.pdf.

Appendix 11.A: Survey, Focus Groups and In-Depth Interviews

Survey

The objective of the survey was to get first impressions to guide subsequent group discussions. The survey had a non-probabilistic sample design, and considered a total catchment population of 1,384 people for the telecenter in the Metropolitan Region (San Francisco de Asis Settlement) and 3,579 people for the telecenter in the O'Higgins Region (San Hernán Town). The survey was conducted between July 26 and September 11, 2010, and was administered to men and women 18 years of age or older, both users and nonusers, who lived within the radius of primary influence of the telecenters.

Focus Groups

The focus groups correspond to user and nonuser profiles. Only five sessions of a proposed initial total of six were held. Focus group participants were selected from among

Table 11.A.1
Number of Survey Interviewees by Center

	San Francisco	San Hernán	Both areas
Women			
Users	51	50	101
Nonusers		25	42
Users of the Internet, nonusers of the Telecenter	26	23	49
Subtotal	94	98	192
Men			
Users	20	22	42
Nonusers	9	18	27
Users of the Internet, nonusers of the Telecenter	20	14	34
Subtotal	49	54	103
Total	143	152	295

those who responded to the survey and indicated their availability to attend and from a list of local residents identified through the contact networks the research assistants were able to build in the two neighborhoods. The invitations were extended in person, followed by a written reminder of the date, time, and place of the meeting.

The sessions took place in August and September 2010 and were recorded with the express permission of the attendees.

In-Depth Interviews

The selection of interviewees was carried out in a non-probabilistic manner, starting with individual invitations to some of the focus group participants and to local

Table 11.A.2
Number of Focus Groups Held by Center

	San Francisco	San Hernán	Both Areas
Women			
Users	2	–	2
Nonusers	1	1	2
Subtotal	3	1	4
Men			
Users	1	–	1
Nonusers	–	–	–
Subtotal	1	–	1
Total	1	0	5

Table 11.A.3
Number of In-depth Interviewees by Center

	San Francisco	San Hernán	Both Areas
Women			
Users	6	4	10
Nonusers	1	3	4
Subtotal	7	7	14
Men			
Users	3	2	5
Nonusers	1	1	2
Subtotal	4	3	7
Total	11	21	21

residents identified through the researchers' contact networks in the two neighborhoods. The interviews were conducted in people's homes by mutual agreement of the two parties, at the telecenter, or at the neighborhood community center, preferably on Thursdays, Fridays, and Saturdays. These interviews, the most time-consuming part of the study, were carried out between September and December 2010.

Four of the women users but none of the nonusers had a home computer connected to the Internet. Two of the men users but none of the nonusers had a home computer connected to the Internet.

12 Cybercafés and Community ICT Training Centers: Empowering Women Migrant Workers in Thailand

Nikos Dacanay, Mary Luz Feranil, Ryan V. Silverio, and Mai M. Taqueban

Abstract

The political and economic crises in Burma[1] have led to the diaspora of more than a million people from different ethnic groups to the Thai border. In the border town of Mae Sot, migrant workers make up more than 50 percent of the population, comprising most of the skilled labor force and organizing into community groups with assistance from nongovernmental organizations (NGOs).

This chapter looks at access to and use of the Internet in cybercafés and community ICT training centers (CITCs) by women migrant workers in Mae Sot and the relation of that access and use to gender empowerment. The migrant population has been largely excluded from the information communication technology (ICT) development plan of the Thai state, but there is strong advocacy for computer and Internet education by migrant organizations aided by the town's two CITCs and its cybercafés. The CITCs are subsidized by NGOs and offer free or low-cost computer and Internet lessons for migrant workers; the cybercafés are private enterprises that provide computer and Internet access for a fee.

Employing mixed methodologies, the research revealed the following: (1) access to cybercafés and CITCs provides gender empowering and emancipatory capacities in social connectivity and cultural invigoration; (2) while there is dynamic networking among migrants to increase public Internet access, that access is constrained by mobility and language barriers, user fees, lack of requisite literacy and numeracy skills, and insufficient computer/Internet technical competence; and (3) migrants have taken to mobile phones faster than to the Internet because phone technology presents fewer user constraints.

In light of the benefits associated with access to cybercafés and CITCs, the research recommends a model structure that merges and supports the educational function of CITCs and the business aspect of cybercafés, as well as the development of programmatic ICT education and infrastructure through partnerships among NGOs, the private sector, and the Thai state. Advocacy efforts should also be directed to encouraging the Thai state to change its policies toward migrants and to implement ICT policies specifically designed to meet the needs of Burmese migrant workers.

Introduction

When I spoke with my son in Bangkok, the first time I've ever handled a cell phone... it felt very inadequate for me. It was so small and there was no mouthpiece. I didn't know whether to keep it near my mouth or near my ears, and I just kept shifting it around. Everybody kept assuring me, "Go on, it's all right. You can say what you want and he can hear you perfectly well."

(Aung San Suu Kyi, Burmese opposition leader and Nobel Peace Prize winner, in a BBC interview on November 15, 2010, shortly after her release from fifteen years of house arrest[2])

Information and communication technology (ICT) has evolved so rapidly over the last ten years that for someone like Aung San Suu Kyi, who had been cut off from the world for more than a decade, it seemed implausible that a small device could allow her to talk to her son across the Pacific. Indeed, ICT's role in communication and other applications has improved the lives of many people.

The Thai government has implemented several ICT policies in its drive to build a knowledge-based society. Unfortunately, the numerous ethnic groups from Burma living in Thailand have been excluded from those plans. The movement of ethnic people from Burma to Thailand that began in the 1950s has intensified in the last thirty years as the Burmese military offensive has pushed the ethnic groups to the Thai border. In Thailand, ethnic Burmese can be classified into two groups: migrant workers and refugees. The migrant workers, who live in towns in key areas of the country, make up a sizable population; most of them belong to lower income groups and are working illegally, without proper work permits. The refugees are confined to enclosed camps on the Thai–Burma border, and their movements and opportunities are restricted by the Thai government. The United Nations High Commissioner for Refugees (UNHCR) has resettled around 60,000 refugees to third countries, but the continuous arrival of new entrants from Burma has merely replaced this number.[3]

Various nongovernmental organizations (NGOs) and community-based organizations (CBOs) have introduced computers and the Internet to migrants through training and informal lessons. Migrants can access the Internet in CBO offices and public venues such as cybercafés and community ICT training centers (CITCs), the latter of which we define as venues that offer computer and Internet training to a target population. CITCs are not typically open to the general public.

Most of the literature on the digital divide has focused on statistical differences in ICT access and use, but little attention has been given to ICT use by women at the margins (e.g., ethnic minorities, displaced persons, and those caught up in armed conflict) (Nsibirano 2009). This research aims to help fill the gap. It examines cybercafés and

CITCs patronized by ethnic women migrant workers in Mae Sot and their impact on the women's sense of empowerment.

The primary objective of the study was to assess the empowering impact of access to and use of the Internet in cybercafés and CITCs by women migrant workers in Mae Sot. Secondary objectives were to determine the limitations and potentials of the empowering effects of cybercafés and CITCs, determine the mediations that affect Internet access, and assess the impact on women migrants of Internet penetration versus mobile phone penetration.

The Context

Burmese Migrant Workers in Mae Sot

Mae Sot is one of the most heavily Burmese populated towns in Thailand: the Burmese population of Mae Sot is said to outnumber the Thai population two to one (McGeon 2007). It is situated in Tak province, in the westernmost region of Thailand, next to the Moei River, which separates Thailand and Burma. The Thai-Myanmar Friendship Bridge connects Mae Sot to Myawaddy, the Burmese town on the opposite bank of the river. Mae Sot is geographically closer to Myawaddy, eighteen kilometers away, than to the provincial capital of Tak, eighty-six kilometers away—in other words, closer to Burmese than to other Thai communities. The river is narrow, allowing Burmese people to travel to and from Mae Sot easily.

There is a long history of cross-border movements of people and goods between Mae Sot and Myawaddy. Primarily an agricultural area, Mae Sot relied on economic trade with Myawaddy, and the two towns shared market and labor force. In the last thirty years, as a result of the Thai state's relocation of industry to border areas, Mae Sot has been transformed from a trade area to an industrial hub linked to Bangkok and other commercial centers. Its development was also aided by the state's implementation of an East–West Economic Corridor as part of the development plan for the Greater Mekong subregion. The Corridor will connect the Indian Ocean and the South China Sea, cutting across borders and connecting trade zones in the Mekong countries. Mae Sot lies on the westernmost point of Thailand, a strategic position in the Economic Corridor.

The development of Mae Sot as an industrial hub and economic trading zone dramatically increased the migrant workforce. According to Arnold (2007), from the early to mid-1990s, small-scale businesses were set up, each employing two to three thousand migrants. The mid-1990s saw the construction of many factories, about twenty of which employed Burmese and other ethnic groups from the nearby refugee camps. Following the Asian financial crisis of 1997, bigger factories were put up, each employing about a thousand workers. Today, Mae Sot is home to a huge informal labor market harnessed by many Thai and foreign entrepreneurs.[4]

The economic development of Mae Sot, together with other pull factors such as ease of crossing the Thai–Burma border and improved transportation in both countries, played a major role in the migration of Burmese to Mae Sot. There were also push factors such as the risk of persecution, human rights abuses, political and ethnic oppression, internal violence, armed conflict, poverty, and economic underdevelopment.

The growth of a large migrant workforce eventually led to exploitative labor practices, including excessive working hours, relatively low wages, and frequent arrest and deportation (Kusakabe and Pearson 2010). Whereas the minimum wage in Tak province is between 140 and 150 Baht per day, the migrant workers in Mae Sot's textile and garment factories earn between 50 and 70 Baht per day (Arnold 2007). The more than 150,000 migrants in Mae Sot are among the 250,000 registered and unregistered migrants in Tak province. Many migrants have work documents typically valid for a year, but the majority are in Thailand illegally and subject to police harassment for not having official work permits. At the same time, they are not well integrated into Thai society: Burmese cannot speak the Thai language and often do not mingle with the local people.

The Ministry of Labor acknowledges the country's current need to employ 1.2 million low-skilled migrant workers, but out of concern for national security, the Thai government has been reluctant to accept migrants and has failed to establish realistic immigration policies (Aung 2010).

Several NGOs and CBOs in Mae Sot provide development assistance to migrant workers. The CBOs are composed of migrants and receive funding from NGOs. Most of them are organized along ethnic lines, but there are also sector groups with members from different ethnic backgrounds: women, youth, ICT, law, education, livelihood, and so on. Today there are more than one hundred CBOs in Mae Sot, most with programs centered on capacity building, including internship programs that cover a variety of topics such as human and gender rights, sexual and reproductive health and rights, computer and Internet lessons, office work, and English and Thai language classes. The internships normally last from three to six months. There are also training courses and workshops, typically lasting one or two days, on these topics and others such as livelihood, business management, basic accounting, gender and sexual health and rights. These internships and training programs are provided by either the CBOs or the NGOs.

The CBOs emerged after the fall in 1995 of the Burmese city of Manerplaw, the headquarters of the Karen National Union (KNU), which resulted in a massive influx of ethnic refugees into Tak province and the relocation to Mae Sot of the bases of the

KNU-led Burmese political organizations. Since then, other exiled Burmese organizations have moved their bases to Mae Sot and used the town not only as a communication hub but as a physical base for the activities of exiled Burmese. Eventually, Mae Sot became a major center for Thai and international NGOs advocating for Burmese refugees and migrant workers.[5]

Development of ICT in Thailand and Mae Sot

Internet use in Thailand grew from 4 percent of the population in 2000 to 29 percent in 2013 (International Telecommunications Union 2013). By 2013, 29 of every 100 people in Thailand had a computer and mobile phone penetration had reached 138 percent (International Telecommunications Union 2013). There are, however, significant differences between rural and urban areas: in 2009, Internet penetration was reportedly 32.7 percent in urban areas but only 14.5 percent in rural areas (Santipaporn 2010).

To bridge the digital divide between urban and rural communities, the Thai government created the ICT and Happiness Plan, which aims to integrate ICT development with the country's Green and Happiness Society Index, the latter being a measure of the well-being of the Thai people and the environment. One component of the plan aims to expand Internet access in rural areas (Sirirachatapong and Pooparadai 2007). This has led to an increase in the number of Internet public access venues. A 2008 survey of cybercafés by the Thailand Information Center at the Chulalongkorn University Center of Academic Resources identified 10,477 cybercafés, of which a significant number (22 percent) were located in northern Thailand. Nearly all these venues are privately run and formally registered; most have between ten and fourteen computers and employ one to five staff (Thailand Information Center 2008).

In Mae Sot, Internet accessibility improved dramatically following the implementation of National Electronics and Computer Technology's (NECTEC's) *IT 2010* policy. In the year 2000, Internet connection was set up in government offices, but there were few cybercafés. By the end of 2010, there were three Internet service providers (TOT, TT&T/3B, and CAT) providing DSL, cable, and dialup service, two mobile phone providers (DTAC and GSM), eighteen to twenty-two cybercafés, and wireless Internet was available in most restaurants, coffee shops, guest houses, and hotels.[6]

Although overall Internet access and usage have increased dramatically, there is still a wide gap between rural and urban Internet users. The Thai government's ICT policies and the projects of the Royal Monarchy include non-Thais but only marginally (through ICT in primary education where non-Thais can enroll), and there is no ICT policy addressing the needs of migrants. The survey conducted by National Electronics and Computer Technology (2009) revealed the glaring disparity between urban and rural Internet users: Internet use was dominated by residents of Bangkok and its suburb (61 percent), followed by other urban areas (21 percent). Only 18 percent of users were from rural areas. Nearly a third of all users were between 30 and 39 years old, and the majority (56 percent) had a bachelor's degree. Non-Thais and rural residents with lower educational levels have limited access to the Internet.

Owing to the Thai state's diplomatic stance on internal politics in Burma and its treatment of Burmese in Thailand as "non-Thais," Burmese migrant workers have been left out of the Thai state's ICT development program. Nonetheless, in Mae Sot, the exiled Burmese opposition leaders who have set up community-based organizations have incorporated modern communication technologies into their political advocacy. According to Aung (2010):

> *Another important factor supporting the growth of exiled BCSOs [Burmese civil society organizations]—which was absent in the traditional ethnic armed struggle—is quick adaptation of these groups to advanced modern communication technologies. BCSOs have been able to create their own websites, through which they lobby the international community for attention and support on the Burma issue. The most important feature of recent technological advancement is that they allow Burmese exiles to stretch out their organizational arms to lobby governments all around the world, international non-governmental organizations, and intergovernmental organizations, increasing the range of support for their activities.* (p. 31)

Networking among CBOs has helped increase computer and Internet literacy through internship, training, workshops, and short-term computer courses. The training programs help migrants working for CBOs to use these skills for political advocacy. Two CITCs for migrants—Community Capacity Building Committee (CCBC) and Knowledge Zone (KZ), discussed below—were established by international NGOs in 2008 and 2010, respectively.

Overall, meager ICT support to the migrant community exists because few CBO internship programs and CITCs offer computer or Internet training. Furthermore, few organizations have computers and Internet connection. Of the more than one hundred CBOs in Mae Sot, fewer than half are equipped with personal computers or laptops.

Methodology and Theoretical Framework

Methodology, Scope, and Limitations

We employed mixed methodologies with an emphasis on qualitative methods. We used long interviews, focus group discussions, participant observation, and a survey. To understand how public access to Internet shapes notions of empowerment, we compared cybercafé usage with CITC usage, public Internet usage (in cybercafés and CITCs) with private usage (in CBO offices), and Internet users with non-Internet users who use cell phones instead.

The research was conducted in Mae Sot, Tak province, over an eighteen-month period beginning in January 2010. It focused on two cybercafés regularly frequented by migrant workers and two CITCs. The primary respondents were migrant women.

The first part of our research involved establishing contact with women from different CBOs and identifying who among them used the cybercafés or CITCs and who did not. We also carried out observations in the two cybercafés and the two CITCs.

The second part of the research was devoted to focus group discussions, long interviews, and participant observation. We conducted one focus group discussion for public users of the Internet and another for users of Internet in private CBO offices. The focus group discussions were meant to establish rapport between the participants and the researchers and to initiate a discussion and sharing of ideas among the participants on the use and nonuse of cybercafés/CITCs and the benefits and drawbacks of ICT use. After the focus group discussions, we conducted one-on-one interviews with the women and probed deeper into the themes that surfaced during the group meetings. Each interview lasted two to three hours. We prepared a set of semistructured questions and allowed the women to expand on topics according to their preferences. Both the focus group discussions and interviews were conducted with the help of translators; they were audio and photo recorded with informed consent and transcribed into English. We also observed the women while they accessed the cybercafés and CITCs and used the Internet in their offices.

The third part of the research was a continuation of the interviews and clarification of responses to questions in the initial interviews. We then conducted a survey of cybercafés (there are twenty or so cybercafés in Mae Sot) in Thai language. We also ran a Burmese language survey of the women who access the cybercafés and CITCs. Fifty-seven women participated in the survey, the majority of them users of the two CITCs and/or attendees of a local Christian church. The women who access cybercafés and CITCs who were interviewed (table 12.1) were also included in the survey.

The context in which the research was conducted presented several limitations and methodological challenges. First, the political situation prevented access to and inclusion of many migrants, who hesitated to interact with strangers for security reasons. The research relied on respondents identified through personal referrals.

Second, because of time and resource constraints, rapport with informants was not fully developed, which may have prevented informants from revealing personal details of their communication practices. These constraints also prevented the full exploration

Table 12.1
Distribution of Interviews/Focus Group Discussions

	Public Internet Use		Private Internet Use	
Women's CBOs	Cybercafé	CITC	Office Internet	Nonusers of Internet
ULYO	1/1	–	–	–
MWU	4/0	–	–	–
MTC	4/0	–	–	–
KWO	–	–	6/1	–
PWO	–	–	4/0	–
BWU	–	–	4/0	–
Non-CBO (KZ)	–	4/0	–	–
Non-CBO (CCBC)	–	4/0	–	–
KHK	–	–	–	0/1
ML	–	–	–	2/2
UM	–	–	–	1/2
Total	9/1	8/0	14/1	3/5

Key:
BWU, Burmese Women's Union
CCBC, Community Capacity Building Committee
KHK, Karen help Karen
KWO, Karen Women's Organization
KZ, Knowledge Zone
ML, Mae La
MTC, Mae Tao Clinic
MWU, Myeik Women's Union
PWO, Palaung Women's Organization
ULYO, United Lahu Youth Organization
UM, Umphiem Mai

of the linkages between mobile phones in refugee camps and Internet usage in migrant towns. The research would have benefited from a richer database if friends and relatives of migrant women who have now been resettled to third countries had also been interviewed.

Third, linguistic barriers prevented nuanced responses to the questions. Although the lead researcher spoke Thai and the collaborators were acquainted with Thai culture, we conducted the interviews in English and Burmese with the help of translators. The interviewees were, however, sometimes more comfortable talking in their native languages.

Theoretical Framework

This chapter looks at empowerment through the lens of development work and gender (women's) rights. The idea of empowerment has a long history rooted in various academic and developmental discourses. For most social activists and development agencies, it is used as a local endeavor, concerned with inspiring the poor to challenge the status quo or upset the established power structures and achieve more equitable communities. The concept is understood as having "the ability to change the world, to overcome opposition" (Rai 2007, p. 3) and is commonly seen as transformative in nature.

Feminists have contributed important insights into the concepts of power and empowerment. Because in many societies power relationships generally marginalize women, feminists have embraced the idea as naturally relevant to women's issues and problems. Third World feminists regard the issue of participation as central to empowerment.[7] Participation in the process of challenging hegemonic discourses has been seen as leading to deeper understanding of the self, which often empowers individuals and inspires political action in both their private and public lives (Rai 2007).

This research takes on the idea of power as process, outcome and participation, in which women experience, challenge, and subvert power relationships. As a process, empowerment takes place through mediations such as capacity building on information technology provided by NGOs and others such as ICT public access and ICT training venues (PAVs and CITCs). As an outcome, empowerment can be measured against expected accomplishments, where accomplishments are viewed as subjective, relative, and perspectival (Kabeer and Subrahmanian 1999). Empowerment as an outcome comes from the individual's subjective self-analysis of his or her "agency" and "power" in maximizing his or her opportunities and options. It is the ability to determine choices in life and to influence the direction of change (Askew 2002, Moser 1993). By looking at empowerment in terms of access to cybercafés and CITCs, the research fleshed out the "participation" aspect through the ways women migrant workers engage in ICT development.

Findings

Cybercafés

The House of Internet The House of Internet (HOI) is a cybercafé located near a Burmese clinic. It is owned and operated by a Thai woman who also manages a kiosk next door. The venue is a long narrow room partitioned into two sections; one has six computers for online computer games, and the other has nine computers for web browsing. HOI is open from 9 A.M. to 10 P.M. and charges 15 Baht (about US$0.50) per hour. The shop also offers printing services.

According to the owner, the users of HOI are predominantly young Thai men between thirteen and twenty-two years old, in *matayom* (high school), who like to play online games from six to ten in the evening. In contrast, the migrant workers who frequent HOI are mostly young women who work at the Mae Tao Clinic. They go to HOI in the morning or at lunchtime when the young Thai boys are not using the computers. They like to download Burmese fonts (WinBurmese 1 & 2); however, because only two computers allow downloading of files, they use the English alphabet when they email or chat online in their ethnic languages.

Net Day Net Day cybercafé is located across the street from a migrant school managed by Myeik Burmese women. It is relatively new (2009), operates from 10 A.M. to 8 P.M., and charges 15 Baht (about US$0.50) per hour. Apart from Internet use, it offers other services such as printing, photocopying, scanning, and selling of refreshments. The shop has fifteen brand-new high-speed computers equipped with gadgets such as earphones, web cams, and joysticks. The shop also allows downloading of files, including Burmese fonts, and the computers can read Burmese language websites. Many of the customers of Net Day are Burmese students and teachers at the migrant school across the street. The young men primarily play online games, and the women (students and teachers) prefer surfing the net. Migrant women from the Myeik Women's Union (MWU) patronize Net Day.

Community ICT Training Centers

There are two community ICT training centers (CITCs) serving the migrant workers: Knowledge Zone (KZ) and Community Capacity Building Committee (CCBC). Both call themselves "telecenters," but they are in fact CITCs. The main service provided is training and access to computers and the Internet is not available to the general public.

The two CITCs are closely linked and have evolved to become effectively "one-stop shop" resource centers for web designers, program operators, computer troubleshooters, and PC assemblers serving the Burmese migrant community. The current few IT experts are teachers and trainers for CCBC and KZ. Through networking, they work with various CBOs to create and develop the CBOs' websites and email systems, fix computer problems, and assemble their personal computers. The teachers from KZ have undergone training at CCBC. Another IT expert from a CBO called the Burma Workers Network (BWN) was also trained at CCBC and now teaches short-term computer courses for migrants within the factories where they work. While most CCBC and KZ students are women, all current IT experts are men, underscoring how control over ICT knowledge is biased in favor of men.

Community Capacity Building Committee Located near factories where there are many migrants, Community Capacity Building Committee (CCBC) is a research and computer/Internet center set up in 2010 and funded by the International Refugee Committee (IRC) and the U.S. Agency for International Development (USAID). It grants scholarships to six individuals from different CBOs to train them in computer and Internet use (MS Office, website and domain hosting, video and photo editing, etc.) for six months, after which time they go back to their own organizations to use their newly acquired ICT skills. CCBC also offers other short-term computer courses for migrants, as well as courses in human rights, office management, strategic planning, and organizational development.

CCBC is part of a network of one hundred CBOs in Mae Sot. It is operated by nine staff members assisted by volunteers from various ethnic groups (Karen, Karenni, Shan, Akha, Palaung, etc.). It has three public computers that are often used by and reserved for the computer teachers; students taking computer lessons bring their laptops with them. They can use the free wireless connection but only for a limited period. They go to CCBC only during class time.

CCBC, in partnership with members of other CBOs, also plans and coordinates short-term computer courses that are conducted in the migrants' workplace. Because there are currently few IT experts in the community, one of CCBC's objectives is to develop a pool of experts (one or two from each ethnic group) who can spread the knowledge and skills to their respective groups.

Knowledge Zone Unlike CCBC, whose focus is computer skills development, Knowledge Zone (KZ) is a quasi-school that offers training courses to migrants in a variety of subjects. It is headed by Thet Naing, a Burmese and a member of Burmese Eligible Teachers (a group of teachers in Burma who oppose the Burmese government), which established KZ in 2008 in partnership with the All Burma Monk Alliance (ABMA).

KZ offers language and computer classes. With five computer/Internet teachers, it runs basic Microsoft Office and Internet classes for one to two hours a day as part of a three-month course that includes English and Thai language lessons. Students are charged 100 Baht (about US$3.10) for the course. The computer and Internet skills taught include downloading video, audio, and photo files and using the Internet and email.

Table 12.2
Main Characteristics of Cybercafés and CITCs Studied

Attribute	Cybercafés: HOI and Net Day	Community ICT Training Centers (CITCs): CCBC and KZ
Nature	Profit-oriented	Development projects funded by foreign NGOs
	Recreational; used to practice Internet skills such as emailing, chatting, and watching music videos	Educational, programmatic and goal-oriented. Students take computer and Internet lessons (basic, intermediate, and advanced)
Fee	15–20 Baht (about US$0.50–0.60) per hour	CCBC: Free computer and Internet classes; free wireless Internet connection (personal laptops)
		KZ: 100 Baht (US$3.10)/three-month computer and Internet course; free Internet use for one hour
Services	Internet connection	Internet and computer classes in website domain hosting; uploading and downloading text files, videos, and photos; creating blog sites and websites; Microsoft Office suite
		Free Internet connection

KZ currently has 287 students, 65 percent of whom are women working in factories or as market vendors. Those who are unemployed are mostly young women (ten to seventeen years old) who depend on their parents. The students are multi-ethnic: Rachine, Mon, Karen, and Shan. Representatives of some CBOs, including the Burmese Women's Union (BWU), visit KZ to teach human rights. Other NGOs, such as the Burma Law Council (BLC), support KZ by providing breakfast and lunch to teachers and students. Computer teachers from KZ improve their ICT skills by participating in computer and other training programs organized by CCBC. KZ has fifteen computers that are regularly used inside the classroom. Students are allowed up to one hour of free Internet use.

A summary of the main features of the cybercafés and CITCs studied is given in table 12.2.

Migrant Users of Cybercafés and CITCs

The majority of the migrant women we interviewed who access cybercafés are in their early twenties, are single, have attained at most ten standard education (equivalent to secondary education), are employed as factory workers, teachers, or medical assistants, and hold work permits that give them limited mobility around the Mae Sot area (essentially confining them to their workplaces and the surrounding neighborhood).

The women have taken short computer courses and/or internship programs. The Internet lessons were informal, introduced in short computer courses and by friends during internship. As a result, their computer skills are rudimentary. They do not own personal computers and access the Internet only at cybercafés or friends' homes. On average, they use the Internet for three hours a week. Because of the Internet user fees in cybercafés, they spend a limited amount of time using the Internet there. Except for those from the Mae Tao Clinic (MTC), the women belong to organizations that are relatively recently set up, small, and composed of fewer than ten active members. These organizations rely on bigger CBOs and NGOs in Mae Sot for funding and are not equipped to provide computer and Internet training.

The women are limited in their online activities and use the Internet primarily for communication. They use email services (Gmail and Yahoo Mail), chat programs (Gchat and Yahoo Messenger), and social networking sites (Facebook and Hi5) to communicate with family members, friends, and other CBO partners and networks. They consider email to be very important, and they rely on it to connect with relatives and friends living in other Thai provinces, Burma, or other countries where some have been resettled.[8] Email is also used for their CBO work and facilitates more efficient communication, such as sending and receiving reports and other information as well as planning activities with other women's groups. The younger women enjoy social networking and have Facebook and Hi5 accounts where they meet new friends who live outside Mae Sot. The women often listen to Burmese songs, watch videos on YouTube, and visit Burmese news websites. In rating the activities they engaged in most frequently while using the Internet in these venues, the highest was checking and sending email (81 percent said they do it every time), chat (53 percent), and listening to or downloading Burmese music (30 percent).

In the survey of migrant women who access the Internet at public venues (both cybercafés and CITCs), the majority of the fifty-seven respondents were students at KZ and CCBC or at migrant schools, and they were living with parents who work in Mae Sot and who provide them with a monthly allowance of 500–1,000 Baht (about US$15.60–31.30).

About a third of respondents rate their level of Internet skills as fairly good, and 53 percent use the Internet once a week. While the majority first learned to use the Internet using a friend's computer and consider this as more important in developing their Internet skills than either cybercafés or CITCs, 54 percent rely on these two types of centers to access the Internet.

Thirty-nine of the women users of cybercafés or CITCs interviewed rated the impact of Internet access on various spheres. The areas perceived to be most impacted are

Table 12.3
Assessment of Impact of the Internet by 39 Women Respondents—Users of Cybercafé or CITCs

	Highly Positive		Slightly Positive		No Impact	
Impact on:	#	%	#	%	#	%
Education	20	51.3	17	43.6	2	5.1
Activities like organizing and involvement in NGOs	17	43.6	19	48.7	3	7.7
Meeting people	17	43.6	19	48.7	3	7.7
Maintaining communication with family and friends	10	25.6	18	46.2	11	28.2
Health	11	28.2	11	28.2	17	43.6
Access to information about the government	11	28.2	11	28.2	17	43.6
Pursuing interests and hobbies	8	20.5	7	17.9	24	61.5
Access to resources and skills necessary for work	8	20.5	6	15.4	25	64.1
Participation in activities to build stronger culture and language	4	10.3	8	20.5	27	69.2
Pursuing leisure activities	5	12.8	8	20.5	26	66.7
Providing support to Burmese in Mae Sot	6	15.4	3	7.7	30	76.9
Sending and receiving money to and from family and friends	2	5.1	6	15.4	31	79.5
Income	2	5.1	3	7.7	34	87.2

education, organizing and involvement in NGOs, meeting people, and maintaining communication with family and friends; least impacted are income, sending or receiving money, and providing support to Burmese in Thailand (table 12.3). This last high "no impact" response may reflect a generalized frustration regarding what can actually be done to help ethnic Burmese migrants living in Thailand.

Emancipatory Capacities of Internet Use in Cybercafés and CITCs

Despite having limited computer skills, the women feel empowered when they visit the cybercafés and CITCs. The empowering capacities of the Internet are based on social connectivity or bringing together scattered members of different ethnic groups, and the creation of virtual communities centered on ethnic cultures.

Social Connectivity For a dislocated diaspora of ethnic people with families, relatives, friends, and work partners living outside Mae Sot—in Chiang Mai, Bangkok, Burma, and resettlement countries—the Internet has become a social avenue. The cybercafés and CITCs have provided women migrants with a doorway to a wider space for maintaining and expanding social relationships beyond the geographical boundaries of Mae Sot. The problems of physical distance are remedied by the proximity of virtual relationships.

For families, the Internet allows for trans-border care arrangement. Through email and video chat using Skype, Yahoo Messenger, and Gchat, women in Mae Sot are able to repair kinship ties and extend their familial obligations as daughters, sisters, cousins, and nieces to relatives who are geographically distant.

For friends, the Internet in cybercafés has opened the doors to interesting social opportunities. Chat programs and social networking sites enable especially the younger women to stay connected with friends who are far away as well as meet new friends. For instance, two girls from the United Lahu Youth Organization (ULYO) reported having "virtual boyfriends" on Hi5 while others entertain virtual suitors.

In the work context, the Internet has allowed migrants to maintain relationships with funders and partners and increase networking opportunities. The nature of the CBOs' work is multigeographic, and the Internet is helpful in this regard: email and chat allow the women to communicate with funders in Western countries and with partners and networks (NGOs/CBOs) outside Mae Sot. Through their websites, the women also recruit new supporters for their CBOs.

The Internet has also fostered unity among CBOs. The activities in Mae Sot that are meant to build closer relationships among CBOs (e.g., conferences, forums, workshops, training, and celebrations of special events) are communicated via email and the CBO websites. Thanks to the Internet, the various Burmese women's organizations are now more closely linked with each other despite differences in ethnic back grounds, as evidenced by their shared activities, communication, and website linkages.

While the Internet has provided a space for maintaining expected social relationships between family members in multiple geographic locations, it has also allowed for expanding social relationships beyond cultural expectations. Women are now more open to the idea of online or virtual romantic relationships, sometimes initiating these relationships themselves. This behavior runs counter to gender norms in their ethnic groups, which discourage women from initiating and pursuing relationships with the opposite sex. The CBO women especially are more daring in challenging these gender norms, even in familial relationships. Some women are the economic providers in the family, sending their allowances to relatives in Burma, while others are the decision makers in their households.

Case Study: Nu Te Nu Te was born in Chin state, Burma. She is thirty-three years old and has an eleven-year-old son. Her mother has passed away, her father and one of her brothers live in Burma, and her sister lives in North Carolina. Her other brother, who lived in Malaysia, has been missing for fifteen years. Nu Te finished high school and was married at an early age. When she was living in Burma, she worked as a weaver and sold handicraft products in the market.

In 2005, after she separated from her husband, she crossed to Thailand to search for a better life for herself and her son. At the time, her sister was working for the Mae Tao Clinic and invited Nu Te to work as a teacher in the migrant school run by the clinic. Before beginning teaching, she took a six-month training program that included English and Thai language and computer lessons. Today, she teaches English to grade school students. Her salary is not high, but the school provides a housing subsidy, a food ration, electricity and water subsidies, and free medicine.

Because the school's Internet connection is regulated, Nu Te spends most of her time at HOI checking her Gmail and using Gtalk to connect with her family and her best friend Ai Khon, who lives and works in Malaysia.

For Nu Te, the Internet has many benefits. It has opened opportunities for connection and information-sharing that were previously unavailable to her. Nu Te is close to her family, and Gmail and Gtalk allow her to keep in touch with them.

I'm happy that I can use the Internet. In Burma, we didn't have anything, not even a cellphone. Life was very different. It was miserable and I was staying in an isolated place. It seemed like the doors to the outside world were closed. But now they're open.

My mother is already gone. I love her so much. We were her priority, and she always put our interests ahead of other things. I inherited that from her, because I think of my son's interests first before anything else. Now that she is gone, my siblings and I take care of our father. I feel happy now because I can reach out to my family even if they are far away. Most of the emails I send are to my sister and brother. I also talk to them through Gtalk. My siblings and I talk about our father's needs. My father is very old now. He goes to different places to preach the gospel. I discuss with my father on Gtalk how to take care of our health. We also talk about Bible verses and about God.

Nu Te regularly keeps in touch with her best friend Ai Khon in Malaysia and other friends in Burma and other countries.

I use Facebook and Hi5, which were introduced to me by Ai Khon. It's a way for us to be connected to each other. I have friends in Burma but I cannot contact them directly so I contact them through other people's emails or cellphones. Some of my friends are Karen and are now in third countries. We send each other emails, but they're very short messages because we cannot speak English very well. If the email I receive from them has a very good message I keep it in my inbox....

Whenever I receive emails from Ai Khon I'm very happy. We always exchange news about ourselves. We share pictures and music. She would say to me, "You did many good things for me. I will never forget you. You're very kind." I don't delete these emails. I keep them because they are very special....

Sometimes we chat using Gtalk. We use Chin language in English script. We talk about everyday life like, "I miss you very much. Do you have problems? How are you?" I remember our encounters with each other, et cetera.

Nu Te also goes to HOI to listen to Chin music on YouTube and to Burmese radio on the BBC website. She also reads news and human rights issues on news sites such as Khitpyaing and the Chin email group. She often forwards the information that she reads to her friends and family.

Internet is very important and useful. I can get all the information that I want and need. I read news and listen to the radio on the Internet. Ono the Khitpyaing website, there are many different kinds of news: politics, entertainment, and stories about the different ethnic people. I have learned many things about the state of Burma from these websites.

Nu Te is a devout Baptist, and the Internet also helps her strengthen her religious faith.

The Internet is important for my religion. I'm a Christian. On YouTube I can find sermons by different pastors. I am occasionally required to preach so I go to the Internet to look for Bible verses that are good for my sermon. My favorite Bible verses are also online, like Proverbs' quotes on humility, or the Beatitudes. I share these with friends....

I inherited my devotion to God from my father. He says, "Even though I cannot put my children in high positions or give them all the things they want, this is okay as long as they are God-fearing." This is the most important thing in life. I teach my son how to love God too.

Nu Te also uses the Internet to earn a small amount of money selling Burmese products to her sister and her sister's friends in the United States. Her sister orders cosmetics and food ingredients from her by email. In addition, the handicraft products made by the Chin Women's Organization, of which she is a member, are advertised on the organization's website and sold at the Borderline shop in Mae Sot.

Nu Te sees the potential of using the Internet to aid her teaching but has not explored the possibility.

I think the Internet is also important for teaching. Although I have not explored this, I know I can get many ideas and information from the Internet. I want to learn how to use the Internet for my work, like search for educational materials in English teaching.

Nu Te relies on her cellphone for instant connection with friends in Mae Sot and her family in Burma.

I also like the cellphone because it's now easier to contact my friends and family. With the Internet, we can send emails and we are sure that our message has been received by our friend or relative. With cellphones, sometimes we cannot contact each other and we are not sure if our text message has been sent.

Cultural Empowerment Because of the dislocation of many ethnic peoples from Burma, women migrants use the Internet as a virtual cultural headquarters, a repository of cultural data, a space for cultural expression, and a source of entertainment. The women express themselves online in their ethnic languages when using email or chat, in either Burmese font (which they download) or English script. The CBO websites are in Burmese and ethnic languages. In addition, the women are active participants in cultural entertainment—downloading, uploading, watching, and listening to Burmese ethnic music videos and celebrations and festivals.

The Internet has become a space for preserving, spreading, and transforming ethnic cultures. The women email and chat with relatives and friends who have been resettled in other countries. They talk about homesickness (e.g., missing the way of life in Burma and Thailand, people, festivals, food, clothes, music, etc.) and mitigate that feeling in various ways (e.g., by celebrating ethnic festivals in distant locations and using email, chat, and blog sites to share photos, videos, and music). The people in third countries also order goods from the women in Mae Sot, such as traditional dresses like the sarong, food products like fish paste and tea, cosmetic items like thanaka, and other goods.

The Internet is also a virtual space for the construction and transformation of ethnic identity. CBO websites present ethnic histories and information about admired leaders, arts, traditions, and customs. In schools and internship programs, for instance, women are taught that the ideal Karen or Mon is somebody who is educated. Consequently, Myeik women look up to women like Aung San Suu Kyi and Dr. Cynthia Maung, who are well educated, as ideals to emulate. The Internet reinforces this educated identity role, as the Internet is seen and used as a purveyor of knowledge.

Internet, Agency, and Empowerment The concept of empowerment in development theory and policy as "a process treating people as agents of change on the road to giving them greater control over and a say about resources and decisions that affect their life prospects" (Koggel 2009, p. 2) brings to the fore the tales of the women who go to cybercafés and CITCs to connect with loved ones and invigorate their ethnic culture by participating in online communities of Burmese ethnic people.

This process of empowerment is underscored by the immense capacity of the Internet to connect women to their loved ones scattered in different parts of the world and to reproduce in online communities the offline sociocultural practices (as in the case of Nu Te of MTC and her online relationship with her father and siblings). The cybercafés and CITCs have provided women migrants with a space in the virtual world where they can break down physical and geographical barriers and maintain their relationships with their dispersed families and friends. By providing migrant women access to the Internet, these places give them the freedom to choose how to control and what to do with online information and connection. This reflects the idea of empowerment as "the expansion of freedom of choice and action to shape one's life...it implies control over resources and decisions" (Narayan 2005, p. 4).

In conceiving empowerment as a process, the women's agency in enabling change in their lives is contextual, relational, and responsive to changing conditions and circumstances (Koggel 2009). It underscores the social contexts in which women operate. The empowering capacities of the Internet are embedded in the women's location, the opportunities they have as migrants, the roles of CBOs, and how their experience is affected by Thai policies and global factors, such as development support on the Thai–Burma border and international sanctions against Burma. Given this social context of restrictions and opportunities, cybercafés and CITCs allow women to decide for themselves how they will use the computer and Internet skills they have acquired, what activities they will do online, and which people they will connect with.

The emphasis on social connectivity with family members and loved ones through a constant affirmation and reaffirmation of social ties and responsibilities, by way of email, Facebook, chat, and so on, underlies the primacy of ethnic identity over other identities formed in this age of modern technology.

Burmese migrant women access cybercafés and CITCs not just to find out how their loved ones are doing but to listen to their ethnic music and Burmese music and watch old Burmese television shows on YouTube (in the case of students).

The women of the MWU go further. They consume news about the human rights violations of the Burmese government and share it with friends and CBO networks. These activities remind us of Castells' (1996) notion of the dialectic of the net and the self in the contemporary condition, wherein the self is viewed as asserting a sense of cultural identity. Whether migrant women's online activities imply a covert social movement that delegitimizes the Burmese military government is not fully proven, as the notion of using the Internet to subvert power structures underestimates the power of governments to control access to information (Wilson and Peterson 2002). What is evident is that individual Burmese migrants, although situated in a marginal context in Thailand that limits how much control they have over their lives, purposefully exercise their agency to remove barriers of political oppression by sharing news about human rights violations perpetrated by the Burmese military government, something that is completely impossible to do inside Burma. As Nu Te of MTC reported,

I'm happy that I can use the Internet. Before, in Burma, we didn't have anything, not even a cellphone. Life was very different. It was miserable and I was staying in an isolated place. It seemed like the doors to the outside world were closed. But now they're open.

Potentials and Limitations of Cybercafés and CITCs as Empowering Places

Access to cybercafés and CITCs is potentially empowering, but issues of mobility, language, cultural differences with the Thais, and cybercafé user fees emerged as barriers to access (table 12.4).

Cybercafés offer Internet access and space for migrants to practice their ICT skills and explore the Internet, but sociocultural factors inhibit open access to cybercafés. The choice of cybercafé is based primarily on the hourly rate for Internet use: the rate of 20–25 Thai Baht (about US$0.60–0.80) per hour is considered exorbitant by Burmese migrant workers, who earn below minimum wages of 80 Baht (about US$2.50) per day.

Another factor is the friendliness of the cybercafé owner and manager to Burmese migrant workers. All the cybercafés in Mae Sot are owned and managed by Thais and are considered Thai spaces patronized mainly by young men—spaces that many migrant workers are reluctant to invade.

The choice is also based on the cybercafé's proximity to the women's workplace because most migrants have no work permit, and their mobility is restricted. When they go out in public, migrants are in constant fear of harassment and extortion by the police. These difficulties are well described by SuhNii, a Mon in her early thirties who works as a librarian for the BWU. SuhNii accesses the Internet at the BWU office and sometimes goes to a cybercafé nearby. She does not feel comfortable going to cybercafés for several reasons.

> *Most Thai people look down on Burmese people. When you enter the Internet shop, the woman will look at you from head to foot to see whether you are Burmese or Thai. If you start to speak, she will know you are Burmese and she will not treat you well.... I also carry a work permit but it is written in my permit that I am a construction worker. That is why I am scared to go to a cybercafé, because the police might discover that I am working for an NGO and not in construction.*

The CITCs, in contrast, are one-stop resource centers for ICT knowledge and skills. They are development projects built as community-based centers to address the lack of training and access to ICT services among migrants. As community centers, both CCBC and KZ have been appropriated by the migrants as "safe" zones where they can escape the harassment of the Thai police. Longstanding inter-ethnic conflicts have been considered one of the reasons for the inability of these ethnic groups to overthrow the Burmese military government. In the CITCs, the camaraderie and closeness among migrant people are evident, and people ask each other for assistance during computer classes. They have been able to unite ethnic groups and erase discrimination based on ethnicity and gender. For instance, MiSeik Chan, a twenty-three-year-old Mon taking computer classes at CCBC, said:

Table 12.4
Comparison between Use of Cybercafés and CITCs

Attribute	Community ICT Training Centers: CCBC and KZ	Cybercafés: HOI and Net Day
Uses by migrants	Focused on lessons and computer training; one hour of Internet surfing is allowed after class is finished (checking email, chatting, watching videos on YouTube) Migrants come from various ethnic groups	Checking email, chatting, watching videos on YouTube, occasionally reading news on Burmese websites
Constraints	Internet access is moderated and regulated CCBC: only three public computers; migrants who don't have personal laptops use their friends' laptops during classes KZ: limited use of Internet because computers are reserved for classes Some migrants travel far to get to the CITC and are sometimes detained by the police	Most migrants are illegal and cannot freely move around Mae Sot and go to cybercafés Cybercafés are viewed as "Thai space" or domain; migrants are reluctant to communicate with Thais because of lack of Thai language skills and perception that Thai people look down on them Cybercafés are male-dominated; female migrants usually visit cybercafés in the company of two or three female friends Limited use of Internet because of fees HOI: computers are old and virus prone; keyboards are Thai and web browsers are set in Thai; downloading Burmese font is not allowed
Benefits	CITCs are viewed as "safe" spaces and Burmese domain; people can communicate with each other in Burmese; easy to ask for assistance from other Burmese people Female-dominated; more female students/CBO members attending courses Internet skills are developed beyond email and chat Provide other resource materials such as development books in Burmese and English CCBC: Allows Burmese migrants to telephone their relatives in Burma for free in emergency situations	Migrants can access Internet for a fee

I don't have a laptop so it's difficult for me to follow the lessons. I just take notes and draw the computer in my notebook. During class, my friend, who is Karen, shares her laptop with me, and the teacher sometimes lets me use his laptop during exercises. I feel at home here and we are all friends and we try to help each other.

Unfortunately, there are only two CITCs in Mae Sot, a number that is insufficient to serve a population of more than one hundred thousand migrants. In addition, the CITCs offer only limited and regulated use of computers and the Internet, thereby hindering the growth and penetration of the Internet among migrants.

Mediated Access Migrant women who use the Internet in CBO offices exhibit more advanced ICT skills and are able to conduct more activities online. They use email to contact their loved ones as well as their funders, partners, and network organizations. They maintain their organization's website and use the Internet to advance political advocacy, education, and income-generation projects. Cybercafé and CITC users, in contrast, have limited Internet skills and use the Internet mainly for email and web browsing.

The women's level of ICT skills depends on the support they receive from their organizations. Private Internet users generally belong to CBOs that are relatively large and financially stable. As staff or interns, they have taken several computer/Internet courses and have unlimited Internet connection in their offices.

Cybercafé and CITC users generally belong to smaller, more informal CBOs with limited or no access to computers or the Internet, which explains why they patronize cybercafés and CITCs. These women have taken short courses and informal Internet lessons from friends. However, access to cybercafés and CITCs alone is not enough to allow them to fully exploit the Internet's potential. Migrant women need quality ICT education that is programmatic and holistic. Their access to PAVs should involve some knowledge of technology, as well as a facility and experience level that embraces the technical as well as the social aspects of Internet-based media and the implications of technology on a wider scale (Wilson and Peterson 2002).

The unequal ICT support that organizations are able to provide for their staff reflects a socioeconomic stratification within the migrant community that affects access to and use of ICT. In the absence of an explicit ICT policy from the Thai state, marginalized groups continue to suffer from limited access to ICT and ICT education.

While the larger and more stable CBOs offer ICT training opportunities, access is restricted. Affiliation with these CBOs is based on ethnicity and is competitive. For instance, the Karen Women's Organization (KWO) and the Palaung Women's

Organization (PWO) offer internships to six to ten students per year but only to migrants who are staff or interns; others only have the option of short ICT courses.

There is also an urgent need for basic and advanced education in numeracy and literacy. Only a minority of migrants are relatively well off. They include professional staff in CBOs and NGOs as well as hotel and restaurant employees, most of whom are college graduates with stable salaries that allow them to acquire better ICT education and computer and Internet connection in their homes and workplaces. The majority of migrants, however, are factory workers and women from farming villages in Burma who have completed only primary or secondary education (Kusakabe and Pearson 2010). Most are illegal workers in factories or on construction sites.

Women Users of Internet in CBO Offices The migrant women who use the Internet in CBO offices are from KWO, PWO, and BWU. Compared with other CBOs in Mae Sot, these organizations are large and relatively stable. Each employs fifteen to twenty staff members and offers several programs, such as education, consciousness-raising, training and capacity building, networking, publication, and economic development.

Most of the women working in these CBOs are in their early to late twenties and single, and they have either finished ten standard education or have reached college. They are either employed in leadership positions within their CBO or are completing internships that typically lead to employment with the CBO. Their work involves heavy computer and Internet use, so they typically participate in several intensive internship programs with computer courses provided by their own and other organizations. These programs run from six months to one year. Courses are offered in Microsoft Office, Adobe programs (Photoshop, PageMaker, InDesign, etc.), movie editing, and CD/DVD burning. Participants use these programs to write reports; design posters, leaflets, fliers, and banners; and maintain their organizations' websites.

The women use computers in their offices, and some have personal laptops. As staff and interns, they live in or near the CBO offices and have unlimited Internet access. They are online more than ten hours per week. Compared with women who use cybercafés and CITCs, they have more time to explore the Internet and often spend their leisure time checking their email, chatting, writing blogs, reading and listening to news, watching movies, downloading and uploading music videos (see table 12.5).

Some of these women have visited cybercafés in the early stages of their ICT learning and now use cybercafés occasionally (e.g., if the Internet connection in their office is slow or not working properly and they need to email something urgently). They leave the cybercafé when they have finished their tasks.

Table 12.5
Comparison of Internet Use in Public Venues and Private Venues (CBO Offices)

Attribute	Public Venues (Cybercafés and CITCs)	Private Venues (CBO Offices)
Access to computer/ Internet	Users do not own computers/ laptops Limited Internet access; users depend on friends' computers, CITCs, and cybercafés to access Internet Use computer/Internet three hours/week	Users have personal laptops Unlimited Internet access; Internet is available 24 hours/day Use computer/Internet 10 hours/ week
Use of Internet in public	CITCs for ICT lessons, and cybercafés for practice of ICT lessons	Accessed cybercafés in the initial stages of ICT learning
Use of Internet	Email: contact relatives and friends; communicate and share information with funders, partners, networks, and supporters Social networking: meet new friends outside Mae Sot Web surfing: visit Burmese websites and watch Burmese music videos on YouTube	Email: contact relatives, friends, office mates, funders, partners, networks, and supporters; communicate and share information (photos, videos, music files, web links, funding applications and reports, etc.) Social networking: communicate with relatives, friends, partners, networks, and supporters Web surfing: visit news websites like Kwekalu, Burma Today, Irrawaddy, BBC, DVB, VOA Political advocacy Livelihood Information/education

The women rely on the Internet for communication and use Gmail, Yahoo Mail, Gchat, Yahoo Messenger, Skype, Facebook, and Hi5 to communicate.

As part of their work on networking, linkages, and political and social advocacy, CBO staff women regularly visit news websites such as Kwekalu, Burma Today, Irrawaddy, BBC, DVB, and VOA. They use these websites to obtain and contribute news about current events in Burma and Mae Sot as well as the activities of CBOs. They also share this news on their CBOs' websites, to which they also upload their posters, brochures, and books.

The women also use the Internet for livelihood opportunities (e.g., using their websites to advertise handicraft products from their income-generation projects or searching for handicraft designs online) and as an information and education resource (e.g., for improving their English language skills by learning English words and grammar or for acquiring information about human rights and women's rights, health issues, and Burmese popular culture).

Dependence on Mobile Phones The use of cellphones and the Internet shows contextual divides. The Internet is context dependent (i.e., it can be used only in specific places such as cybercafés, CITCs, NGO offices, and private homes). It requires basic levels of literacy and numeracy, computer and Internet skills, and Thai, Burmese, and English language skills. Migrants in Mae Sot rely more heavily on cellphones than on the Internet for communication because phone technology is less dependent on context.

Although the benefits of mobile phone use are not as wide reaching as those of Internet use, they have nevertheless empowered migrant women. The positive aspects of mobile phones include minimal support requirement in learning the technology, affordability, and portability. Migrants rely on cell phones to set up and coordinate meetings and activities, and they use text messaging to mobilize their peers to rally in support of certain issues (women's rights, reproductive and sexual rights, economic rights, etc.). They get news updates about Burma during phone conversations with relatives and friends in that country.

Mobiles also empower women economically. Women can use a cellphone to ask for financial assistance from relatives abroad or to coordinate with other CBOs and NGOs to implement income-generation projects such as handicraft production.

Mobiles also have a social empowerment effect. Safety and security are important for migrants in Mae Sot, and in that context, communication with family and secondarily with CBOs/NGOs is crucial. Cellphones provide immediate communication and allow users to maintain their social ties to loved ones outside Mae Sot (in other Thai provinces, in Burma, and in third countries). Women can easily contact their husbands or boyfriends, children, other relatives, and friends. In the workplace, cellphones allow easy access to funders such as international donor agencies and partners such as NGOs, CBOs, and church groups.

In terms of cultural empowerment, mobile phones are used to express ethnic identity through ringtones and to facilitate the exchange of cultural goods (e.g., traditional dresses such as the sarong, food such as fish paste and tea, cosmetic items such as thanaka, and other goods) with relatives and friends in third countries.

Conclusions and Recommendations

Access to and use of the Internet has provided ethnic women with opportunities for new ways of communication that were not available to them while they were still living in Burma. This access is constrained by security issues, cybercafé user rates, language barriers, cultural differences, low literacy and numeracy skills, lack of ICT education, and shortage of CITCs and Burmese-friendly cybercafés. As a result, only a handful of computer and Internet literate migrants—perhaps fewer than 10 percent of the total migrant population—access public venues and are able to use computers and the Internet regularly.[9]

The absence of an ICT policy and programs addressing the specific needs of migrants, the different educational and professional backgrounds of migrants, and the Thai state's strict policies toward migrants further limit the extent of Internet use among displaced peoples. While Thailand offers sophisticated communication media to its people, it deliberately excludes migrants, who rely more on mobile phones rather than the Internet, as phone technology is less dependent on sociopolitical context.[10] The great ICT challenge on the Thai–Burma border, where thousands of Burmese continue to cross into Thailand, is to increase Internet penetration among migrants by addressing these limitations.

The few existing CITCs and migrant-friendly cybercafés help satisfy the needs of migrant women for Internet education and access. The CITCs are used for computer and Internet training and the cybercafés for practicing Internet skills. The CITCs are an important source of ICT knowledge and expertise for the migrant community. The ways the Burmese ethnic people have contextually localized and appropriated the CITCs to meet specific objectives, ICT-related or otherwise, present an interesting overlap of a development project with ICT entrepreneurship activities (source for web designers, computer system operators, PC troubleshooters, PC assemblers, etc.), political advocacy, and social unity among ethnic groups. In these specific social environments, ICT diffusion is related not just to development but also clearly to economic and other ventures (Rangaswamy 2007).

In order for ICT to penetrate the Burmese community, cybercafés and CITCs, which are beneficial and complementary to each other, should be increased and adapted for migrants. The developmental nature of CITCs should incorporate the business aspects of cybercafés, and cybercafés can play a complementary role to CITCs. As a commercial venture, potentially run by migrant women or even CBOs, CITCs could be a source of income and be self-sustaining with minimal development assistance.

Moreover, computer and Internet education needs to be comprehensive. Programmatic ICT education needs to be developed and implemented through the cooperation of NGOs, private sector agencies, and the Thai state. Infrastructure development should also take place, notably through an increase in the number of CITCs and cybercafés and the translation of computer software programs into local languages. In addition, because cellphones are by far the easiest technology to accommodate, the ICT industry should develop or allow cheap, Internet-enabled cellphones (such as those available in China). Currently, mobile Internet is offered only on smart phones, which are beyond the financial reach of migrant workers.

There is also a need for NGOs and international agencies to urge the Thai government to change its policies toward migrants and implement ICT policies for marginalized non-Thais living in Thailand. Without these changes, ICT penetration among migrants cannot progress significantly.

Finally, one of the greatest challenges in harnessing ICT for the social transformation of women is to see the women not simply as consumers but as ICT producers, developers, and decision makers in order to promote the equal participation of women in the information society (Kuga Thas, Garcia Ramilo, and Cinco 2007). Although CITCs are open to both men and women, and both CCBC and KZ have more female students than male, there is no program that addresses the specific ICT needs and demands of women, such as building knowledge around female gender and sexual health and rights even when these subjects are well covered in workshops and training and internship programs offered by women's CBOs. CITC education programs should address specific women's needs (Jorge 2000). Currently, the two CITCs for migrants in Mae Sot merely provide ICT skills training and assume that once they have acquired and developed these skills, women (as well as men) can apply them in conducting online advocacy for human rights and women's rights. The pool of Burmese ICT experts who are being trained by CCBC is all male, and women's role in ICT development for Burmese migrants is merely that of recipients or consumers of ICT. *This state of affairs makes no sense.*

The Internet has been highly successful in enabling change. The current dynamic networking of ICT enthusiastic migrant women, coupled with the implementation of the specified recommendations, augurs well for a greater transformation of their lives: from being marginalized because of their gender to being empowered by ICT, not merely as consumers but as developers and active agents in determining how the technology will be appropriated to meet their personal objectives and reshape their future.

Notes

1. In this research, we refer to the Republic of the Union of Myanmar by its former name, Burma, out of respect for the ethnic groups that participated in this research.

2. BBC interview of Aung San Suu Kyi from which this quote is taken may be viewed online. It starts around minute 9 in the following clip: http://www.youtube.com/watch?v=jFSE6BfBksY/.

3. Thailand's ten refugee camps host about 150,000 people, of which about 80,000 live in the three camps in Tak province. Members of the Karen ethnic group comprise 61 percent of the refugees. In the same period, the United Nations High Commissioner for Refugees (UNHCR) recorded 102,418 registered refugees, half of whom (about as many men as women) were staying in the three camps. (UNHCR data is for June 2010 available from The Border Consortium website: http://theborderconsortium.org/camps/2010-06-jun-map-tbbc-unhcr.pdf). Many of them remain in the camps; they cannot get across the borders and have become internally displaced persons (IDPs) inside Burma (McGeown 2007).

4. There are 150 to 200 factories, both registered and unregistered, employing thousands of factory workers. The textile and garment factories alone employ some 80,000 migrants. This is in addition to an estimated 100,000 migrants who are wage workers in other factories, agriculture, hotels, shops, restaurants, construction, domestic service, and a number of other jobs (Arnold 2007).

5. According to the Committee for Coordination of Services to Displaced Persons in Thailand (http://www.ccsdpt.org/our-members), NGOs providing humanitarian and development support to refugees in Thailand include:
ADRA (Adventist Development and Relief Agency)
AMI (Aide Médicale Internationale)
ARC (ARC International)
COERR (Catholic Office Emergency Relief and Refugees)
HI (Handicap International)
IRC (International Rescue Committee)
JRS (Jesuit Refugee Service)
MI (Malteser International)
NCA (Norwegian Church Aid)
RTP (Right to Play)
Ruammit-DARE
Solidarités International
SVA (Shanti Volunteer Association)
TBBC (Thailand Burma Border Consortium)
TOPS (Taipei Overseas Peace Service)
WE (World Education)
WEAVE (Women's Education for Advancement and Empowerment)
ZOA (ZOA Refugee Care Netherlands)
The following NGOs/CBOs focus on migrants:

AWU (Arakan Workers' Union)
BLC (Burma Lawyers' Council)
BLSO (Burma Labor Solidarity Organization)
BMWEC (Burmese Migrant Workers Education Committee)
BWU (Burmese Women's Union)
FTUB (Federation of Trade Unions—Burma)
HRDP (Human Resource Development Program)
HREIB (Human Rights Education Institute of Burma)
MTC (Mae Tao Clinic)
NDD (Network for Democracy and Development)
OIA (Overseas Irrawaddy Association)
YCOWA (Yaung Chi Oo Workers' Association)

6. Data is from Mae Sot municipal office and venue survey results.

7. For a comprehensive discussion of feminism and empowerment, see Sen and Grown (1987), Rai (2007), and Sen (1990).

8. Many migrants formerly stayed in refugee camps, where they were issued UNHCR identification entitling them to be resettled to third countries such as the United States, Canada, and Australia, as well as European countries.

9. Based on demography and statistics, only a few hundred migrants have taken computer classes at the CITCs. Comparing this number with the more than 130,000 migrant workers in Mae Sot, most of them women who have completed secondary education, it is safe to conclude that fewer than 10 percent of migrants are able to access and use computers and the Internet.

10. Raul Pertierra, who has conducted extensive research on mobile phone use in the Philippines (see e.g., Pertierra et al. 2003), gave technical advice in support of this study. He noted that in comparing use of mobile phones and the Internet, it is important to realize that Burmese migrant women in Thailand are more dependent on context because: (1) refugees are excluded from using the Internet, (2) the Burmese need technical and social skills to be able to use the Internet, and (3) most of the cybercafés are accessible physically but not culturally.

References

Arnold, Dennis. 2007. *Capital Expansion and Migrant Workers: Flexible Labor in the Thai-Burma Border Economy. Human Rights in Asia Series*. Bangkok: Mahidol University, Office of Human Rights Studies and Social Development, Faculty of Graduate Studies.

Askew, Marc. 2002. *Bangkok: Place, Practice, and Representation*. London: Routledge Press.

Aung, Zaw. 2010. *Burmese Labour Rights Protection in Mae Sot*. Bangkok: Chulalongkorn University, Center for Social Development Studies.

Castells, Manuel. 1996. *The Rise of the Network Society: The Information Age: Economy, Society and Culture, Volume 1*. Malden, MA: Blackwell.

International Telecommunications Union (ITU). 2013. Statistics webpage. Geneva: ITU. http://www.itu.int/en/ITU-D/Statistics/Pages/stat/default.aspx?utm_source=twitterfeed&utm_medium=twitter/.

Jorge, Sonia. 2000. Gender Perspectives on Telecenters. Paper presented at ITU Telecom Americas 2000 Telecom Development Symposium on Communications, Universal Access and Community Telecenters, Rio de Janeiro, April 11. http://www.bridge.ids.ac.uk/docs/jorge_telecenters.pdf.

Kabeer, Naila, and Ramya Subrahmanian, eds. 1999. *Institutions, Relations and Outcomes: Framework and Tools for Gender-Aware Planning*. Delhi: Kali for Women Publishers and ZedPress (UK).

Koggel, Christine M. 2009. Agency and Empowerment: Embodied Realities in a Globalized World. In *Embodiment and Agency*, ed. Sue Campbell, Susan Sherwin, and Letitia Maynell, 250–267. University Park, PA: Pennsylvania State University Press.

Kuga Thas, Angela, Chat Garcia Ramilo, and Cheekay Cinco. 2007. *Gender and ICT. United Nations Development Programme—Asia-Pacific Development Information Programme and Association for Progressive Communications (Melville, South Africa)*. New Delhi: Elsevier.

Kusakabe, Kyoko, and Ruth Pearson. 2010. Transborder Migration, Social Reproduction and Economic Development: A Case Study of Burmese Women Workers in Thailand. *International Migration (Geneva, Switzerland)* 48 (6): 13–43.

McGeon, Kate. 2007. Life on the Burma-Thai Border. BBC news item, February 26. http://news.bbc.co.uk/2/hi/asia-pacific/6397243.stm.

Moser, Caroline O. N. 1993. *Gender Planning and Development: Theory, Practice and Training*. London, New York: Routledge Press.

Narayan, Deepa. 2005. *Measuring Empowerment: Cross-Disciplinary Perspectives*. Washington, DC: World Bank.

National Electronics and Computer Technology. 2009. *Internet User Profile of Thailand 2009*. Bangkok: Author.

Nsibirano, Ruth. 2009. Him and Her—Gender Differentials in ICT Uptake: A Critical Literature Review and Research Agenda. *International Journal of Education and Development Using Information and Communication Technology* 5 (5): 33–42.

Pertierra, Raul, Eduardo F. Ugarte, Alicia Pingol, Joel Hernandez, and Nikos Dacanay. 2003. *Txting Selves: Cellphones and Philippine Modernity*. Manila: De La Salle University Press.

Rai, Shirin M. 2007. (Re)defining Empowerment, Measuring Survival. Paper prepared for workshop on Empowerment: Obstacles, Flaws, Achievements, 3–5. Ottawa, Canada: Carleton University, May. http://www.ethicsofempowerment.org/papers/RaiEmpowerment.pdf.

Rangaswamy, Nimmi. 2007. ICT for Development and Commerce: A Case Study of Internet Cafés in India. In *Proceedings of the 9th International Conference on Social Implications of Computers in Developing Countries*. São Paulo, Brazil, May. http://www.ifipwg94.org.br/fullpapers/R0071-1.pdf.

Santipaporn, Sureerat. 2010. Information and Communication Technology Statistics in Thailand. Paper presented at International Seminar on Information and Communication Technology Statistics. Seoul, Korea, July 19–21. http://unstats.un.org/unsd/economic_stat/ICT-Korea/Documents/Santipaporn_Thailand.pdf.

Sen, Gita, and Caren Grown. 1987. *Development Crises and Alternative Visions: Third World Women's Perspectives*. New York: Monthly Review Press.

Sirirachatapong, Pansak, and Kasititorn Pooparadai. 2007. ICT for Happiness in Thailand: Revisiting Past, Understanding Present, and Envisioning Future Roles of NECTEC. Paper presented at the International Conference on Happiness and Public Policy. Bangkok, July 18–19. http://www.happysociety.org/ppdoconference/session_papers/session19/session19_pansak.pdf.

Thailand Information Center. 2008. *Internet Café Survey—Report 2008* [in Thai]. Bangkok: Center of Academic Resources, Chulalongkorn University.

Wilson, Samuel M., and Leighton C. Peterson. 2002. The Anthropology of Online Communities. *AR Reviews in Advance* 31: 449–467.

IV A Place to Learn, a Place to Play, a Place to Dream, a Place to Fall from Grace

13 Public Access Impact and Policy Implications

Francisco J. Proenza
with the collaboration of Erwin A. Alampay, Roxana Barrantes, Hernán Galperín, Abiodun Jagun, George Sciadas, Ramata Molo Thioune, and Kentaro Toyama

Abstract

This chapter summarizes the findings of previous chapters and, for completeness, also draws on significant findings from prior studies in search of patterns of use and impact that apply across countries and inform public access policy. Three themes emerge.

First, public access enables most users to achieve personal objectives such as learning, communicating with family and friends, enhancing work skills and job prospects (Rwanda), and entertaining themselves (China). Not all impacts are positive: overuse can adversely affect school performance (Cameroon) and personal life spheres (China).

Second, public access enables users to expand their social networks and build up social capital (Malaysia, Jordan), facilitates social inclusion (Argentina), and makes it easier for rural grassroots organizations to develop specific capacities, such as interacting with external agents (Peru).

Third, although women and underprivileged groups can benefit significantly, their access to the most ubiquitous type of venue, cybercafés, is frequently limited, in some countries severely. This major obstacle must be overcome if public access benefits are to be widespread and equitable.

The chapter ends with a discussion of policy design considerations regarding mobiles and public access, information and communication technology (ICT) skills training, telecenter establishment, cybercafé regulation, and options for redressing cybercafé gender imbalance.

Introduction

Cybercafés thrive in urban areas, but their survival is challenged in the rural setting (Instituto Nacional de Estadistica e Informática 2008; Proenza 2001, 2006a, 2006b; Proenza, Bastidas-Buch, and Montero 2001; Stern, Townsend, and Monedero 2007). Two other common venue types are libraries, usually funded and operated by government, and telecenters, generally government funded and run by various institutions such as nongovernmental organizations (NGOs), universities, and local government.

Figure 13.1 gives an overview of the public access landscape based on data primarily from Gomez (2012). The overwhelming dominance of cybercafés stands out: in

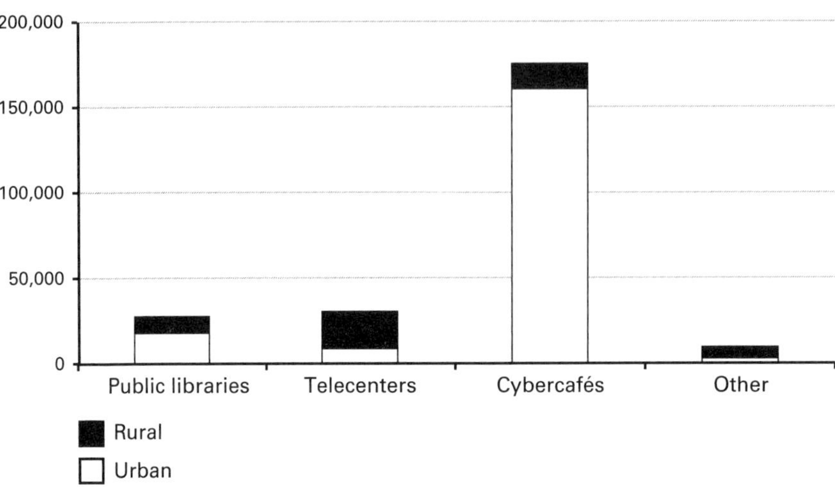

Figure 13.1
Distribution of public access in 25 landscape study countries, by venue type (Gomez 2012).

eighteen of the twenty-five countries considered, there are more cybercafés than libraries and telecenters combined.[1]

Public access has universal appeal as a low-cost way of providing widespread access to technology by sharing resources. Johan Ernberg (1997, 1998), the conceptual father of telecenters as instruments of development policy, was a driving force behind pilot initiatives of the International Telecommunications Union (ITU) that established multipurpose community telecenters, which would provide a broad range of information and communication technology (ICT)-enabled services traditionally lacking in rural communities. Service aggregation would enhance impact and generate the revenue needed to ensure sustainability. The International Development Research Centre (IDRC) was another early player, sponsoring action-oriented research and the formation of telecenter networks (Gomez 1999).

Significant public investments have been made, mainly in rural telecenters, under the presumption that the better-substantiated impacts of Internet use can be obtained through public access. Some negative effects have been observed, usually in connection with urban cybercafés, and have been used to justify operational restrictions. Research on socioeconomic impacts has been sparse and scattered and has seldom informed public access policy.

This chapter aims to help fill this gap. It summarizes the findings of ten research studies on three continents, covering urban cybercafés in seven countries, telecenters in four rural and four urban settings, and community ICT training centers (CITCs) in two countries (table 13.1). CITCs are not public access venues (PAVs) because they are not open to the public at large, but because they provide comparable ICT skills training services they are often considered to be telecenters and thus are often counted as such in formal surveys. Libraries are not covered, which is unfortunate because there is at least one exemplary library experience, in Chile (Salas, Yacometti, and Bustos 2005; Román and Guerrero 2005), and there may be more. A mix of quantitative and qualitative analyses were used, but the dominant approach was qualitative in four countries and quantitative in six (table 13.1).

Table 13.2 presents basic features that can affect computer and Internet use in our ten study countries and in another six countries. Myanmar (formerly Burma) is included because it is the country of origin of the migrants in our Thailand study. Sri Lanka has had a significant telecenter project underway since 2005 (741 telecenters as of 2013) and has generated useful indicators (Proenza 2008; Shadrach 2013; Skill International Private Limited 2010). The Global Impact Study (GIS) conducted valuable surveys in one of our study countries, Chile, and in four other countries: Bangladesh, Brazil, Ghana, and the Philippines (Sciadas et al. 2012; Sey et al. 2013; Survey Working Group 2012).

In the countries listed in table 13.2, the mobile and Internet penetration frontiers are in rural areas. The access challenge is formidable where the majority of people live in rural areas: Thailand (66 percent), Myanmar (67 percent), India (68 percent), Rwanda (81 percent), and Sri Lanka (85 percent). Low literacy rates pose another obstacle to expanding computer and Internet use in Bangladesh (58 percent), India (63 percent), Ghana (71 percent), Cameroon (71 percent), and Rwanda (66 percent).

Growth in mobile phone use has been phenomenal in the past decade, but Internet use also grew quite rapidly (table 13.2). In fact, in the last five years, 2008–2013, Internet penetration grew as fast or faster than mobile phone subscriptions in ten of the sixteen countries considered: Argentina, Chile, Bangladesh, Jordan, China, Ghana, India, Philippines, Sri Lanka, and Thailand.[2]

Use and User Features

Age and Gender

Public access users are young. Chile has a relatively higher number of elderly users (7.3 percent older than age 50), but users younger than age 25 represent 56 percent of all public access users (table 13.3), a high number considering this age group accounts for only 39 percent of the country's population (table 13.2). Users under 25 represent 76 percent of cybercafé users in China, 64 percent in Jordan, and 59 percent in Uttar

Table 13.1
Country Studies, by Rural-Urban Status, Type of Venue, Dominant Data Approach, and Theoretical Framework Used

Chapter	Region / Study Country	Urban (U)/ Rural (R)	Type of Venue: Café	Telecenter	CITC	Dominant Approach	Data Gathered	Theoretical Framework
Africa and Middle East								
2	Jordan	U	X			Quant	336 users of 24 cybercafés	Perceptions of impact
3	Rwanda	U R	X	X		Quant	418 white-collar workers	Logic model of training
6	Cameroon	R		X		Quant	1,015 secondary students/ 5 telecenters	Theories of education
Asia								
4 & 5	China	U	X			Quant	975 users of 22 cybercafés; 964 nonusers of Internet	Self-determination & PIU theories
8	Malaysia	R		X		Quant	299 users of 15 centers	Connectedness
10	India	U	X			Quant	100 women users of 2 cafés; 100 women nonusers	Gender analysis
12	Thailand	U	X		X	Qual	31 Burmese migrant women users, 3 nonusers; 2 Focus groups of users, 5 Focus groups of nonusers	Empowerment theories
Latin America								
7	Argentina	U	X		X	Qual	1 cybercafé, 2 CITCs	Comparative sociology
9	Peru	U R	X	X		Qual	9 community-based organizations	Lusthaus et al. theory of organizational capacities
11	Chile	U		X		Qual	2 telecenters	Grounded theory/ gender analysis

Table 13.2
Basic Features of Study Countries and Other Selected Countries

		Population			Mobile Subscriptions[e]		Individual Use of the Internet[e]		Adult Literacy rate (% adults > 15)[c,g]	Per Capita Income (PPP) (2012 $)[c]
Region/Country[a]		Millions (2013)[b]	% rural (2012)[c]	% age < 25[d]	As % of 2013 pop.[f]	5-yr % annual Δ[e]	As % of 2013 pop.[f]	5-yr % annual Δ[e]		
Africa and Middle East										
1	Cameroon	22	47	62	70	17	6	13	71	2,550
2	Rwanda	12	81	64	57	34	9	14	66	1,390
3	Jordan	7	17	54	142	10	44	14	96	11,420
	Ghana	26	47	58	108	17	12	24	71	3,510
Asia										
4	China	1,386	48	37	89	13	46	15	95	10,900
5	India	1,252	68	50	71	19	15	28	63	5,080
6	Malaysia	30	27	48	145	7	67	4	93	25,430
7	Thailand	67	66	37	138	8	29	10	94	13,270
	Myanmar	53	67	45	13	78	1	40	93	n.a.
	Bangladesh	157	71	51	67	17	7	21	58	2,640
	Philippines	98	51	58	105	7	37	43	95	6,170
	Sri Lanka	21	85	40	96	12	22	30	91	8,840
Latin America										
8	Argentina	41	7	42	159	6	66	16	98	n.a.
9	Chile	18	11	39	134	9	67	12	99	20,450
10	Peru	30	22	49	98	6	39	5	90	11,070
	Brazil	200	15	43	135	11	52	9	90	14,320

Notes and sources:

[a]Study countries are those numbered 1 through 10.

[b]Population: UNFPA 2013.

[c]Percent rural population, literacy rates, and purchasing power parity gross national income per capita: World Bank Indicators 2014.

[d]% age < 25: 2010 estimate, www.wolframalpha.com.

[e]Annual equivalent rates of growth in penetration rates for the period 2008–2013 for both mobiles and Internet use calculated using ITU 2013 data.

[f]% of individuals using the Internet and mobile subscriptions as % of population are from ITU 2013 data.

[g]Literacy rates are from various estimates 2005–2012.

Table 13.3
Use of Public Access Venues, by Age: Global Impact Study Survey Countries

Age	Bangladesh	Brazil	Chile	Ghana	Philippines
≤ 19	27.8	49.0	33.7	31.3	59.7
20–24	32.1	23.2	22.3	35.1	25.2
25–50	38.6	26.0	36.7	32.6	14.7
> 50	2.6	1.8	7.3	1.0	0.4
Total	100.0	100.0	100.0	100.0	100.0

Source: Sciadas, Lyons, Rothschild, and Sey (2012).

Table 13.4
Age and Gender Composition of Cybercafé Users in Three Study Countries

Age	Male (%)	Female (%)	Total (%)
China*			
≤ 19	12	5	17
19 to < 25	44	16	59
25 to < 49	17	6	23
Subtotal	73	27	100
Jordan*			
≤ 19	17	4	21
20–24	32	12	43
25–49	18	7	26
49+	9	1	10
Subtotal	76	24	100
India—Uttar Pradesh (initial survey)**			
≤ 19	18	–	18
19 to < 25	39	2	41
25 to < 49	38	1	39
49+	2	–	2
Subtotal	97	3	100

*See China and Jordan chapters.
**The initial India survey covered 298 users of two cybercafés.

Pradesh, India (table 13.4). Users of rural telecenters are also young: those ages 25 and under account for 57 percent of Malaysia's Rural Information Center (RIC) users and 78 percent of Sri Lanka's Nenasala users (table 13.5).

Women represent 27 percent of cybercafé users surveyed in China, 24 percent in Jordan, and 3 percent in Uttar Pradesh (table 13.4). There are within-country

Table 13.5
Age and Gender Composition of Rural Telecenter Users in Malaysia and Sri Lanka

Age	Male (%)	Female (%)	Total (%)
Malaysia—RIC users*			
≤ 17	4	11	15
18–24	12	30	42
25–50	18	20	37
> 50	3	2	5
Subtotal	37	63	100
Sri Lanka—Nenasala users**			
< 11	1	1	2
12–25	29	47	76
> 26	7	15	22
Subtotal	37	63	100

*See Malaysia chapter.
**1,008 users of Sri Lanka's Nenasalas (Skill International Private Unlimited 2010).

differences: for instance, in seven of the twenty-four cybercafés surveyed in Amman, women accounted for 59 percent of users. These seven cafés are situated near the University of Jordan or in upper middle-class neighborhoods. In the remaining seventeen cybercafés, male user dominance is overwhelming (87 percent). In China, in only one of the twenty cybercafés sampled were women in the majority (54 percent), and in only three did the proportion of women users reach 40 percent.

Telecenters are apparently more gender inclusive. About 63 percent of Malaysia's RIC users are women. A high proportion of women users is also found in Sri Lanka's Nenasalas (Skill International Private Limited 2010). In both of these countries, however, women users are underrepresented in cybercafés: 20 percent in Malaysia (Shah Alam and Abdullah 2009) and 26 percent in Sri Lanka (Gomez 2009).

Figure 13.2 shows the gender distribution of cybercafé users in twenty-three countries.[3] With two exceptions (Mongolia and Kazakhstan), survey after survey points to a gender imbalance that is quite acute in some countries in Asia and the Middle East. Aggregating over these twenty-three countries, women as a proportion of users account for 39 percent in cybercafés, 43 percent in telecenters, and 51 percent in libraries.

Distance to Venue

In China, 91 percent of users travel two kilometers or less to the venue they visit regularly, 83 percent one kilometer or less, and 67 percent five hundred meters, or about a ten-minute walk. Women use cybercafés that are slightly closer to home than men.

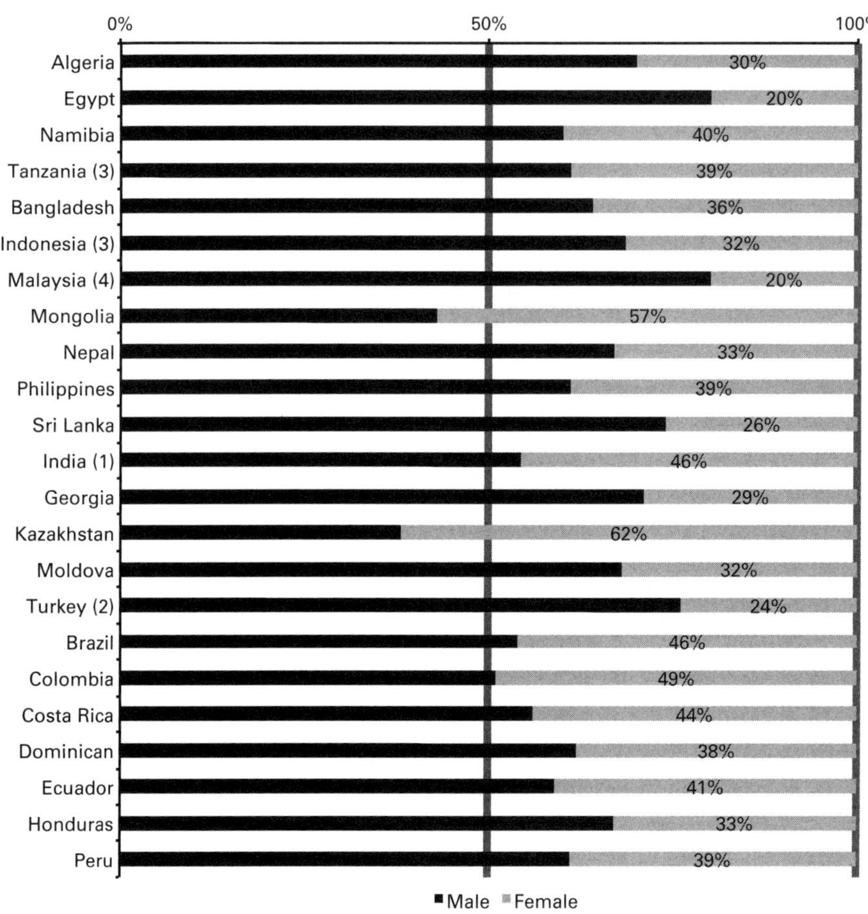

Figure 13.2
Gender distribution of users in select urban cybercafés.

Nearly 14 percent of China's rural residents who visit urban cafés travel more than two kilometers from home, compared with 8 percent of urban residents. Users in Jordan travel longer distances than those in China. In contrast to China and even Peru in 2000 (Proenza, Bastidas-Buch, and Montero 2001), women in Amman travel farther to visit cybercafés than men do (table 13.6) perhaps because of the limited number of "women-friendly" cybercafés.

Places of Access

Although it has a limited number of telecenters and Internet equipped libraries, China probably has more PAVs than any other country in the world—around 144,000 (Kan

Table 13.6
Distance Traveled to Cybercafés in Jordan and China in 2010 and in Peru in 2000 and to Telecenters in Sri Lanka in 2010

Jordan 2010*	Male (%)	Female (%)	
< 1 km	44	31	
1–2 km	31	39	
2–5 km	20	21	
> 5 km	6	9	
China 2010*	Urban male (%)	Urban female (%)	Rural users (%)
< 1 km	84.7	85.3	75.8
1–2 km	7.0	7.1	10.5
> 2 km	8.3	7.6	13.7
Peru 2000**	Male (%)	Female (%)	
< 1 km	45	42	
1–5 km	36	36	
> 5 km	20	22	
Sri Lanka 2010***		All users (%)	
< 1 km		59	
1–2 km		10	
2–5 km		15	
> 5 km		15	

*See Jordan and China chapters.
**Proenza, Bastidas Bush, and Montero (2001).
***Skill International Private Limited (2010).

2011) to 170,000 (Junlong Culture Communication 2010) net bars, as cybercafés are locally known, most of them located in urban centers in eastern China. This figure is not far from the 183,000 calculated by the Landscape Study (Gomez 2009, 2012) for twenty-three countries. By the end of 2008, China had 298 million Internet users, and the proportion of users connecting from net bars reached a peak of 42.4 percent (China Internet Network Information Center 2009). By the end of 2012, the number of Internet users had risen to 564 million (an increase of nearly 90 percent in four years), and the proportion connecting from net bars had declined to 22.4 percent (China Internet Network Information Center 2013).

Access preferences of China's net bar users are similar to those observed in relatively wealthier countries such as Brazil or Chile (table 13.7). Public access users in all three countries frequently connect from cybercafés and home; the main differences are the number of options used and the relative importance of connection from schools and

Table 13.7
Places of Access Most Often Used by Internet Users of China's Urban Cybercafés and by Internet Users of PAVs in GIS Countries (%)

	China*	Bangladesh**	Brazil**	Chile**	Ghana**	Philippines**
Cybercafé	52	43	52	31	82	81
Telecenter	–	41	8	9	1	3
Library	–	–	2	25	1	5
Home	23	9	31	20	10	7
Office/work	4	4	4	5	3	2
School	15	2	1	2	3	3
Friend's house	1	–	2	3	1	–
Other	5	–	1	6	–	–
Total	100	100	100	100	100	100

Notes: Percentages for China represent users of Urban cybercafés interviewed, whereas the calculations for the five GIS countries cover all types of venues and the whole country.
* The China column was calculated for a subsample of 760 observations of cybercafé users (of the total sample of 976) who selected the options listed either as their sole predominant place or in combination with mobiles as a predominant place. The observations not considered exhibit more complex patterns, either with more than two predominant places or with no predominant place of access.
For China, the "Other" category represents the proportion of café users who connect from mobiles as sole predominant place. Note, however, that of the 726 observations with a predominant place other than mobiles, 64% connect to the Internet from their mobiles at least occasionally.
** Sciadas et al. (2012).

mobiles. The proportion of public access users who also connect to the Internet from schools is 15 percent in China but only 2 percent in Chile and 1 percent in Brazil. In China, about 25 percent of cybercafé users interviewed connect to the Internet "every time" or "most of the time" using their mobile and about 64 percent at least occasionally. Overall, Internet users in China have many access options: about 90 percent connect from their home and 81 percent using their mobile (China Internet Network Information Center 2014).

Public access users with up to two years of computer experience represent 53 percent of users in Bangladesh, 23 percent in Brazil, 17 percent in Chile, 25 percent in Ghana, and 24 percent in the Philippines (Sciadas et al. 2012). Given China's low overall Internet penetration (from table 13.2: 46 percent in 2013), we expected to observe a similar pattern in our survey of 976 users, but, in practice, only 6 percent of Chinese users interviewed had two years or less of Internet experience whereas 80 percent had five years or more.[4]

What comes across from our Chinese sample of experienced urban cybercafé users is that when options are available, a complex pattern of Internet access and use develops (tables 13.8a, 13.8b, and 13.8c). Thirty percent listed net bars as their sole predominant place of connection and used them either every time or most of the time. An additional 11 percent were predominant users of both cafés and mobiles. Some users connected "every time" or "most of the time" from one or two venues other than cybercafés (e.g., about 18 percent from home, 12 percent from school, and 3.3 percent from the office, table 13.8c). Only 9 percent used net bars *exclusively* (table 13.8b). Men were more frequent users of net bars than women, and women users were more likely than men to connect to the Internet from their home or their mobile (table 13.9).

Table 13.8a
China: Places of Access to the Internet of Cybercafé Users, by Frequency of Use

	Frequency of Use					
Venue	Every Time	Most of the Time	Sometimes	Seldom	Never	All
Cybercafé	141	341	221	218	55	976
Home	60	201	166	127	422	976
Mobile phone	51	190	229	152	354	976
School	30	141	125	145	535	976
Office	13	49	76	118	720	976
Friend's house	5	14	93	326	538	976
Library	3	22	33	82	836	976
Other	2	6	9	49	910	976

Table 13.8b
China: Cybercafé Users—Frequency of Use and Number of Other Venues Used

			Cybercafé Users Who Also Use Other Venues: # of Additional Venues Besides Café			
Frequency of Use of Internet Café	All Café Users	Exclusive Café (No Other Venue)	1 More	2 More	3 More	4 More +
All the time	141	60	31	15	16	19
Most of the time	341	25	74	75	74	93
Sometimes	221	3	30	42	57	89
Seldom	218	1	32	47	65	73
Never	55	1	28	11	4	11
Total	976	90	195	190	216	285

Table 13.8c
China: Predominant Place of Access of Internet Café Users

Predominant Place of Access	#	%
No predominant place	82	8
Only one predominant place		
Cybercafé	289	30
School	99	10
Home	130	13
Office	25	3
Friend's house	8	1
Library	3	–
Mobile phone	34	3
Predominant mobile users who are also predominant users of:		
Cybercafés	107	11
Home	48	5
School	15	2
Office	2	0.3
Users with 2 predominant places, excluding mobiles	87	9
Users with 3 or more predominant places	46	5
All user respondents	975	100

Note: A place is considered predominant if the respondent used it to access the Internet "Every time" or "Most of the time."

Table 13.9
Places of Access to the Internet of China's Cybercafé Users, by Gender (%)

	Male Users			Female Users		
Venue	Every Time or Most of the Time	Sometimes or Seldom	Use of Venue as % of Male Users	Every Time or Most of the Time	Sometimes or Seldom	Use of Venue as % of Female Users
Cybercafé	52	48	100	41	59	100
Home	25	30	55	31	30	61
Mobile	24	39	63	27	38	65
School	17	27	45	18	28	46
Office	6	20	26	6	20	27
Friend's house	2	42	44	2	45	46
Library	1	12	13	6	11	17
Other	1	6	7	1	6	6

A surprisingly high number of public access users also access the Internet from home, and in general, there is greater home access to computers than to the Internet (table 13.10).

Why do people who can access the technology from elsewhere visit public access venues? The GIS survey (Survey Working Group 2012) and our China survey asked users to select their main reason for using public access from six predefined possibilities (table 13.11). In five of the six countries considered, more than 40 percent of respondents selected "No other option for computer/Internet access." Brazil is the exception: only 15 percent of users indicated lack of Internet access options. "To work or be with friends or other people" was chosen by 29 percent of respondents in Chile, 24 percent in the Philippines, and 30 percent in China. "Availability of better equipment" was another frequent answer, particularly in Chile (29 percent). "Getting help" was not considered important, except for help from venue staff in Bangladesh (9 percent), a country with low digital literacy and where telecenters are dominant.

Use Patterns and Activities

PAV users who visit every day or nearly every day are in the majority in Jordan (62 percent) and Sri Lanka (70 percent; table 13.12).[5] Users in the five countries surveyed by the GIS are also frequent visitors. In contrast, the Chinese net bar users surveyed are more occasional users, many of them (42 percent) using urban cybercafés once or twice a week. Chinese users spend more time during each visit to net bars than public access

Table 13.10
Percentage of Public Access Users Who Also Access Computers or the Internet from Home

	Cybercafés		All PAV Types	
	Male	Female		
	Internet			Computers
China*	55	61		
Jordan*	45	40		
Chile**			33	76
Bangladesh**			14	36
Brazil**			40	60
Ghana**			26	66
Philippines**			25	42

* See China and Jordan chapters.
** Sciadas et al. (2012).

Table 13.11
Main Reason for Using Public Access Venues (%)

Reason Given	Users of All Types of Venues					China Net Bar Users
	Bangladesh	Brazil	Chile	Ghana	Philippines	
No other option for computer access	16	8	9	11	15	26
No other option for Internet access	35	15	44	47	33	16
To work or be with friends and other people	17	29	8	14	24	30
To get help from other users	1	4	2	3	2	na*
To get help from venue staff	9	4	2	4	2	3
Better equipment than home or work	17	29	16	15	15	19
Other	5	12	19	6	8	6
Total	100	100	100	100	100	100

Reason given	China Internet café users					
				Predominant users from:		
	Urban males	Urban females	Rural	Cafés	Home	Mobile
No other option for computer access	23	19	41	36	7	29
No other option for Internet access	16	18	15	18	9	21
To work or be with friends and other people	29	36	27	20	46	24
To get help from venue staff	3	2	4	2	3	3
Better equipment than home or work	23	18	9	17	30	24
Other	6	6	4	7	5	–

Source: Sciadas et al. (2012).
*na: This option was not a possible survey response.

Table 13.12

Users of Cybercafés in China and Jordan, of Sri Lanka's Telecenters, and of All Venue Types in Global Impact Study Survey Countries: Frequency of Visits, Visit Duration, and Time of Visit (%)

	China*		Jordan*		Sri Lanka**		Global Impact Study Survey Countries***				
	Male	Female	Male	Female	Male	Female	Bangladesh	Brazil	Chile	Ghana	Philippines
Frequency of visits											
Daily or almost daily	19	7	78	44	67	72	38	41	33	41	50
At least once a week	42	42	10	42	27	22	45	38	43	47	43
At least once a month	21	26	8	7	4	5	12	13	10	8	4
A few times a year	18	25	4	6	2	1	5	9	13	4	3
Subtotal	100	100	100	100	100	100	100	100	100	100	100
Usual duration of visit											
Up to 2 hours	21	17	39	60	52	69					
Around 2–3 hours	54	54	33	30	36	24					
More than 3 hours	25	29	28	10	12	7					
Subtotal	100	100	100	100	100	100					
Usual time of visit											
Morning	9	9									
Noon	7	4									
Afternoon	35	41									
At dusk	20	23									
Evening	23	18									
Late night/early morning	1	2									
Overnight	5	3									
Subtotal	100	100									

* China and Jordan chapters.

** Skill International Private Limited (2010).

*** Sciadas et al. (2012).

users in Jordan or Sri Lanka (table 13.12). Female cybercafé users in China and Jordan visit less frequently than male users, and in Jordan for shorter periods.

Users generally engage in more than one activity when they visit PAVs. In China, out of ten activities offered as options, users marked an average of 2.1 activities "every time" and 4.4 activities "at least sometimes." There appears to be a more intense engagement of males with online games in cybercafés, but in both China and Jordan, women's engagement with gaming is significant. Training is more frequent and varied in telecenters than in cybercafés (table 13.13).

Occupation and Income

Students account for 35 percent of public access users in the Philippines, 39 percent in Brazil, 42 percent in Chile, and 51 percent in both Bangladesh and Ghana (Sciadas et al. 2012). Students make up 48 percent of our cybercafé user samples in Jordan and China (table 13.14). There are more female than male student users, particularly in Jordan (58 percent vs. 44.5 percent). Nonstudent users are mostly working people (42 percent in China, 30 percent in Jordan) or self-employed (8 percent in China, 16 percent in Jordan). Only a few unemployed or retired people use public access (2 percent in China, 6 percent in Jordan).

The World Bank (2011) estimates that 36 percent of China's population and 3.5 percent of Jordan's population earn less than US$2 per day. Table 13.15 would suggest that few if any of the users interviewed in China and Jordan fall below this international poverty line. Most Chinese users (68 percent) earn less than US$2,671 per year, an amount significantly lower than the 2011 national income per capita of US$5,700. These findings are compatible with the view of Sciadas et al. (2012) that public access users generally fall in middle- to low-income categories.

For high-income users, accessing the Internet from *cabinas públicas*, as cybercafés are locally known in Peru, appears to be a matter of convenience, whereas for low-income users it is more of a necessity. Consider, for example, Internet use and places of access in Peru's capital, Lima. High-income groups (i.e., those in categories A and B) account for 30 percent of all Internet users, whereas low-income users are found in categories D and E, for 31 percent (figure 13.3a). High-income users have more access options, which is why when we add up percentages across places of access in figure 13.3b, A-type users reach 142 percent and B-type users 149 percent, compared with 116 percent for the combined group of D- and E-type users. The majority of A and B users (85 percent and 55 percent, respectively) access the Internet from their homes, but home access is rare among low-income users (only 2 percent in the D and E groups). The proportion of A-type Internet users who use *cabinas* is 25 percent, compared with 62 percent of B-type users and 97 percent of D- and E-type users (figure 13.3b).

a

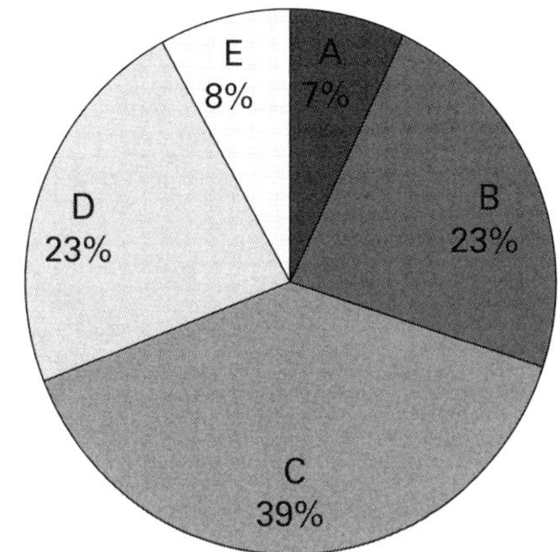

b

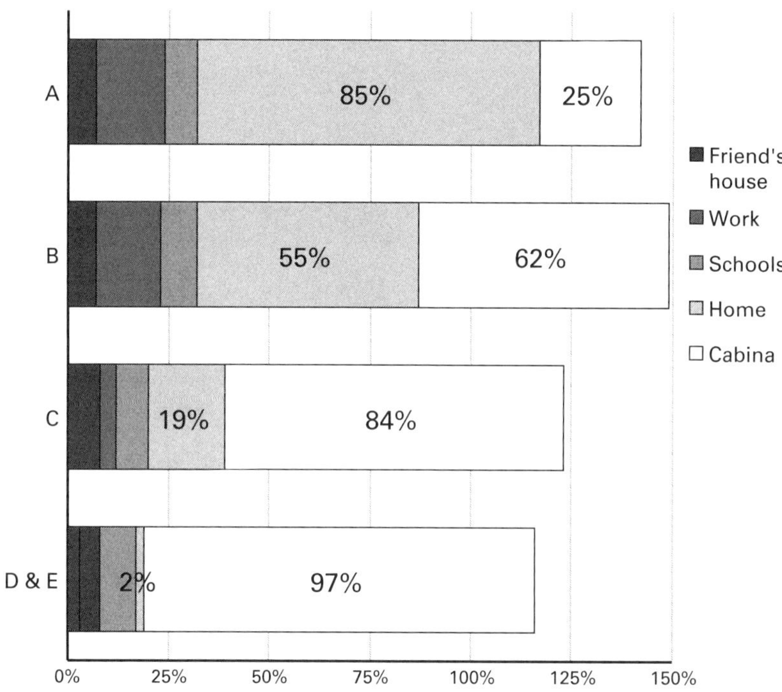

Figure 13.3

Lima. (a) Distribution of Internet users by socioeconomic category.
(b) Places of access to Internet by socioeconomic category.

Table 13.13

Frequency (%) With Which Users Engage in Select Internet Activities When They Visit Public Access Venues: China, Jordan, Malaysia, and Sri Lanka

		Cybercafés						Telecenters		
		China*				Jordan* (Usual Activity)		Malaysia* (Always or Frequently)		
		Male		Female						
Activity		Every Time	At Least Sometimes	Every Time	At Least Sometimes	Male	Female	Male	Female	Sri Lanka**
1	Send and receive email	6	27	6	29	61	73	55	44	40
2	Chat	25	77	28	82	64	60	56	46	24
3	Browse the web, surf the Internet	15	64	16	61	–	–	66	53	24
4	Write blog	2	16	3	22	–	–	17	18	–
5	Use social networking (e.g., Happy Network)	4	25	5	26	–	–	56	45	–
6	Watch movies, TV, or videos online	9	56	14	65	4	1	23	17	–
7	Play online games	27	71	13	48	42	28	63	64	21
8	Download and listen to music	8	54	11	57	23	25	29	20	–
9	Watch or read about current events	9	41	7	34	36	23	49	30	–
10	Shop on the web	1	10	3	13	20	42	15	16	–
11	Use computer	–	–	–	–	–	–	–	–	79
12	Use computers for self-learning/to get ICT skills	–	–	–	–	–	–	–	–	31
13	Use Internet to search for jobs	–	–	–	–	20	15	–	–	2

14	Use computer for skills training class	–	–	–	–	–	–	43	52	14
15	Use computer to record bio-data, create a résumé, CV, etc.	–	–	–	–	–	–	–	–	51
16	Use computers for self-learning/to get ICT skills (today or on previous visits)	–	–	–	–	–	–	–	–	19
17	Use Internet for educational services	–	–	–	–	–	–	–	–	7
18	Access government information and services	–	–	–	–	–	–	32	27	8

Notes and Sources:

1. The actual wording of the options offered to survey respondents varies from country to country.

2. The Sri Lanka information comes from two parts of the questionnaire. Items 1 through 12 refer to "equipment and services you use at the Nenasala" and are comparable with information available for the 3 study countries. Items 13 through 18 refer to what the respondent did during his or her "last or previous visit." For items 14 and 18, we include data for Malaysia and Sri Lanka in the same row, but because of the different time frame, these indicators are not directly comparable.

* See China, Jordan, and Malaysia chapters in this book.

** Skill International Private Limited (2010).

Table 13.14
Percentage of Public Access Users Who Are Students

	% Students	
	By Gender	All Respondents
Study countries		
China		43
Male	41	
Female	48	
Jordan		48
Male	45	
Female	58	
GIS countries		
Bangladesh		51
Brazil		39
Chile		42
Ghana		51
Philippines		35

Impact

Our focus is on socioeconomic *impacts* as opposed to inputs or outcomes, although in practice the distinction is sometimes blurry (Sey and Fellows 2011). For the most part our studies rely on self-reports of impact. Because user perceptions do not always match realized impact, our ability to attribute observed changes to public access use is limited (Heeks and Molla 2009). Where public access is practically the only way to access computers or the Internet (e.g., in Cameroon, Rwanda, Sri Lanka, and many rural areas in Malaysia), user perception of impact is closely linked to public access. In contrast, interviewees who access from more than one place (e.g., urban users in China) cannot tell whether impact is derived from public access or from use of the technology elsewhere.

We examine impact in three areas: (1) personal achievement and well-being, (2) social interaction, and (3) negative effects of public access. These broadly defined domains are convenient, but people's experiences are multifaceted and not always readily compartmentalized. Inevitably, the discussion of these topics overlaps.

Table 13.15
China and Jordan: Select Statistics and Annual Personal Income of Nonstudent Users of Cybercafés

	China	Jordan
% poor[a]	36.2	3.5
GNI per capita (current)[b,c]	5,700	4,350
GNI per capita (PPP)[b,c]	7,520	5,770

China: All nonstudent users			Jordan: All nonstudent users		
Personal income in US$	#	%	Personal income in US$	#	%
< 890	21	4	3,390–6,780	69	45
890–2,671	196	35	6,780–11,864	46	30
2,671–3,561	164	29	11,864–16,949	29	19
3,561–5,341	121	22	16,949–25,424	8	5
5,341–8,902	38	7	25,424–33,898	–	–
8,902–14,243	9	2	> 33,898	2	1
> 14,243	8	1	Total	154	100
Total	557	100			

Notes: Personal income user data were collected by China and Jordan studies.
[a]% poor is based on the World Bank's 2011 international threshold of US$2/day (i.e., US$730/year) in PPP. The China survey on which these estimates are based was conducted in 2005 and the Jordan survey in 2006.
[b]World Bank (2011).
[c]National per capita income figures serve as a point of reference for each country, but should not be compared directly with users' personal income because the latter ignores family size and the number of income earners in the family. Also, reported personal incomes in China cannot be compared with Jordan's. Personal income in Jordan is high probably because the user reporting income is likely to be the only income earner (or one of only a few) in a large household. Average household size in Jordan is about 5.4 persons (Department of Statistics 2004), compared with only 3.1 in China (Xinhua 2008). Women's participation in Jordan's labor force is minimal: 9.1% (Department of Statistics 2004), compared with 77% in China (Schneiderman 2010).

Personal Achievement and Well-Being

User Motivations and Realization of Objectives In China we sought to understand user motivations to visit cybercafés and to assess impact from the extent to which user objectives were met. From the list of Internet use activities in the Pew Internet Project (2012) questionnaire, we identified twenty-eight likely underlying *situational goals* of net bar users. (See chapter 4, table 4.1). The relationship between activities and the situational objectives thus constructed is indirect. For example, email may be used to fulfill one or more objectives, such as "Keep in touch with family and friends," "Meet new friends," or "Get health information to improve physical health." A twenty-ninth situational goal is unrelated to ICT use: "Socialize and make friends with people in net bars."

We also identified seventeen broadly defined life aspirations or *life goals*. These life goals are linked to situational goals with varying degrees of proximity. To illustrate, a person may visit a net bar to improve school performance, acquire skills to become a better worker or a better entrepreneur, get a better job, or learn ICT skills. Based on these four situational objectives, we defined "Learn more knowledge" as a life goal that users as well as nonusers can identify with.

According to self-determination theory (SDT), intrinsic goals are pursued for their own sake because they satisfy one or a combination of the human psychological needs for autonomy (to act freely on your own volition), competence (to feel competent at what you are doing), and relatedness (to care for others and feel cared for). Extrinsic goals are pursued because a person feels compelled by a contingency beyond the control of the self (Deci and Ryan 2000; Sheldon et al. 2003). Extrinsic goals are not always bad or detrimental. One may be required to perform an unpleasant study- or work-related task or engage in an arduous exercise routine to become healthier. Over time, a desirable extrinsically motivated behavior can become part of a person's values and turn the extrinsic goal into a goal that is internalized (albeit not intrinsic) and "owned" by the person.

Of the twenty-nine possible situational goals, four cannot be classified, twenty-one are classified as intrinsic, and four are extrinsic. Of the seventeen life goals, three cannot be classified, twelve are intrinsic, and only two can be clearly identified as extrinsic. Considering that survey goals were constructed from common Internet use activities, *our analysis suggests that the goal content of Internet and cybercafé use is predominantly intrinsic*. Furthermore, this finding *applies to Internet and public access use in general everywhere.*[6]

Users engage in Internet activities and visit PAVs for powerful reasons: as part of their efforts to satisfy basic human needs. To the extent that public access use furthers the satisfaction of these needs, personal well-being in the form of mental health and vitality increases.[7]

ICT Skills Learning PAVs are often where people first come into contact with computers and the Internet (Sciadas et al. 2012). In Malaysia, out of twenty possible options (including "Other"), the top objective for using the RICs selected by the users interviewed was "To improve my ability to use the computer and the Internet." Eighty-five percent of male and 90 percent of female RIC users chose this goal, and its popularity was independent of age. It was chosen by 85 percent of young users (ages 24 and under) and by 93 percent of mature users (ages 25 and over).

In China, this same goal was the sixth most popular out of twenty-nine situational goals. It was chosen by 36 percent of users and was particularly popular among young (under age 19) males (56 percent) and young females (50 percent). As users gain experience with the technology, the motivational value of this goal appears to wane: 50 percent of users with up to two years of experience chose this goal, but only about a third of experienced users did.

Do Users Achieve Their ICT Skills Learning Objectives? In Jordan, 336 cybercafé users were asked whether their lives had been impacted in different spheres. Forty-eight percent rated the impact on "improving computer skills" as highly positive and 45 percent as slightly positive. Only 4 percent felt there had been a negative impact, and 2 percent perceived no impact at all.

Eighty-four percent of Malaysia's telecenter users interviewed either agreed or strongly agreed with the notion that "the information available through the telecenter" had empowered them to "use the computer to type letters, etc."

In China, net bars were the most important place for learning ICT skills. Thirty-eight percent of the net bar users interviewed learned how to use computers, and 52 percent learned how to use the Internet in these venues. Second in importance were schools, where 37 percent of interviewees learned how to use computers and 24 percent the Internet.

In Cameroon, 57 percent of the 700 computer-literate secondary students interviewed learned how to use computers in schools, and 17 percent learned in telecenters. Because the *télécenters communautaires polyvalents* (TCPs) are the only place of Internet connection in the five villages studied, they play an even greater role in Internet skills training. Of 550 Internet-literate students interviewed, 51 percent learned Internet skills through TCP training, and another 17 percent taught themselves at the TCP.

A marked distinction between cybercafés, on the one hand, and telecenters and CITCs, on the other, reappears in our studies. Cybercafés provide access and often serve as a gathering place to meet friends. Telecenters also fulfill this role, but normally they also provide training in ICT skills and other subjects. CITCs usually have ICT skills training as a mandate.

Learning and School Performance Jordan's cybercafé user ratings of the educational impact of cybercafés were 38 percent highly positive, 22 percent slightly positive, 8 percent somewhat or very negative, and 31 percent no impact.

In Argentina, a link between schoolwork and public access and CITCs has been emerging. Teachers often tell students to look up information on the web, but low-income students unable to do so (for lack of access or lack of ICT skills) use CITCs more readily than cybercafés for these purposes, in part, because in CITCs they can get help from a friend or the CITC instructor.

In Sri Lanka, 98 percent of beneficiaries consider that the telecenters have helped change livelihoods in the community. When asked what aspect of livelihoods had been affected, 84 percent indicated "Learn new skills." Increased access to government information came in a distant second, mentioned by 21 percent of beneficiaries (Skill International Private Limited 2010).

Malaysia's rural telecenter user ratings of the impact on "knowledge and education" were 69 percent strongly positive, 27 percent somewhat positive, 1 percent somewhat or very negative, and 3 percent no impact.

Users' motivations vary by demographics. In China, about 41 percent of young students identify improving their school performance as a goal for visiting cybercafés, compared with 28 percent of the overall user population. When we turn to life goals, "Learn more knowledge" is the highest ranked goal (of seventeen possible choices) for 53 percent of Chinese users. It ranked third in popularity among nonusers, chosen by 44 percent.[8] Among young (under age 19) urban students, it was the top life goal choice of both users (64 percent) and nonusers (60 percent). Most telling, users pursuing this goal reported a statistically significant performance advantage over nonusers who were also pursuing this goal for three critical subsamples: urban males under age 35, urban male students, and urban female students.

In Cameroon, we examined the effect of rural telecenters on the performance of secondary school students. Self-reporting of academic performance over the past three years—falling, rising, or stable—was used as an indicator. A higher proportion of high-performing students learn how to use the Internet than other secondary students using the telecenter, and the high-performing group tends to use public access more intensively for school-related purposes. Furthermore, even after controlling for critical variables (gender, age, motivation, computer skills, hours of study, and hours of TCP use), we find that mid and upper secondary level students (but not lower level) with Internet skills outperformed those who did not have these skills. Because the telecenters were the only place providing Internet connectivity in these villages, the performance edge may be attributed to public access.

To claim that young urban males and urban student users in China learned more than nonusers, or that the academic performance of Cameroon secondary school student users of public access improved, would require measures of actual performance as opposed to self-reports. It is nevertheless remarkable that Chinese young urban males and urban students who use cybercafés *perceive* higher achievement of the high-priority goal "Learn more knowledge" than nonusers, and that mid and upper level secondary students in Cameroon *feel* that Internet access through these centers gives them a school performance edge.

Employment and Income Evidence of impact was least significant in this domain. In Jordan, the percentage of cybercafé users perceiving no impact was 65 percent for "Increasing your income," 71 percent for "Getting a promotion at work," and 52 percent for "Finding a job." With respect to "Finding a job," some impact was perceived, particularly by males, among whom 12 percent marked strong impact and 22 percent high impact.

Malaysia's telecenter user responses were more positive, but impact questions were worded in modest terms. Seventy-four percent of telecenter users interviewed agreed or strongly agreed that they felt empowered by the RIC because it had made it easier for them to find information on employment opportunities and to apply for jobs or university placement.

In China, we included six income employment-related goals for using net bars in the list of twenty-nine possible situational goals. One might expect these six goals to be popular among nonstudent users, a group consisting mostly of wage workers, but this is not the case (table 13.16). "Entertainment," "Keeping in touch with family and friends," and "Accessing information" were chosen by 73 percent, 61 percent and 51 percent of nonstudents, respectively, compared with 34 percent for the top employment-related goal, "Improve my job skills to work better," and by lower percentages for the other five.

Our Rwanda study's purposive sample of office workers sought to determine whether ICT skills training in PAVs improved job prospects. The consensus among Rwandan interviewees is that ICT skills are indispensable in today's white-collar work environment. Similar manifestations as to the importance of computer skills as a path to a job were observed in other countries. According to a young Argentinian cybercafé user,

Knowing how to use a PC is always useful. For whatever job, they ask if you have computer skills, just in case. Even for a street-sweeping job they ask for computer skills.

Many Rwandan interviewees (56 percent) were recruited because they had ICT skills, and 41 percent had to take an ICT test during recruitment. Of the three venue types,

Table 13.16
China: Ranking and Percentage of Nonstudent Users Choosing Their Top 4 Situational Goals for Using Internet Cafés, and of the 6 Income-Related Situational Goals

	Popularity	
	Rank	%
Entertainment (play games, listen to music, watch movies, play online video, etc.)	1	73
Keep in touch with family and friends (email, QQ, etc.)	2	61
Access information (news, weather forecasts, stock info, sports, gossip, etc.)	3	51
Relax, relieve tension	4	41
Improve my job skills to work better	5	34
Improve my skills to get better/new job	8	29
Find an additional/new job	12	25
Make money (e.g., online store, doing web pages, etc.)	16	20
Better manage my company or farm (e.g., check market info)	21	18
Shop online or get product information online	22	18

Notes: The term *situational goal* is used to refer to the twenty-nine possible goals for using Internet cafés offered to respondents of the user survey.
Shading indicates the six income-related goals.
In all, 547 nonstudent observations were considered.

telecenters appear to have the most effective training programs. Overall, impact on job acquisition was limited. Fewer than 7 percent of respondents used the Internet to find vacancies, and only 3 percent applied for jobs online. These findings are not surprising considering that even in an advanced labor market such as the United States, it is only now, after Internet use has become widespread, that Internet job search is perceived to be effective (Kuhn and Mansur 2014).

The impact of public access on employment or income may in fact be higher than can be observed directly. As discussed in the next section, public access increases the size of personal networks, and personal ties, many of which may seem weak, are in practice significant links that end up being crucial when searching for a job (Granovetter 1983, 2005).

Social Benefits

Communication and Networking Of all impact indicators considered in Jordan, cybercafé users gave the highest ratings to "Maintaining communication with family and friends": 61 percent highly positive, 22 percent slightly positive, 6 percent slightly or highly negative, and 11 percent no impact. "Meeting new people online" was also rated favorably: 38 percent highly positive, 33 percent slightly positive, 12 percent slightly negative, and 20 percent no impact. "Knowing about other cultures" was also appreciated: 76 percent highly or slightly positive, 7 percent negative, and 17 percent no impact.

Malaysian RIC users perceive an enhanced sense of connectedness due largely to increased communications. Of twenty options, users' third most popular objective was "Keep in touch/communicate with family, friends, and acquaintances" (74 percent). Seventy-nine percent reported that telecenter use had increased communications with family and 82 percent with distant friends. Overall, 74 percent felt they now had a wider social network.

In China, "Keep in touch with family and friends" is the second most popular goal for using cybercafés, chosen by 64 percent of users.

In Chile, telecenters are primarily used for communications. As one woman user explained,

The Internet changed my life and allowed me to contact my relatives who live outside of the country

Argentinian youths spend most of their time communicating, especially in cybercafés, because a popular means used to interact, namely, online games, is discouraged in CITCs. ICT-enabled communications help youngsters build new friendships and strengthen existing relationships. When asked whether he could have met as many people without the Internet, Gabriel, a twenty-one-year-old Argentinian youth, responded,

No. It's not possible. A computer without Internet is like having... ears and not being able to hear....

Bessière, Kiesler, Kraut, and Boneva (2008, 2010) have shown how the use of the Internet to communicate with family and friends can lower depression levels. People who connect to the Internet on a regular basis from PAVs probably experience similar health benefits.

Are There Benefits from Socializing in the Venue? Argentina's youngsters with home access visit cybercafés largely in search of friends and companionship. Gabriel, the Argentinian youth we just met, answers this section header's question:

My dad had died and my friends brought me to the cybercafé.... I hadn't been here for a long time. It was good to be here because at home I was bored, I was sad. Here, I'm with people. I spend a while here and I clear my head a bit.

Among China's net bar users, 46 percent of predominant home users give "To work or be with friends" as their main reason for visiting these venues. In Jordan, 23 percent of men and 12 percent of women visit cybercafés because their friends go there.

Table 13.11 allows only one reason for visiting PAVs, when in practice people may have more than one. The appreciation for socialization at the venue comes across even more strongly when this is acknowledged. In Malaysia, for example, "Meet friends, socialize, and make new friends at the RIC" was the fourth most popular of twenty goal options for using the telecenter, chosen by 66 percent of users. In China, where users were presented with twenty-nine options, "Socialize and make friends with people in Internet cafés" was the sixth most popular goal, chosen by 33 percent of users. Among young (under age 19) urban respondents, this goal was even more popular: it was chosen by 41 percent of males and 45 percent of females.

Do Infomediaries Add Value? Some venues use information brokers to help specific groups, such as women and the elderly, get started using the technology. We found infomediaries in telecenters in Chile and Malaysia as well as in CITCs in Argentina and Thailand. In cybercafés, operators help but usually informally and with minor tasks.

Help from an operator is not the main reason for using public access, except for a small minority that reaches 9 percent in Bangladesh where telecenters abound and overall digital literacy is minimal, and 4 percent or less in the five other countries considered in Sciadas et al. (2012). Nevertheless, our own studies show that in telecenters and CITCs, operators and teaching staff play a critical role teaching basic ICT skills to novice users, particularly older adults. Our findings are compatible with those reported in Gomez, Fawcett, and Turner (2012).

Strengthening Rural Organizations Our Peru study examined impact on the capabilities of nine grassroots organizations in Daniel Hernández, an impoverished rural district of the Peruvian Andes. We found that some organizational capabilities are more likely to be impacted by ICT (e.g., those related to leadership, infrastructure, and external communication) than others (e.g., tracking, monitoring, and evaluating plan implementation). In all, impact is greatest when the tools made available by public access are linked to the organization's goals and when they are used to search for funding opportunities.

Is Public Access Empowering? We use the term *empowerment* to mean "a process treating people as agents of change on the road to giving them greater control over and a say about resources and decisions that affect their life prospects" (Koggel 2009).[9] The evidence from Chile, Argentina, Thailand, and Peru shows that empowerment involves a struggle to redress injustices or alter the balance of power, even if that progress is often slow.

In Chile our study looked at the impact of two small telecenters: one located in Villa San Francisco, a suburb of Santiago, and the other in Villa San Hernán, a smaller town. In both districts, drugs, alcoholism, and crime are everyday challenges reported by interviewees. Social relations are characterized by mistrust and the perception that public spaces are dangerous places where you learn "bad things." In this setting, children are the main users of the telecenters, and they use them to do their homework and for entertainment. Adult women are more frequent users than men. Both venues studied are also used as community centers. Since the telecenters started operating early in 2010 and our study was conducted in mid-2010, our assessment of impact is based on short-term impressions. Digital literacy training is appreciated and the free Internet service is valued in these two low income communities, especially by women users who face significant constraints to venture beyond the neighborhood and also by what is expected of them. For women in these two communities the telecenter affords a unique proximate opportunity to learn and use technology. This is probably why women's strongest valuations of the telecenter were expressed in terms of pride for having a place of learning "of their own."

Our Argentina study focused on the effects of a cybercafé and two CITCs on low-income youth from La Matanza, a district of greater Buenos Aires of about 1.7 million people with high indices of poverty and unemployment and a large population of young people who are neither in school nor working (i.e., *ni-nis* [*ni estudia ni trabaja*]). Several interviewees were *ni-nis* at some point in their lives. Young men perceive training at the two CITCs as a path to gainful employment. Those enrolled in the computer refurbishing courses appreciate being able to earn some income while they learn. Women trainees value ICT skills training and view training time as a way to achieve independence from their husbands and the confining aspects of their roles as mothers. Men and women highlight the communications and sociability value of the technology.

Far from their homes, with few skills and limited rights of association or mobility (Saltsman 2011), Burmese women migrants living in Mae Sot find their community online. The Internet lets them read in their own language, listen to their music, and read and hear news about their community and their heroes. They communicate with family and friends relocated to other countries, make new friends, fall in love, express themselves, and find comfort in virtual space. They organize for causes they care for and fundraise online.

Asociación de desplazados del Nor-Oriente de Tayacaja (ADESNORTAY—Association of Displaced People of Northeastern Tayacaja) was founded in 2003 in Daniel Hernández District, Huancavelica, Peru. Its approximately ninety members were displaced from conflict areas and resettled in the District. The organization's leader escaped death as a child when rebels attacked his village and murdered his family. ADESNORTAY members are extremely poor and have no property; they are frequently discriminated against and regarded as ignorant by long-term residents of the District. ADESNORTAY's work consists of identifying and formally registering displaced people so that they qualify for support from the National Reparations Council.

The Daniel Hernández telecenter was set up the same year that ADESNORTAY was founded. The center's assistance was essential during the organization's early years when it provided a meeting space and ICT training for members and assistance in identifying and contacting aid agencies, other organizations working with displaced people, and government officials in charge of the registration of victims of conflict. ADESNORTAY is constantly challenged and remains a weak organization. When the municipal government changed in 2007, evening hours of telecenter operation—which are most convenient for working people—were cut, and the staff support that ADESNORTAY used to enjoy is no longer forthcoming.

The Dark Side of Public Access

Learning, Playing, or Wasting Time? In China, "Improve my performance in school" was a goal for using cybercafés selected by 41 percent of young (under age 19) urban student males and 43 percent of young urban females. These percentages are not insignificant but pale in comparison with the popularity of the goal "Entertainment," chosen by 81 percent of males and 82 percent of females. The allure of videogames is strong because they are intrinsically motivating and help users satisfy their mental health needs for autonomy, competence, and relatedness (Ryan, Rigby, and Przybylski 2006) and make them feel close to their idealized selves (Przybylski et al. 2012). For many young Chinese, net bars feel like a "second home," a place where they can pass the time in the evenings, meet with friends on- and offline, and "try adventures, play with friends, and feel free to do what they could not do at school or even at home" (Sun 2010).

Our China study identified some negative impacts:

1. Urban male nonstudent users of net bars make up 36 percent of the user sample. Urban male nonstudents who do not use the Internet account for 39 percent of the nonuser sample. These urban male nonstudents, both users and nonusers, are predominantly workers. When we compare self-reported achievement regarding life goal "Get

stable, high-paying job, better business opportunities," nonusers of the Internet outperform net bar users.

2. Rural residents who are predominant users of urban net bars (190 observations) report lower achievement of the life goal "Improve the mental health of myself or my family" than non-Internet users (140 observations).

The first finding suggests that male urban nonstudent users of net bars may feel they are wasting time (with respect to the goal "Get stable, high-paying job, better business opportunities") in comparison with the more positive perception of male urban nonstudents who do not use cafés. Alternatively, it could be that male urban nonstudent users are self-selected and visit cafés because they are frustrated with their current work situation. Similarly, rural residents who visit urban net bars may be those afflicted with mental health issues who are searching for solace in virtual space. Sorting out what lies behind these findings requires greater scrutiny than our data allow.

In Cameroon, our finding that upper and mid-level high school students who use the telecenters and know how to use the Internet report a school performance advantage over those who do not must be tempered with two caveats. First, having a strong motivation to learn and spending long hours studying remain key factors and far outweigh the observed academic advantage that Internet or computer access seems to confer. Second, some of the evidence gathered suggests that spending too much time at the telecenter may hinder academic achievement.

In summary, many public access users play, many learn, and some waste time.

Problematic Internet Use Chinese net bars are generally perceived in negative terms.

Internet cafés have become an important place for juvenile delinquents and in particular for crimes committed by primary and middle school students. (Hongkou District Procurator in Shanghai, cited in Xueqin 2009)

The Internet is not much use. My son used to come home for lunch every day, but now he's going to bars every noon after classes without eating his lunch. I have to search for him every day in those damned bars, running from one to another. It's very frustrating. In my opinion, the net bar is no good at all, and it ruins our children. I'll buy him a computer only if he is admitted to a university, so he's got to study hard this year. (Mother looking for her seventeen-year-old son at a net bar; cited in Sun 2010)

Our studies show that about 2 percent of Chinese cybercafé users may be classified as Internet "addicts" and another 16 percent as overusers. We detected some negative consequences linked to overuse: (1) Urban male nonstudent net bar overusers report lower achievement of life goal "Keep up to date" than regular users and nonusers, and (2) rural resident overusers report lower achievement than ordinary users and nonusers regarding the life goal, "Get stable, high-paying job, better business opportunities."

Are cybercafé users more at risk of overuse than home users? Our research suggests otherwise. Wang et al. (2011) estimate that 12 percent of high school users of the Internet in Guandong Province may be considered addicted. Because about 73 percent of their sample connects from home, problematic Internet use does not appear to be confined to public access users. In our study, Chinese net bar users who access the Internet mainly from home (and declare only one place as "predominant") exhibit about the same rate of overuse (10 percent) as those who connect primarily from cafés (8 percent).[10]

Chinese overusers typically spend long hours using the Internet, connect very frequently and using every possible means (café, home, school, office), and frequent not one but many net bars.

It is unclear whether Internet overuse causes behavioral and health problems or is instead a reflection of antecedent conditions that lead to or correlate with overuse (Czincz and Hechanova 2009). Moreover, China's regulations limit the possibilities for using the technology for instrumental reasons. Net bar computers do not have storage devices, word processing, spreadsheet, and presentation and educational software, nor are they connected to printers, photocopiers, or fax machines. In essence, China's regulatory regime has reinforced the use of cafés for activities frequently associated with overuse such as gaming (Linchuan Qiu 2009).

Social Exclusion in Public Access Venues In the border town of Mae Sot, only a few Thai-owned cybercafés are friendly to migrants.

Most Thai people look down on Burmese people. When you enter the Internet shop, the woman will look at you from head to foot to see whether you are Burmese or Thai. If you start to speak, she will know you are Burmese and she will not treat you well. . . . I also carry a work permit but it is written in my permit that I am a construction worker. That is why I am scared to go to a cybercafé, because the police might discover I am working for an NGO and not in construction. (Mon woman in her thirties)

In Peru, Quechua people who do not speak or write Spanish well are often rejected or mistreated by cybercafé staff. In Daniel Hernández, a predominantly rural district with few access options, leaders of grassroots organizations have been forced to look for alternative places of access.

We also found a *consistent pattern of exclusion of women in cybercafés*. Our quantitative studies show that women are underrepresented among cybercafé users in China (27 percent), Jordan (24 percent), and Uttar Pradesh (3 percent). A similar pattern of exclusion kept coming up in our qualitative analyses. In Peru's Daniel Hernández District, the space in cybercafés is small and prevents accompanied women from sharing the same workstation. In Argentina, few women visit the cybercafé studied, and when they do visit, they do not stay long. Most cybercafé customers are young men. The venue has tinted glass, and the workstations have cubicles allowing for privacy while surfing. In Malaysia, women prefer to use the RIC, where they feel safer and more comfortable than in cybercafés. In Chile, also, women prefer telecenters.

The telecenter is a study center and not a place to hide and download whatever you want. There is a big difference between an Internet café and a telecenter. (Woman, occasional user)

In India, after a first survey found that only 3 percent of cybercafé users were female, we conducted a follow-up purposive survey of nonusers to try to figure out why. Table 13.17 summarizes our findings.

About two-thirds of women nonusers do not visit cafés because of parentally imposed curfews. Being too busy with household obligations was cited by a third of nonusers. Even among the few women who do use cafés, these two reasons (curfews and household chores) are significant deterrents.

I go to the cybercafé along with my brother or father.... The environment there is unfriendly, with a crowd of unemployed men. When these men see a girl alone, they make lewd comments or want to take undue advantage. (Woman interviewee, India)

Cybercafé gender exclusion reflects societal norms reinforced by a service demand primarily driven by young men: "The tendency of young men in Internet public access points to view pornography deters many young women from frequenting such places" (Huyer et al. 2005, p. 169).

What makes gender exclusion in cybercafés so pernicious is the overwhelming dominance of these venues in the public access landscape (figure 13.2). Because public access is often where people first learn how to use the technology, the exclusion of women from cybercafés deserves far more attention from scholars and policymakers than it has been afforded.

Policy Design Considerations

Public Access and Mobiles

The demise of the Internet Café has long been foreshadowed. Individual access to the Internet, be it from home or smart phones, is generally preferred to shared access, especially for communication purposes, and access through mobiles is becoming increasingly affordable. Cybercafé decline was reported in the United States as far back as 1998 and is often the subject of current news in other countries.[11]

Table 13.17
Primary Barriers Preventing Women's Access to Cybercafés in Uttar Pradesh, India

	Users			Nonusers		
	#		%	#		%
Social and family restrictions		40	48.8		50	68.5
Parentally imposed curfews	23			50		
Household chores	20			24		
Unfavorable environment at the cybercafés		19	23.2		25	34.2
Predominance of male users	17			15		
Lack of toilet facilities	1			–		
Not enough space to sit properly	7			7		
Absence of female operators and instructors	2			7		
Inappropriate content on the desktop	3			–		
High costs		14	17.1		20	27.4
Internet fees at cybercafés	12			19		
Cost of transportation to cybercafés	4			8		
Infrastructure and capacity problems		52	63.4		38	52.1
Inadequate transportation facilities	14			9		
Not enough computer systems	12			8		
No power backup during power failures	18			7		
Slow Internet speed	18			7		
Lack of English language skills and financial problems	2			5		
Total # of women responding	82	82	100.0	73	73	100.0
Observations with no response	18			27		
Total # of interviewees	100			100		

The relationship between mobile phone use and Internet and cybercafé use may be appreciated in Peru, a country that for years has had a high density of urban *cabinas públicas*. In 2002, 71 percent of Lima's Internet users accessed from *cabinas* and only 8 percent from home (table 13.18). In 2002, *cabinas públicas* were essentially the only way to connect to the Internet, and only fixed phone lines were available. At the time, about 13 percent of Lima's *cabina* users visited these venues to make calls using Voice over Internet Protocol (VoIP), and 40 percent had done so at some point in the past. Between 2007 and 2013, mobile phone use rose rapidly in Peru, from 40 to 81 percent. Home Internet connections also increased but not as fast: from 5 percent in 2007 to an estimated 26 percent in 2013. VoIP use in *cabinas* is now much less frequent and is no longer recorded in surveys. The proportion of households with at least one person

Table 13.18
Peru: Internet, Places of Access, and Fixed and Mobile Phones 2002–2013

	Lima*	Peru	
		Jan–Mar	
	2002	2007**	2013 Projections***
% of access place of adult (> 6) Internet users			
Home	8	12.5	42.1
Workplace	7	10.3	15.7
Educational institution	11	3.1	7.2
Cybercafé	71	82.1	47.6
Elsewhere	2	2.3	12.3
Total	100	110.3	124.9
% of households			
With fixed telephone service		27.8	33.5
With mobile phone service		35.9	81.5
With home Internet connection		4.6	25.5
With at least 1 member using cybercafés		42.1	37.6
% of households with home access to Internet			
Peru		4.6	25.5
Lima Metropolitan Area		10.8	44.1
Other urban areas		4.2	12.5
Rural areas***		0.1	0.6

Notes: Apoyo (2002) data cover Lima's population > 8 years old and reflect predominant place of access (i.e., add up to 100%). Instituto Nacional de Estadistica e Informática data cover the population of Peru (> 6 years old) and allow for more than one place of access (i.e., totals exceed 100%).

* Apoyo (2002).

** Instituto Nacional de Estadistica e Informática (2008, pp. 4, 6, 21, 31).

*** Instituto Nacional de Estadistica e Informática (2013, pp. 4, 5, 40).

using *cabinas* declined, from 42 percent in 2007 to 38 percent in 2013, the sum across percentage of users for each of the five access options increased from 110 percent in 2007 to 125 percent in 2013 (table 13.18). As Internet use has expanded, user options have also increased, and Peru's access patterns have become more varied.

In China, as Internet use has become more widespread users have diversified their modes of access. Between 2006 and 2013 individualized forms of access, i.e. from the

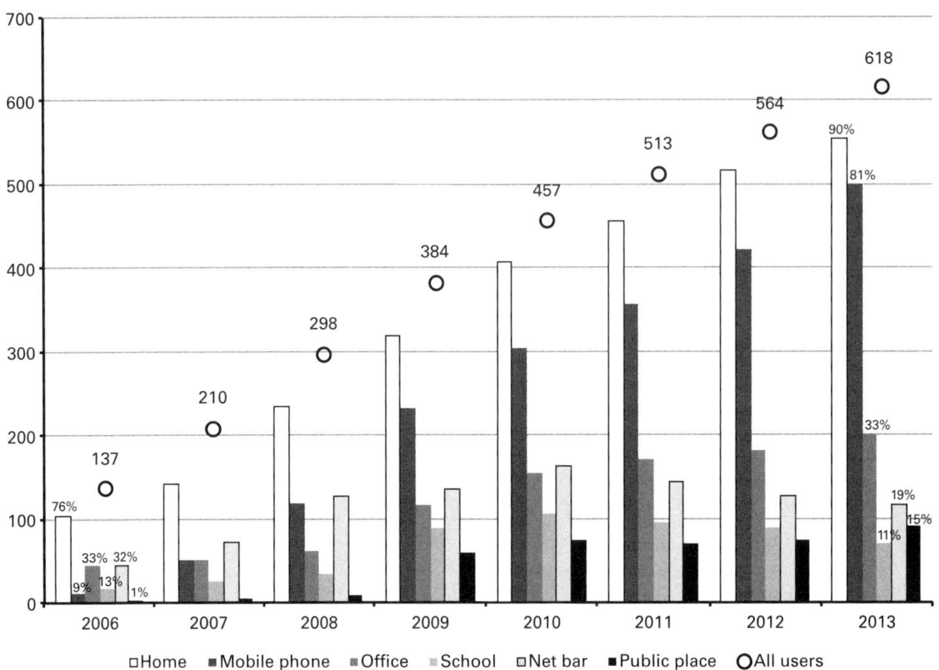

Figure 13.4
China: Millions of Internet users by year and access mode, and frequency of mode used in 2006 and 2013.

home or using mobiles, grew in tandem with overall Internet use (figure 13.4). The number connecting from mobiles was 9 percent in 2006, but by 2013 represented 81 percent of all Internet users. The number who accessed from the office also grew during this period and remained at roughly 33 percent of all Internet users. Access from Schools and Internet Cafés grew numerically and in relative terms until about 2010, but subsequently declined. The number of people connecting from public places (i.e. telecenters), was insignificant in 2006, but grew to 90 million or nearly 15 percent of all Internet users in 2013 (figures 13.4 and 13.5).[12,13]

The increased diversification in access mode that has occurred in China may be appreciated, as in Peru, by adding the percentage of users across the country's six access options. This total was 164% in 2006 compared to 249% in 2013.[14] Diversity in modes of access in China is also reflected in our Internet Café user survey. Only 90 of the 976 Internet café users interviewed were exclusive users of cafés. Most café users also used other modes of access, with about 50 percent using three or more additional modes.

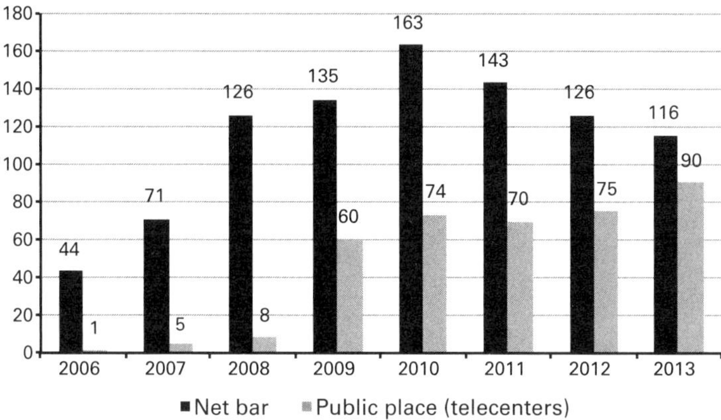

Figure 13.5
China: Millions of public access users by PAV type.

Migrant Burmese women in Mae Sot, Thailand, have limited possibilities to access the Internet from either home or mobiles. They spend more on cellphone credit than at cybercafés. Nevertheless, they say cybercafés give better value for their money because for 15 Baht (about US$0.50) per hour, they can do many things online: communicate with loved ones, listen to music, watch videos, read news, keep up with Burmese culture, obtain information useful for their work, and even fundraise.

Different technologies and modes of access provide different affordances. As ICT options expand, instead of a single place of access, what appears to develop is a "communications ecosystem" where people use the various options available (Walton and Donner 2012). A combination of home use, mobiles, and low-cost smart phones may eventually displace many (most?) PAVs, but shared access to computers and the Internet is likely to remain significant in the foreseeable future.

ICT Skills Training

ICT skills training is a key service of CITCs in Argentina and Thailand and a significant activity of telecenters in Cameroon, Rwanda, Malaysia, Peru, and Chile. ICT skills are also acquired in cybercafés, mainly through self-directed learning.

Nearly 52 percent of China's urban population uses the Internet. Young people (under age 30) who do not use the technology are few in number, both in our sample and as a proportion of China's urban population. In contrast, urban adults ages 30 and older account for 70 percent of all urban nonusers. We asked adult nonusers to choose their main reason (out of six options) for not using the Internet (table 13.19): nearly

Table 13.19
China: Percentage of Urban Nonusers of the Internet According to Reason for Not Using, by Age Group

Reason for Not Using	Young (< 30)	Mature (≥ 30)
No time	40	18
No need or interest	24	26
No access	13	7
No skills	11	47
Expensive	9	2
Other	4	1
Total	100	100
# of observations	270	554

half (47 percent) chose "No skills"—this in an urban setting where technology is commonplace.

Introducing technology is an even greater challenge in rural settings, where Internet use is uncommon, illiteracy is high, and English language skills and local language content are limited. Nonusers do not know the benefits that ICT skills can bring. Johan Ernberg (1998) was well aware of this challenge: "Most people are unable to imagine the potential of ICT until they see, and actually try out the tools."

The whole day, I am too busy doing household work.... I am not interested in knowing about the Internet as it is of no use to me. Further, it can't help me with household chores. (Woman nonuser, Uttar Pradesh, India)

Basic ICT skills training is a potentially high-impact area of public intervention, which if well targeted can help empower disenfranchised peoples. De la Maza and Abbagliati (2004) describe an eighteen-hour digital literacy training program that gives users foundational capacities and has been successfully implemented in Chile by the BiblioRedes program.[15] Curiousity or casual interest in acquiring ICT skills does not necessarily translate into willingness to pay for training, particularly among older adults, because of information asymmetries: nonusers do not know the benefits they might derive from such skills. Encouragement and the opportunity to try out the tools are required. This is an area where government intervention is justified on both efficiency and equity grounds.

Telecenter Establishment

Cybercafés have served as a model for governments and donors to set up rural telecenters in the expectation that these would eventually become self-sustaining. In practice, the evidence of rural telecenter failure is substantial (Best and Kumar 2008; Kuriyan and Toyama 2007; Proenza 2003, 2006a, 2007, 2008; Toyama 2010; Toyama et al. 2005), even if overshadowed by calls to launch new initiatives.

The positive impact findings in Chile, Argentina, and Thailand suggest that it may be feasible to design and implement high-impact, well-targeted *urban* development telecenter or CITC initiatives. Because these are generally subsidized centers, to avoid unfair competition, they should be situated far from existing commercial venues. Sustainability will not be an issue if, after donor funding has ended, users who have acquired ICT skills can access computers and the Internet from other places (e.g., from home or, even if somewhat more distant, from other PAVs).

The situation is different with regard to *rural* telecenters.

We did not examine rural telecenter projects per se, and yet in Cameroon, we stumbled on a phenomenon too common to ignore. Since 2008, the government has established thirty-four rural telecenters. When we searched for centers that met minimum operational conditions, we found only five. Of the other twenty-nine, eighteen were discarded for lack of access to the Internet, five experienced frequent power cuts that prevented regular functioning, five did not respond to our request for a meeting, and one was too new to have had an observable impact.

Rural telecenters face three formidable challenges: (1) high connectivity costs, (2) high maintenance costs, and (3) few users.

Connectivity costs are generally higher in rural areas. Currently, the only way to bring connectivity to the many small but sparsely distributed rural communities of the Peruvian, Ecuadorean, Colombian, and Bolivian highlands is through VSAT (satellite Internet) at a cost of $250 per month or more. In Chile, the cost of connecting 44 percent of BiblioRedes libraries using VSAT (i.e., those situated in rural areas) exceeded $220 per month in 2008 (table 13.20). Servicing two hundred of Sri Lanka's telecenters in 2008 cost US$370 per month (Proenza 2008). Such high costs can only be met with government support.

Maintenance costs are higher in rural areas, where few if any local personnel are skilled in computer repair or are in a position to address connectivity problems. The Sustainable Access in Rural India (SARI) project, supported by a consortium of government, donors, and academia, managed to achieve connectivity costs of $15 per month per kiosk, but failure to provide reliable service was a major factor leading to the closing of the seventy-eight kiosks (Best and Kumar 2008). In Colombia, the main problems cited by the operators of CITCs set up under the government's Compartel communications program (Centro de Estudios sobre Desarrollo Económico 2007) as disrupting their functioning were connectivity (64 percent), equipment (58 percent), and energy (51 percent).

Table 13.20
BiblioRedes: Connectivity Costs—2008

Technology	Number of Centers (Libraries)	Average Cost/Month (US$)
Asymmetric Digital Subscriber Line (ADSL)	81	221
Digital Subscriber Line (XDSL)	131	182
Gigabit Digital Subscriber Line (GDSL)	69	153
Wireless Local Loop (Will)	2	119
Fiber optics	16	323
Microwave	4	141
VSAT	69	277
Total	372	208

Without users there can be no impact from or justification for government subsidies. Yet time and again, rural telecenters are under-utilized. According to Toyama et al. (2005), the number of customers of Drishtee and n-Logue kiosks in India was very low, with a third to half of the franchisees reporting fewer than five customers a day. Centre for Electronic Governance at the Indian Institute of Management Ahmedabad (2002) and Cecchini and Raina (2004) reported only one to four users per day at Gyandoot telekiosks. eChoupal kiosks and computers are rarely used by people other than the designated operator (Kumar 2004, 2009; Veeraraghavan, Yasodhar, and Toyama 2009.[16] Mahmood's (2005) review of the experience of three rural telecenters in Pakistan concludes that users are unaware of the benefits of the technology. In one of these centers, there were ten to twelve visitors a day at inception but only four or five a day three months later (Mahmood 2005). Fifty-one percent of Colombia's 922 rural telecenters surveyed by Centro de Estudios sobre Desarrollo Económico (2007) had fewer than ten customers a day.

Three main factors underlie the low use rates of rural telecenters. First, in communities where hardly anyone uses the technology, there is no way for people to learn what it can be used for or how it can help them. The benefits of computers or the Internet cannot be explained. There is no substitute for sitting down in front of a computer and experiencing its power by writing a document, sending an email, chatting with a friend, or browsing the web.

Second, programs that have relied primarily on government service provision have failed to build up a regular user base: examples include Gyandoot (Bailur 2006; Cecchini and Raina 2004; Centre for Electronic Governance at the Indian Institute of Management Ahmedabad 2002) and the SARI kiosks (Best and Kumar 2008).

Third, communicating via the Internet is subject to network effects. When relatives and friends can be contacted through email, chat, Facebook, or videoconferencing, people find a powerful reason to learn how to use the technology. But achieving network effects in impoverished, largely disconnected rural communities is a daunting task, likely to require costly efforts to provide basic ICT skills training to large segments of a population that often lacks basic education. To illustrate what is required to achieve network effects in rural environs, appendix 13.A summarizes two large-scale digital literacy programs: one in Chile and one in India.

Self-sustainability is not indispensable, nor is it necessary for all publicly funded telecenters to survive over time. Cybercafés are not all individually sustainable. Like small businesses everywhere, some fail while others thrive. The system is resilient as long as there are paying customers. What is important is *dynamic sustainability: that a valued service continues to be provided*, be it by a publicly sponsored telecenter, by a cybercafé that takes over, or by some other means, such as home access, even if it needs to be galvanized by an initial public investment.

If impacts are demonstrably high, governments of high-income developing countries such as Chile and Malaysia may be in a position to subsidize rural telecenters on a continuing basis, even surviving changes in government administrations. In low-income countries with weak governance and limited implementation capabilities, the dynamic sustainability prospects of rural telecenter projects are bleak.

Cybercafé Regulation

Cybercafés are regulated for a variety of reasons: in India to combat terrorism (Associated Press 2004), in Thailand to stop the exploitation of children (Assavanonda 2007), in Pakistan to protect children from inappropriate content (Ali 2006), and in China for fear youngsters are being corrupted and harmed (Kan 2011; Sun 2010; Xueqin 2009).

Cybercafé regulation is extensive in China: operators need eight different permits that can take up to eight months to obtain. All workstations have monitoring software that tracks users' activities. Owners must designate staff to monitor and report irregularities, such as visits by minors, users without an ID, and visits to "yellow" (pornographic) or "reactionary" websites. Official sweeps are carried out several times a year to identify violations and fine or close down the establishment (Sun 2010). As many as 130,000 cafés were shut down over a recent six-year period (Kan 2011).

China's efforts to regulate cybercafés have been expensive but largely unsuccessful. The proscription of minors, the ban on "yellow" websites, and the prohibition of staying overnight are often ignored. The government has tried to get all small cafés to join ten large chain operators, but only 30 percent (Kan 2011) to 40 percent (Earp 2013) of China's net bars are affiliated with chains.

Regulations? If I'm too strict with the students, who'll come to my bar? Nobody will come! (Net bar operator; quoted in Sun 2010)

Chinese media and official concerns over adolescent use of net bars have stoked parental fears and led to the emergence of a private unregulated industry that purports to cure "Internet addiction" for high fees, and at times with tragic consequences (Stewart 2010).

Insofar as most users are concerned, fears regarding the extent of Internet addiction appear unfounded. Nevertheless, the lives of some users may be adversely impacted by Internet use and overuse. Therefore, it is sensible for governments to use their regulatory power to protect minors. It is also important to design such programs with a full understanding of user motivations. Adolescents use cybercafés for powerful reasons: to assert their identity and autonomy, to play games that are intrinsically motivating, and to feel competent (Przybylski et al. 2012); to socialize with friends and classmates; and, ultimately, because they want to have fun just like young people all over the world.

Interventions that recognize these powerful motivations and support users' own self-control, rather than undermine their autonomy, are likely to be more successful.

Cybercafés are driven by profits. Instead of imposing restrictive, expensive, and largely ineffective controls, governments should consider offering financial incentives to help operators increase their profits. Establishments that create a safe environment for minors and women could be rewarded, for example, with tax breaks or low registration fees.[17] The criteria for awarding incentives could include:

1. *Venue layouts that encourage a communal work and social environment as opposed to privacy* Open settings tend to curtail viewing of socially unacceptable sites and create a safe environment for women visitors.
2. *Venues that provide services that encourage more instrumental uses of ICT* For example, computers equipped with storage devices, word processing, spreadsheet and presentation and educational software, printers, and photocopying and fax machines.
3. *Venues that make explicit formal arrangements with educational institutions*, by either providing training or allowing the use of the facilities for the conduct of classes or the completion of homework.

Redressing Cybercafé Gender Imbalance

The potential developmental role of cybercafés is frequently noted (Finquelievich and Prince 2007; Haseloff 2005; Rangaswamy 2007a). Cybercafés are also often perceived as "male spaces." Nevertheless, we have not found any recorded acknowledgment by policymakers of cybercafé gender imbalance as a policy issue, not even in countries or regions where the exclusion of women is evident and severe (e.g., Jordan and small towns in Uttar Pradesh).

Gender discrimination is commonly ingrained in culture and invisible. Few operators will admit that they allow viewing of pornographic sites (Rangaswamy 2007b). It is doubtful that they are "proud" or even aware that their venues are unsafe for women; they are merely responding to the demand for a service.

Creating a safe environment for women and minors in cybercafés is feasible. In the Philippines, Netopia's cybercafés are located in well-lit, high-traffic public areas, and their customer base is gender balanced. In Jordan, cafés near the university have many women customers because it is in the operators' interest. Chile's BiblioRedes libraries do not filter content, and their workstations are arranged so that content being viewed is visible to library visitors. Similarly, there are no partitions between workstations in Chile's Infocentros (Klein 2011).

Officials who wish to foster a safe environment should consider supporting ICT skills training for adult women in cybercafés that meet standards of safety along the lines discussed in the previous section. Such programs would increase women's opportunities to benefit from the most ubiquitous venue type and amplify operators' markets. By involving mothers, understanding of the power and allure of technology should also increase and facilitate parental engagement in efforts to curb overuse.

Concluding Remarks

Pervasive poverty amid plenty and inequality are the major threats to prosperity, stability, and peace in the twenty-first century. Overcoming these threats will in large measure require increasing the engagement of people in the use of technology, their enjoyment of its benefits, and their participation in the creative processes that technology enables. *Widespread access to information and communication technology is essential.*

Significant challenges have constrained the reach and impact of public access ICT. First, access by women to the most ubiquitous type of venue, cybercafés, is frequently limited, severely in some countries. Second, whereas some well-targeted projects manage to empower traditionally marginalized groups (see chapters on Argentina, Chile, Peru, and Thailand), by and large the impact of public access on very poor people has been limited. Third, rural access has been constrained by high connectivity and equipment maintenance costs and digital illiteracy.

Mobile phones are helping mitigate the effects of these limitations. Mobiles enable communications networks to reach deeper to serve low-income users and rural communities and, in principle, mobiles are within women's reach. In practice, only the most sophisticated costly broadband handsets enable the interactive exchange needed to build up social networks. At present, the provision of access to computers and the Internet is better suited to helping people learn and develop, that is, to magnifying their capacities to learn, find work, advocate on their own behalf, and innovate. A pragmatic development approach would focus on community needs and draw on mobiles and on public access initiatives to increase participation in the network society, as Amy Mahan might put it, to diversify access and redress social inequities and invest to "build up community resources."

Our studies show that the overwhelming majority of users consider public access ICT to have impacted their lives positively, on personal achievement and well-being, and expanding networks and opportunities to communicate, exchange ideas and collaborate. The evidence cuts across countries and settings. Detrimental effects can be observed (e.g., excessive use), but these can be managed and minimized. When people are able to use the technology on a regular basis, its usefulness becomes evident, and public access can then affect their lives, at times in powerful personal ways.

A place where I leave my pots and pans behind in search for my dreams of becoming a poet . . . writing poetry in the computer. (Significance of the telecenter to domestic worker in Chile; cited in Garrido, Morales, and Villarroel 2002)

Notes

1. Seven countries had more libraries and telecenters than cybercafés: Kazakhstan, South Africa, Sri Lanka, Namibia, Moldova, Colombia, and Bangladesh. The reasons the number of donor or publicly sponsored centers exceeds the number of cybercafés in these countries vary, but there are two critical variables: digital literacy and the existence of a substantial subsidized public access program. In Sri Lanka, for example, the 640 Nenasala telecenters installed with government sponsorship and World Bank financial assistance largely account for the relatively large number of telecenters. With limited digital literacy prior to the Nenasala program, there was little demand for services to spur the emergence of self-sustaining cybercafés.

2. We define *penetration rate* as the number of mobile phone subscribers and/or Internet users as a percentage of a country's population. Currently, in most countries, mobile phone penetration rates are much higher than Internet penetration rates, in part, because of differences in the way these rates are measured. It is common for one person to have more than one mobile phone subscription, but only one person or user is counted when estimating Internet penetration rates.

3. Figure 13.2 is based on surveys reported in Gomez (2009), supplemented with estimates for India (Haseloff 2005), Turkey (Eskicumali 2010), Tanzania and Indonesia (Furuholt, Kristiansen, and Wahid 2008), and Malaysia (Shah Alam and Abdullah 2009). We associate these estimates of

gender distribution with the countries where the survey was undertaken, but most of these estimates are based on a limited number of sample venues.

4. We are comparing Internet use experience in China with computer use experience in GIS countries. Because computer use normally precedes Internet use, the proportion of users in GIS countries with two years or less of Internet experience would be lower than the proportion given in the text.

5. Because these are user surveys, infrequent users would be difficult to capture, and their numbers would tend to be underestimated. This bias would be less of a problem in the more carefully crafted surveys conducted by the GIS.

6. This finding comes from our research in China (chapter 4) based on a list of Internet use activities in the United States. These activities are commonplace everywhere, and the principles of SDT have been shown to hold true across many countries and cultures (see e.g., Grouzet et al. 2005).

7. Following Huta and Ryan (2010), the term *well-being* is used here "broadly to refer to one or more subjectively experienced states or evaluations of one's life that could be rated as desirable or undesirable, such as positive affect, negative affect, life satisfaction, inspiration, awe, transcendence, sense of meaning, feeling carefree, and vitality." Ryan and Frederick (1997) define vitality as "a positive feeling of aliveness and energy."

8. The life goal chosen as either "Most Important" or "Very Important" by the highest proportion of nonusers (57 percent) was "Improve the physical health of myself or my family," followed by "Keep in touch with friends and family who don't live nearby," chosen by 45 percent of nonusers. Considering that nonusers were much older than users, it makes sense that these two life goals took precedence over "Learn more knowledge" among nonusers.

9. This definition of empowerment builds on Amartya Sen's work on the development of individual human capabilities by gaining education and skills to improve their lives as individuals (Rai 2007). The emphasis is on enhancing capabilities for agency, including the ability to join forces, as part of an online or offline network, to improve the quality of life of the community however defined. The term *empowerment* has been the subject of extensive scholarship. The reader is referred to Koggel (2009), Rai (2007), and the Thailand chapter in this book (chapter 12).

10. The China sample is not a sample of Internet users but of cybercafé users. Accordingly, we cannot say that our overuse estimate applies to all home users. Notice also that the questionnaire and criteria used by Wang et al. (2011) to estimate addiction differs from the ones we used to estimate "overuse." For details, please refer to chapter 5 on problematic Internet use in China.

11. See Michell Marriott. The Sad Ballad of the Cybercafé. *New York Times*, April 16, 1998. http://www.nytimes.com/1998/04/16/technology/the-sad-ballad-of-the-cybercafe.html. Sean Hargrave. Terminal Decline? The *Guardian*, March 8, 2004. http://www.theguardian.com/media/2004/mar/08/mondaymediasection9/print/. Harsimran Singh. Growth of Cybercafés Declining

Sharply. *The Economic Times,* July 15, 2008. http://articles.economictimes.indiatimes.com/2008-07-15/news/27697952_1_cyber-cafes-sify-naresh-ajwani/. Miquel Hudin. The Decline of Senegalese (and maybe all) Internet Cafés. September 15, 2009. https://www.hudin.com/blog/jgf1252987551/. Alejandro Millán Valencia. Locutorios y cybers en problemas para sostenerse. Podrán? October 21, 2010. http://soydondenopienso.wordpress.com/2010/10/22/locutorios-y-cybers-en-problemas-para-sostenerse-podran/. James F. Larson. The Rise and Fall of Korea's PC Rooms (a.k.a. Internet Cafes). April 15, 2012. http://www.koreainformationsociety.com/search?q=+korea%27s+pc+rooms/. *BBC*. Decline and Fall of the Internet Café. November 13, 2012. http://www.bbc.com/news/world-us-canada-20307609/. Eric Jou. China's Internet Cafés Are Disappearing: What's Going On? December 19, 2013. http://kotaku.com/chinas-internet-cafes-are-disappearing-whats-going-o-1479419777/. Sarah Mishkin. Internet cafés losing out in China's online battle. December 26, 2013. http://www.ft.com/cms/s/0/2860d312-62ea-11e3-a87d-00144feabdc0.html#axzz3EJGfI4CL/. *Daily Independent (Lagos)*. Nigeria: How Cyber Cafes Bowed to Smartphones, Internet Charges. August 15, 2014. http://allafrica.com/stories/201408180669.html?viewall=1/.

12. The combined number of users accessing from PAVs (i.e., from Internet Cafés and telecenters) may have grown during this period, but this cannot be determined from the available data. The total number of PAV users cannot be estimated just by adding the number of Internet Café users to the number of users of public places because some Internet users may use both modes of access.

13. Figures 13.4 and 13.5 were constructed using CNNIC data available in China Internet Network Information Center (2007a, 2008, 2009, 2010, 2011a, 2011b, 2012, 2013, 2014) reports published in January and based on surveys conducted in December of the previous year.

14. The sum of the percentages that each access mode is used in any given year will exceed 100 and gives a rough indication of the extent to which users access the Internet using more than one mode. In 2013, very few mobiles in Peru had the capability to connect to the Internet; only 17 percent of Peru's mobiles were smartphones (Oleaga 2014). In contrast, Internet access has been a central feature of China's mobiles and Internet access through mobiles was already being tracked in national statistics in 2006. This is why we add percentages for 5 access options in Peru and for 6 options in China. For Peru we do not consider mobile access, for China we do. This is also why adding the percentages of various Internet access modes is much higher in China than in Peru.

15. A description in English of this training program appears in Annex D of Proenza (2008).

16. India's eChoupal network of 5,400 kiosks are not PAVs: they have been installed by a large private company, ITC, and are run by a designated operator. They provide a marketing infrastructure supported by computer and connectivity (Narsalay, Coffey, and Sen 2012).

17. In 2007, Thailand launched a White Internet Café project that was to be implemented by the Ministries of Culture, Interior, Social Development and Human Security, Education, and the Royal Thai Police (National News Bureau of Thailand 2007). According to the Taiwan Services Trade Information Platform 2011, the project's objective is to promote a healthy environment for minors in cybercafés and includes the identification of cafés that meet program requirements

(no alcohol served, no service to minors after 10 P.M.) and awards them benefits such as software discounts. No information on the implementation performance of this program is available online.

References

Ali, Zulficar. 2006. Pakistan: Cabinet Approves Bill to Regulate Cyber-cafés. Dawn, May 26, reproduced in UCLA Asia Institute web page. Pakistan: Asia Media Archives; http://www1.international.ucla.edu/article.asp?parentid=46879/.

Apoyo Opinión y Mercado. 2002. Uso y actitudes hacia Internet 2002. www.apoyo.com.

Apoyo Opinión y Mercado. 2007. Uso y actitudes hacia Internet 2007. www.apoyo.com.

Assavanonda, Anjira. 2007. Thailand: Paiboon Seeking Tighter Internet Café Rules. UCLA International Institute. *Bangkok Post* reprint. November 3. http://www1.international.ucla.edu/article.asp?parentid=81187/.

Associated Press. 2004. India's Cybercafé Cops Make a Meal of Net Crackdown. *Sydney Morning Herald,* January 26. http://www.smh.com.au/articles/2004/01/26/1075087944419.html?from=storyrhs/.

Bailur, Savita. 2006. Using Stakeholder Theory to Analyze Telecenter Projects. *Information Technologies and International Development* 3 (3): 61–80.

Bessière, Katherine, Sara Kiesler, Robert Kraut, and Bonka S. Boneva. 2008. Effects of Internet Use and Social Resources on Changes in Depression. *Information Communication and Society* 11 (1): 47–70.

Bessière, Katherine, Sara Kiesler, Robert Kraut, and Bonka S. Boneva. 2010. Effects of Internet Use on Health and Depression. *Journal of Medical Internet Research* 12 (1): e7.

Best, Michael, and Rajendra Kumar. 2008. Sustainability Failures of Rural Telecenters: Challenges from the Sustainable Access in Rural India (SARI) Project. *Information Technologies and International Development* 4 (4): 31–45.

Cecchini, Simone, and Monica Raina. 2004. Electronic Government and the Rural Poor: The Case of Gyandoot. *Information Technologies and International Development* 2 (2): 65–75.

Centre for Electronic Governance at the Indian Institute of Management. Ahmedabad. 2002. Gyandoot: Rural Cybercafés on Intranet, Dhar, Madhar Pradesh, India, a Cost Benefit Evaluation Study. Centre for Electronic Governance. October. http://www.iimahd.ernet.in/egov/documents/gyandoot-evaluation.pdf.

Centro de Estudios sobre Desarrollo Económico. 2007. Informe Final de Medición de Impacto y Análisis de los Programas COMPARTEL-Internet Social. March 27. Bogotá: Universidad de Los Andes.

China Internet Network Information Center. 2007. *Statistical Survey Report on the Internet Development in China*. January. 19th Survey Report. Beijing: Author. http://www.apira.org/data/upload/pdf/Asia-Pacific/CNNIC/19threport-en.pdf.

China Internet Network Information Center. 2008. *Statistical Survey Report on the Internet Development in China*. January. 21st Survey Report. Beijing: Author. http://www.apira.org/data/upload/pdf/Asia-Pacific/CNNIC/21streport-en.pdf.

China Internet Network Information Center. 2009. *Statistical Report on Internet Development in China*. 23rd Survey. January. Beijing: Author. http://www1.cnnic.cn.

China Internet Network Information Center. 2010. *Statistical Survey Report on Internet Development in China. January. 25th Survey Report*. Beijing: Author.

China Internet Network Information Center. 2011. *Statistical Report on Internet Development in China*. January. 27th Survey Report. Beijing: Author. http://www1.cnnic.cn/IDR/ReportDownloads/201209/P020120904420388544497.pdf.

China Internet Network Information Center. 2012. *Statistical Report on Internet Development in China*. January. 29th Survey Report. Beijing: Author. http://www1.cnnic.cn/IDR/ReportDownloads/201209/P020120904421720687608.pdf.

China Internet Network Information Center. 2013. *Statistical Report on Internet Development in China*. 31st Survey. January. Beijing: Author. http://www1.cnnic.cn/IDR/ReportDownloads/201302/P020130221391269963814.pdf.

China Internet Network Information Center. 2014. *Statistical Report on Internet Development in China*. January. 33rd Survey Report. Beijing: Author. http://www1.cnnic.cn/IDR/ReportDownloads/201404/U020140417607531610855.pdf.

Czincz, Jennifer, and Regina Hechanova. 2009. Internet Addiction: Debating the Diagnosis. *Journal of Technology in Human Services* 27 (4): 257–272.

Deci, Edward L, and Richard M. Ryan. 2000. The 'What' and 'Why' of Goal Pursuits: Human Needs and the Self-Determination of Behavior. *Psychological Inquiry* 11 (4): 227–268.

de la Maza, Maria Luisa, and Enzo Abbagliati. 2004. BiblioRedes: Abre tu Mundo, su modelo de alfabetización digital. Paper presented at the World Library and Information Congress: 70th IFLA (International Federation of Library Associations and Institutions) General Conference and Council. Buenos Aires, August 22–27. http://archive.ifla.org/IV/ifla70/papers/012s-Maza_Abbagliati.pdf.

Department of Statistics. 2004. Jordanian Mothers, Facts and Figures (web page), Government of Jordan. http://www.dos.gov.jo/dos_home_e/mother.htm.

Earp, Madeline. 2013. *Throttling Dissent: China's New Leaders Refine Internet Control*. Washington, DC: Freedom House.

Ernberg, Johan. 1997. Universal Access through Multipurpose Community Telecenters: A Business Case? Global Knowledge Conference, Toronto, Canada, June 22–25.

Ernberg, Johan. 1998. Universal Access for Rural Development: From Action to Strategies. Paper presented at the First International Conference on Rural Telecommunications, Washington, DC, November 30–December 2. http://www.itu.int/ITU-D/univ_access/telecentres/papers/NTCA_johan.html.

Eskicumali, Ahmet. 2010. The Effect of Internet Cafés on Social Change in Turkey: The Case of Hendek. *Turkish Online Journal of Educational Technology* 9 (2): 196–204.

Finquelievich, Susana, and Alejandro Prince. 2007. *El (involuntario) rol social de los cibercafés*. Buenos Aires: Editorial Dunken. http://www.oei.es/tic/rolcibercafes.pdf.

Furuholt, Bjørn, Stein Kristiansen, and Fathul Wahid. 2008. Gaming or Gaining? Comparing the Use of Internet Cafés in Indonesia and Tanzania. *International Information & Library Review* 40: 129–139.

Garrido, Rodrigo, Manuel Morales, and Alejandra Villarroel. 2002. Aportando a la disminución de la brecha digital en comunidades de bajo desarrollo humano de la Araucanía: El rol de la red de operadores de telecentros comunitarios. Conference lecture at Virtual Educa in Valencia. June. http://e-spacio.uned.es/fez/view.php?pid=bibliuned:1255/.

Gomez, Ricardo. 1999. Telecenter Evaluation: A Global Perspective. Report of an International Meeting on Teletelecenter Evaluation. Ottawa: IDRC. http://web.idrc.ca/uploads/user-S/10244248430Farhills.pdf.

Gomez, Ricardo. 2009. *Measuring Global Public Access to ICT: Landscape Summary Reports from 25 Countries Around the World*. CIS Working Paper No. 7. Seattle: Technology & Social Change Group (formerly the Center for Information & Society), University of Washington Information School. http://tascha.uw.edu/publications/measuring-global-public-access-to-ict-landscape-summary-reports-from-25-countries-around-the-world/.

Gomez, Ricardo. 2012. *Libraries, Telecenters, Cybercafés and Public Access to ICT: International Comparisons*. Hershey, PA: IGI Global.

Gomez, Ricardo, Phil Fawcett, and Joel Turner. 2012. Lending a Visible Hand: An Analysis of Infomediary Behavior in Colombian Public Access Computing Venues. *Information Development* 28: 117–131.

Granovetter, Mark S. 1983. The Strength of Weak Ties: A Network Theory Revisited. *Sociological Theory* 1: 201–233.

Granovetter, Mark S. 2005. The Impact of Social Structure on Economic Outcomes. *Journal of Economic Perspectives* 19 (1): 33–55.

Grouzet, Frederick M. E., Tim Kasser, Aaron Ahuvia, Miguel Fernández Dols José, Youngmee Kim, Sing Lau, Richard M. Ryan, Shaun Saunders, Peter Schmuck, and Kennon M. Sheldon. 2005. The Structure of Goal Contents Across 15 Cultures. *Journal of Personality and Social Psychology* 89 (5): 800–816.

Gurumurthy, Anita, Parminder Jeet Singh, and Gurumurthy Kasinathan. 2005. The Akshaya Experience: Community Driven Local Entrepreneurs in ICT Service. Case Study 5 in *Community-based*

Networks and Innovative Technologies, ed. Seán Ó Siochrú and Bruce Girard, 143–157. New York: United Nations Development Programme.

Haseloff, Anikar M. 2005. Cybercafés and Their Potential as Community Development Tools in India. *Journal of Community Informatics* 1 (3).

Heeks, Richard, and Alemayehu Molla. 2009. *Impact Assessment of ICT-for-Development Projects: A Compendium of Approaches.* Development Informatics Working Paper No. 36. University of Manchester, Institute for Development Policy and Management, Development Informatics Group. http://www.sed.manchester.ac.uk/idpm/research/publications/wp/di/documents/di_wp36.pdf.

Huta, Veronika, and Richard M. Ryan. 2010. Pursuing Pleasure or Virtue: The Differential and Overlapping Well-Being Benefits of Hedonic and Eudaimonic Motives. *Journal of Happiness Studies* 11: 735–762.

Huyer, Sophia, Nancy Hafkin, Heidi Ertl, and Heather Dryburgh. 2005. Women in the Information Society. In *From the Digital Divide to Digital Opportunities: Measuring Infostates for Development,* ed. George Sciadas, 135–196. Montreal: Orbicom/NRC Press.

Instituto Nacional de Estadistica e Informática. 2008. Las Tecnologías de Información y Comunicación en los Hogares, Enero–Marzo 2008. Technical bulletin No. 2 (June) covering January–March. Lima: Author. http://www.inei.gob.pe/media/MenuRecursivo/boletines/7457.pdf.

Instituto Nacional de Estadistica e Informática. 2013. Las Tecnologías de Información y Comunicación en los Hogares, Enero–Marzo 2013. Technical bulletin No. 6 (June) covering January–March. Lima: Author. http://www.inei.gob.pe/media/MenuRecursivo/boletines/b_16709.pdf.

International Institute of Information Technology. 2005. *Information and Communication Technologies for Development: A Comparative Analysis of Impacts and Costs from India.* Report prepared for the Department of Information Technology of the Ministry of Communications and Information Technology and Infosys Technologies. July. Bangalore: Author. http://www.iiitb.ac.in/sites/default/files/uploads/Complete%20report.pdf.

International Telecommunications Union. 2008. *Measuring Information and Communication Technology Availability in Villages and Rural Areas.* May. Geneva: Author. http://www.itu.int/ITU-D/ict/material/Measuring%20ICT_web.pdf.

International Telecommunications Union. 2013. Statistics webpage. Geneva: Author. http://www.itu.int/en/ITU-D/Statistics/Pages/stat/default.aspx?utm_source=twitterfeed&utm_medium=twitter/.

Junlong Culture Communication Co. Ltd. 2010. *China Internet Café Holdings.* Investor presentation presented at China Rising Investment Conference, December. http://a.eqcdn.com/junlongculturecommunicationcoltd/media/18c09d90db0ee3883808e8db089dc0d1.pdf.

Kan, Michael. 2011. China Closes 130,000 Internet Cafés as It Seeks More Control. *PCWorld,* March 18. http://www.pcworld.com/article/222531/china_shuts_net_cafes.html.

Kiran, Gopakumar Rajalekshmi. 2007. E-Governance Services Through Telecenters: The Role of Human Intermediary and Issues of Trust. *Information Technologies and International Development* 4 (1): 19–35.

Klein, Dorothea. 2011. The Men Never Say that they Do Not Know: Teletelecenters as Gendered Spaces. In *ICTs and Sustainable Solutions for the Digital Divide: Practical Approaches*, ed. Jacques Steyn, Jean-Paul van Belle, and Eduardo Mansilla Villanueva, 189–255. Hershey, PA: IGI Global.

Koggel, Christine M. 2009. Agency and Empowerment: Embodied Realities in a Globalized World. In *Embodiment and Agency*, ed. Sue Campbell, Letitia Maynell, and Susan Sherwin, 250–267. University Park, PA: Pennsylvania State University Press.

Kuhn, Peter, and Hani Mansour. 2014. Is Internet Job Search Still Ineffective? *Economic Journal* (April). doi:10.1111/ecoj.12119.

Kumar, Richa. 2004. eChoupals: A Study on the Financial Sustainability of Village Internet Centers in Rural Madhya Pradesh. *Information Technologies and International Development* 2 (1): 45–73.

Kumar, Richa. 2009. The Yellow Revolution in Malwa: Alternative Arenas of Struggle and the Cultural Politics of Development. PhD diss., Massachusetts Institute of Technology (MIT), Cambridge, MA. http://dspace.mit.edu/handle/1721.1/47825#files-area/.

Kuriyan, Renee, and Kentaro Toyama. 2007. *Review of Research on Rural PC Kiosks*. April 14. http://research.microsoft.com/en-us/um/india/projects/ruralkiosks/Kiosks%20Research.doc.

Linchuan Qiu, Jack. 2009. *Working Class Network Society: Communications Technology and the Information Have-less in Urban China*. Cambridge, MA: MIT Press.

Mahmood, Khalid. 2005. Multipurpose Community Telecenters for Rural Development in Pakistan. *Electronic Library* 23 (4): 204–220.

Mishra, Shridhar Mubarak, John Hwang, Dick Filippini, Reza Moazzami, Lakshminarayanan Subramanian, and Tom Du. 2005. Economic Analysis of Networking Technologies for Rural Developing Regions. *Lecture Notes in Computer Science* 3828: 184–194.

Narsalay, Raghav, Ryan T. Coffey, and Aarohi Sen. 2012. *ITC: Sourcing from Small Rural Suppliers on a Mass Scale*. Accenture. http://www.accenture.com/Microsites/emerging-markets/Documents/pdf/Accenture-ITC-Case-Study-Final.pdf.

National News Bureau of Thailand. 2007. Government Launches White Internet Café Project. December 20. http://202.47.224.92/en/news.php?id=255012200016/.

Oleaga, Michael. 2014. Mexico Tops Smartphone Market in Latin America with 50 Percent Growth in 2013, Becomes Interest for Mobile Ad Marketers. http://www.latinpost.com/articles/6946/20140206/mexico-tops-smartphone-mobile-market-latin-america-50-percent-growth.htm.

Pal, Joyojeet. 2007. Examining E-literacy using Telecenters as Public Spending: The Case of Akshaya. In *Proceedings of the 2nd IEE/ACM International Conference on Information and Communication Technologies and Development*, 59–67. Bangalore, India, December 15–16. http://research.microsoft.com/en-us/um/india/events/ictd2007/ICTD2007_Proceedings_CD.pdf.

Pal, Joyojeet, and G. R. Kiran. 2005. E-literacy and Connectivity for Development in India: The Akshaya Approach. *Community Technology Review* (Spring–Summer): 35–37.

Pal, Joyojeet, Sergiu Nedevschi, Rabin K. Patra, and Eric A. Brewer. 2006. A Multi-Disciplinary Approach to Shared Access Village Computing Initiatives: The Case of Akshaya. *E-learning* 3 (3): 291–316.

Pew Internet Project. 2012. Usage Over Time. Excel spreadsheet available for download. http://www.pewinternet.org/data-trend/internet-use/internet-use-over-time/.

Proenza, Francisco J. 2001. Telecenter Sustainability-Myths and Opportunities. *Journal of Development Communication* 12 (2): 94–109.

Proenza, Francisco J. 2003. *Argentina: Establecimiento y experiencia inicial de los Centros Tecnológicos Comunitarios*. FAO Investment Centre Working Paper, May. Rome: Food and Agriculture Organization of the United Nations.

Proenza, Francisco J. 2006a. *Guatemala: Programa de Acceso Rural a Internet*. FAO Investment Centre Working Paper, May 9. Rome: Food and Agriculture Organization of the United Nations. http://www.e-forall.org/pdf/GuatemalaAccesoRural_9mayo2006.pdf.

Proenza, Francisco J. 2006b. The Road to Broadband Development in Developing Countries is through Competition Driven by Wireless and Internet Telephony. *Information Technologies and International Development* 3 (2): 21–39.

Proenza, Francisco J. 2007. *Tecnologías de la Información y Comunicación para la Reducción de a Pobreza en localidades atendidas por el Proyecto Sierra Sur*. FAO Investment Centre Working Paper, December 19. Rome: Food and Agriculture Organization of the United Nations. http://www.e-forall.org/pdf/IFAD_SierraSur_19Dic2007.pdf.

Proenza, Francisco J. 2008. Towards High Impact Sustainable Telecenters in Sri Lanka. Consultancy report prepared for the World Bank, December 7.

Proenza, Francisco J., Roberto Bastidas-Buch, and Guillermo Montero. 2001. *Telecenters for Socio-economic and Rural Development in Latin America and the Caribbean*. Washington, DC: FAO-ITU-IDB, May. http://www.itu.int/ITU-D/ict/mexico04/doc/doc/10_telecenters_e.pdf.

Przybylski, Andrew K., Netta Weinstein, Kou Murayama, Martin F. Lynch, and Richard M. Ryan. 2012. The Ideal Self at Play: The Appeal of Video Games That Let You Be All You Can Be. *Psychological Science* 23 (1): 69–76.

Rai, Shirin M. 2007. (Re)defining Empowerment, Measuring Survival. Paper prepared for workshop on Empowerment: Obstacles, Flaws, Achievements, 3–5. Ottawa, Canada: Carleton University, May. http://www.ethicsofempowerment.org/papers/RaiEmpowerment.pdf.

Rangaswamy, Nimmi. 2007a. ICT for Development and Commerce: A Case Study of Internet Cafés in India. In *Proceedings of the 9th International Conference on Social Implications of Computers in Developing Countries*. São Paulo, Brazil, May. http://www.ifipwg94.org.br/fullpapers/R0071-1.pdf.

Rangaswamy, Nimmi. 2007b. Representing the Non-formal: The Business of Internet Cafés in India. *Ethnographic Praxis in Industry Conference Proceedings* 1: 115–127.

Román, Marcela, and Alexis Guerrero. 2005. *Impact Evaluation of the "BiblioRedes Abre tu Mundo" Project*, September. Previously available at http://www4.biblioredes.cl/NR/rdonlyres/EF066796-154B-4380-B52D-687C080E6B2C/171194/ImpactEvaluationoftheBiblioredesAbretuMundoProject.pdf.

Ryan, Richard M., and Cristina Frederick. 1997. On Energy, Personality, and Health: Subjective Vitality as a Dynamic Reflection of Well-Being. *Journal of Personality* 65 (3).

Ryan, Richard M., C. Scott Rigby, and Andrew Przybylski. 2006. The Motivational Pull of Video Games: A Self-Determination Theory Approach.*Motivation and Emotion* 30: 347–363.

Salas, O. Victor, Ornella Yacometti, Z., and Atilio Bustos, G. 2005. Informe Final de Evaluación: Programa Red de Bibliotecas Públicas, BiblioRedes. Chile: Ministerio de Educación, Dirección de Bibliotecas, Archivos y Museos (DIBAM), June. http://geminis.dipres.cl/virlib/docs/Gestion/2005/doc21-228-200797_EPF090502072005_IF.pdf.

Saltsman, Adam. 2011. *Developing a Profiling Methodology for Displaced People in Urban Areas-Case Study: Mae Sot, Thailand*. Boston: Feinstein International Center, Tufts University.

Sciadas, George, Hil Lyons, Chris Rothschild, and Araba Sey. 2012. *Public Access to ICTs: Sculpting the Profile of Users*. Global Impact Study Working Paper. Seattle: Technology & Social Change Group, University of Washington Information School. http://www.globalimpactstudy.org/wp-content/uploads/2012/01/Global-Impact-Study-User-Profiles-Survey-Working-Paper-1.pdf.

Schneiderman, R. M. 2010. Chinese Women Are More Ambitious Than Americans. *Newsweek*, August 27. http://www.newsweek.com/chinese-women-are-more-ambitious-americans-71375/.

Sey, Araba, Chris Coward, François Bar, George Sciadas, Chris Rothschild, and Lucas Koepke. 2013. *Connecting People for Development: Why Public Access ICTs Matter*. Global Impact Study Research Report. Seattle: Technology & Social Change Group, University of Washington Information School. http://tascha.uw.edu/publications/connecting-people-for-development/.

Sey, Araba, and Michelle Fellows. 2011. *Loose Strands: Searching for Evidence of Public Access ICT Impact on Development*. Global Impact Study, iConference 2011, Seattle, February 9–11. http://www.globalimpactstudy.org/wp-content/uploads/2011/02/p189-sey.pdf.

Shadrach, Basheerhamad. 2013. *Nenasala: The Sri Lankan Telecenter Experience*. Colombo: Information and Communication Technology Agency of Sri Lanka. http://www.academia.edu/4141329/Nenasala_the_Sri_Lankan_telecentre_experience/.

Shah Alam, Syed, and Zaini Abdullah. 2009. Cyber Café Usage in Malaysia: An Exploratory Study. *Journal of Internet Banking and Commerce* 14 (1).

Sheldon, Kennon M., Daniel B. Turban, Kenneth G. Brown, Murray R. Barrick, and Timothy A. Judge. 2003. Applying Self-Determination Theory to Organizational Research. *Research in Personnel and Human Resources Management* 22: 357–393.

Skill International Private Limited. 2010. *Outcome Evaluation Report of Nenasala Project*. Report prepared for the Information Communication Technology Agency of Sri Lanka (ICTA), October. http://www.icta.lk/en/get/category/3-p.html?download=62%3Anenasala-outcome-evaluation-final-report-october-2010/.

Stern, Peter, David Townsend, and José Monedero. 2007. *New Models for Universal Access to Telecommunications Services in Latin America: Lessons from the Past and Recommendations for a New Generation of Universal Access Programs for the 21st Century*. Bogotá: Latin American Forum of Telecommunications Regulators. http://regulationbodyofknowledge.org/wp-content/uploads/2013/03/Stern_New_Models_For.pdf.

Stewart, Christopher S. 2010. Obsessed with the Internet: A Tale from China. *Wired*, January 13.

Sun, Helen. 2010. *Internet Policy in China: A Field Study of Internet Cafés*. Lanham, MD: Lexington Books.

Survey Working Group. 2012. *Global Impact Study Surveys: Methodologies and Implementation*. Global Impact Study Working Paper. Seattle: Technology & Social Change Group, University of Washington Information School. http://www.globalimpactstudy.org/wp-content/uploads/2012/02/Global-Impact-Study-survey-methodology-report.pdf.

Taiwan Services Trade Information Platform. 2011. Internet Café Franchise in Thailand. December 15. http://www.taiwantrade.com.tw/MAIN/en_front/searchserv.do?method=listNewsDetail&information_id=39430&locale=2/.

Toyama, Kentaro. 2010. Can Technology End Poverty? *Boston Review* (November/December). http://www.bostonreview.net/forum/can-technology-end-poverty/.

Toyama, Kentaro, Karishma Kiri, Deepak Menon, Joyojeet Pal, Suneet Sethi, and Janaki Srinivasan. 2005. PC Kiosk Trends in Rural India. *E-learning* 3 (3): 317–324.

United Nations Population Fund. 2013. *The State of World Population 2013: Motherhood in Childhood—Facing the Challenge of Adolescent Pregnancy*. New York: Author.

Veeraraghavan, Rajesh, Naga Yasodhar, and Kentaro Toyama. 2009. Warana Unwired: Replacing PCs with Mobile Phones in a Rural Sugarcane Cooperative. *Information Technologies and International Development* 5 (1): 81–95.

Walton, Marion, and Jonathan Donner. 2012. Public Access, Private Mobile: The Interplay of Shared Access and the Mobile Internet for Teenagers in Cape Town. Global Impact Research

Report. October. Seattle: Technology & Social Change Group, University of Washington Information School. https://digital.lib.washington.edu/researchworks/bitstream/handle/1773/20956/Public%20access%20private%20mobile%20final.pdf?sequence=1/.

Wang, Hui, Xiolan Zhou, Ciyong Lu, Jie Wu, Xueqing Deng, and Lingyao Hong. 2011. Problematic Internet Use in High School Students in Guangdong Province, China. *PLoS ONE* 6 (5).

World Bank. 2006. *World Development Report 2007: Development and the Next Generation*. Washington, DC: Author.

World Bank. 2011. *World Development Report 2012: Gender Equality and Development*. Washington, DC: Author.

Xinhua. 2008. Family Size Keeps on Shrinking. January 4. http://www.china.org.cn/english/health/238007.htm.

Xueqin, Wang. 2009. Internet Cafés: What Else Can Be Done in Addition to Rectification? In *Good Governance in China—A Way Towards Social Harmony: Case Studies by China's Rising Leaders*, ed. Wang Menkui, 86–97. London: Routledge.

Appendix 13.A Two Approaches to Digital Literacy Training

Between 2002 and 2004, two digital literacy programs were implemented: one in Chile by BiblioRedes and the other in India by the Akshaya project. Summary parameters are given in table 13.A.1.

The BiblioRedes fourteen-hour digital literacy training program targeted users of Chile's network of 368 libraries (some in urban areas, but many in small rural communities) and 17 regional training laboratories. Through the project, each library was equipped with two to seven computers and each laboratory with eleven computers. The project was funded by the Chilean national government in partnership with participating municipalities, and it received a US$10 million grant from the Bill and Melinda Gates Foundation. Initially, BiblioRedes also installed seventeen mobile units, each equipped with eleven laptops, that traveled from library to library to impart the training. Trainees could use the computers during the class or practice on their own afterward.

Trainees were taught computer basics (e.g., how to use the mouse and keyboard) and fundamental skills in how to use word processing software, the Internet, and email. About 120,000 people received digital literacy training, and an additional 21,000 participated in more advanced training modules. Every training participant received a certificate of attendance, provided he or she attended at least 80 percent of the course sessions. To encourage potential adult trainees and let them feel confident and comfortable, no tests or exams were given.

Table 13.A.1
Summary Parameters: BiblioRedes (Chile) and Akshaya (India) Digital Literacy Programs

	BiblioRedes—Chile	Akshaya—Malappuram, Kerala, India
Income per capita[a]	US$5,870	US$390
Adult literacy rate	96%	87%
Implementation period	2002–2004	April 2002–March 2004
Investment	US$19.8 million[d]	US$6.6 million[e]
Training sites		
Municipal libraries	368	–
Pre-existing e-centers (cybercafés)	–	160
New e-centers	–	475
Computers per center	2–7	5–6
Monthly connectivity costs per center[b]	US$208 (average)	US$20
E-literacy training[c]	–	
Target	114,595	600,000
Achieved	121,262 (+21,029 trained in advanced skills)	152,361[f]

Notes and Sources:

BiblioRedes: de la Maza and Abbagliati (2004), Román and Guerrero (2005), and Salas et al. (2005).

Akshaya: Pal (2007), Pal et al. (2006), Pal and Kiran (2005); International Institute of Information Technology (2005), Gurumurthy, Singh, and Kasinathan (2005), and Mishra et al. (2005).

[a]For Chile, World Bank (2006); for Kerala, Pal et al. (2006).

[b]In Chile, these costs are paid by municipal governments. Actual cost varies depending on viability of technological options. In Kerala, connectivity costs are paid by e-center operators to Tulip, the wireless provider.

[c]In Kerala, training was e-awareness; in Chile, computer/Internet literacy proper.

[d]Includes a US$10 million donation from the Bill and Melinda Gates Foundation.

[e]Estimate based on figures given by International Institute of Information Technology (2005). Includes US$1.4 million from local government for e-literacy campaign, US$1.4 million from state government to establish connectivity and develop content, and US$3.75 million from entrepreneurs to set up kiosks.

[f]Pal (2007) found that only 29.7 percent of households participated in the program, and of those, 14.5 percent attended only the first hour of the course. The 152,361 figure is 29.7 percent of 600,000 (178,200) minus 14.5 percent of that number.

The fifteen-hour Akshaya e-literacy program in Malappuram, Kerala, India, focused on increasing awareness as opposed to giving users hands-on experience with computers and the Internet. Awareness did increase among the population, but few of the trainees learned to use or became regular users of the technology. Training took place in 635 Akshaya e-centers, including 160 previously existing cybercafés recruited into the program. After the first phase subsidies were discontinued, many of the newly created e-centers had to shut down (Pal 2007; Pal et al. 2006), and by late 2005 only 415 e-centers were still operating (Kiran 2007). Fewer than 6 percent of the total "e-literates" were able to use the computer for any application, and most trainees could only turn the computer on and off.

Cost per trainee was higher in Chile, about US$208, compared with US$20 in Malappuram, but BiblioRedes appears to have had a higher impact than Akshaya's "awareness" approach.

About the Authors

Lead Editor

Francisco J. Proenza is a PhD economist (University of Florida, 1981) and an authority on rural access to information and communication technologies (ICTs) and ICT applications for poverty reduction. After a thirty-five-year career working in forty countries for various international agencies (including the United Nations Food and Agriculture Organization, the World Bank, the Inter-American Development Bank, the African Development Bank, the International Fund for Agricultural Development, and the United Nations Development Programme), he returned to academia to direct the Amy Mahan Research Fellowship Program to Assess the Impact of Public Access to ICT (www.upf.edu/amymahan). He is presently Visiting Professor of Information and Communication Technology at Universitat Pompeu Fabra, Barcelona.

Contributing Editors

Erwin A. Alampay is an associate professor at the National College of Public Administration and Governance at the University of the Philippines and a former director of its Center for Leadership, Citizenship, and Democracy. He is the editor of the book *Living the Information Society in Asia* (ISEAS Press 2009) and senior editor of the *Electronic Journal of Information Systems in Developing Countries*. He also serves as a senior research fellow with LirneAsia. Dr. Alampay graduated from the University of Manchester with a PhD in development administration and management.

Roxana Barrantes is an economist (PhD, University of Illinois, 1992), executive director and associate researcher at the Institute of Peruvian Studies, and a professor of economics and business law at the Pontifical Catholic University of Peru. She has specialized in applied microeconomics with a focus on regulation and privatization of infrastructure sectors, and environment and natural resources. Dr. Barrantes currently serves on the steering committee of the Regional Dialogue on the Information Society, an ICT policy research consortium for Latin America and the Caribbean. She has published extensively on ICT for development. Her recent papers include "The Shifting Digital Paradigm in Latin America," co-authored with Valeria Jordán and Fernando Rojas (2013), and "Mobile Telephony in Rural Areas: A Case Study in Puno, Peru," co-authored with Mireia Fernández-Ardèvol and Aileen Agüero García (2013).

Hernán Galperín (PhD, Stanford University) is an associate professor at the University of San Andrés (Argentina) and director of its Center for Technology and Society. He is a former associate professor (with tenure) at the Annenberg School for Communication at the University of Southern California. Dr. Galperin is also a member of the steering committee of the Regional Dialogue on the Information Society. His most recent books are *Accelerating the Digital Revolution in Latin America and the Caribbean* (ECLAC, 2010) and *Mobile Communications and Socioeconomic Development in Latin America*, co-authored with Dr. Manuel Castells and Dr. Mireia Fernández-Ardèvol (Ariel 2011).

Abiodun Jagun obtained her PhD in management science in 2006 at the University of Strathclyde Business School, where she also served as a research fellow in the Management Science Department. She worked as the Africa policy officer for the Association for Progressive Communications and was a part-time lecturer (information systems and development) at the Institute for Development Policy Management, University of Manchester. Dr. Jagun has also worked as a part-time lecturer (ICT, society, and the network knowledge economy) at the Graduate School of Public and Development Management, University of Witwatersrand, South Africa. She is currently a special assistant to the Honorable Minister for Communication Technology of the Federal Republic of Nigeria.

George Sciadas is a manager at Statistics Canada. He has written and edited numerous papers in the area of connectedness—including *Unveiling the Digital Divide* (STC, 2003) and *Our Lives in Digital Times* (STC 2007)—and compendia publications on the information society (*Networked Canada* [STC 2001] and *Canada's Journey to the Information Society* [STC 2003]). He has also worked at the OECD in the area of indicators and policy analysis for the digital economy. As a visiting scholar at the International Development Research Centre, he worked extensively with its major research networks in South America, Asia, and Africa.

Ramata Molo Thioune is a senior program officer in the Nairobi-Kenya regional office of the International Development Research Centre. She has been involved in research programs ranging from ICT4D to women's rights and citizenship, as well as governance, security, and justice. She has published and contributed to publications in the field of ICT for community development as well as on women's rights to land and water.

Kentaro Toyama is an associate professor at the University of Michigan School, where he conducts research at the intersection of technology and human development. Previously, he was a researcher at University of California, Berkeley, and until 2009, assistant managing director of Microsoft Research India, which he co-founded in 2005. Dr. Toyama graduated from Yale with a PhD in computer science and from Harvard with a bachelor's degree in physics.

Chapter Authors

Ali Farhan AbuSeileek is an associate professor at the College of Education at Al al-Bayt University, Jordan, and the former director of the E-learning and Distance Learning Center at the College of Languages and Translation, King Saud University, Saudi Arabia. He has served on the editorial board of *The JALT CALL Journal* published by the Japan Association for Language Teaching.

Carolina Aguerre is a researcher and lecturer at the Technology and Society Center, University of San Andrés in Buenos Aires, Argentina, and a visiting lecturer at the Catholic University of Uruguay. She is pursuing her doctoral studies at the Consejo Nacional de Investigaciones Científicas y Técnicas (National Scientific and Technical Research Council) in Buenos Aires, conducting research on national Internet governance policies in Argentina and Brazil.

Oluwasefunmi 'Tale Arogundade has a PhD in computer software and theory from Graduate University, Chinese Academy of Sciences in Beijing, and an MSc in computer science from the Federal University of Agriculture in Abeokuta, Nigeria. She has published articles in journals and conference proceedings with a primary focus on human–computer interactions and aligning information technology with business security management practices.

Nor Aziah Alias is the director of e-learning and an associate professor of instructional technology at Universiti Teknologi MARA, Malaysia. She is the co-editor (with Sulaiman Hashim) of *Instructional Technology Research, Design and Development* (IGI Global, USA, 2012) and has contributed to eight other books on technology and higher education. She also sits on the review panel of journals such as *Educational Technology and Society*, *International Journal of Education and Development using Information and Communication Technology*, *MERLOT Journal of Online Learning and Teaching*, and *International Review of Research in Online Distance Learning*.

Sebastián Benítez Larghi has a master's degree in sociology of culture from the National University of San Martín and a PhD in social sciences from the University of Buenos Aires. He is a professor of sociology of ICT in the Department of Sociology at the National University of La Plata and an assistant researcher at Argentina's National Scientific and Technical Research Council. He is principal investigator of the project "Youth, Inequalities and ICT: A Qualitative Study of Youth Paths to the Incorporation of Computer and Internet in the Frame of the Plan Conectar Igualdad in La Plata and Gran La Plata," sponsored by the Sirca II program of IDRC/Nanyang Technological University, Singapore. He is the author of many scholarly articles, including "Internet y la computadora como estrategias de inclusión social entre los sectores populares: Imaginarios y prácticas desde la exclusion" (*Revista Comunicação & Inovação*, No. 20, Sao Paulo, 2010), "De brechas, pobrezas y apropiaciones: Juventud, sectores populares y TIC en Argentina" (*Revista Versión. Estudios de Comunicación y Política*, No. 27, Universidad Autónoma Metropolitana, Mexico, 2011), and "La apropiación del acceso a computadoras e Internet por parte de jóvenes de sectores populares urbanos en la Argentina" (*El impacto del acceso público a las computadoras e Internet en Argentina, Chile y Perú*, Lima: Amy Mahan Research Fellowship Program, DIRSI, 2012).

Jorge Bossio has an MBA and an MSc in public policy and is currently director of knowledge management at Universidad Peruana de Ciencias Aplicadas (Lima) and researcher at the Institute of Peruvian Studies. He has more than fifteen years of experience in the field of telecommunications and ICTs for development. He is the former coordinator of the Regional Dialogue on the Information Society and a researcher at the Pontifical Catholic University of Peru, and he has held positions of responsibility in the Peruvian Telecommunications Regulatory Agency (OSIPTEL), including representation of the institution in international fora and in negotiations of international trade agreements with the United States, the European Union, member countries of the European Free Trade Agreement, Chile, and Canada.

Juan Fernando Bossio works as a lecturer at the Pontifical Catholic University of Peru (PUCP) and as a private consultant. He has an MSc in analysis, design, and management of information systems from the London School of Economics and a bachelor's degree in librarianship from PUCP. Since 1998 he has been working on ICT for development, with a special focus on rural development, project design and management, social studies, application of qualitative research methodologies, social facilitation, information system design (e.g., indigenous peoples, agriculture), and project evaluation, always working closely with stakeholders—NGOs, government officials, donors, and beneficiaries.

Marina Laura Calamari is a research and teaching assistant at the University of San Andrés in Buenos Aires, where she coordinates the Technology and Society Center. She has a master's degree in organizational studies. Her main research interests are ICT for development and the use of ICT by governments.

Nikos Dacanay is currently pursuing an MSc in practicing sustainable development (ICT4D track) at Royal Holloway, University of London. Following his research on telecenter and cybercafé use by ethnic women's organizations in northern Thailand, he completed a study on the organizations' general use of Internet and mobile phones. He has also studied the use of ICT to increase uptake and access of HIV testing and counseling by young Thai and migrant men who have sex with men, transgenders, and male sex workers, sponsored by Save the Children International. He is currently involved in a cyber-security project with Burmese human rights organizations, sponsored by the Citizen Lab, University of Toronto. He is co-author of the book *Txting Selves: Cellphones and Philippine Modernity* (De La Salle University Press 2002). He is also a consultant with the Human Rights Education Institute of Burma, a non-profit organization based in Chiang Mai, Thailand.

Jean Damascène Mazimpaka is a researcher, teacher, and training coordinator at the Geographic Information Systems and Remote Sensing Centre of the National University of Rwanda, where he also coordinates the postgraduate diploma program in applied geo-information science. He has published papers on spatial databases, including "Towards an Automated Conversion between Spatial Data Models in Spatial Databases" (*International Journal of Mathematics and Computation*, Vol. 9, D10, December 2010).

Laurent Aristide Eyinga Eyinga is a junior researcher and volunteer with Protège QV Cameroon, an NGO working on ICT4D. He has a master's degree in project management from Senghor University in Alexandria, Egypt. In 2008, he co-authored (with Sylvie Siwam Siwe) a study on the use of universal access funds in Cameroon, *Le financement de l'accès universel: Le Fonds spécial des télécommunications au Cameroun,* published by the Association of Progressive Communications.

Mary Luz Feranil is an independent researcher and gender consultant based in the Philippines. She completed a master's degree in gender and development studies at the Asian Institute of Technology in Thailand. She is the author of *Local-Global Connections: Gender, Land and Labor* (LAP 2010) and of a chapter in the book *Contradictions of Palm Oil Promotions in the Philippines in the Palm Oil Controversy: A Transnational Perspective* (ISEAS 2013). Other published articles cover gender and agrarian change, food security, and crop industry studies. Currently, she works as a gender consultant for projects in

Thailand and the Philippines, funded respectively by the International Fund for Agricultural Development and the Asian Development Bank.

Ariel Fontecoba is a political scientist and a professor of social economy at the University of Buenos Aires, where he is currently pursuing doctoral studies in social sciences.

Omar Fraihat has a master's degree in linguistics from the University of Jordan. He is an English language lecturer at the Prince Hussein bin Abdulla II Academy of Civil Protection in Amman, Jordan, and is currently a PhD candidate at Universiti Sains Malaysia.

Martin S. Hagger is a professor of psychology in the School of Psychology and Speech Pathology at Curtin University, Perth, Australia. Professor Hagger's research interests are the motivation and self-regulation of social behavior. He is interested in how people's beliefs, attitudes, intentions, and motives affect their behavior and what health professionals can do to change social behavior. He is editor-in-chief of *Health Psychology Review* and *Stress and Health*, and he serves on the editorial board of nine other international peer-reviewed journals.

Jianbin Hao is a senior engineer at the China Internet Network Information Center (CNNIC). He has been involved in various projects, such as CNNIC's *Statistical Survey Report on Internet Development in China*, China's online shopping market research, and the Ministry of Commerce of the People's Republic of China's online retailing regulation legislation.

Sulaiman Hashim is a senior lecturer in the Department of Management Information Systems, Centre of Technology Management, Institut Aminuddin Baki (formerly the National Institute of Educational Management and Leadership), Ministry of Education, Malaysia.

Izaham Shah Ismail is an associate professor at Universiti Teknologi MARA, Malaysia. His areas of research include computer-assisted language learning, educational and instructional technology, and teacher education.

Haziah Jamaludin is an associate professor at Universiti Teknologi MARA, Malaysia. Her area of research is online learning and instructional design and technology. She has co-authored papers and contributed book chapters in publications such as *Instructional Technology Research, Design and Development* (edited by Nor Aziah Alias and Sulaiman Hashim; IGI Global, 2012) and *Understanding Learning-Centred Higher Education* (CBS Press 2008).

Xuemei Jiang is an assistant professor at the Laboratory of Management, Decision and Information Systems, Academy of Mathematics and Systems Science, Chinese Academy of Sciences. She was awarded a PhD in management science and engineering from the Chinese Academy of Sciences in 2008 and a PhD in economics from the University of Groningen in 2011. She has published one English book and several papers in professional journals, including *Environment and Planning A*, *Regional Studies*, and *Asia-Pacific Journal of Accounting and Economics*.

Laura León is a researcher at the Institute for Peruvian Studies and a lecturer at the Pontifical Catholic University of Peru. She holds an MSc in ICT for development from the University of Manchester. Her main research interest is the adoption and appropriation of ICTs in marginalized communities.

Guoxin Li is a professor in the School of Management of the Harbin Institute of Technology in China. She has been a visiting scholar at the University of British Columbia, the University of Guelph in Canada, and at Hong Kong Polytechnic University. She has specialized in online consumer behaviors with a focus on consumers' co-creation in virtual environments, and has published research papers in several academic journals, including *Journal of Product Innovation Management*, *Journal of Business Research*, and *Electronic Commerce Research and Applications*. She is a committee member of the Chinese Network for Social Network Studies.

Balwant Singh Mehta is an assistant professor at the Institute of Human Development, New Delhi, and visiting faculty at Birla Institute for Management Technology, Greater Noida, Uttar Pradesh, India. He has a PhD in development economics from the Centre for Jawaharlal Nehru Studies at Jamia Millia Islamia, New Delhi. He has contributed several research papers on the labor market, livelihood, and ICT to reputed national and international journals and books. In 2013, he completed a working paper, "Capabilities, Costs, Networks and Innovations: Impact of Mobile Phones in Rural India," for the Institute for Human Development, New Delhi.

Nidhi Mehta is the director of The Vision, Lucknow, Uttar Pradesh, India. She has an MPhil in social work from the University of Lucknow. She has published on gender issues and been involved in advocacy activities on children's and gender issues in rural Uttar Pradesh. Her studies on *Impact of Mobile Phone on Women in Rural Areas*, *Socio-Economic Impact of Widening of Rural Roads on People in Rural India*, *Child and Maternal Health Problems in Rural India*, and *Social Exclusion and Income* are widely known and appreciated.

Marina Moguillansky is a postdoctoral fellow at the Consejo Nacional de Investigaciones Científicas y Técnicas (National Scientific and Technical Research Council) in Buenos Aires and an assistant professor of sociology at the National University of San Martín. She has a PhD in social sciences and a master's degree in sociology of culture from the University of Buenos Aires. She is the editor of the international journal *Rethinking Development and Inequality*.

Marhaini Mohd Noor earned her PhD in policy studies from the University of Southern Queensland, Australia, in 2013. She is a senior lecturer at Universiti Teknologi MARA, Malaysia. Her area of research is community informatics, social capital, and community development. She has published papers on digital literacy and on the use and effectiveness of Malaysia's e-government services. Her dissertation is titled "Evaluating the Contribution of Community Informatics to Rural Development: The Case of Malaysia's Rural Internet Centers." Dr. Mohd Noor is a member of the Australian and New Zealand Academy of Management.

Avis Momeni is an environmentalist in Cameroon's energy research program and co-author of numerous program publications. He is secretary general of Protège QV Cameroon, an NGO working on ICT4D, and coordinator of a program to promote the appropriation of ICTs by underprivileged primary school students in Yaoundé, Cameroon.

Théodomir Mugiraneza is a researcher in the Centre for Geographic Information Systems and Remote Sensing (CGIS-NUR) at the National University of Rwanda. In 2009, he obtained a master's degree in geo-information science and Earth observation, with specialization in geo-information management for land administration. He also holds a BSc (2006) in physical and human geography from the National University of Rwanda. Currently, he is the head of the Society and Land Management Department at the CGIS-NUR and teaches courses related to land administration, GIS, and cartography in the Faculty of Science, particularly the Geography Department. His areas of research interest include ICT impact, geo-ICT application in land administration, land tenure systems, land use planning, land policy, land management, and spatial data infrastructure for land administration.

Jimena Orchuela holds a bachelor's degree in sociology and has been a lecturer at the National University of La Plata. She is currently pursuing her master's degree at the Facultad Latinoamericana de Ciencias Sociales. She has worked on health and development topics for different NGOs and government agencies.

Patricia Peña is an assistant professor and researcher in digital communication and journalism at Instituto de la Comunicación e Imagen at the University of Chile. She has a master's degree in communication from Diego Portales University, Chile, and an MSc in communication, information, and society from The London School of Economics and Political Science. In recent years, she has published articles related to Chilean social movements and uses of social media, young rural women in Latin America, and ICT and social media and participation.

Alejandra Phillippi is a professor of philosophy at the Pontifical Catholic University of Valparaíso. She has a master's degree in education and multimedia and is currently pursuing doctoral studies at the Universitat Autònoma de Barcelona. She works as a professor at the School of Journalism at Diego Portales University in Santiago de Chile and as a researcher for the National Television Council (Chile). Her recent publications include "Communicative Empowerment: Narrative Skills of the Subjects," co-authored with Claudio Avendaño and published in Report No. 36 of the *Scientific Journal of Media Literacy* (2011).

Jimena Ponce de León is a doctoral fellow at the Consejo Nacional de Investigaciones Científicas y Técnicas (National Scientific and Technical Research Council) in Buenos Aires and a PhD candidate in social sciences at the National University of General Sarmiento. She holds a bachelor's degree in social anthropology and is currently completing her master's thesis on "Local Development" at the National University of San Martín.

Ghaleb Rabab'ah is an associate professor of English at the University of Jordan. He has a PhD from the University of Newcastle upon Tyne, UK. He has worked for various academic institutions in the Middle East, including Etisalat Academy in Dubai, King Saud University and Alfaisal University in Riyadh, and the University of Jordan. He has served on the editorial board of the *Indian Journal of Applied Linguistics* and the *International Journal of Translation.*

Saif Addeen Alrababah is a lecturer at Al al-Bayt University in Jordan. He received his master's degree in computer information systems from Yarmouk University, Jordan.

Wei Shang is an associate professor in the Laboratory of Management, Decision and Information Systems, Academy of Mathematics and Systems Science, Chinese Academy of Sciences. She is co-editor of the Chinese translation of the book *Strategies for E-business Success* and editor of *Advances in Information Sciences and Service Sciences*. She has published research papers in leading academic journals, including *Decision Support Systems* and *International Journal of Information Technology & Decision Making.*

Ryan V. Silverio has an MA. in human rights from Mahidol University, Thailand. He is currently a lecturer in the College of International, Humanitarian and Development Studies at Miriam College in the Philippines, where he teaches courses on peace studies, human rights, and qualitative social research. He has worked for various human rights organizations, including the Philippine Human Rights Information Center, Southeast Asia Coalition to Stop the Use of Child Soldiers, and Child Rights Coalition Asia.

Sylvie Siyam Siwe is a senior engineer in electro-mechanics and holds a master's degree in energetics. She is coordinator of Protège QV Cameroon, an NGO working on ICT4D. She is active in civil society, and in 2008, she co-authored (with Laurent Aristide Eyinga Eyinga) an important report on telecommunication reform in Cameroon and a study on the use of universal access funds, *Le financement de l'accès universel: Le Fonds spécial des télécommunications au Cameroun*, published by the Association of Progressive Communications. Since 2007, she has co-authored the Cameroon paper in the *Global Information Society Watch*, published annually by the Association for Progressive Communications.

Mai M. Taqueban is currently a reader in political economy of chemical use and youth for a PhD in anthropology at the University of Amsterdam. She has conducted research on gender and indigenous peoples and has worked with several non-profit organizations, including as deputy director for the Legal Rights and Natural Resources Center in the Philippines. She is Assistant Professor of Anthropology at the University of the Philippines, Diliman campus, where she teaches courses in gender and political and applied anthropology.

Olga Balbine Tsafack Nguekeng works as a volunteer at Protège QV Cameroon, an NGO working on ICT4D. She has a BSc in political science from the University of Buea (2008) and a professional master's degree in international communication and public action from the International Relations Institute of Cameroon (2013). She has experience in community development and website management, and as a translator (French to English) and digital security trainer.

Xiaoguang Yang is a professor and the director of the Laboratory of Management, Decision and Information Systems, Academy of Mathematics and Systems Science, Chinese Academy of Sciences. He is on the editorial boards of the following journals: *Journal of Systems Science and Complexity*, *Acta Mathematicae Applicatae Sinica*, *Systems Engineering: Theory and Practice* (Chinese journal), and *Operations Research and Management* (Chinese journal).

Index

Note: Page numbers followed by "f," "t," and "n" refer to figures, tables, and endnotes, respectively.